THE CAMBRIDGE COMP/
TO VICTORIAN WOMEN'S \

*The Cambridge Companion to Victorian Wome*ı chapters by leading scholars to provide innovative and comprehensive coverage of Victorian women writers' careers and literary achievements. While incorporating the scholarly insights of modern feminist criticism, it also reflects new approaches to women authors that have emerged with the rise of book history; periodical studies; performance studies; postcolonial studies; and scholarship on authorship, readership, and publishing. It traces the Victorian woman writer's career – from making her debut to working with publishers and editors to achieving literary fame – and challenges previous thinking about genres in which women contributed with success. Chapters on poetry, including a discussion of poetry in colonial and imperial contexts, reveal women's engagements with each other and with male writers. Discussions on drama, life-writing, reviewing, history, travel writing, and children's literature uncover the remarkable achievement of women in fields relatively unknown.

LINDA H. PETERSON is Niel Gray, Jr. Professor of English at Yale University. She is the author of *Traditions of Victorian Women's Autobiography: The Poetics and Politics of Life Writing* (1999) and *Becoming a Woman of Letters: Myths of Authorship, Facts of the Victorian Market* (2009).

A complete list of books in the series is at the back of the book.

THE CAMBRIDGE COMPANION TO
VICTORIAN WOMEN'S WRITING

EDITED BY
LINDA H. PETERSON
Yale University

CAMBRIDGE
UNIVERSITY PRESS

University Printing House, Cambridge CB2 8BS, United Kingdom

Cambridge University Press is part of the University of Cambridge.

It furthers the University's mission by disseminating knowledge in the pursuit of education, learning and research at the highest international levels of excellence.

www.cambridge.org
Information on this title: www.cambridge.org/9781107659612

© Cambridge University Press 2015

This publication is in copyright. Subject to statutory exception and to the provisions of relevant collective licensing agreements, no reproduction of any part may take place without the written permission of Cambridge University Press.

First published 2015

Printed in the United Kingdom by Clays, St Ives plc

A catalogue record for this publication is available from the British Library

Library of Congress Cataloguing in Publication data
The Cambridge Companion to Victorian women's writing / edited by Linda H. Peterson
pages cm. – (Cambridge Companions to literature)
ISBN 978-1-107-65961-2 (paperback)
1. English literature – Women authors – History and criticism.
2. Women and literature – Great Britain – History – 19th century.
3. English literature – 19th century – History and criticism.
4. Publishers and publishing – Great Britain – History – 19th century.
I. Peterson, Linda H., editor.
PR115.C36 2015
820.9'928709034–dc23
2015011595

ISBN 978-1-107-06484-3 Hardback
ISBN 978-1-107-65961-2 Paperback

Cambridge University Press has no responsibility for the persistence or accuracy of URLs for external or third-party internet websites referred to in this publication, and does not guarantee that any content on such websites is, or will remain, accurate or appropriate.

CONTENTS

List of illustrations vii
Notes on contributors viii
Acknowledgments xii
Chronology of publications and events xiii

Introduction: Victorian women's writing and modern literary criticism 1
LINDA H. PETERSON

PART I VICTORIAN WOMEN WRITERS' CAREERS

1 Making a debut 15
ALEXIS EASLEY

2 Becoming a professional writer 29
JOANNE SHATTOCK

3 Working with publishers 43
LINDA H. PETERSON

4 Assuming the role of editor 59
BETH PALMER

5 Achieving fame and canonicity 73
ALISON CHAPMAN

PART II VICTORIAN WOMEN WRITERS' ACHIEVEMENTS:
GENRES AND MODES

6 Poetry 89
LINDA K. HUGHES

7	Silver-fork, industrial, and Gothic fiction ELLA DZELZAINIS	105
8	The realist novel DEIRDRE D'ALBERTIS	119
9	Sensation and New Woman fiction LYN PYKETT	133
10	Drama and theater KATHERINE NEWEY	144
11	Life-writing CAROL HANBERY MACKAY	159
12	Travel writing TAMARA S. WAGNER	175
13	Colonial and imperial writing MARY ELLIS GIBSON AND JASON R. RUDY	189
14	History writing DEBORAH A. LOGAN	206
15	Periodical writing MARGARET BEETHAM	221
16	Reviewing JOANNE WILKES	236
17	Children's writing CLAUDIA NELSON	251
	Guide to further reading	265
	Index	276

ILLUSTRATIONS

1 "The Fraserians," *Fraser's Magazine* 11 (January 1835), 2–3. Courtesy of the Yale University Library.   53

2 "Regina's Maids of Honour," *Fraser's Magazine* 13 (January 1836), 80. Courtesy of the Yale University Library.   53

3 Title page, *The White Wampum*, by E. Pauline Johnson (London: John Lane, 1895). Courtesy of the University of Michigan Library.   201

4 Frontispiece, Sarojini Naidu, *The Bird of Time: Songs of Life, Death & the Spring* (London: William Heinemann; New York: John Lane, 1912). Courtesy of the Yale University Library.   202

NOTES ON CONTRIBUTORS

MARGARET BEETHAM publishes on nineteenth-century print culture, particularly women's magazines and Lancashire dialect publications; on theorizing the periodical; and on popular reading. Her scholarship includes *A Magazine of her Own? Domesticity and Desire in the Woman's Magazine, 1800–1914* (1996), *The Victorian Woman's Magazine: An Anthology* (2001) with Kay Boardman, and numerous articles and chapters in books. She is an associate editor of the *Dictionary of Nineteenth-Century Journalism* (2009).

ALISON CHAPMAN is an associate professor at the University of Victoria, Canada. She is the author of *The Afterlife of Christina Rossetti*, coauthor of *A Rossetti Family Chronology*, and editor or coeditor of several collections including *A Companion to Victorian Poetry* and *Victorian Women Poets*. A new monograph, *Networking the Nation: British and American Women Poets and Italy, 1840–1870*, is forthcoming. She continues to work on the digital project *A Database of Victorian Periodical Poetry* (http://web.uvic.ca/~vicpoet/database-of-victorian-periodical-poetry/).

DEIRDRE D'ALBERTIS is a professor of English at Bard College and the author of *Dissembling Fictions: Elizabeth Gaskell and the Victorian Social Text*, as well as essays on Margaret Oliphant, Charlotte Brontë, Eliza Lynn Linton, Hannah Cullwick, and Mary Howitt among others. Her current research is focused on transnational feminist networks and social reform in nineteenth-century Britain, America, and Europe.

ELLA DZELZAINIS is a lecturer in nineteenth-century literature at Newcastle University. Her research is interdisciplinary, located in the intersection between literature, feminist history, and economic history in the long nineteenth century. Recently, her work on manners and commerce has taken a transatlantic turn, producing an essay collection (coedited with Ruth Livesey), *The American Experiment and the Idea of Democracy in British Culture, 1776–1914* (2013), that includes her own piece on "Dickens, Democracy and Spit."

Notes on Contributors

ALEXIS EASLEY is a professor of English at the University of St. Thomas in St. Paul, Minnesota. She is the author of *First-Person Anonymous: Women Writers and Victorian Print Media* (2004) and *Literary Celebrity, Gender, and Victorian Authorship* (2011). Her most recent publications appeared in three 2012 essay collections, *Women Writers and the Artifacts of Celebrity*, *Women in Journalism at the Fin de Siècle*, and *Centenary Essays on W. T. Stead*. She is coediting the *Ashgate Companion to Nineteenth-Century Periodicals and Newspapers* (with John Morton and Andrew King) and serves as the editor of *Victorian Periodicals Review*.

MARY ELLIS GIBSON is a professor of English at the University of Glasgow and the Elizabeth Rosenthal Distinguished Professor Emerita at the University of North Carolina at Greensboro. Her most recent books are *Anglophone Poetry in Colonial India, 1780–1913: A Critical Anthology* and *Indian Angles: English Verse in Colonial India from Jones to Tagore* (2011). She recently coedited the Robert Browning bicentenary issue of *Victorian Poetry* with Britta Martens and *Victorian India*, a special issue of *Victorian Literature and Culture*.

LINDA K. HUGHES, Addie Levy Professor of Literature at Texas Christian University in Fort Worth, Texas, specializes in Victorian literature and culture with particular interests in historical media studies (poetry and print culture, periodicals, serial fiction), gender and women's studies, and transnationality. She is the author of *The Cambridge Introduction to Victorian Poetry* (2010) and coeditor with Sharon M. Harris of *A Feminist Reader: Feminist Thought from Sappho to Satrapi* (4 vols., Cambridge, 2013).

DEBORAH A. LOGAN is a professor of English at Western Kentucky University and editor of *Victorians Journal of Culture and Literature*. The author of four monographs, she has edited many of Harriet Martineau's works, including six volumes of letters. Forthcoming publications include *The Indian Ladies' Magazine: Raj and Swaraj* and an edition of Maria Weston Chapman's *Memorials of Harriet Martineau*.

CAROL HANBERY MACKAY is the J. R. Millikan Centennial Professor of English Literature at the University of Texas at Austin, where she teaches Victorian fiction, women's and gender studies, and autobiography. The author of *Soliloquy in Nineteenth-Century Fiction* (1987) and *Creative Negativity: Four Victorian Exemplars of the Female Quest* (2001), she is also the editor of *The Two Thackerays* (1988) and *Dramatic Dickens* (1989). She has recently published a critical edition of Annie Besant's *Autobiographical Sketches* (2009).

CLAUDIA NELSON is a professor of English at Texas A&M University. Her research focuses primarily on Victorian family studies and childhood studies. Her fifth and most recent monograph is *Precocious Children and Childish Adults: Age*

Inversion in Victorian Literature (2012); with coeditor Rebecca Morris, she published in November 2014 a collection of essays entitled *Representing Children in Chinese and U.S. Children's Literature*. She is a former president of the Children's Literature Association and editor (2014–19) of the *Children's Literature Association Quarterly*.

KATHERINE NEWEY is a professor of theater history at the University of Exeter. Her research focuses on the theater of the nineteenth century and women's writing. Recent publications include *Women's Theatre Writing in Victorian Britain* (2005) and *John Ruskin and the Victorian Theatre*, coauthored with cultural historian Jeffrey Richards (2010). She is currently leading the Arts and Humanities Research Council-funded project "A Cultural History of English Pantomime, 1837–1901" with Jeffrey Richards and Peter Yeandle.

BETH PALMER is a lecturer in English literature at the University of Surrey. Her published work includes a monograph *Women's Authorship and Editorship in Victorian Culture: Sensational Strategies*, a coedited volume entitled *A Return to the Common Reader: Print Culture and the Novel, 1850–1900*, and other essays on aspects of Victorian women's writing and print culture. She is currently working on a new project investigating the relationships between sensation fiction and the theater.

LINDA H. PETERSON is the Niel Gray, Jr. Professor of English at Yale University. Her books include *Victorian Autobiography* (1986), *Traditions of Victorian Women's Autobiography* (1999), and most recently *Becoming a Woman of Letters: Myths of Authorship and Facts of the Victorian Market* (2009). She is currently working on *The Victorian Poetic Debut: From Originality to Iconicity* – a study of *debut* volumes of poetry as aesthetic, material, and textual objects.

LYN PYKETT, professor emerita at Aberystwyth University, has published widely on nineteenth- and early twentieth-century literature and culture. Her books include *"Improper" Feminine: The Women's Sensation Novel and the New Woman* (1992) and *The Nineteenth-century Sensation Novel* (2011, 2nd edition).

JASON R. RUDY is an associate professor of English at the University of Maryland, College Park. Author of *Electric Meters: Victorian Physiological Poetics* (2009) and essays on the poets Felicia Hemans and Mathilde Blind, he is currently finishing a book on poetry written in the context of British colonialism.

JOANNE SHATTOCK is an emerita professor of Victorian literature at the University of Leicester. Her recent publications include the *Selected Works of Margaret Oliphant*, 25 vols. (2011–16) of which she is general editor with Elisabeth Jay, and an edition of *The Works of Elizabeth Gaskell*, 10 vols.

(2005–6). She edited *The Cambridge Companion to English Literature 1830–1914* (2010).

TAMARA S. WAGNER obtained her PhD from Cambridge University and is currently an associate professor at Nanyang Technological University in Singapore. Her recent books include *Financial Speculation in Victorian Fiction: Plotting Money and the Novel Genre, 1815–1901* (2010), as well as the edited collections *Victorian Settler Narratives: Emigrants, Cosmopolitans and Returnees in Nineteenth-Century Literature* (2011) and *Domestic Fiction in Colonial Australia and New Zealand* (2014).

JOANNE WILKES teaches nineteenth-century literature and criticism at the University of Auckland, New Zealand. She has published on Lord Byron and his literary links with French literature and most recently *Women Reviewing Women in Nineteenth-century Britain: The Critical Reception of Jane Austen, Charlotte Brontë and George Eliot* (2010). She has edited or coedited three volumes of Margaret Oliphant's periodical criticism and literary writing for the *Selected Works of Margaret Oliphant* in the Pickering Masters series.

ACKNOWLEDGMENTS

Thanks belong, first and foremost, to the contributors to this volume, whose knowledge, insight, and enthusiastic collaboration have guided me throughout the process of thinking and writing about Victorian women authors and their work. Thanks also belong to Linda Bree, Senior Commissioning Editor at Cambridge University Press, for inviting me to take on this editorial project and giving crucial advice along the way, and to Anna Bond, Assistant Editor, for guiding me through the many details of production. Assistance from Alexis Chema, Sarah Mahurin, and Andrew Willson, at Yale, proved invaluable in late stages. All of us who wrote chapters owe thanks to our home libraries and librarians for supplying the scholarly materials we needed to complete our work. Special thanks to three libraries for permission to reproduce images from their book collections: The James Smith Noel Collection of Louisiana State University for the cover inset image of Harriet Martineau, the University of Michigan Library for the title page of *The White Wampum* (1895) by E. Pauline Johnson, and Yale University Library for the frontispiece to Sarojini Naidu's *The Bird of Time: Songs of Life, Death & the Spring* (1912) and two illustrations from *Fraser's Magazine*, "The Fraserians" (January 1835) and "Regina's Maids of Honour" (January 1836).

CHRONOLOGY OF PUBLICATIONS AND EVENTS

This chronology features important "firsts" and major achievements in the careers of Victorian women writers. It highlights significant publications and events discussed in the chapters that follow. Birth and death dates are given at the woman writer's first entry.

1819   Mary Russell Mitford (1787–1855) launches her popular prose sketches, *Our Village*, in the *Lady's Magazine*.
1820   Elizabeth Barrett (later Browning, 1806–61) receives fifty privately printed copies of *The Battle of Marathon: A Poem* from her father on her fourteenth birthday.
       Laetitia Elizabeth Landon (1802–38) places her first poems in the *Literary Gazette*, signed "L" (later "L.E.L.").
1821   Elizabeth Barrett publishes "Stanzas Excited by Reflections on the Present State of Greece" in the *New Monthly Magazine*, her first public appearance as a poet.
       Harriet Martineau (1802–76) publishes her first essay, "Female Writers on Practical Divinity," in the *Monthly Repository*.
1823   Mary Howitt (1799–1888) co-publishes her first volume of poetry, *The Forest Minstrel and Other Poems*, with her husband William.
       Julian, the first of several plays by Mary Russell Mitford, is performed at Covent Garden Theatre.
1824   *The Improvisatrice* by Laetitia Elizabeth Landon (L.E.L.) appears in print.
1825   Felicia Hemans (1793–1835) publishes *The Forest Sanctuary*.
1828   Felicia Hemans publishes *Records of Woman*, her most popular volume of poetry.
1829   Anna Maria Hall (1800–81) publishes *Sketches of Irish Character*, followed by a second volume in 1831.

1832   First Reform Bill passes.
        Harriet Martineau launches *Illustrations of Political Economy* (1832–34), a best-selling monthly series that establishes her reputation as professional writer.
        Frances Trollope (1779–1863) publishes *Domestic Manners of the Americans*.
1834   Marguerite Gardiner, the Countess of Blessington (1789–1849), assumes the editorship of *The Book of Beauty*.
        Christian Johnstone (1781–1857) becomes editor of *Tait's Edinburgh Magazine*.
1835   Eliza Cook (1818–89) publishes *Lays of a Wild Harp*.
        Emma Roberts (1794–1840) publishes *Scenes and Characteristics of Hindustan*.
1836   Elizabeth Gaskell (1810–65) and her husband William co-publish *Sketches among the Poor*, a poetry cycle, in *Blackwood's Magazine*.
        Catherine Parr Traill (1802–99) publishes *The Backwoods of Canada*.
1837   Victoria (1819–1901) becomes queen of the United Kingdom of Great Britain and Ireland.
        Harriet Martineau publishes *Society in America*.
        Christian Johnstone initiates an annual anthology of working-class poetry in *Tait's Edinburgh Magazine*.
1838   Harriet Martineau publishes *Deerbrook*, a domestic novel.
        Anna Jameson publishes *Winter Studies and Summer Rambles in Canada*.
1839   Custody of Infants Act passes.
        Charlotte Elizabeth Tonna (1790–1846) serializes her industrial novel *Helen Fleetwood*, in the *Christian Lady's Magazine*.
        Rosana Bulwer (1802–82) publishes *Cheveley; or, the Man of Honour*, with an antihero based on her husband Edward.
        The Zenana and Other Poems by L.E.L. is edited by Emma Roberts and posthumously published after Landon's mysterious death in Africa.
        Four women authors (Joanna Baillie, Harriet Martineau, Mary Russell Mitford, and the Countess of Blessington) sign the "Authors' Petition" on behalf of a new domestic copyright law.
1840   Agnes (1796–1874) and Elizabeth (1794–1875) Strickland begin their multivolume *Lives of the Queens of England*.

	Frances Trollope publishes *The Life and Adventures of Michael Armstrong, the Factory Boy* in support of the Ten Hours Bill.
	Australian poet Fidelia Hill (1794–1854) publishes *Poems and Recollections of the Past*.
1841	Catherine Gore (1798–1861) publishes *Cecil, or the Adventures of a Coxcomb*, her most popular silver-fork novel.
	The Countess of Blessington becomes editor of the popular annual *The Keepsake*.
	Charlotte Elizabeth Tonna publishes *Personal Recollections* (1841).
	Anne Katharine Elwood (1796–1873) publishes *Memoirs of the Literary Ladies of England*, an early attempt to compile biographies of canonical women writers.
1842	Copyright Act extends term to forty-two years from publication or seven after author's death.
1843	Eliza Meteyard (1816–79) serializes her first novel, *Scenes in the Life of an Authoress*, in *Tait's Edinburgh Magazine*.
	Charlotte Elizabeth Tonna begins *The Wrongs of Woman*, four tales in support of the Factory Act that limited the working hours of women and children.
	Elizabeth Barrett publishes "The Cry of the Children" in *Blackwood's Magazine*.
	Factory Act passes, limiting women and children under eighteen to a twelve-hour working day.
1844	Catherine Gore wins a prize competition set by the Royal Theatre, Haymarket, for the best modern comedy.
1845	Eliza Lynn (later Linton, 1822–98) moves to London to start a literary career, publishing *Azeth, the Egyptian* two years later.
	Anna Jameson (1794–1860) publishes *Early Italian Painters*, followed by *Sacred and Legendary Art* in 1848.
	Elizabeth Barrett begins writing *Sonnets from the Portuguese*, given to Robert Browning after their marriage.
1846	Mary Ann Evans (George Eliot, 1819–80) publishes an English translation of David Strauss's *Das Leben Jesu* as *The Life of Jesus, Critically Examined*.
	The Brontë sisters publish *Poems*, using the pseudonyms Currer Bell (Charlotte Brontë, 1816–55), Ellis Bell (Emily Brontë, 1818–48), and Acton Bell (Anne Brontë, 1820–49).
1847	The Brontë sisters publish *Jane Eyre* (Charlotte), *Wuthering Heights* (Emily), and *Agnes Grey* (Anne).

	Mary Howitt and her husband William launch and edit *Howitt's Journal*.
	Verses: Dedicated to Her Mother by Christina Rossetti (1830–94) is privately printed by her grandfather.
1848	Elizabeth Gaskell publishes her first novel, *Mary Barton*.
	Elizabeth Barrett Browning publishes "Runaway Slave at Pilgrim's Point" in the American periodical *The Liberty Bell*.
	Elizabeth Rigby (later Eastlake, 1809–93) anonymously places a negative review of *Jane Eyre* in the *Quarterly Review*.
	Eliza Lynn Linton joins the staff of the *Morning Chronicle*, becoming the first paid woman journalist.
1849	Margaret Oliphant (1828–97) publishes her first novel, *Passages in the Life of Margaret Maitland*.
	Eliza Cook founds *Eliza Cook's Journal*, writing most of the material herself but also soliciting contributions from working-class women writers.
	Harriet Martineau begins publishing her multivolume *History of the Thirty Years' Peace 1816–46*.
1850	The Pre-Raphaelite Brotherhood launches *The Germ*, with lyrics by Christina Rossetti as "Ellen Allyne."
	Fanny Parkes (1794–1875) publishes *Wanderings of a Pilgrim in Search of the Picturesque*.
1851	Elizabeth Barrett Browning publishes *Casa Guidi Windows*.
	Gaskell's *Cranford* begins serialization in *Household Words*.
	Charlotte Yonge (1823–1901) launches *The Monthly Packet*, aimed at young female readers.
1852	Margaret Oliphant serializes *Katie Stewart* in *Blackwood's Magazine*, the beginning of a forty-five-year engagement that includes contributing fiction, biography, essays, and reviews.
	Harriet Beecher Stowe (1811–96) publishes *Uncle Tom's Cabin*.
	Susannah Moodie (1803–85) publishes *Roughing It in the Bush*.
	Samuel Beeton launches the *Englishwoman's Domestic Magazine*, with columns on fashion, food, and household management written by his wife Isabella.
1853	Charlotte Brontë publishes her last novel, *Villette*.
1854	Elizabeth Gaskell's *North and South* begins serialization in *Household Words*.

	Caroline Leakey (1827–81) publishes *Lyra Australis: or Attempts to Sing in a Strange Land*.
1855	Harriet Martineau writes and prints her *Autobiography*, although it is not released until 1877 after her death.
	Elizabeth Gaskell publishes *North and South*, her second industrial novel.
1856	Elizabeth Barrett Browning publishes *Aurora Leigh* (1856, date stamped 1857).
	Mary Ann Evans (George Eliot) publishes "Silly Novels by Lady Novelists" in the *Westminster Review*.
	Charlotte Yonge publishes her best-selling novel *The Daisy Chain*.
1857	George Eliot places her first piece of fiction, "The Sad Fortunes of the Reverend Amos Barton," in *Blackwood's Magazine*, collected the next year in *Scenes of Clerical Life*.
	Elizabeth Gaskell publishes *The Life of Charlotte Brontë*.
	Harriet Martineau publishes *A History of British Rule in India*, followed by *Suggestions for the Future Rule of India* the next year.
	The Englishwoman's Review begins publication.
1858	Bessie Rayner Parkes (1829–1925) and Barbara Leigh Smith Bodichon (1827–91) found the *English Woman's Journal*.
	Adelaide Procter (1825–64) publishes *Legends and Lyrics*, first series.
1859	George Eliot publishes her first novel, *Adam Bede*.
	Isa Craig (1831–1903) wins the Burns Centenary Prize for the best poem submitted to the competition.
1860	Ellen (Mrs. Henry) Wood (1814–87) serializes *East Lynne*, a best-selling sensation novel, in the *New Monthly Magazine*, followed by book publication the next year.
	Harriet Grote (1792–1878) publishes *Memoir of the Life of Ary Scheffer*, a painter, the first of several biographies.
1861	Margaret Oliphant launches *The Chronicles of Carlingford* in *Blackwood's Magazine* with "The Executor."
1862	Elizabeth Barrett Browning's *Last Poems* is posthumously published.
	Christina Rossetti publishes *Goblin Market and Other Poems*.
	Mary Elizabeth Braddon (1835–1915) publishes *Lady Audley's Secret*, a popular sensation novel later adapted for the stage.
	George Eliot's *Romola* is serialized in the *Cornhill*.

1863	Emily Faithfull founds and edits *Victoria Magazine*.
	Julia Kavanagh (1824–77) publishes *English Women of Letters*, using the title phrase to designate professional women authors.
1864	First Contagious Diseases Act passes, allowing arrest and compulsory medical examination of prostitutes.
1865	Ellen Wood purchases and edits the *Argosy* magazine.
	Elizabeth Gaskell's novel *Wives and Daughters* is partially serialized in the *Cornhill Magazine*, when the author dies suddenly.
1866	Mary Elizabeth Braddon founds and edits *Belgravia* magazine.
	Jessie Boucherett (1866–1910) founds and edits the *Englishwoman's Review*, a feminist periodical.
	Margaret Gatty founds *Aunt Judy's Tales*, a children's magazine, using the title of her popular 1859 collection of juvenile fiction.
	Augusta Webster (1837–94) publishes *Dramatic Studies*.
1867	Second Reform Act passed.
	Working-class writer Ellen Johnston (1835–73) publishes *Autobiography, Poems and Songs*.
1868	Frances Power Cobbe (1822–1904) begins writing leaders (editorials) for the London halfpenny paper, the *Echo*.
	Eliza Lynn Linton publishes "The Girl of the Period" in the *Saturday Review*, considered an attack on the women's rights movement.
1869	John Stuart Mill publishes *On the Subjection of Women*, likely coauthored with Harriet Taylor Mills.
1870	Married Women's Property Act is passed, allowing women to own the money they earned and to inherit property.
	Lydia Becker (1827–90) founds the *Women's Suffrage Journal*.
1871	George Eliot's *Middlemarch* begins serial publication.
1872	Christina Rossetti publishes *Sing-Song: A Nursery Rhyme-Book*.
1874	Christina Rossetti publishes her first book of devotional prose, *Annus Domini: A Prayer for Each Day of the Year*.
1875	Alice Thompson (later Meynell, 1847–1922) publishes her first volume of poetry, *Preludes*.
1876	*Daniel Deronda*, George Eliot's last novel, is issued by William Blackwood and Sons.

	Margaret Oliphant publishes the first of her urban histories, *The Makers of Florence*, followed by *Makers of Venice* (1887), *Jerusalem* (1891), and *Makers of Modern Rome* (1895).
1877	Anna Sewell (1820–78) publishes *Black Beauty*.
	Edith Nesbit (1858–1924) publishes her first juvenile tale in the *Sunday Magazine*.
1878	The actress Frances ("Fanny") Kemble (1809–93) publishes her memoirs *Records of a Girlhood*, followed by *Records of Later Life* (1882) and *Further Records, 1848–1883* (1890).
1880	*The Lady's Pictorial* begins, featuring interviews with women writers by the journalist Helen C. Black (1838–1906).
	Isabella Bird Bishop (1831–1904) publishes *Unbeaten Tracks in Japan*.
	The Religious Tract Society launches the *Girls' Own Paper*.
1881	Christina Rossetti's "Monna Innominata: A Sonnet of Sonnets" appears in *A Pageant and Other Poems*.
1882	Married Women's Property Act grants women's right to own and control property after marriage.
	Ancient Ballads and Legends of Hindustan by Toru Dutt (1856–77) is released in London by John Lane of the Bodley Head Press.
1883	Charlotte Riddell publishes *A Struggle for Fame*, a fictional account of the challenges she faced in the literary marketplace.
	Olive Schreiner (1855–1920) publishes *The Story of an African Farm*.
1884	Third Reform Act passes.
	Society of Women Journalists is founded.
	Annie Wood Besant (1847–1933) founds *Our Corner*, a literary magazine with socialist leanings.
	Amy Levy (1861–89) publishes *A Minor Poet and Other Verse*.
	Augusta Webster (1837–94) begins reviewing books of poetry for *The Athenaeum*.
1885	J. W. Cross, George Eliot's widower, edits and publishes *George Eliot's Life as Related in Her Letters and Journals*.
	Annie Wood Besant publishes *Autobiographical Sketches*.
	Marie Corelli (pen name of Mary Mills Mackay, 1855–1924) publishes her first signed article, "One of the World's Wonders," in *Temple Bar*.

1886	Margaret Oliphant publishes a two-volume *Literary History of England*.
1887	Queen Victoria's Golden Jubilee.
	"Sarah Grand" (Frances Elizabeth McFall, 1854–1943) publishes *The Beth Book*.
	L. T. Meade (1844–1914) founds *Atalanta*, a magazine for young middle-class women.
1888	*The Dawn: A Journal for Australian Women* is founded.
1889	Literary Ladies dining club holds its first dinner.
	"Michael Field" (pen name of Katherine Bradley, 1846–1914, and Edith Cooper, 1862–1913) publishes *Long, Long Ago*, a rewriting of Sappho.
	Alice Meynell begins contributing reviews and short essays to the *Scots Observer*.
1890	The penny weekly *Woman* is launched.
1891	Olive Schreiner (1855–1920) publishes *Dreams*.
1892	"Michael Field" publishes *Sight and Song*.
1893	Alice Meynell publishes *The Rhythm of Life*, an essay collection, and *Poems*, a reissue of poems from her 1875 *Preludes*, with John Lane of the Bodley Head Press.
	"George Egerton" (Mary Chavelita Dunne, 1859–1945) publishes *Keynotes*, a collection of experimental short stories, with John Lane of the Bodley Head Press.
	Sarah Grand publishes *The Heavenly Twins*.
1894	Frances Power Cobbe publishes *Life of Frances Power Cobbe, by Herself*.
	Mona Caird publishes the New Woman novel *The Daughters of Danaus*.
1895	Coventry Patmore "nominates" Alice Meynell for the poet laureateship in the *Saturday Review*.
	E. Pauline Johnson (1861–1913) publishes *The White Wampum*.
1896	Margaret Oliphant writes "The Anti-Marriage League," a review of Thomas Hardy's *Jude the Obscure* and Grant Allen's *The Woman Who Did*, for *Blackwood's Magazine*.
	Christina Rossetti's *New Poems*, edited by W. M. Rossetti, is posthumously published by Macmillan.
1897	Queen Victoria's Diamond Jubilee.
	Prominent women writers, including Margaret Oliphant, Eliza Lynn Linton, and Charlotte Yonge, contribute to *Women Novelists of Queen Victoria's Reign*.

National Union of Women's Suffrage Societies is founded.

Mary Kingsley (1862–1900) publishes *Travels in West Africa*.

1898 Henry Mackenzie Bell publishes *Christina Rossetti: A Biographical and Critical Study*.

1899 *Red Pottage* by Mary Cholmondeley (1859–1925) becomes a best-selling New Woman novel.

The Autobiography and Letters of Mrs. M.O.W. Oliphant, edited by her cousin Annie Coghill, is released by William Blackwood and Sons.

Isabella Bird Bishop publishes *The Yangtze Valley and Beyond*.

1901 Queen Victoria dies on January 22.

Beatrix Potter (1866–1901) privately prints *The Tale of Peter Rabbit*, the first of a series of animal stories for children.

LINDA H. PETERSON

Introduction
Victorian women's writing and modern literary criticism

In 1852, G. H. Lewes published an omnibus review of Charlotte Brontë's *Jane Eyre*, Elizabeth Gaskell's *Mary Barton*, George Sand's *oeuvre*, and the work of other nineteenth-century "lady novelists" in the *Westminster Review*. Lewes used the occasion to probe the significance of "the appearance of Woman in the field of literature" and to argue that "the advent of female literature promises woman's view of life, woman's experience ... a new element."[1] Although Lewes assumes gender differences that many readers today would question, most notably that intellect dominates in men, emotion in women, his recognition of a distinctive women's literary tradition expresses his personal view of an important trend in Victorian literature and a belief that became common among critics of the age. In *The Subjection of Women* (1869), John Stuart Mill would echo Lewes's assessment of women's achievement in the novel – noting that "our best novelists in point of composition, and of the management of detail, have been mostly women" – though he would demur at the claim of "a new element," finding little "high originality of conception" in contemporary women's work.[2] Nonetheless, both men acknowledged the emergence of a category – women's writing – that has continued to influence our thinking about Victorian women writers to the present day.

It was not only male critics who highlighted the literary achievements of Victorian women. Throughout the century, women critics and biographers similarly assessed the work of their colleagues and traced the emergence of a distinctive "female literature," to use Lewes's phrase, especially in the novel. Prior to Lewes, Anne Katharine Elwood (1796-1873) produced *Memoirs of the Literary Ladies of England* (1841) out of a preference for "the literary performances of her own sex" and a desire "to obtain information concerning the lives and characters of those individuals in whose production she took an interest."[3] In 1863, Julia Kavanagh (1824-77) published *English Women of Letters*, concentrating on women writers who had contributed to the development of the modern novel.[4] Later in the century, in her two-volume

Literary History of England (1886), Margaret Oliphant would point to the appearance of Maria Edgeworth, Jane Austen, and Susan Ferrier as "three sister novelists" who "opened up for women after them a new and characteristic path in literature."[5] Oliphant expressed uncertainty about the origins of this new path: "Whether it was Rousseau and the French Revolution who did it, or whether it was the waking up in divers places of such genius among women as creates its own audience and works its own revolution, it is difficult to tell."[6] Yet for her, as for Lewes, Elwood, and Kavanagh, women's writing represented "a branch of art worthy and noble, and in no way inferior, yet quite characteristically feminine."[7]

This Victorian view of a women's tradition influenced – sometimes directly, sometimes subtly – the emergence of a feminist approach to literature in the later twentieth century. In her groundbreaking *Literary Women* (1976), Ellen Moers voiced an initial skepticism about the value of "separating major writers from the general course of literary history on the basis of sex," but she acknowledged that as a critical approach, "it has turned out to be surprisingly productive."[8] In *A Literature of Their Own* (1977), a title taken from Mill's *Subjection of Women*, Elaine Showalter similarly argued the importance of constructing a women's literary history; without it, "each generation of women writers has found itself, in a sense, without a history, forced to rediscover the past anew, forging again and again the consciousness of their sex."[9] Then, in their influential *The Madwoman in the Attic: The Woman Writer and the Nineteenth-Century Literary Imagination* (1979), Sandra Gilbert and Susan Gubar began by asserting, "even when we studied women's achievements in radically different genres, we found what began to seem a distinctively female literary tradition."[10] Although these scholarly studies of the 1970s have different emphases – Moers and Showalter focusing on how women studied and developed the work of prior women writers, Gilbert and Gubar highlighting the struggle with a patriarchal tradition – they nonetheless established the critical value of considering women's writing as a distinctive body of work.

Of course, in the forty years since their appearance, the judgments of these feminist critics have been modified, challenged, and developed – including by themselves.[11] And all along we have recognized that there are other productive approaches to the study of women writers and their work. For example, women writers can be studied alongside their male contemporaries as contributors to a period or movement in literary history. Women writers can be treated as members of a regional coterie or professional group. Or women writers can be viewed within genre categories in conjunction with, or in contrast to, male writers. All these approaches appear in Victorian criticism, in scholarship of the late twentieth century, and in this volume of essays.

Illustrating the first approach, one of the earliest collective biographies of authors as a working professional group – John Watkins and Frederic Shobal's *Biographical Dictionary of the Living Authors of Great Britain and Ireland* (1816) – treats male and female writers alphabetically and even-handedly, giving more space to writers of both sexes who have produced substantial literary work than to minor figures with only a title or two. Thus, Mary Bishop gets two lines listing her books of verse (*Poetical Tales and Miscellanies* [1812], *St. Oswald and Other Poems* [1813]), whereas the achievements of Hannah More (1745–1833), poet, dramatist, educational and devotional writer, occupy well more than a page and include a career biography.[12] The same relative treatment applies to Thomas Moore, a novelist with one published work, *The Bachelor* (1809), to his name, who gets a single-line entry, versus Thomas Moore, the Irish poet, classical translator, and friend of Byron, who merits half a page. In a sense, a similar even-handedness emerges in this *Cambridge Companion*, given that highly productive, publicly prominent writers such as Harriet Martineau (1802–77), George Eliot (1819–80), and Margaret Oliphant (1828–97) appear in multiple chapters, and their achievements, often in multiple genres, receive substantial discussion. (The need to claim this achievement, however – as in Moer's subtitle, *The Great Writers* – is no longer a rhetorical necessity.)

Most Victorian critics took multiple approaches to women's writing – as did Margaret Oliphant within her comprehensive *Literary History of England in the End of the Eighteenth Century and Beginning of the Nineteenth Century*. Like many contributors to this collection, Oliphant treats male and female writers together as part of historical movements, as members of literary coteries, and as practitioners of established or emerging genres, evaluating their work both quantitatively (by paragraphs allotted) and qualitatively (by comments inserted). For example, Anna Seward (1747–1809), the "Swan of Litchfield," is significant to Oliphant mostly as a member of a regional coterie, her memoir of Eramus Darwin and the Litchfield literary circle receiving more praise than her poetry: "It is a pity," Oliphant comments, "she had not left poetry alone, and given us more of those graphic if high-flown descriptions."[13] In contrast, Mary Wollstonecraft (1759–97), though included in a chapter deflatingly titled "London: The Lower Circle" – receives substantial and respectful treatment for her *Vindication of the Rights of Women*, a "plea for women" that Oliphant describes as "of the mildest description": "All that Mary Wollstonecraft asks is education for her clients and an exemption from that false and mawkish teaching specially addressed to 'the fair.'"[14] As noted earlier, the "three sister novelists" whose innovations opened new paths in fiction receive an entire chapter – and detailed analyses of their achievements – in Oliphant's *History*. Readers of this *Cambridge Companion* will find extensions, adaptations, and new versions of these approaches to women writers and their work.

Even so, the fundamental insight of Moers's and Showalter's studies – that attending to "the continuities in women's writing"[15] allows us to better understand Victorian literature and recognize a distinctive women's tradition within it – underlies many chapters. In her discussion of poetry (ch. 6), for instance, Linda K. Hughes notes the high esteem in which Felicia Hemans (1793–1835) was held by fellow poets, including William Wordsworth, and her significant impact on Christina Rossetti (1830–94) and Elizabeth Barrett (1806–61), whose plot in *Aurora Leigh* (1856) looks back to Hemans's *Records of Woman* (1828). Hemans's influence was felt well beyond England – as Mary Ellis Gibson and Jason Rudy demonstrate in their discussion of women's colonial and imperial writing (ch. 13). Periodicals in Australia and New Zealand frequently reprinted British poetry, with Hemans's verse as a favorite, and colonial poets paid tribute in their adaptations of her style. The Canadian poet Sarah Herbert (1824–46) "demonstrated her admiration for Hemans and expressed emotion through tropes of distance, whether from emigration, death at sea, or infant mortality." Similarly, Australian poet Fidelia Hill (1794–1854) channeled "Hemans's domestic affections in lyrics composed after arriving in the fledgling town of Adelaide in 1836," and Eliza Hamilton Dunlop (1796–1880), another Australian, borrowed stylistically from Hemans's "Indian Woman's Death Song" to evoke sympathy for Indigenous peoples. Nonetheless, in these chapters the continuities involving women poets are not restricted to female-female transmission. Hemans influenced Alfred Tennyson in England and H. L. V. Derozio in India; Barrett Browning drew on Wordsworth's *The Prelude* and Hill on Wordsworth's landscape poetry. Thus, in new modes of literary history, influence crosses gender lines easily and frequently, making female-male influence and male-female influence part of the story.

This is not to suggest that all transmission came without struggle or that no woman writer had to resist patriarchal norms. Alexis Easley begins her account of women authors' careers, "Making a Debut" (ch. 1), by quoting Isaac Disraeli on the sorrows of the authoress and the difficulties of "find[ing] success in a male-dominated literary marketplace": "Women who chose the literary life often faced social censure, received substandard pay, and fell subject to a critical double standard," Easley adds. So, too, Carol MacKay, in her discussion of life-writing (ch. 11), notes a fundamental social obstacle faced by women who wished to write autobiographies: "A Victorian woman was in a bind when it came to writing her own life story, for her autobiographical impulse met with charges of pride or egotism for writing an autobiography in the first place." Katherine Newey, in the chapter on drama and theater (ch. 10), points to the many "invisible" Victorian women playwrights, whose work was performed in their day but has been forgotten now. Victorian professional authoresses, female autobiographers, and playwrights certainly resisted patriarchal norms, or we would not have the rich body of literature on which to draw for these chapters.

Yet, as Joanne Wilkes's chapter (ch. 16) on reviewing makes clear, some forms of struggle involved two women with opposing views, not women opposing male reviewers or cultural codes of proper feminine behavior. The now famous *Quarterly* review of *Jane Eyre* chastises the novelist for "violat[ing] every code human and divine abroad, and foster[ing] Chartism and rebellion at home," and then speculates that the author could not be female, or if a woman, then she must be "one who has, for some sufficient reason, long forfeited the society of her own sex" – these harsh words were composed by another woman writer, Elizabeth Rigby (later Lady Eastlake). Clearly, these two Victorian women writers – Charlotte Brontë and Elizabeth Rigby – held different views of Christianity, morality, femininity, and fictional conventions.

Within this volume, most discussions of women writers emphasize supportive or enabling aspects of their relations – and here some new approaches to women's writing emerge. What Oliphant labeled a "coterie," several contributors to this volume treat as a "network" – a group of writers tightly or loosely linked by region, religion, politics, or shared interests. As Alexis Easley reminds us in "Making a Debut" (ch. 1), networks often enabled women to enter the literary field and place their work. Mary and William Howitt helped Elizabeth Gaskell publish her first piece of fiction (in *Howitt's Journal*) and place her first novel, *Mary Barton* (1848), with Chapman and Hall. Joanne Shattock further describes, in "Becoming a Professional Writer" (ch. 2), the importance of networks in advancing a professional career. Eliza Meteyard belonged to "a circle of radical Unitarians at W. J. Fox's South Place Chapel that included a number of women writers, among them Mary Leman Grimstone and Harriet Martineau." Meteyard used her membership in the Whittington Club, a self-improvement society founded in 1846, for meeting other writers and networking with professional women such as Mary Howitt and Eliza Cook, who befriended and aided her. Informal networks were crucial to women's success because, as Shattock explains, they "had fewer opportunities to participate in the interlocking networks of writers, publishers, editors, and proprietors that operated in the capital than their male colleagues."

Some networks emerged from specific social movements and generated forms of literature that advanced the cause. *Howitt's Journal* (1847–49), coedited by William and Mary Howitt, and *Eliza Cook's Journal* (1849–54), edited as its name suggests by Eliza Cook, were radical mid-century "magazines with interests in the intellectual and social progress of 'the people,' and in humanitarian and progressive causes";[16] they featured biographies of successful artisanal and middle-class figures and poetry that voiced the sentiments of "the people." As the century progressed, women came increasingly to edit such periodicals, and many Victorian women writers (and some who were not writers) moved into political editorships. In her discussion of women editors (ch. 4), Beth Palmer traces the routes by which participation in a "political or activist group ... presented opportunities for women to extend their personal convictions through editorship." One early example is Christian Isobel Johnstone (1781–1857), who became editor of the reformist *Tait's Edinburgh Magazine* (1832–61) in 1834 and used her position, as Palmer notes, to "express her convictions on class reform and gender equality by encouraging contributions from the artisan classes and from female writers such as Mary Russell Mitford and Eliza Meteyard." A later example is Annie Besant (1847–1933), who after losing her Christian faith assisted Charles Bradlaugh in editing the *National Reformer* and then, when her socialist convictions crystalized, moved on to edit her own periodical, *Our Corner* (1883–88).

If we can illumine the careers of women writers by locating them within literary, social, and political networks, we can also place them within larger literary movements and recognize their contributions to established and emerging genres. In her *Literary History of England*, Oliphant, as we have seen, emphasizes the importance of Austen, Edgeworth, and Ferrier for the development of domestic fiction (what she terms novels "considered suitable for domestic reading").[17] In her *Blackwood's Magazine* reviews and essay in *Women Novelists of Queen Victoria's Reign* (1897), Oliphant highlights Charlotte Brontë's enduring achievement in *Jane Eyre* as it changed the treatment of romantic love in English fiction: "Charlotte Brontë was the first to overthrow this superstition" (that a woman should "maintain a reserve in respect to her feelings").[18] Chapters in this volume explore the contributions of women writers to other forms of fiction, including silver-fork, industrial, and Gothic fiction (ch. 7), the realist novel (ch. 8), and sensation and New Woman fiction (ch. 9). In "The Realist Novel" (ch. 8), Deirdre d'Albertis highlights George Eliot's central role as a practitioner but, more importantly, as a theorizer of realism: "Surprisingly few writers in the English tradition referred directly to, much less theorized, realism until the great work of mid-Victorian fiction was underway. ... George Eliot (1819–80) changed all of that." In Eliot's thought-provoking essays in the *Westminster Review* and her novelistic practice from *Adam Bede* (1860) to

Daniel Deronda (1876), she developed a form of realism that attended, in d'Albertis's words, "both to the neglected surfaces of the world and to underlying truths they body forth." Eliot also influenced other novelists, including Elizabeth Gaskell and Thomas Hardy. This new direction in realism involved, however, a rejection of the techniques and genres of prior women novelists, whose work Eliot (then Mary Ann Evans) dismissed as "frothy ... prosy ... pious, or ... pedantic" in "Silly Novels by Lady Novelists," published anonymously in the *Westminster Review* before she made her own debut in fiction.[19] Ella Dzelzainis discusses the actual achievements of these earlier women novelists in ch. 7, including their pioneering work in social reform.

Contemporaneously with Eliot's practice of realism, women novelists pioneered the development of sensation fiction and stage melodrama. As Lyn Pykett points out (ch. 9), sensation fiction allowed women novelists to explore the same social and political issues that essayists discussed in periodicals such as the *English Woman's Journal* (1858–64) and the *Englishwoman's Review* (1866–1910):

> Concerns about the nature of women's role within the family; the limited opportunities available to middle-class women outside of the family; the economic and emotional dynamics of marriage and its unequal power relations under the current state of the laws governing marriage, inheritance, and women's property rights; the desirability (or otherwise) of divorce, and the circumstances under which it might be obtained; the operations of the sexual double standard (in which chastity before marriage and sexual fidelity after it were expected of women but not of men).

The transgressive heroines of sensation fiction, notably in such avant-garde novels as *East Lynne* (1861) and *Lady Audley's Secret* (1862), "are propelled into marriage by the pressure of their unfortunate financial and parental circumstances and ... subsequently misunderstood, infantilized, and abandoned or neglected by their respective husbands." These marital discontents lead to their crimes and misdemeanors. When these novels were adapted for the stage, as Katherine Newey shows in "Drama and theater" (ch. 10), they – and other melodramas like them – "shifted the Victorian theater into a new period of creativity and change." New Woman fiction, so called because its heroines embody or act on the principles of intellectually advanced women, extended the techniques of realism and sensationalism to expose the plight of women trapped in degrading marriages or in unsatisfying jobs – or facing a choice between one or the other.

The innovations of women novelists in Victorian fiction are well known and well documented in this collection. Other chapters treat women's writing that innovates in surprising, previously unknown ways and whose significance was unrecognized by the Victorians. One reason for our current recognition of these women's achievements lies in recent scholarly interest in print culture and the various media in which "literature" appeared during the nineteenth century: magazines, newspapers, literary annuals, and so on. Victorian women writers were active participants in all these print media. Another, related reason stems from a renewed interest in the history of authorship, readership, and publishing, and its attendant concern with women's career trajectories (the focus of Part I of this volume). Finally, modern scholars tend to reject (or at least resist) the hierarchy of genres that Alison Chapman discusses in "Achieving Fame and Canonicity" (ch. 5): whereas Victorians valued original poetry and serious fiction published in book form, we tend today to explore the various, multiple genres that comprised the literature of Britain. This broadening of the sense of literature has brought other Victorian women writers to the fore.

In discussing one of these other genres, "History Writing" (ch. 14), Deborah Logan treats the remarkable achievement of Harriet Martineau, the only Victorian woman writer "whose history can be called *national*" and whose work would thus have been considered "real" history by Victorian norms. Otherwise, as Logan notes, "the masculine professionalization of History as a rarefied scholarly discipline cast Victorian women historians as unprofessional, amateur, and intellectually shallow." In fact and contrary to this Victorian view, Logan argues that we can see today how women writers were not unprofessional but pioneered in forms of "alternative history," most notably "biographies of individual figures and dynastic reigns, in both English and European contexts, which furthered the work of interpreting human social experience." These forms anticipate the mid-twentieth-century movement to produce social history, sometimes called the "new social history," which attends to the experiences of ordinary people and undercuts the assumption "that History can only mean national history (wars, conquests, reigns, politics)."

Women writers innovated in other Victorian genres, throughout the century but especially toward its end when increasing numbers entered journalism. In her discussion of periodical writing (ch. 15), Margaret Beetham traces women's contributions to religious journalism and leader (editorial) writing for social and political causes; she also highlights their seminal work in such journalistic genres as the "special columns or causeries, which might include gossip, snippets of news, and moral stories or jokes," and the "celebrity interviews," which became an important aspect of the "New Journalism." *Fin-de-siècle* authors such as Rosamund Marriott Watson and Alice Meynell wrote regularly for the "Wares of Autolycus" column in the *Pall Mall*

Gazette, with many of Meynell's essays later collected in beautifully produced books such as *The Children* (1897) and *The Spirit of Place* (1898). Indeed, the aesthetic essay is another genre in which Victorian women made important innovations. Meynell came to prominence as an aesthetic essayist by publishing brief, brilliant, highly wrought pieces for the *Scots Observer*, and this work led to the invitation to write for the *Pall Mall Gazette* and publish books of essays with the prominent aesthetic publisher John Lane at the Bodley Head press.

In some genres, women writers were essential contributors, both as originators and as continuing innovators in the form. As Tamara Wagner notes (ch. 12), travel writing by British women predates the nineteenth century, with its particular emphasis on domestic manners and "the details of everyday living arrangements." Without losing this emphasis, Victorian travel writers reflect a growing "interest in 'unbeaten tracks' about which little had then been written," with Isabella Bird and Mary Kingsley "epitomiz[ing] the solitary woman traveler who sought to leave civilization behind and write about unknown places." In "Children's Writing" (ch. 17), Claudia Nelson similarly observes both continuity in and development of the genre. On the one hand, Victorian women writers "were already well ensconced in this profession, having inherited a thriving tradition of women's writing for children from their Georgian predecessors"; often their tales fulfill the assumption that "children's literature would communicate something worthwhile – morals or information or both – to its young consumers," whether the lesson be "setting a virtuous example," as in Anne Maria Sargeant's "Edith and Her Ayah," or treating animals humanely, as in Anna Sewell's *Black Beauty*. At the end of the century, however, women (and men as well) often employed fantasy and fairy tales "to comment on the shortcomings not of children but of the adult world."

As I have read – with many an eye-opening moment – the chapters in this collection, I have been reminded of the recuperative impulse that has generated, and continues to generate, important scholarship on writing by women. "Recuperation" is a tricky term – not one much used by the scholars who contributed the following chapters. As Susan Stanford Friedman noted twenty-five years ago, "The word *recuperation* means to 'recover from sickness of exhaustion', to 'regain health or strength', to 'recover from loss'. Embedded in the term is a notion of disease."[20] The sense of Victorian women's writing conveyed by the contributors here is quite different: it is of authors and works brimful of vigor and vitality, of imagination and innovation, of optimism and confidence in what women achieved. Nonetheless, it is worth remembering the recuperative aspect of scholarship published by both Victorian women writers and modern feminist scholars who have "recovered from loss" the literature of the nineteenth century. As Betty Schellenberg, a scholar of eighteenth-century women's literature, observes, "the formation of literature as one discipline within a newly professionalized system of intellectual labor" involved a "great forgetting" – a forgetting that women wrote in many different genres (not just the novel), that they wrote with popular and often critical success, and that they were fundamental to the establishment of literature as a profession.[21]

Schellenberg notes that eighteenth-century women writers were sometimes complicit in this "great forgetting," whether by destroying their personal papers, erasing public knowledge of their lives, or maintaining silence about the career achievements of fellow women writers. Victorian women writers, I believe, were less likely to forget, more likely to remember and document their achievements. They edited collective biographies, as did Elwood and Kavanagh; they wrote literary histories, as did Oliphant; and they assembled critical collections about their predecessors and contemporaries, as in the multi-authored *Women Novelists of Queen Victoria's Reign* (1897) and Helen C. Black's *Notable Women Authors of the Day* (1893). Of course, we can quote Elizabeth Barrett on strategic forgetting ("I look everywhere for Grandmothers & see none"),[22] or cite Harriet Martineau on destroying personal correspondence ("I made up my mind to interdict publication of my private letters").[23] But these individual decisions go against the Victorian norm of documenting achievement as part of the record of the professionalization of authorship, women's as well as men's.

The chapters that follow extend this documentation. In Part I, the chapters trace the stages of a woman writer's career, noting women's engagements within the Victorian publishing world and their efforts to professionalize their work. In Part II, the chapters turn to women writers' achievements in important Victorian literary genres. All testify to the remarkable achievements of Victorian women in many arenas.

NOTES

1. [George Henry Lewes], "The Lady Novelists," *Westminster Review* 58 (July 1852), 129, 131.
2. John Stuart Mill, *The Subjection of Women* (London: Longmans, Green, Reader, and Dyer, 1869), pp. 128–29. Online at www.gutenberg.org.
3. Mrs. [Anne Katharine] Elwood, *Memoirs of the Literary Ladies of England* (Philadelphia: G. B. Zieber, 1845), p. 3. This is a pirated American edition of the 1841 London text published by Henry Colburn.
4. Julia Kavanagh, *English Women of Letters: Biographical Sketches*, 2 vols. (London: Hurst and Blackett, 1863).

5. Mrs. [Margaret] Oliphant, *The Literary History of England in the End of the Eighteenth and Beginning of the Nineteenth Century* (New York: Macmillan, 1886), p. 328.
6. Ibid., p. 326.
7. Ibid., p. 328.
8. Ellen Moers, *Literary Women: The Great Writers* (New York: Oxford University Press, 1976), p. xi.
9. Elaine Showalter, *A Literature of Their Own: British Women Novelists from Brontë to Lessing* (Princeton: Princeton University Press, 1977), pp. 11–12.
10. Sandra M. Gilbert and Susan Gubar, *The Madwoman in the Attic: The Woman Writer and the Nineteenth-Century Literary Imagination* (New Haven: Yale University Press, 1979), p. xi.
11. See Elaine Showalter, "'A Literature of Their Own' Revisited," *NOVEL : A Forum on Fiction* 31:3 (Summer 1998), 399–413.
12. John Watkins and Frederic Shobal, eds., *Biographical Dictionary of the Living Authors of Great Britain and Ireland* (London: Henry Colburn, 1816), s.v. "Mary Bishop" and "Hannah More."
13. Oliphant, *Literary History*, vol. 1, p. 193.
14. Ibid., vol. 2, pp. 38–39.
15. Showalter, *A Literature of Their Own*, p. 7.
16. Brian Maidment, "Magazines of Popular Progress & the Artisans," *Victorian Periodicals Review* 17:3 (1984), 83.
17. Oliphant, *Literary History*, vol. 2, p. 325.
18. See Mrs. Oliphant, "The Sisters Brontë," in *Women Novelists of Queen Victoria's Reign* (London: Hurst & Blackett, 1897), pp. 23–24.
19. [George Eliot], "Silly Novels by Lady Novelists," *Westminster Review* 66 (October 1856), 442.
20. Susan Stanford Friedman, "Post/Poststructuralist Feminist Criticism: The Politics of Recuperation and Negotiation," *New Literary History*, 22:2 (Spring 1991), 476.
21. Betty A. Schellenberg, *The Professionalization of Women Writers in Eighteenth-Century Britain* (Cambridge: Cambridge University Press, 2005), p. 164.
22. Letter of 1845, in *The Browning Correspondence*, 21 vols., ed. Philip Kelley and Ronald Hudson (Winfield, KS: Wedgestone Press, 1984–2013), vol. 10, p. 14.
23. Harriet Martineau, *Autobiography*, ed. Linda H. Peterson (Peterborough: Broadview Press, 2007), p. 34.

PART I

Victorian women writers' careers

I

ALEXIS EASLEY

Making a debut

In *Calamities of Authors* (1812), Isaac Disraeli writes, "Of all the sorrows in which the female character may participate, there are few more affecting than that of an Authoress."[1] Throughout the century, it was challenging for women to find success in a male-dominated literary marketplace. Women who chose the literary life often faced social censure, received substandard pay, and fell subject to a critical double standard. As a result of separate spheres ideology, it was difficult for women to gain access to masculine social and professional networks. Yet by the end of the nineteenth century, women's opportunities in the literary marketplace seemed to have improved. Between 1871 and 1891, the number of women listing themselves as authors on the census increased from 255 to 660.[2] As a writer for *All the Year Round* put it in 1889,

> Do but think how, with the spread of elementary education, and the growth of the press, the field for writers has been enlarged since Isaac Disraeli's time. . . . And in no particular is the revolution more strongly foreshadowed than in the prevailing multitude of women who, by means of their pens, disseminate the influence of their minds over all the civilised parts of the globe.[3]

Many Victorian women writers began their careers by publishing a novel or poetry collection in book form. Elizabeth Barrett Browning (1806–61), for example, began her literary career at age eleven by writing a Homeric epic, *The Battle of Marathon*, a poem privately printed by her father three years later. Likewise, Christina Rossetti (1830–94) wrote her first poem at age twelve, and her first collection, *Verses: Dedicated to Her Mother*, was privately published by her grandfather when she was just seventeen. Both poets' entry into the literary field was made possible by their precocious, exceptional talent, which was then authorized and enabled by patriarchal authority. Supportive family contexts enabled both writers to define themselves as writers during a time when few middle-class women were encouraged to pursue work beyond the domestic sphere.

The publication of privately printed collections had the effect of nurturing youthful talent, but it did not provide an opportunity for either poet to write for a public audience. As Margaret Forster puts it, Barrett Browning at age twenty-one found herself "stuck in Hope End in out-of-the-way Herefordshire [where] she had no chance of coming into contact with any poets of her generation. . . . It was through publication in London literary magazines and newspapers that she knew she could catch the eye of other poets and those appreciative of 'true' poetry."[4] The appearance of her first poems in the *New Monthly Magazine* in 1821 provided much-needed affirmation. Likewise, Rossetti found a public voice as a contributor to the Pre-Raphaelite journal the *Germ*, founded by her brother Gabriel and his artistic collaborators. Although Barrett Browning published her first poems anonymously and Rossetti adopted a pseudonym, their entry into the public world of print represented an important first step in their careers as writers, leading ultimately, in both cases, to their high-profile status as celebrity poets.

Margaret Oliphant (1828–97) also began writing at a young age, composing her first novel *Christian Melville* at age sixteen. Unlike Barrett Browning and Rossetti, she claimed to have fallen into writing almost by accident, taking up the craft merely because she "had no liking then for needlework" and had to "secure some amusement and occupation" while tending her mother during an illness.[5] Such a self-effacing explanation does not square with the facts of Oliphant's early career, which demonstrate her seriousness and ambition as a writer. At age twenty-one, she published her first novel, *Passages in the Life of Margaret Maitland* (1849); after placing several additional novels with London publishers, she sold *Katie Stewart* (1852), a serial novel, to *Blackwood's Magazine*. This eventually led to her influential role as a regular reviewer for the magazine, a career that spanned forty-five years. For Oliphant, as for many other women writers, networking was essential for gaining a foothold in the literary marketplace.

Elizabeth Gaskell's (1810–65) entry into the world of print vividly illustrates the benefit of networking for a novice woman writer. In 1838, Gaskell sent an unsolicited travel sketch, "Clopton Hall," to William and Mary Howitt, who accepted it for publication in *Visits to Remarkable Places* (1840). Seven years later, the Howitts published Gaskell's first work of fiction, "Life in Manchester: Libby Marsh's Three Eras," in *Howitt's Journal*. Once the manuscript of *Mary Barton*, Gaskell's first novel, was complete, she submitted it to a variety of publishers without success. The manuscript finally found a home when William Howitt presented it to John Forster, a reader for Chapman and Hall. Such intermediaries performed an important function for women writers, especially those, like Gaskell, who lived outside of London publishing networks.

Women who were single or otherwise free to relocate often moved to London to seek literary opportunities. For example, in 1845 Eliza Lynn Linton (1822–98), age twenty-three, persuaded her father to provide her with the funds necessary to spend a year in London writing her first novel. Later reflecting on her departure from home, Linton remarked,

> My choice was made. Selfish, or only self-respecting, I took my place with Mr. Loaden in the coach which was to carry us to the railway station; and thus and for ever broke down my dependence on the old home and set my face towards the Promised Land—the land where I was to find work, fame, liberty, and happiness.[6]

Before departing, Linton had published two poems in *Ainsworth's Magazine*, but in the city she was able to give her literary ambitions full reign. She wrote *Azeth, the Egyptian* (1847) and arranged to have the book published by Thomas Newby at her own expense. "London," she later wrote, "is my Home, and there are all my best friends, my work, my Ambition, my surrounding."[7] At the termination of her year in the city, she returned home but soon made her way back to the capital, where she wrote a second novel, *Amymone: A Romance in the Days of Pericles* (1848), which she sold to Bentley for £100.[8]

As these examples illustrate, publication in periodicals and newspapers played an important role in many women's literary careers. The expansion of the press during the nineteenth century – brought about by the spread of literacy, advances in printing technology, and the gradual elimination of taxes on print – provided a host of new venues for women writers that were often more accessible than the conventional book trade. Periodicals aimed at women and children provided particularly welcoming outlets for women's writing. Kathryn Ledbetter notes that "while many titles confirm stereotypical domestic roles ... they also aggressively examined topics such as women's work, philanthropy, education, equality, and social issues."[9] Women further expanded their literary range by contributing to other niche-market periodicals, such as religious, philanthropic, family, and juvenile magazines.

During the early and mid-Victorian era, the convention of anonymous or pseudonymous publication adopted by most periodicals enabled many women to begin their writing careers without having to assume "feminine" identities. By contributing their work anonymously to major quarterlies and monthlies – for example, the *Westminster Review*, the *Quarterly Review*, or *Blackwood's Magazine* – women could write on politics, economics, and other conventionally masculine topics, thereby extending their scope beyond traditional domains of feminine writing. George Eliot's first prose publications, for example, appeared in a local paper, the *Coventry Herald and Observer*. As Fionnuala Dillane points out, writing anonymously for a newspaper owned by mentor Charles Bray provided Eliot (then Marian Evans) with a "comfortable first entry into the world of publishing" where she could experiment with narrative styles and negotiate the "relationship with her audience and her editor through her journalistic personae."[10]

Anonymous publication was also useful for women novelists because it enabled them to situate their work outside a narrowly defined feminine literary tradition. In her essay "Silly Novels by Lady Novelists" (1856), Eliot draws attention to the critical double standard faced by women writers: "By a peculiar thermometric adjustment, when a woman's talent is at zero, journalistic approbation is at the boiling pitch; when she attains mediocrity, it is already at no more than summer heat; and if ever she reaches excellence, critical enthusiasm drops to the freezing point."[11] Eliot's awareness of this double standard partly explains why she chose to assume a pseudonym when negotiating publication of her first stories in *Blackwood's Magazine* and why she maintained this persona even after her identity as Marian Evans was revealed to the public.

Even though women writers employed pseudonyms defensively as a means of avoiding stereotypes associated with female authorship, some did so with a degree of playfulness. For example, when seeking a publisher for their poetry collection in 1846, Charlotte, Emily, and Anne Brontë assumed gender-neutral names – Currer, Ellis, and Acton Bell – so that they could negotiate with publishers without fear of falling subject to a critical double standard. They maintained these pseudonyms when placing their novel manuscripts with publishers Thomas Newby and Smith, Elder. After the appearance of *Jane Eyre*, *Wuthering Heights*, and *Agnes Grey* in 1847, there was some speculation in the press that the novels had been written by a single author. To correct this mistaken assumption, Charlotte and Anne traveled to London where they presented themselves to George Smith, publisher of *Jane Eyre*. In a letter to her friend Mary Taylor, Charlotte recounts the exchange that unfolded. Smith walked into the waiting room, asking,

> "Did you wish to see me, Ma'am?"
> "Is it Mr. Smith?" I said, looking up through my spectacles at a young, tall, gentlemanly man.
> "It is."
> I then put his own letter into his hand directed to "Currer Bell." He looked at it—then at me—again—yet again—I laughed at his queer perplexity—A recognition took place—
> I gave my real name—"Miss Brontë—."[12]

Such lighthearted accounts of having passed as a man but being acknowledged privately as a woman pervade many women's autobiographical writings. In her *Autobiography* (1877), Harriet Martineau similarly recounts the moment when she revealed her authorial identity to her brother. In 1829, she published her first article in the *Monthly Repository* signed only with the letter "V." Her elder brother soon came across the essay, reading it aloud to her and exclaiming over the work of a "new hand." When Martineau finally admitted that she was the author of the article, her brother put his hand on her shoulder, saying, "Now, dear, leave it to other women to make shirts and darn stockings; and do you devote yourself to this." Martineau later remembered how she "went home in a sort of dream, so that the squares of the pavement seemed to float before my eyes. That evening made me an authoress."[13] The sense of triumph – of being recognized as a talented author and being endorsed by benign patriarchal authority – characterizes many women's accounts of the genesis of their writing careers.

Working-class women writers

Because working-class women writers lacked the networking opportunities available to middle- and upper-class women, they were often forced to rely on middle- and upper-class editors and patrons. As Martha Vicinus has shown, they also formed clubs and nurtured friendships with fellow working-class authors.[14] Women writers benefited from the rapid expansion of cheap periodicals and newspapers aimed at a working-class audience. Magazines of popular progress such as the *People's Journal* (1846–49), *Howitt's Journal* (1847–49), *Eliza Cook's Journal* (1849–54), and the *Working-Man's Friend and Family Instructor* (1850–53) were important early outlets for working-class women writers. As Brian Maidment notes, these periodicals were "essentially literary magazines with interests in the intellectual and social progress of 'the people,' and in humanitarian and progressive causes." The editors of these magazines, he adds, "saw themselves as patrons and cultural entrepreneurs of artisan literary values" yet published examples of working-class poetry and prose that "favoured the literary traditions of middle-class writing."[15]

Even though magazines of popular progress may have played a censoring role, they nevertheless served as significant venues for amateur working-class writing. For example, in her mid-fifties Scottish poet Janet Hamilton (1795–1873), wife of a shoemaker, published her first essay, "Counteracting Influences" (1850), in the *Working-Man's Friend*, published by John Cassell. She had originally submitted this pro-temperance essay to a competition sponsored by the magazine, which offered prizes to working-class entrants whose works were selected for publication. However, as an editorial note appended to the essay made clear, the contribution "from a Working Man's Wife, was intended to have been inserted in our Supplementary Number; but our communications for that number were so numerous from WORKING MEN themselves, that in conformity with our design, were compelled to make it give way."[16] Clearly, the magazine's essay competition privileged male over female compositions. Nevertheless, Cassell "found a place" for Hamilton's essay in the April issue.[17] As Florence Boos points out, six of Hamilton's essays were subsequently published in Cassell's *Literature of Working Men*, making her the most frequent contributor to the series.[18] Cassell also published her poems and essays in the *Working-Man's Friend* and the *Quiver*.[19] She went on to publish three volumes of poetry and prose, including *Poems and Essays of a Miscellaneous Character* (1863).

As Hamilton's example illustrates, working-class women writers depended on the sponsorship of editors dedicated to the "improvement" of the working classes. Cassell, like many other editors of popular education periodicals, believed that creative writing was a healthy intellectual pursuit for working-class operatives. When introducing his "Literature of Working Men" competition, Cassell noted that an "opportunity will thus be afforded to the working classes for furnishing hints and suggestions as to the improvement of their own order, whether physically, socially, or morally."[20] Unlike Cassell, who came from humble roots, most sponsors of working-class poetry were middle class. For example, in 1837 middle-class editor Christian Johnstone instituted an annual anthology of working-class poetry in *Tait's Edinburgh Magazine* (1832–61) called the "Feast of the Poets." In her introduction to the series, Johnstone asserted that her aim was to provide space for the "modest Muse," where the poet "may niche herself, and sing at freedom"; although most poems published in the series were signed with initials, the inclusion of the occasional female pen name – "Inez" or "Lavinia" – suggests that Johnstone's "unpatronized genius" was sometimes a woman.[21] *The People's Journal* (later the *People's and Howitt's Journal*) also became an important venue for amateur working-class women poets. For example, "Marie," a factory dye-worker, published twenty-six poems in the journal from 1846 to 1850.[22] In addition, as Kirstie Blair has shown, the *People's Journal* (1858–1986) and other Scottish weeklies published poetry correspondence columns that offered advice to working-class poets. These columns "functioned as a venue for the discussion of poetry submissions, regularly proffering advice on the appropriate subject matter, language, form, and style that poets should adopt if they wished their poems to be published."[23]

Newspapers, like magazines of popular progress, were particularly accessible venues for aspiring working-class writers. Eliza Cook published a book of poems, *Lays of a Wild Harp*, in 1835, but it was not until she published her work in the *Weekly Dispatch* that her poetry began to receive notice. Beginning in 1836, her poems regularly appeared in the newspaper's "Facts and Scraps" column under the initial "C" and later under the moniker "E. C." The popularity of poems such as "The Old Armchair" led to demands for her identity to be revealed. In 1837, the "Answers to Correspondents" column released Eliza Cook's name "in reply to a great many inquiries" and pronounced that she was a poet "destined to occupy a distinguished station among the metrical writers of our country."[24] As a contemporary biographer put it, this praise provided a catalyst for her career as a poet, giving purpose to her "burning desire to pour out [her] soul's measure of music."[25] The fact that Cook's poems were initially published in the "Facts and Scraps" column of the *Weekly Dispatch* suggests the low status often afforded to working-class poetry in newspapers; indeed, the work of most amateur poets was viewed more as filler than as valuable literary content. However, the broad circulation of newspapers like the *Weekly Dispatch*, which achieved a circulation of more than sixty thousand by 1840, sometimes made it possible for a poet to break out of the anonymous ranks and establish herself as a literary celebrity. Indeed, after her successful run in the *Weekly Dispatch*, Cook went on to produce two popular volumes, *Melaia and Other Poems* (1838) and *Poems, Second Series* (1845). After she founded her own periodical in 1849, she became a mentor to other working-class women poets such as "Marie," who published nine poems in *Eliza Cook's Journal* from 1850 to 1852.

Women and social reform

Magazines of popular progress were not only important venues for working-class women writers but for middle-class women writers as well. Three of the most significant of these periodicals – *Howitt's Journal*, *Tait's Edinburgh Magazine*, and *Eliza Cook's Journal* – were edited by women and regularly included female contributors. During the early to mid-Victorian period, magazines of popular progress were thus vitally important in opening up the literary field to women. They not only incorporated conventionally feminine content such as sentimental poetry and domestic fiction but also featured articles describing women's activism on behalf of the poor, thus providing opportunities for middle-class women to translate their philanthropic work into print. For example, the first volume of *Howitt's Journal* featured "Life in Manchester: Libbie Marsh's Three Eras" by Elizabeth

Gaskell, signed poems by Mary Howitt and Anne Bartholomew, an article on working-class housing by Mary Gillies, and a short story by Mrs. Hodgson.

Eliza Meteyard (1816–79) got her start writing for magazines of popular progress. Her first publication was a novel, *Scenes in the Life of an Authoress*, which was serialized in *Tait's Edinburgh Magazine* in 1843–44. After her father died in 1842, Meteyard relocated from Shrewsbury to London, where she met Douglas Jerrold, who suggested her pseudonym "Silverpen." By 1845, she was publishing her work in *Jerrold's Weekly Newspaper* and was an active member of the Whittington Club, a self-improvement society founded in 1846 that offered educational and social opportunities to a largely lower-middle-class constituency. One of the most striking features of the club was its active incorporation of women among its membership; this provided Meteyard with valuable opportunities to network with prominent women writers such as Mary Howitt and Eliza Cook.[26]

Meteyard would go on to publish several books and a variety of short stories and essays, but in these early days of her career, Mary Howitt remembered her as a "poor dear soul," who struggled to support her family by her pen:

> She is sitting by me at this moment with her lips compressed, a look of abstraction in her clever but singular face, and her hair pushed back from her forehead, while she is busy over a story ... Indeed, she is both father and mother to her family; yet she is only seven-and-twenty, and a fragile and delicate woman, who in ordinary circumstances would require brothers and friends to help her. How many instances one sees almost daily of the marvelous energy and high principle and self-sacrifice of woman! I am always thankful to see it, for it is in this way that women will emancipate themselves.[27]

For Meteyard, as for many women writers who came of age at mid-century, writing was a form of self-expression and a means of financial support. Authorship was one of very few fields of employment open to middle-class women, yet the vagaries of the literary life made it a difficult profession for women who had no other source of funding. Nevertheless, Meteyard, like many other middle-class radicals, was fueled by a passion for social reform. Magazines of popular progress thus provided both the motivation and the means for many women to enter the literary profession.

Making a debut after 1860

Beginning in the 1860s, the movement toward signed publication in the periodical press to some extent constrained the range of topics women could pursue, yet it also provided opportunities for women to engage in strategic self-marketing. For example, while early on in her career Christina Rossetti used a pseudonym or initials when publishing her work, it was not until 1861 when she began publishing signed poetry in *Macmillan's Magazine* that she was able to achieve literary fame. As Jennifer Phegley has shown, *Macmillan's* and other literary magazines founded in the late 1850s and 1860s were particularly supportive venues for women's writing. These periodicals located women "firmly in the center of the nineteenth-century literary marketplace as participants in a cultural debate rather than as subjects to be debated."[28] Even though women made great strides as periodical journalists, men still outnumbered women throughout the final decades of the century. The *Cornhill Magazine* was particularly welcoming to women writers, yet, as Janice Harris has shown, from 1860 to 1900 women contributed only about 20 percent of its content.[29] The rates of pay for journalists also tended to be lower for women than for men. Indeed, in 1891 editor W. T. Stead created a stir when he announced that the female staff of his weekly periodical, the *Review of Reviews*, would be paid at the same rate as male journalists.

In the later decades of the nineteenth century, women were increasingly defined as important consumers of novels, periodicals, and newspapers as well as the commercial goods featured in advertising pages. As a result, women writers were recruited in increasing numbers as producers of "feminine" content. Yet, through strategic networking, some women journalists were able to enter into traditional masculine domains. For example, with the encouragement of John Ruskin, Flora Shaw (1852–1929) began her career as a fiction writer; in the 1880s, another male mentor, George Meredith, introduced her to W. T. Stead, who employed her as a staff writer for the *Pall Mall Gazette*, a position that eventually led to a prestigious assignment as colonial editor of the *Times*, a position she held from 1893 to 1900. For the lucky few, an initiation into the workaday world of journalism sometimes led to a long-lasting and successful career.

Even though by the second half of the nineteenth century the literary field seemed more open to women than ever before, it presented a host of new challenges, especially for women novelists. As Gaye Tuchman and Nina Fortin demonstrate in their analysis of the Macmillan publishing archive, from 1867 to 1917 women were "edged out" of the high-culture marketplace for fiction, with men enjoying higher acceptance rates and securing more advantageous publishing contracts. They further reveal that "by the 1880s Macmillan paid men more than women—even for novels that sold as well and, within the confines of the critical double standard, were as well received."[30] When pursuing book publication, amateur women novelists first had to get past readers who provided advice to publishers on manuscript submissions. Through an analysis of publishers' archives, John Sutherland has shown that the odds of making it beyond this first hurdle were poor. Between 1868 and 1870, Macmillan received 143 unsolicited novel manuscripts, eighty of which were explicitly known to have been written by women.[31] Out of this slush pile, only six novel manuscripts were selected for publication: terrible odds indeed. Unsolicited manuscripts were the most difficult to place; women with contacts in the literary world had a much better chance of success.

On one hand, the literary marketplace at century's end promised financial and creative freedom. As novelist Marie Corelli (1855–1924) put it, "Chiefest among the joys of the Life Literary are its splendid independence, its right of free opinion, and its ability to express that opinion."[32] On the otherhand, the publishing world was a fiercely competitive marketplace where only the most talented and stalwart could survive. Corelli warned the young woman writer to expect to "fight like the rest, unless she prefers to lie down and be walked over."[33] In the early years of her career, Corelli certainly demonstrated her willingness to fight for a place in the literary marketplace. Born Mary Mackay, in 1883 she assumed the stage name "Marie Corelli" and moved to London intent on pursuing a career as a concert pianist. She soon turned to journalism, publishing her first signed article, "One of the World's Wonders," in *Temple Bar* in 1885. As Annette Federico points out, Corelli consciously invented a fictional persona, presenting herself to George Bentley as a "Venetian" lady temporarily residing with the Mackays who "could trace her lineage back to Arcangelo Corelli."[34] Just two months after Bentley published this novel, *A Romance of Two Worlds*, she urged him to place an advertisement "*prominently* before the public, with a judicious selection of one line from the press notices."[35] As Federico demonstrates, this advanced form of self-marketing was made possible by the widespread celebrity culture at the *fin de siècle*, which relied on women as print consumers and as sensationalized objects of public interest.

Of course, most women writers at the *fin de siècle* had more difficulty finding their way in the literary marketplace. Marian Yule, a character in George Gissing's *New Grub Street* (1891), expresses the angst felt by many women writers of the period. As she sits in the British Museum Reading Room,

> Such profound discouragement possessed her that she could not even maintain the pretence of study.... She kept asking herself what was the use and purpose of such a life as she was condemned to lead. When already there was more good literature in the world than any mortal could cope with in his lifetime, here was

she exhausting herself in the manufacture of printed stuff which no one even pretended to be more than a commodity for the day's market. What unspeakable folly![36]

Gissing depicts the reading room as an oppressive atmosphere where literary work is both solitary and ineffectual. Such cynicism was to be expected during a time when mass-market publishing was viewed as being both grossly commercial and increasingly feminine. Yet, as Susan David Bernstein has shown, the British Library Reading Room was a vitally important location for women writers "to experience kinds of exteriority that proved absolutely crucial to their writing." Here "they met and created networks of friendship, found mentors and publishers, [and] inspired and encouraged one another in their literary careers."[37] From 1875 to 1884, women made up approximately 10 to 20 percent of library users.[38]

Women's literary clubs and associations provided even more structured occasions for professional development. At the *fin de siècle*, women were admitted as members of the Society of Authors, the Institute of Journalists, and the Society of Women Journalists, founded in 1884, 1890, and 1894, respectively. By 1888, the number of clubs for women had increased so significantly that Amy Levy pronounced, "The female club must be regarded as no isolated and ludicrous phenomenon, but as the natural outcome of the spirit of an age which demands excellence in work from women no less than from men, and as one of the many steps towards the attainment of that excellence."[39] The formation of the Literary Ladies dining club in 1889 brought together prominent women writers of the day, including L. T. Meade, Matilde Blind, and Sarah Grand. As Linda Hughes has shown, the "founding of the Literary Ladies was on one hand a claim to equal status and privileges enjoyed by male authors, and on the other part of the larger entrance of women into the public spaces of London."[40]

In addition to networking in libraries and clubs, aspiring women writers sought advice on how to succeed in the literary marketplace through print sources. With the expansion of employment opportunity during the 1880s, "how-to" employment guides proliferated along with periodical essays providing advice to novice authors. Literary careers were featured in vocational guidebooks such as Phillis Browne's *What Girls Can Do* (1880) and Mercy Grogan's *How Women May Earn a Living* (1883). Such guides offered encouragement and practical advice but also admonished women not to set their literary sights too high. For example, in *Press Work for Women* (1904), Frances Low introduces the writing profession in sobering terms:

> If, then, I were asked to sum up my advice to the beginner, it would be as follows: Take up one or more expert subjects. Dress, employments, complexion, what

you will (so long as it is *in demand*), and make your name known as an authority thereon; but, at the same time, *refuse nothing* which you can do without dishonour. I do not pretend that this is consistent with elevated taste and culture; but I am here addressing the woman who must make a fair income if she is to live in any degree of comfort and refinement, and who sensibly acknowledges to herself, maybe not without a pang, that she cannot *afford* to reform the "journalistic stable."[41]

Following on this dose of practical advice, Low provides tips on proof correction, the locations and membership fees of various literary clubs, and rates of remuneration offered by major periodicals in Britain and the United States. Periodicals also published articles offering practical advice on entering the literary profession and held contests for novice writers. For example, Holden Pike, writing for the *Girl's Own Paper* in 1891, provides some encouragement to women interested in pursuing a career in journalism, noting that a "great deal of the most effective work on our newspapers has been done by women"; however, he emphasizes that "journalism is an arena in which the disappointments greatly outnumber the successes."[42] A year later, W. T. Stead writes in the *Young Woman* that a woman journalist can "go about her business at all hours in English-speaking countries, without serious risk either of safety or reputation," but he adds that women should not expect to "be judged more leniently than if [they] were only a man," which includes being "admonished as freely as their male comrades."[43] This combination of encouragement and caution characterized much of the advice literature for women writers at the *fin de siècle*.

Regardless of the discouragement women sometimes received, they continued to write. As novelist Eliza Humphreys (1850–1938) put it,

> I began to write ... when I was fourteen years of age, and for the one and only reason that is possible—namely, because I felt I *had* to write. The first thing to be accepted and published was a newspaper article. Oh, the excitement and ecstasy of that first acceptance! I feel the thrill to this day, and no subsequent success that I had ever *quite* equaled that moment."[44]

For Humphreys, as for so many other women writers, making a debut in the literary world was not only about seeking financial independence but also about the "excitement and ecstasy" of finding a public voice.

NOTES

1. Isaac Disraeli, *Calamities of Authors* (London: John Murray, 1812), p. 297.
2. Sally Mitchell, "Careers for Girls: Writing Trash," *Victorian Periodicals Review* 25:3 (1992), 109.

3. "Authorship: Past and Present," *All the Year Round* 1 n.s. (March 23, 1889), 273, 276.
4. Margaret Forster, *Elizabeth Barrett Browning: A Biography* (New York: Doubleday, 1989), p. 35.
5. Margaret Oliphant, *Autobiography*, ed. Laurie Langbauer (Chicago: University of Chicago Press, 1988), p. 16.
6. Quoted in George Somes Layard, *Mrs. Lynn Linton: Her Life, Letters, and Opinions* (London: Methuen, 1901), p. 49.
7. Eliza Lynn Linton to Mrs. Cooper, September 15, 1869, qtd. in Lynda Nead, *Victorian Babylon: People, Streets, and Images in Nineteenth-Century London* (New Haven: Yale University Press, 2000), p. 77.
8. Layard, *Mrs. Lynn Linton*, p. 56.
9. Kathryn Ledbetter, "Periodicals for Women," in *The Ashgate Companion to Victorian Periodicals and Newspapers*, ed. Alexis Easley, Andrew King, and John Morton (Aldershot: Ashgate, 2015).
10. Fionnuala Dillane, *Before George Eliot: Marian Evans and the Periodical Press* (Cambridge: Cambridge University Press, 2013), pp. 74, 73.
11. [George Eliot], "Silly Novels by Lady Novelists," *Westminster Review* 66 (October 1856), 460.
12. Charlotte Brontë to Mary Taylor, September 4, 1848, in *The Letters of Charlotte Brontë*, ed. Margaret Smith (Oxford: Oxford University Press, 2000), vol. 2, p. 112.
13. Harriet Martineau, *Autobiography* (1877; rpt. London: Virago, 1983), vol. 1, pp. 119–20.
14. Martha Vicinus, *The Industrial Muse* (New York: Harper & Row, 1974), pp. 158–60.
15. Brian Maidment, "Magazines of Popular Progress & the Artisans," *Victorian Periodicals Review* 17:3 (1984), 83, 90.
16. Editorial note to "Counteracting Influences," *Working-Man's Friend and Family Instructor* 2 (April 6, 1850), 24.
17. Ibid.
18. Florence Boos, "The 'Homely Muse' in Her Diurnal Setting: The Periodical Poems of 'Marie,' Janet Hamilton, and Fanny Forrester," *Victorian Poetry* 39:2 (2001), 265.
19. See Florence Boos, *Working-Class Women Poets in Victorian Britain* (Peterborough, ONT: Broadview, 2008), p. 43.
20. "The Literature of Working Men," *Working Man's Friend* 1:3 (February 9, 1850), 192.
21. [Christian Johnstone], "Our Feast of the Poets for September," *Tait's Edinburgh Magazine* 4 (September 1837), 566.
22. See Boos, "The 'Homely Muse' in Her Diurnal Setting," 281.
23. Kirstie Blair, "'Let the Nightingales Alone': Correspondence Columns, the Scottish Press, and the Making of the Working-Class Poet," *Victorian Periodicals Review* 47:2 (2014), 188–89.
24. Quoted in *Notable Women of Our Own Times* (London: Ward, Lock, 1883), p. 142.
25. Ibid.

26. See Christopher Kent, "The Whittington Club: A Bohemian Experiment in Middle-Class Social Reform," *Victorian Studies* 18:1 (1974), 46, 37.
27. Mary Howitt, *Autobiography* (1889; rpt. Cambridge: Cambridge University Press, 2010), vol. 2, pp. 61–62.
28. Jennifer Phegley, *Educating the Proper Woman Reader: Victorian Family Literary Magazines and the Cultural Health of the Nation* (Columbus: Ohio State University Press, 2004), p. 7.
29. Janice Harris, "Not Suffering and Not Still: Women Writers at the *Cornhill Magazine*, 1860–1900," *Modern Language Quarterly* 47:4 (1986), 385.
30. Gaye Tuchman and Nina Fortin, *Edging Women Out: Victorian Novelists, Publishers and Social Change* (New Haven: Yale University Press, 1989), p. 18.
31. John Sutherland, *Victorian Novelists & Publishers* (Chicago: University of Chicago Press, 1976), p. 210.
32. Marie Corelli, "The Happy Life," *Strand Magazine* 28 (July 1904), 71.
33. Ibid., p. 74.
34. Annette Federico, *Idol of Suburbia: Marie Corelli and Late-Victorian Literary Culture* (Charlottesville: University of Virginia Press, 2000), p. 23.
35. Quoted in ibid., p. 17.
36. George Gissing, *New Grub Street* (London: Smith, Elder, 1891), vol. 1, p. 194.
37. Susan David Bernstein, *Roomscape: Women Writers in the British Museum from George Eliot to Virginia Woolf* (Edinburgh: Edinburgh University Press, 2013), p. 76.
38. G. B. Burgin, "Some British Museum Stories: A Chat with Dr. Garnett," *Idler* 5 (July 1894), 374.
39. Amy Levy, "Women and Club Life," *Woman's World* 1 (1888), 364.
40. Linda Hughes, "A Club of Their Own: The 'Literary Ladies,' New Women Writers and Fin-de-siècle Authorship," *Victorian Literature and Culture* 35:1 (2007), 236.
41. Frances Low, *Press Work for Women: A Text Book for the Young Woman Journalist* (London: L. Upcott Gill, 1904), p. 6. Emphasis in original.
42. Holden Pike, "Young Women as Journalists," *Girl's Own Paper* (March 1891), 396, 395.
43. W. T. Stead, "Young Women in Journalism," *Review of Reviews* 6 (October 1892), 373.
44. "How I Broke into Print," *Strand Magazine* 50 (1915), 574. Emphasis in original.

2

JOANNE SHATTOCK

Becoming a professional writer

> Neither necessity, nor the unsatisfied solitude of a single life, nor, as I fancy, an irresistible impulse, threw her into the paths of literature. She wrote, as the birds sing, because she liked to write; and ceased writing when the fancy left her.

David Masson's obituary for Elizabeth Gaskell (1810–65), published shortly after her death in November 1865, struck a note that was echoed in other tributes. Gaskell had written, he suggested, not because she needed to earn her living or to fill a gap in her life, but because she enjoyed writing. That alone drove her creativity. Her works, he went, on possessed "a degree of perfection and completeness rare in these days, when successful authoresses pour out volume after volume without pause or waiting."[1]

Writing in 1865, Masson's "successful authoresses" could have referred to any number of women writers, but probably included Mary Elizabeth Braddon (1835–1915) and Ellen Wood (1814–87), both of whom were then celebrated as writers of "sensation" novels, and who were producing fiction at a prodigious rate. Other possibilities include Dinah Maria Craik (1826–87), Margaret Oliphant (1828–97), and Eliza Meteyard (1816–79), whose rates of publication in the 1860s were steady rather than relentless, but who had each achieved public recognition.

Masson was careful to make a distinction between Gaskell's "complete" and "perfect" works, which were not produced by financial exigency, and those of her contemporaries, which he believed were. His use of the feminine "authoress" acknowledged their presence in the marketplace but implied a secondary status, which was also his point. Whether he thought of the successful authoresses as professionals because they earned a living and Gaskell as a gifted amateur by contrast is not clear. The mid-nineteenth-century's perception of what constituted a professional writer and women writers' increasing sense of their own professionalism are in part the subjects of this chapter.

Debates about the need for appropriate work for women, and middle-class women in particular, proliferated from the 1850s onward. Writing in the same year as Masson's obituary, the feminist and journalist Bessie Rayner Parkes argued passionately for a range of new professions for women who needed to support themselves. In her *Essays on Woman's Work* (1865), she acknowledged that literature already *was* a profession in which women had made their mark, particularly in the periodical press:

> As periodicals have waxed numerous so has female authorship waxed strong. The magazines demanded short graphic papers, observation, wit, and moderate learning,—women demanded work such as they could perform at home, and ready pay upon performance; the two wants met, and the female sex has become a very important element in the fourth estate. If editors were ever known to disclose the dread secrets of their dens, they only could give the public an idea of the authoresses whose unsigned names are Legion; of their rolls of manuscripts, which are as the sands of the sea.[2]

Women writers' contributions to the periodical press, she suggested, were indicative of a stage in their development, a process that eventually led to full professional status and recognition in a range of genres and subjects.

Writing for the periodical press conferred status and respectability, as the journalist G. H. Lewes declared in an influential article in 1847.[3] It also encouraged variety and experiment. Writers of both sexes seized opportunities to write reviews and articles, thereby extending their repertoire, and at the same time securing an income or augmenting an existing one. This extended repertoire was, in part, what made them "professional" in the eyes of their contemporaries. By virtue of the range and variety of their literary production, they also qualified for the term "woman of letters," one that Linda Peterson has shown came into use in the later nineteenth century as men and women writers sought personal and collective status as authors.[4] In what follows, I propose to examine three nineteenth-century women writers whose careers spanned the 1840s through to the 1890s, each of whom regarded herself as a professional writer even if she did not use the term.

Eliza Meteyard (1816–79) was the Liverpool-born daughter of an army surgeon who grew up in Shropshire. Early in her life, she assumed responsibility for her siblings and moved to London in the 1840s to establish herself as a writer. Elizabeth Gaskell (1810–65) was born into a comfortable, well-connected Cheshire family with Unitarian affiliations; she spent her adult life in Manchester, the wife of a Unitarian minister and mother of four daughters. Margaret Oliphant (1828–97), born in Wallyford, near Edinburgh, grew up in Liverpool and Birkenhead, the daughter of a clerk in the Customs House. She moved to London in 1852 following her marriage to a stained-glass designer. Widowed at the age of thirty-one, she supported her two sons and later several of her close relations by her writing.

These three women were of the same writing generation, although eighteen years separated the oldest, Gaskell, from the youngest, Oliphant. They achieved success and recognition at different stages in their careers. Meteyard and Oliphant wrote, in Masson's phrase, "of necessity," to support themselves and their dependents. Money mattered to Gaskell as well, but her earnings contributed to the family budget and purchased luxuries such as holidays, rather than constituting the only source of income.

All three women took advantage of the periodical press. One of those advantages, as Parkes emphasized, was anonymity, which until the 1860s remained the norm in most publications. Another was the opportunity to work from home, which in the case of Gaskell and Oliphant was imperative, given their domestic responsibilities. For writers of both sexes, living in London, or within easy reach of it, was an advantage. A London base proved a key factor in the development of Meteyard's career. It was less important to Gaskell, who overcame the disadvantage of living in a provincial city by her instinctive sociability and a penchant as well as the means for travel. Oliphant's career was less dependent on metropolitan contacts, although she lived in London until 1865 and then settled in Windsor, within reach of the capital.

Women writers had fewer opportunities than their male colleagues to participate in the interlocking networks of writers, publishers, editors, and proprietors that operated in London. Publishers' offices became meeting places for writers, and the wheels of literary London were oiled by publishers' dinners and soirées from which women were largely excluded, as they were from the various literary clubs that sprang up in the 1840s.[5] Networks that included women writers existed, nevertheless, from the 1830s onward. Eliza Meteyard was part of a circle of radical Unitarians emanating from W. J. Fox's South Place Chapel at Finsbury.[6] Through William and Mary Howitt, the proprietors of *Howitt's Journal* who were on the fringes of this circle, she was introduced to a group of editors and writers with liberal sympathies that included Douglas Jerrold, editor of *Douglas Jerrold's Shilling Magazine* and *Douglas Jerrold's Weekly Newspaper*. Possibly also through the Howitts, she met Christian Johnstone, editor of *Tait's Edinburgh Magazine* and like Mary Howitt an active patron of women writers. It was through Mary Howitt that she met Eliza Cook, who in 1849 launched *Eliza Cook's Journal*, which became Meteyard's next periodical outlet. And so her literary career, precarious as it proved to be, was launched.

The Howitts proved influential patrons for Elizabeth Gaskell as well as Meteyard.[7] It was through them that her first novel *Mary Barton* (1848) was placed with the publishers Chapman and Hall. That connection led to an introduction to Dickens, which in turn prompted an invitation to contribute to his new weekly magazine *Household Words* in 1850. These early contacts were crucial to Gaskell's career.

By her own admission Margaret Oliphant was not a good networker. Her most important contact, with the firm of William Blackwood and Sons, was made before she moved to London. She became, in her words, the Blackwoods' "general utility woman," contributing "miscellaneous papers," as she and John Blackwood referred to them, to *Blackwood's Magazine* on a regular basis from 1854 until her death in 1897.[8] It was a role she accepted gratefully, one that provided a steady income when she most needed it.

Meteyard, Gaskell, and Oliphant entered the literary marketplace within ten years of one another, between 1838 and 1849. In each case, the early contacts made and the contracts secured played a vital part in their professional writing lives and influenced the outcomes as much as their innate abilities.

Eliza Meteyard

Eliza Meteyard's radical political beliefs shaped her early writing and were in turn shaped by her various personal associations. Much of her writing career was dependent on the periodical press. She published a series of novels, beginning with *Struggles for Fame* (1845), which was previewed as "Scenes in the Life of an Authoress" in *Tait's Edinburgh Magazine* (1843–44).[9] Few of her novels made a positive impact, either on the reading public or on the critics. Consequently, she relied on the press to keep afloat financially. The periodicals for which she wrote in the 1840s, *Tait's Edinburgh Magazine*, *Douglas Jerrold's Shilling Magazine*, *Douglas Jerrold's Weekly Newspaper*, *Howitt's Journal* and its precursor the *People's Journal*, paid little. Most of them were short lived. In the 1850s, she wrote for, among others, *Eliza Cook's Journal*, *Sharpe's London Magazine*, and *Chambers's Edinburgh Journal*, all of which were aimed at an artisan and lower-middle-class readership similar to *Douglas Jerrold's Shilling Magazine* and *Howitt's Journal*. Despite her productivity, she was forced to apply to the Royal Literary Fund for financial assistance on five separate occasions, the first as early as 1851.[10]

The subject matter of Meteyard's stories and articles, which reflected the journals' concerns as much as her own, included the cooperative movement, the regulation of working hours in shops and offices, women's employment, women's education, temperance, prostitution, reform of the poor laws, and women's rights. She was one of the first women to serve on the council of the Whittington Club, a project promoted by Jerrold and others to provide the benefits of a London gentlemen's club for shopmen and office workers of both sexes: meeting rooms, a library, and dining facilities. In "The

Whittington Club and the Ladies" in *Douglas Jerrold's Weekly Newspaper* (October 24, 1846), she celebrated the "liberal spirit" that promoted equality of the sexes within the club. Writing as "Silverpen," a pseudonym suggested by Jerrold, and with her gender scarcely concealed, she noted: "Necessity now enforces woman to earn her bread (and we think happily) by what were once considered the masculine prerogatives of the pen, the pencil, or the voice" (343). Women writers' full participation in the facilities of the club, particularly the library and meeting rooms, would have the same humanizing effect as their presence in the reading room of the British Museum. It would enable them to participate in the reforming agenda of the age as intellectual equals. Women writers, the article implied, were acquiring an increasingly public role and voice.

Writers and publishers appear in Meteyard's fiction in both major and minor roles. Barbara, the author heroine of *Struggles for Fame*, is an orphan who after brutal treatment in early life and many improbable adventures is befriended by Adam Leafdale, a kindly book dealer by whom she is educated. Leafdale advocates the importance of "eating the bread of independence" (vol. 2, chap. 1). At the end of the novel, when her fortunes have gone through three volumes' worth of peaks and troughs, Barbara has to choose between an advantageous marriage and her writing; she sacrifices the former for the latter. "Miss Byron," the silver-fork novelist in "Time versus Malthus" (*Douglas Jerrold's Shilling Magazine* 1846, vol. 3, no. 17) is rescued from her lonely life by marriage to "the moralist," a reformed Malthusian who now endorses parenthood. "The Works of John Ironshaft" (*Douglas Jerrold's Shilling Magazine*, 1847, vol. 6, no. 35) is the story of a self-educated working man who rises to become a nationally famed industrialist and philanthropist. A writer with an "iron pen" as well as a blacksmith, he seeks out a London publisher, "Mr Proof," who condescends and then dismisses his efforts while his underling fawns over "her ladyship," a fashionable novelist. At the end of his life, Ironshaft is celebrated, not only for his success as an industrialist but for his other "Works," which have influenced the lives of working people for the better.[11] None of the author subjects is transparently a self-portrait, but many of them show the price, in terms of drudgery and exploitation, of pursuing a literary career.

The transition to a more stable professional status came in the 1860s when Meteyard seized an opportunity to write the biography of Josiah Wedgwood, the famous Staffordshire potter. The raw materials for the biography had been acquired by her friend Joseph Mayer, who was unable to carry out the project. Mary Howitt claimed to have been instrumental in securing a thousand pound advance for the biography from the publishers Hurst & Blackett,[12] but the end product, the two-volume *Life of Josiah Wedgwood from his private correspondence and family papers* (1865–66), was a triumph for Meteyard alone. She found her subject, a man of talent and abilities who had risen from humble origins by his own exertions, immensely sympathetic. He was a real-life version of the heroes of several of her stories. The biography demonstrated her command of a wide range of source materials and her ability to write not only a compelling narrative but also an authoritative history of pottery making.

Yet success, when it came, was short lived. Despite the popularity of the biography, Meteyard's financial position seems never to have been secure. In 1869, Gladstone's government awarded her a Civil List pension of £100. Her reputation quickly waned after her death in 1879. Meteyard was eminently qualified for the title of a "woman of letters" by her competence in many genres: novels, short stories, biography, history, and children's books as well as her extensive journalism. The *Dictionary of National Biography* designates her as an "author," an acknowledgment of her professional status and the range of her writing. What the entry does not convey is the uphill struggle her professional writing life had been. Like her heroine Barbara in *Struggles for Fame*, she had "eaten the bread of independence," but it had proved a meager diet, bringing neither lasting success nor financial security.

Elizabeth Gaskell

The publication of Gaskell's first novel, *Mary Barton* (1848), brought a mixed response from readers and reviewers, but in terms of her professional writing life it opened new doors and established her securely in the literary marketplace. From 1849 onward, she was in receipt of invitations from the editors and proprietors of weekly and monthly magazines directed at a wide spectrum of readers. Dickens's fulsome invitation to write for *Household Words* in 1850 – "I do honestly know that there is no living English writer whose aid I would desire to enlist, in preference to the authoress of Mary Barton"[13] – was undoubtedly the most flattering, but it was preceded and followed by a stream of similar solicitations from other editors.

Through Mary Howitt, she was introduced to John Sartain, the proprietor of *Sartain's Union Magazine*, an illustrated monthly published in Philadelphia, to which she contributed her stories "The Last Generation in England" (July 1849) and "Martha Preston" (July 1850), the latter later expanded into "Half a Life-time Ago" (*Household Words*, October 6–20, 1855). It was probably also through Mary Howitt that she was introduced to Eliza Cook, who urged her to contribute to her newly established *Eliza Cook's Journal*, an invitation she did not accept. William and Robert Chambers were reported to be in pursuit of the author of *Mary Barton* as a potential contributor to *Chambers's Edinburgh Journal*, although there is no record of her having written for their weekly. An approach in 1853 by the novelist Fanny Mayne, the editor of the *True Briton*, was politely refused.[14]

The steady flow of invitations must have been encouraging to a young writer who was only just finding her way into metropolitan literary circles. Gaskell's choice of publishing outlets was seemingly fortuitous, although initially she inclined to publications with a wide range of readers rather than more elite journals intended for the educated reading public. The invitation to write for *Household Words* was an opportunity to be grasped, and she did so; her three-part story "Lizzie Leigh" followed Dickens's "A Preliminary Word" in the opening number of March 30, 1850. *Cranford*, one of her best-known works, began as a sketch in *Household Words* and grew into a nine-part series (1851–53), republished in volume format in 1853. Her novel *North and South*, which, like *Mary Barton*, tackled the tensions between working people and their employers in mid-century Manchester, was serialized in weekly parts in *Household Words* in 1854, following Dickens's own *Hard Times*. Despite an at times fraught relationship with its hands-on "Conductor," as Dickens called himself, she wrote for *Household Words* until it came to an end in 1858 and continued to write for the "new Dickensy periodical,"[15] as she described *All the Year Round*, which succeeded it.

Gaskell's commitment to mass-market journalism, or at least a desire for her stories to reach as wide a readership as possible, is emphasized by her willingness to write two stories, "Hand and Heart" and "Bessy's Troubles at Home," for her friend Travers Madge's *Sunday School Penny Magazine* in 1849 and 1852 and to allow her story "Christmas Storms and Sunshine" (1848) to be reprinted in the penny weekly *Christian Socialist* in 1851.[16]

Elizabeth Haldane, one of her early twentieth-century biographers, lamented that Gaskell's "journalism" had been an error of judgment, and that had she resisted contributing short stories and articles to periodicals, she would have had more time to write the full-length novels on which her reputation rested.[17] This judgment, it could be argued, misinterprets Gaskell's view of her writing life. At no point did she demonstrate the single-mindedness of George Eliot, who determined to forgo reviewing and concentrate on writing novels once *Scenes of Clerical Life* became successful.[18] To the contrary, Gaskell seemed to thrive on a mixture of short-term projects such as stories and articles that ran alongside more ambitious book projects, no doubt attracted by the extra income they provided. Angus Easson notes that when she was at her busiest and most preoccupied, notably at the height of the furor surrounding the publication of her *Life of Charlotte Brontë* in 1857, she was nevertheless willing to undertake some well-paid literary chores. On that occasion, she agreed to contribute a preface to an English edition of *Mabel Vaughan* (1857), a little-known novel by the American novelist Maria S. Cummins, and a short story in *Harper's New Monthly Magazine*.[19]

One aspect of Gaskell's work that attests to her professionalism and adds to an understanding of the range of her talents is her book reviewing. Her anonymous review of Longfellow's long poem *The Golden Legend* (1850) was the lead review in the *Athenaeum* for December 13, 1851. A brief notice of Margaret Sandbach née Roscoe's novel *Spiritual Alchemy* (1849) appeared in the "New Novels" section of the same issue.[20] Like many writers, she found that the process of reviewing the works of others acted as a stimulus to her own writing and provided an opportunity to reflect on her own creative process. The cross-fertilization between her well-judged and knowledgeable review of Longfellow's poem and the plot of her novel *Ruth* (1853), on which she was working at the same time, is clear. Both contain a weak hero, an innocent heroine, and a story that turns on, among other things, whether the heroine can be saved by marriage and whether she lives or dies. In her notice of Sandbach's *Spiritual Alchemy*, Gaskell commented on "the folly exhibited by many an author of a moderately successful novel who hurries forward a second on the reputation of the first,"[21] a possible reflection of her own anxiety about laying herself open to another onslaught from the critics, this time with a controversial story of a working-class woman seduced and betrayed by an upper-class lover.

One unexpected outlet for her reviewing talents was *Household Words*, in which on two occasions she chose a book around which to weave one of her characteristically inventive articles. "Modern Greek Songs" (February 25, 1854) was ostensibly a review of Jean Claude Fauriel's *Chants Populaires de la Grèce Moderne* (1824–25). The prompt for "Company Manners" (May 20, 1854) was an article in the *Revue des Deux Mondes* on Madame de Sablé (1599–1678), the eminent seventeenth-century salon hostess, by the French philosopher Victor Cousin, which was later published as a book. In the *Household Words* tradition, her deftly pitched review-essays combined information and serious thought with entertainment without making unrealistic assumptions about what her readers may have read.

Gaskell's last known book review, of W. T. M. Torrens's *Lancashire's Lesson; or the Need of a Settled Policy in Times of Exceptional Distress* (1864), was written for Alexander Macmillan's weekly review the *Reader* (March 25, 1865) at the same time as her last and most ambitious novel *Wives and Daughters* (1866) was being serialized in the *Cornhill Magazine*. The review demonstrates an ability to enter the political fray and to argue her case with a toughness and precision she had not shown until then. The issues raised in her review are those she had articulated in *Mary Barton* and *North and South* – the dignity of workers and the responsibility of employers and now of the state to provide employment for those thrown out of work by causes beyond their control, in this instance, the Lancashire cotton famine of 1862, an indirect consequence of the U.S. Civil War.

As well as demonstrating a new dimension to Gaskell's talents and competencies, her book reviews endorse the point that she was a professional woman of letters in the Victorian mold, writing across many genres – novels, biography, poems, short stories, articles, and reviews – and contributing to a range of publications from penny and two-penny weeklies to literary weeklies such as the *Athenaeum* and the *Reader* and middle-class magazines such as *Fraser's* and the *Cornhill*. She had no hierarchy of publishing outlets but responded to invitations and opportunities as they arose. She was an assiduous "book maker," collecting her short stories and articles into volumes at regular intervals. She planned another biography – of Madame de Sévigné, the celebrated seventeenth-century French intellectual and letter writer – which was not completed. Professor A. W. Ward, who wrote her entry in the *Dictionary of National Biography*, designated her a novelist, a designation he later reinforced by the structure of his 1906 Knutsford edition of her works, which omitted the *Life of Charlotte Brontë* and consisted of eight volumes of her five full-length novels and three novellas. The memorializing of Elizabeth Gaskell by her obituarists and her early editors and biographers seriously obscured the range of her literary production and her many professional talents, which are only now being fully acknowledged.

Margaret Oliphant

"I have written because it gave me pleasure, because it came natural to me, because it was like talking or breathing, besides the big fact that it was necessary for me to work for my children," Margaret Oliphant wrote candidly in her fragmentary autobiography in 1885. She went on:

> When people comment on the number of books I have written, and I say that I am so far from being proud of that fact that I should like at least half of them forgotten, they stare—and yet it is quite true ... They are my work, which I like in the doing, which is my natural way of occupying myself, which are never so good as I meant them to be.[22]

One of the attractive features of Oliphant's *Autobiography* is the honesty of her self-assessment and the complex tension between her insistence that she had to write to support her family set against her obvious pleasure in her work, the way her writing structured and gave meaning to her life. The writing, as she says at one point, "ran through everything."[23] Also running through the *Autobiography* is the question whether, if she had written less, if she had not felt pressured to write incessantly to support her family, she might have done better work, written "a fine novel" as she calls it, and have earned "nearly as much for half the production."[24] It was a question she could not resolve.

The anxiety of overproduction was not Oliphant's alone – it haunted many writers of both sexes in the second half of the nineteenth century, enabled and encouraged as they were by a diversified literary market to earn a reasonable living, driven by personal circumstances, anxious too about their legacy, and as the century progressed, pursued by a celebrity culture. For Oliphant, however, the sense of being driven to write and an awareness of the consequences seem to have been borne in on her at an early stage. Recalling a happy time in the 1850s when she and her husband were just making ends meet, she wrote, "I was, of course, writing steadily all the time, getting about £400 for a novel, and already, of course, being told that I was working too fast and producing too much."[25] An anonymous review of her novel *The Quiet Heart* (1854) in the *Athenaeum* echoed this perception, noting the similarities between the novel and its predecessor: "the author seems to have written herself quite out, for the present at least."[26] The shrewd reviewer – it was Geraldine Jewsbury – had put her finger on an issue that would characterize Oliphant's entire career.

Oliphant was in no doubt that she was a professional writer. Recalling her various workplaces, from the family dining room to the back sitting room in the houses in Harrington Square and Ulster Place, she noted that the first time she had ever secluded herself for her work was "years after it had become my profession and sole dependence."[27] Like many writers of her generation, she had several projects on the go at once and secured multiple contracts with publishers. Henry Blackett of the firm Hurst & Blackett, who published her books from 1853 onward, became a friend as well as a professional colleague. Alexander Macmillan, with whom she initiated her first contract in 1859, regularly received requests for advances on books still to be written, as did John Blackwood, for whom she then worked off her debt.

As betokened her professionalism, the reviews and articles for *Blackwood's Magazine* ran in tandem with her novels, biographies, literary histories, and whatever else she was contracted for. The early reviews focused primarily on contemporary fiction, but she also reviewed poetry, history, biography, books of travel, and occasionally books on art and theology. Her "miscellaneous pieces" included articles on the Scottish church, accounts of her travels at home and abroad, and reviews of current exhibitions. She wrote on issues affecting women, including divorce and later the vote, some of her views disquieting to a modern sensibility, although these were moderated toward the end of her life. She became sufficiently fluent in French and Italian to review books in both languages, concentrating on contemporary literature and culture. German, too, she tackled although less easily.

Regular reviewing provided an income stream, but she was also energized by it. Her voracious reading of the works of others fed her own creativity, often in direct ways. Her reviews of two novels by F. W. Robinson, a little-known novelist, influenced the plot and characters of *The Perpetual Curate*, one of the acclaimed "Chronicles of Carlingford."[28] Critics have suggested that the research and writing of her biography of the Scottish preacher Edward Irving (1862) fueled an interest in a religious vocation that found its way into several of the Carlingford novels.[29] So many of her articles were biographical sketches that one could also see her journalism at this point as a training ground for the full-scale biographies she later wrote. But it would be wrong to see Oliphant's reviewing as an apprenticeship for something else. Her critical judgments in these early years were sure footed. She could be opinionated, wrong headed at times, but she was also perceptive and shrewd. If she was in training for anything in these reviews, it was to become the influential critical voice of her generation, an achievement signaled by her obituarists – memorably in Henry James's double-edged comment that "no woman had ever, for half a century, had her personal 'say' so publicly and irresponsibly."[30]

Oliphant constantly sought larger projects that would provide a steady income rather than the hand-to-mouth existence of article writing. Blackwood proposed a series of biographical sketches of eighteenth-century figures that became *Historical Sketches of the Reign of George II*, serialized first in *Blackwood's* and then published in two volumes in 1869. Other series followed in the magazine, but disappointingly none turned into books. In 1876, Blackwood proposed that she edit a book series, "Foreign Classics for English Readers," to which she contributed three volumes herself.

David Finkelstein, the modern historian of the House of Blackwood, notes that from 1870 onward, the firm began to move away from three-volume novels to concentrate on biography, general history, and books of travel. After 1870, Blackwood published only seven of Oliphant's remaining novels. Instead, she was contracted by them for biographies, for short stories, and eventually for *Annals of a Publishing House* (1897), the official history of the firm, all of which made a profit. For her novels after 1870, she turned to Macmillan; to Hurst & Blackett; and to periodicals such as *Good Words*, the *Cornhill*, the *Graphic*, *St Paul's Magazine, and Longman's Magazine*; and to Tillotson's fiction agency through which her novels were serialized in newspapers.

In the late 1880s, Oliphant attempted to adapt to new journalistic practices with columns of short articles on topical subjects, including social and political concerns. The titles, "A Fireside Commentary" in the daily *St James's Gazette* (1888), "A Commentary from an Easy Chair" in the weekly *Spectator* (1889–90), and "Things in General" in the monthly *Atalanta* (1893–94), convey the more relaxed tone and fluid format of the new ventures. They were only moderately successful. Her work for *Blackwood's Magazine* continued, as did the steady stream of novels, some from 1894 adopting a one-volume format in the wake of the demise of the circulating libraries. "I am a wonder to myself, a sort of machine so little out of order, able to endure all things, always fit for work whatever has happened to me," she wrote in 1890 at the age of sixty-two.[31] She became increasingly conscious, though, that newer writers were overtaking her and, in the analogy she used in a poignant preface to a collection of stories, aware that her career was on its "ebb tide."[32]

Oliphant's reflection on Trollope's career in her obituary for the novelist might have served as a justification for her own writing life:

> It would be vain to calculate what Mr Trollope might have done had he ... left us only the half-dozen stories which embody the History of Barset ... Our own opinion is that every artist finds the natural conditions of his working, and that in doing what he has to do according to his natural lights he is doing the best which can be got from him. But it is hopeless to expect from the reader either the same attention or the same faith for twenty or thirty literary productions which he gives to four or five. The instinct of nature is against the prolific worker. In this way a short life, a limited period of activity are much the best for art; and a long period of labour, occupied by an active mind and fertile faculties, tell against, and not for, the writer.[33]

Her reflection might also have served as an epitaph for many professional women writers, driven by necessity and perhaps urged on by the need to keep their name before the public, into writing too quickly and producing too much.

Conclusion

After their deaths, Meteyard, Gaskell, and Oliphant suffered the sharp decline in their reputations common to many Victorian writers at the turn of the twentieth century. By any objective measure, Meteyard's was the least successful career of the three. Her writing life, with its unremitting struggle to earn an adequate living, was more common in the nineteenth century than has been acknowledged.[34] In her obituaries, Gaskell was routinely compared with her more famous writing sisters, Jane Austen, Charlotte Brontë, and George Eliot, to her disadvantage. It was Margaret Oliphant who in 1887 declared that "Mrs Gaskell has fallen into that respectful oblivion which is the fate of a writer who reaches a sort of secondary classical rank and survives, but not effectually, as the greater classics do."[35] Oliphant's obituarists respectfully acknowledged her achievements across a wide range of publications including the novel and her impact as a critic, but there was a general sense that she had outlived her time. The writing lives of all three confirm Parkes's sense that by 1865, literature had become an acknowledged profession for women. But the collective experience of these three women of letters also demonstrates that it remained a precarious one, that success, when it came, could be short lived, and that the judgment of posterity could be harsh.

NOTES

1. [David Masson], "Mrs Gaskell," *Macmillan's Magazine* 13 (December 1865), 154.
2. Bessie Rayner Parkes, *Essays on Woman's Work* (London: Alexander Strahan, 1865), p. 120.
3. [G. H. Lewes], "The Condition of Authors in England, Germany and France," *Fraser's Magazine* 35 (March 1847), 285–95.
4. Linda H. Peterson, *Becoming a Woman of Letters. Myths of Authorship and Facts of the Victorian Market* (Princeton: Princeton University Press, 2009); see Introduction and chap. 1.
5. See Joanne Shattock, "Professional Networks: Masculine and Feminine," *Victorian Periodicals Review* 44:2 (Summer 2011), 128–40.
6. See Kathryn Gleadle, The *Early Feminists: Radical Unitarians and the Emergence of the Women's Rights Movement, 1831–1850* (Basingstoke: Macmillan, 1995).
7. See Easley, "Making a Debut," pp. 15–28 in this volume, for details of this connection.
8. Mrs. Oliphant, *Annals of a Publishing House. William Blackwood and his Sons* (Edinburgh: William Blackwood and Sons, 1895), vol. 2, p. 475.
9. "Scenes in the Life of an Authoress," *Tait's Edinburgh Magazine* 99 (December 1843), 765–75; (January 1844), 36–42; and (April 1844), 245–54. These were extracts from the first volume of the novel, not a full serialization.
10. Kay Boardman, "Struggling for Fame: Eliza Meteyard's Principled Career," in *Popular Victorian Women Writers*, ed. Kay Boardman and Shirley Jones (Manchester: Manchester University Press, 2004), p. 48.
11. I am grateful to Tomoko Kanda for directing me to this story.
12. See *Mary Howitt. An Autobiography*, ed. Margaret Howitt (London: Wm. Isbister, 1889), vol. 2, p. 149.
13. *The Letters of Charles Dickens*, ed. Madeline House, Graham Storey, and Kathleen Tillotson (Oxford: Clarendon Press, 1988), vol. 6 (1850–52), p. 22.

14. *Further Letters of Mrs Gaskell*, ed. John Chapple and Alan Shelston (Manchester: Manchester University Press, 2000, 2003), pp. 106–7.
15. *The Letters of Mrs Gaskell*, ed. J. A. V. Chapple and Arthur Pollard (1966; Manchester: Manchester University Press, 1997), p. 538.
16. *Christian Socialist*, March 29, April 5 and 12, 1851, vol. 1, pp. 175–76, 183–84, 191–92.
17. Elizabeth Haldane, *Mrs Gaskell and her Friends* (London: Hodder and Stoughton, 1930), pp. 5, 208.
18. Joanne Shattock, "Publishing and Publication," in *George Eliot in Context*, ed. Margaret Harris (Cambridge: Cambridge University Press, 2013), p. 15.
19. Angus Easson, "'An Incident at Niagara Falls' and the Editing of Mabel Vaughan," *English Language Notes* 17:4 (June 1980), 273–77.
20. Angus Easson, "Elizabeth Gaskell and the Athenaeum: Two Contributions Identified," *Modern Language Review* 85:4 (October 1990), 829–32.
21. "Reviews in the Athenaeum," *The Works of Elizabeth Gaskell*, vol. 1, ed. Joanne Shattock (London: Pickering and Chatto, 2005), p. 216.
22. *The Autobiography of Margaret Oliphant*, ed. Elisabeth Jay (Oxford: Oxford University Press, 1990), pp. 14–15.
23. Ibid., p. 30.
24. Ibid., p. 16.
25. Ibid., p. 63.
26. [Geraldine Jewsbury], *Athenaeum*, November 23, 1854, p. 1577. I am grateful to Isabel Seidel for bringing this review to my attention.
27. *Autobiography of Margaret Oliphant*, p. 31.
28. Wilkie Collins's *No Name* similarly had an indirect influence on the plot. See Joanne Shattock, ed., "Introduction," *The Perpetual Curate*, in *Selected Works of Margaret Oliphant* (London: Pickering & Chatto, 2014), vol. 17, pp. xvi–xix.
29. Trev Lynn Broughton, ed., "Introduction," *Writings on Biography*, in *Selected Works of Margaret Oliphant* (London: Pickering & Chatto, 2012), vol. 7, pp. xiii–xviii.
30. Henry James, "London Notes, August 1897," in *Notes on Novelists* (London: Charles Scribner, 1914), pp. 357–60.
31. *Autobiography of Margaret Oliphant*, p. 56.
32. Margaret Oliphant, "On the Ebb Tide," preface to *The Ways of Life* (London: Smith, Elder, 1897).
33. "Anthony Trollope," *Good Words*, 1883; rpt. in *Literary Criticism, 1877–86*, ed. Valerie Sanders, in *Selected Works of Margaret Oliphant* (London: Pickering & Chatto, 2011), vol. 3, p. 368.
34. See Nigel Cross, *The Common Writer: Life in Nineteenth Century Grub Street* (Cambridge: Cambridge University Press, 1985), chap. 6.
35. "The Old Saloon," *Blackwood's Magazine* 151 (June 1887), 758.

3

LINDA H. PETERSON

Working with publishers

Perhaps it goes without saying that a Victorian writer could not become a professional author without securing a publisher to issue her work. Today, the crucial figure in an author's career may be her agent or editor, as the acknowledgments in many books attest; the modern publisher represents an imprint, sometimes with a distinguished history of book production, but often is just a subsidiary of a national or international conglomerate. In the Victorian period, however, publishing houses were smaller, and most publishers engaged actively in soliciting, reading, and evaluating manuscripts. Some – such as William Blackwood and Sons – were family-run businesses with several generations conducting personal and professional affairs directly with their authors; others – such as Hurst and Blackett – were businessmen who bought a failing firm (in this case Henry Colburn) and grew to become international powerhouses with offices in London, New York, and Melbourne. Whatever their origins or destinations, most Victorian publishers knew their authors personally, supported their professional careers, and helped advance their status in the literary realm. Although the relations between authors and publishers changed over the course of the century, as the last section of this chapter suggests, they remained for the most part cordial and even intimate.

Launching a career

The career of Charlotte Brontë provides a well-documented example of a publisher's role in launching an authorial career – just as her sisters' counter-experiences provide a negative case. All three sisters sent the manuscripts of their first novels – *The Professor* by Currer Bell, *Wuthering Heights* by Ellis Bell, and *Agnes Grey* by Acton Bell – to London firms known for publishing popular fiction. An unsuccessful inquiry went to Henry Colburn in July 1846; another went to Thomas Newby, who declined *The Professor* but accepted *Wuthering Heights* and *Agnes Grey* on terms "somewhat impoverishing to the two authors."[1] In her biographical account of her sisters' lives and works, Charlotte recalled that the three "MSS. were perseveringly obtruded upon various publishers for the space of a year and a half; usually their fate was an ignominious and abrupt dismissal." Eventually, Charlotte found a sympathetic reader in William S. Williams of Smith, Elder, who in consultation with George Smith, the young proprietor of the firm, sent a letter declining *The Professor* "for business reasons" but encouraging its author to submit a three-volume work of a more striking character. Charlotte was pleased that this publisher and his literary advisor "discussed its merits and demerits so courteously, so considerately, in a spirit so rational, with a discrimination so enlightened, that this very refusal cheered the author better than a vulgarly-expressed acceptance would have done."[2] Within two months, Brontë sent the manuscript of *Jane Eyre*, which Smith, Elder promptly accepted and published with phenomenal success in 1847.

Although she initially received only £100 for copyright and another £400 for subsequent editions, Brontë valued her publisher for more than financial reasons. Almost immediately, she and Williams began a correspondence about contemporary novels – her own, her sisters', Thackeray's, as well as lesser, ephemeral works – that allowed her to analyze the achievements (and demerits) of English fiction and articulate her *ars poetica*. George Smith sent parcels of books his firm had published, thus giving access to recent novels and major prose such Ruskin's *Modern Painters*, Hazlitt's *Essays*, and Emerson's *Representative Men*.[3] If the correspondence with Smith remained businesslike for the first year or two, the letters to Williams soon became personal, with Charlotte offering advice about his daughters' future careers as governesses and Williams offering medical information when Emily became seriously ill, and then solace when Emily and then Anne died. Charlotte's publisher truly sustained her career, not only providing needed intellectual stimuli but also prodding her to write when she seemed depressed or discouraged.

Emily's and Anne's dealings with Thomas Newby offer a different case of author-publisher relations. Newby accepted their first novels on terms that reflected their amateur status: the sisters were required to pay £50 in advance, with the promise that the money would be refunded if their novels sold enough copies to cover expenses. Although they promptly paid the fee, Newby was dilatory in bringing out their work. As their biographer Juliet Barker notes, "While *Jane Eyre* was completed, typeset, bound, published, and getting its earliest reviews, [their novels] still languished at Mr Newby's."[4] Newby's shoddy practices resulted, moreover, in books that had not been proofread and thus were riddled with printing errors. Even after the novels met with a modest commercial success, he failed to live up to his contract. After their deaths, when pressed for a financial account by Charlotte, Newby asserted that "he realized no profit" and had "sustained actual loss," further claiming that any profits from sales had gone toward advertisements, as the authors had wished.[5] Charlotte wryly observed to George Smith that no ads had ever been seen. Only when Smith intervened and brought out a new edition of *Wuthering Heights* and *Agnes Grey* in 1850, with a biographical preface composed by Charlotte, did these novels gain a secure future. Indeed, both might have sunk into oblivion without Smith, Elder's intervention.

Although the Brontë sisters provide the best-known cases of positive and negative relations with publishers, the contrasts recur in the biographies of other Victorian women, sometimes within the career of a single author. In her autobiographical novel *A Struggle for Fame* (1883), for instance, Charlotte Riddell (1832–1906) describes the mentoring she received as a young novelist from an old-fashioned publisher, Mr. Vassett, modeled on Charles Skeet of King William Street. When her heroine Glen asks for advice, Vassett claims that he cannot give her a formula for a successful novel: "If I could publish a key to the problem you want to solve[,] it would sell so well, I should never need to bring out another book. The land you want to enter has no itinerary—no finger posts—no guides" (I, 123). Despite the lack of professional tips, Riddell later praised Skeet for his early support and enduring friendship, noting in an interview for the *Lady's Pictorial* that he had published her youthful fiction *The Rich Husband* (1858), *Too Much Alone* (1860), and *The World and the Church* (1862), and thus launched her career. She also praised George Bentley, "though he, like everyone else, refused my work; still I left his office not unhappy, but thinking much more about how courteous and nice he was." Riddell even commented favorably on Thomas Newby, who accepted her first novel, *Zuriel's Child* (1856): "I could always, when the day was frightfully cold ... turn into Mr. Newby's office in Welbeck Street, and have a talk with him and his 'woman of business,' Miss Springett."[6]

In Riddell's view, these early Victorian publishers were closer to amateurs than professional businessmen. In *A Struggle for Fame*, she contrasts an amateur "then" with a professional "now," the former an era when "in the literary world females still retained some reticence, and males the traditions at least of self-respect" (I, 103), the latter a professionalized era when authors became more businesslike and market conscious, if also more "pushing" and "hopelessly impecunious" (I, 103). Like Riddell, her heroine leaves the old-fashioned, gentlemanly Vassett for the trendy firm of Felton and Laplash (based on the Tinsley Brothers). Once she moves, she achieves great popular success – as Riddell did with *George Geith of Fen Court* (1864). But now male authors and reviewers treat her as a professional rival, using periodical reviews to damn or downgrade her work. Even her publisher gives little support in sustaining her career and eventually throws her over when her novels fail to sell. Thus, in negotiating with commercial publishers like Tinsley Brothers, Riddell left behind the gentler, kinder world of early Victorian publishing, where relations between author and publisher were cordial, if sometimes also paternal, and entered a new publishing world of market-driven choices, industrialized production, and commercial profit over literary product. This brave new world dominated, in Riddell's view, the late Victorian literary scene.

Developing a career

If publishers were essential to launching a woman writer's career, they also played an important role in its development. The literary successes of Margaret Oliphant (1828–97), novelist, biographer, and reviewer; of Christina Rossetti (1830–94), poet and devotional writer; and of Alice Meynell (1847–1922), poet and essayist, show this role in different ways.

Oliphant launched her career more or less on her own, using her brother Willie to negotiate with London publishers and place her work with firms known for popular fiction, Henry Colburn and Hurst & Blackett. When she wrote *Katie Stewart* (1852), a Scottish historical novel based on family tales, she turned to the Edinburgh publisher William Blackwood and Sons. With Blackwood, she found a publisher who would support her during hard times, assign book reviews and columns to supplement income, and eventually make her "general utility woman" to the house organ, *Blackwood's Magazine*. After the success of *Katie Stewart*, Oliphant serialized other novels in *Blackwood's Magazine* and added columns about past and recent fiction to her dossier; throughout the 1850s, she anonymously reviewed Thackeray, Dickens, Bulwer, and other modern novelists in "Maga," as William Blackwood called it. In 1859, when her husband became ill with tuberculosis, the family traveled to Italy for the warmer climate, with Blackwood accepting travel pieces, offering translation work, and sending financial advances to aid the family. As Oliphant's biographer Elisabeth Jay notes, "John Blackwood undoubtedly became her banker, reviewer, literary adviser, and friend."[7]

When her husband died and left her a widow with three young children, Oliphant hit a low point, unable to write articles or stories that the Blackwoods would accept. In her *Autobiography* (1899), she tells of summoning up the courage to visit the firm's Edinburgh office and offer a novel face-to-face to John Blackwood and "Major" Blackwood, "both very kind and truly sorry for me," but shaking their heads and saying "it would not be possible to take such a story."[8] In fact, this encounter marked the turning point in her career and her relations with the firm. Oliphant returned home that night to compose "The Executor" (1861), the first story of her Carlingford series, "which made a considerable stir at the time, and *almost* made me one of the popularities of literature" (70). Thereafter, she published more than twenty volumes of fiction, biography, and history with Blackwoods and typically placed half a dozen articles in "Maga" each year, including regular columns, "The Old Saloon" and "The Looker-on," during the last decade of her life. Yet, as Jay notes, this close relationship "remained essentially one of patronage" and perhaps hindered Oliphant's career,[9] if only because she never felt she could negotiate prices with a publisher to whom she was in debt. Nonetheless, during this period, 1860–95, she also sustained cordial friendships and publishing relations with George Craik of Macmillans and Henry Blackett of Hurst & Blackett, with whom she published roughly thirty books each. Oliphant's friendships with these men and their families, especially with Isabella Blackwood and Ellen Blackett, became the core of her social life, giving her much pleasure and stability – not just commercial outlets for her work.

Christina Rossetti never developed this sort of intimate relationship with her publisher, Alexander Macmillan, but when his editor David Masson accepted several lyrics for *Macmillan's Magazine*, Macmillan himself wrote to encourage a collection that became *Goblin Market and Other Poems* (1862) – and thus helped launch her adult career. As an adolescent, Rossetti had published verse under the pseudonym "Ellen Allyne" in *The Germ*, the periodical of the Pre-Raphaelite Brotherhood edited by her brother William Michael Rossetti. When the short-lived *Germ* folded after three issues, Christina lost an outlet for her poetry. She reverted to contributing to a ladies' magazine, *The Bouquet from Marlybone Gardens*, funded by subscription, and to placing occasional poems in minor literary annuals. The appearance of "Uphill" and "A Birthday" in *Macmillan's Magazine* in 1861 changed all this – including Rossetti's psychological state. Initially deferential, she soon was writing enthusiastically to Macmillan about the projected collection, happily acknowledging her desire "to attain fame(!) and guineas by means of the Magazine."[10] Macmillan, in turn, worked to promote a poet whose excellence he recognized. He asked for a photograph to include in his magazine, urged a second volume after the success of *Goblin Market*, and served as primary publisher of her poetry, issuing *The Prince's Progress and Other Poems* (1866), *New Poems* (1896), and the posthumous *Poetical Works of Christina Georgina Rossetti* (1904), edited by William Michael.

This relationship with a distinguished publisher allowed Rossetti to develop her skills and status as a leading Victorian poet.

Alice Meynell (née Thompson), a poet of the late nineteenth century who admired Rossetti's work and composed love lyrics in her strain, started her own literary career with *Preludes* (1875), a collection published by Henry S. King. Although Meynell's father most likely financed the volume, it was a *coup* in that Meynell placed her work with a firm known for literary excellence, especially in poetry. With *Preludes*, Meynell garnered private praise from Alfred Tennyson, Coventry Patmore, Aubrey de Vere, and John Ruskin, as well as positive reviews in such periodicals as the *Pall Mall Gazette*. Unfortunately, as Meynell recounts the story, the poems disappeared from public view when King's warehouse burned to the ground and the volumes were lost. Fortunately, Meynell's poetry was rediscovered fifteen years later when an editor and a publisher – William Henley of the *Scots Observer* and John Lane of the Bodley Head Press – recognized the high quality of Meynell's work.

By then, the early 1890s, Meynell had established a professional reputation as an art critic and essayist; she wrote regular reviews for the *Magazine of Art* and *Art Journal*, occasional pieces for the *Spectator*, *Saturday Review*, *Illustrated London News*, and others, and she edited *Merry England* and the *Weekly Register* with her husband Wilfrid.[11] Yet it was the appearance of her brief essays in the *Observer* – all stylishly polished, despite their spontaneous, almost breathless effect – that brought her to the attention of John Lane and secured her fame. Via Henley, Lane asked if he might publish a volume of essays drawn from Meynell's *Observer* columns. The result was *The Rhythm of Life and Other Essays* (1893), with its title taken from one of her most famous pieces, and *Poems* (1893), a reissue of verses from *Preludes* with the addition of some new lyrics. Although Meynell's relationship with Lane was always polite and professional, never deeply personal or intimate, it was crucial to her career. Lane's role as the leading publisher of aesthetic and decadent writers enabled her to make a transition from professional journalist to prominent woman of letters in *fin-de-siècle* literary culture. His continuing support – from 1892 with *Poems* and *The Rhythm of Life* to 1901 with *Later Poems* – stamped Meynell's work as top flight. Lane's shrewd eye for advertising, moreover, kept her poetry in the public view – as in his 1895 interview for *The Sketch*, in which he presents Meynell as a modern Sappho and lists her first among the "five great women poets of the day."[12] As we shall see in the next section, maintaining an ongoing relationship with a publisher was crucial to sustaining literary status and a professional career.

Consolidating a career

Novelists like Oliphant and poets like Rossetti and Meynell could count on their publishers to regularly accept and issue their submissions. This assurance enabled them to place work in their signature genres, develop skills in others, and consolidate their literary reputations. In no cases was the publisher more crucial (positively) than in the career of George Eliot (1819–80) and (negatively) in the experience of her admirer, the novelist Mary Cholmondeley (1859–1925).

Marian Evans, who adopted the *nom-de-plume* George Eliot, was a notoriously sensitive author. She entered the London literary world as assistant editor to John Chapman on the *Westminster Review*, eventually fulfilling most of the editorial duties and contributing original, but anonymous articles to the periodical. Although her contributions were known to insiders, the policy of anonymity shielded her from public scrutiny and assessment. After eloping with fellow writer George Henry Lewes, Eliot continued this periodical work but, at Lewes's suggestion, in 1856 she turned her hand to writing fictional sketches, "Scenes of Clerical Life." Lewes sent the first "Scene" to John Blackwood as the manuscript of "a friend who desires my good offices with you"; Lewes added, "I confess that before reading the m.s. I had considerable doubts of my friend's power as a writer of fiction; but after reading it those doubts were changed into very high admiration."[13] Blackwood concurred with this judgment, writing that "this specimen of Amos Barton is unquestionably very pleasant reading" and asking to see more stories for publication in *Blackwood's Magazine*.

Typically but unwisely in this instance, Blackwood continued his letter of acceptance with an evaluation of Eliot's submission, "The Sad Fortunes of the Reverend Amos Barton." He praised the death of Milly as "powerfully done" but called the "windup" the "lamest part of the story"; he admired the descriptions as "very humourous and good" but criticized "the error of trying too much to explain the characters."[14] In making these comments, Blackwood was following his usual practice with submissions: offering a balanced account from a typical, but shrewd reader. Eliot did not see the balance, however, only the critique. After receiving Blackwood's letter, Lewes wrote that his "clerical friend" was "somewhat discouraged by it," adding that he rated "the story much higher than you appear to do from certain expressions in your note."[15] When Blackwood continued sending his evaluations of strengths and weaknesses, Lewes had to explain that his friend was "unusually sensitive" and "afraid of failure though not afraid of obscurity"; at one point, after witnessing the depressing effect of a letter on Eliot, he advised outright: "Entre nous let me hint that unless you have any *serious* objection to make to Eliot's stories, *don't* make any."[16] Blackwood took the hint and became, as Gordon Haight notes, "next to Lewes," the one who "did most to develop and sustain George Eliot's genius as a novelist."[17]

This sustenance included more than repeated reassurances and unstinting praise for Eliot's fiction. After the publication of her first novel, *Adam Bede* (1859), Blackwood sent his cousin to search "in all the dog-fancying regions of London" for a pug – having heard that Eliot liked this breed and had recently lost an elder sister.[18] The day after her sister's funeral, Blackwood sent the manuscript of *Adam Bede*, "beautifully bound in red russia."[19] On a more practical level, Blackwood kept Eliot in the public eye with ample and frequent advertisements of her work. Taking the advice of his London manager, Joseph Langford – "George Eliots [sic] books sell more like Holloway Pills than like books and it pays to keep them before the public by advertising" – Blackwood agreed, writing to Langford: "By all means keep them before the public."[20]

Even when she defected to another publisher who offered more money for her novel *Romola* (1863), Blackwood maintained cordial relations. To Langford, he privately wrote: "The going over to the enemy without giving me any warning and with a story on which from what they both said I was fully intitled [sic] to calculate upon, sticks in my throat but I shall not quarrel—quarrels especially literary ones are vulgar."[21] With Eliot, however, he adopted the principle of "not quarreling," noting in a speech he later gave at the centenary of Scott's birth that Sir Walter's relations with publishers had been notably stormy but that, for him, "authors were among his dearest friends."[22] Eliot concurred. After her brief defection, she returned to Blackwoods with her next novel, *Felix Holt* (1866), and stayed with the firm for the rest of her career. In October 1876, when John Blackwood was seriously ill, Eliot wrote to thank him for all his encouragement throughout the years.[23] On hearing of his approaching death, she commented: "He will be a heavy loss to me. He has been bound up with what I most cared for in my life for more than twenty years, and his good qualities have made many things easy to me that without him would often have been difficult."[24]

Of course, John Blackwood and his nephew William, who joined the firm in 1857, had more than friendship at stake in their relationship with George Eliot. As David Finkelstein notes in *The House of Blackwood*, Eliot's books represented a "tangible capital asset," in that they became a "mainstay of the company profits between 1860 and 1900," regularly generating more than £1000 per year.[25] On the novelist's side, the relationship was profitable too, in that Eliot moved from the relative poverty of periodical writing to the financial comfort that Blackwoods' solid, if not extraordinary payments for fiction brought: from *Adam Bede* (£800 in 1858, another £800 in 1859) to *Daniel Deronda* (£4000 in 1873–76).

Such mutual benefit did not always pertain in author-publisher relations. Mary Cholmondeley, a writer who admired Eliot's fiction and incorporated Eliot's aphoristic style into her own novels, lacked the sustaining relationship with a publisher that her predecessor achieved. Cholmondeley's career started well with George Bentley, of Richard Bentley & Son, whom she met in the mid-1880s via friend and fellow novelist Rhoda Broughton. Bentley accepted Cholmondeley's first novel *The Danvers Jewels* (1887), praising "your bright and humorous story" in his acceptance letter and urging that she "continue to give me the benefit of such papers."[26] He accepted her next two novels for publication in periodical and book format, paying £50 for the copyright of *Sir Charles Danvers* (1889), increasing her royalties as her sales and reputation rose,[27] and offering £400 for *Diana Tempest* (1893), then adding a £100 bonus after the novel went into a fifth edition.[28] These rates fall below those paid to George Eliot by Blackwoods or by Bentley to Broughton, who often sold the copyright of her popular novels for £800, but they represent Bentley's estimate of Cholmondeley's solid worth.

Bentley soon became an intimate correspondent, offering medical advice and encouragement when Cholmondeley found herself seriously ill with asthma and addicted to morphine for relief. Perhaps because he too suffered from asthma, she found his letters sincere and helpful. Her biographer, Carolyn Oulton, suggests that empathy with Bentley as a fellow asthmatic and an ongoing struggle to meet his deadlines "led her to confide in him about the details of her illness in ways that are not paralleled elsewhere in her correspondence." Oulton adds that Cholmondeley may not have continued her writing career without this personal support.[29]

When George Bentley died in 1895, however, and his son Richard sold the business to Macmillan, Cholmondeley lost a steady, reliable outlet for her fiction. The publisher's archive does not make clear if Macmillan wished to drop this woman author, known for writing sensational fiction, a genre that was going out of fashion, or if he simply did not keep up with the correspondence required by the business transition. In any case, Cholmondeley felt neglected and unwanted. When Macmillan did not inquire about her new work, she took her next novel *A Devotée* (1897) and the plan for *Red Pottage* (1899), her most famous, to Edward Arnold. After *Red Pottage*'s phenomenal success (it went into a fifth edition within a year), Macmillan wrote to ask why she had left the firm. She responded that she supposed "you would have written to me had you wished for the new book on which Mr. Bentley knew I was engaged," admitting that she was "disappointed that I only heard from you when several months had elapsed, and when I was in treaty with another publisher." In a subsequent letter, written after Macmillan apologized for his lapse, Cholmondeley added:

> I was a very small writer and you are a very great publisher. It never entered my head to write to you. But I will frankly own I was deeply disappointed at not hearing from you ... Until I received your letter of June 24th [1900] I had remained under the impression that the firm did not value my books.[30]

Cholmondeley's impression – that Macmillan had quietly dropped her and resumed correspondence only after she published a best seller – seems accurate, given the five-year hiatus in the correspondence. Whether Macmillan had initially intended to "edge out" this particular woman writer, as Gaye Tuchman and Nina Fortin suggest that the firm systematically did to other women,[31] remains unknown, but it raises a larger question of how gender aided or disabled Victorian women in their relations with publishers.

Gender variants in author-publisher relations

Analyzing the Macmillan publishing archive of the mid-to-late nineteenth century, Tuchman and Fortin argue that 1840–79 saw male authors in "a period of invasion," challenging women's dominance in "the novel as a cultural form"; they posit that a "period of redefinition," 1880–99, followed this invasion, "when men of letters, including critics, actively redefined the nature of a good novel" and demoted women's fiction to the status of popular (low) culture.[32] These insights into late-Victorian publishing have sometimes led scholars to assume that women authors tended *always* to be edged out or that publishers *routinely* valued their work less than that of their male counterparts. Such assumptions are troublesome because, as Tuchman and Fortin carefully note, some publishers (e.g., Tinsley) "viewed themselves as specialists in popular fare" and thus, unlike Macmillan, which began as an academic publishing house, actively sought and even preferred women's fiction.[33] Furthermore, such assumptions are troublesome because they fail to account for different genres, different publishing media, and changing literary norms across the century – factors that affected both male and female authors.

If we turn to the 1830s and consider two famous illustrations of prominent authors – "The Fraserians" and "Regina's Maids of Honour," published in *Fraser's Magazine* in January 1835 and January 1836, respectively – we might conclude that a gender division similarly dominates the early Victorian literary field, promoting male authors and demoting women (see Figures 1 and 2). "The Fraserians" depicts twenty-six male

Figure 1. "The Fraserians," *Fraser's Magazine* 11 (January 1835), 2–3.

Figure 2. "Regina's Maids of Honour," *Fraser's Magazine* 13 (January 1836), 80.

authors and their publisher seated around a table, lifting their glasses in toast of the magazine, its editor, and their recently deceased comrade Edward Irving.[34] "Regina's Maids of Honour," in contrast, depicts eight women – poets, novelists, and editors of literary annuals – drinking tea and engaging in conversation, "with volant tongue and chatty cheer," as the text explains, "welcoming in, by prattle good, or witty phrase, or comment shrewd, the opening of the gay new year."[35] Notably, the illustration of male authors includes a publisher – James Fraser, who took an active interest in the magazine and its contributors – whereas the women authors appear publisher-less. Is this absence the result of women's actual lack of close relations with publishers, or does it rather represent a careful minimizing of certain professional aspects of authorship that might harm a woman's social status? Probably both. Some women writers depicted in "Regina's Maids" had no well-established relationship with a publisher; others had productive, often long-standing relations with publishers and their firms, though they may not have foregrounded these relations in their public self-presentations.

For example, Mary Mitford (1787–1855), one of the women authors in "Regina's Maids," had a regular publisher for her drama, George Whittaker – though, unfortunately for her, she sold him the copyright of most of her plays and of *Dramatic Scenes, Sketches, and Other Poems* (1827) and never realized the significant profits of their commercial success.[36] Later, after the enormous popularity of her prose sketches *Our Village*, published serially in the *Lady's Magazine* between 1822 and 1824, Mitford easily placed her work with various popular publishers such as Saunders and Otley, Colburn and Bentley, and Hurst & Blackett. In contrast, the poetess Laetitia Landon (1802–38) bounced from publisher to publisher with the early volumes of her verse: J. Warren for *The Fate of Adelaide* in 1821; Hurst and Robinson for *The Improvisatrice* in 1824 and *The Troubadour* in 1825; Longman, Brown, Green, and Longmans for *The Golden Violet* in 1827. Ironically, her most reliable publisher was the American firm Carey and Hart of Philadelphia, which regularly pirated her books (paying no royalties, needless to say). Harriet Martineau (1802–76), Landon's contemporary, found a steady outlet for her early essays and reviews in the Unitarian magazine *Monthly Repository*, and for her juvenile tales with the religious publisher Houlston and Son. But when she attempted to place *Illustrations of Political Economy* (1832–34), a series of didactic prose tales, with a London publisher, she encountered repeated refusals. At a time of economic slump, with cholera in London and the first Reform Bill in Parliament, they feared readers would never pay ready money for such tales. Martineau had to settle for demeaning terms with Charles Fox, who nonetheless profited from the *Illustrations*' enormous success. By 1836, when *Fraser's* published "Regina's Maids," in which Martineau was included, she was an acknowledged successful author for whose books publishers competed.

The varying experiences of women authors in the 1820s and 1830s are not so different from those of their male counterparts in that they reflect the slump in book publishing, the downturn in markets for poetry, and a rising interest in prose. Coleridge (1772–1834), included in "The Fraserians" but dead by the time it appeared in print, used various printers to issue his poetry and prose, though by the 1820s the London firm, W. Pickering, became the regular publisher of his verse. Thomas Carlyle (1795–1881), a young author in 1835, had placed articles in London and Edinburgh periodicals but faced almost insurmountable obstacles in securing a book publisher for his satirical masterpiece *Sartor Resartus* and initially settled for serialization in *Fraser's Magazine*. In 1835, William Thackeray (1811–63) did not even have a publisher to turn to; as Peter L. Shillingsburg quips, "During the years of struggle to establish himself as a writer, Thackeray can hardly be said to have 'had a publisher.'"[37] Once Thackeray established a relationship with Smith, Elder at mid-century, he could count on dual publication of his fiction in the *Cornhill Magazine* and in three-volume (triple-decker) format. The experiences of these male authors, like those of their female counterparts, confirm the volatility of the publishing world in the early Victorian period – in contrast to the relative stability that mid-Victorian authors such as Brontë, Oliphant, and Eliot enjoyed with their steady relationships with Smith, Elder and Blackwood.

Stability does not mean that author-publisher relations were gender neutral. As "The Fraserian" hints, male authors enjoyed an easy conviviality with publishers, the latter often hosting dinners on their premises for leading contributors. Moreover, as Joanne Shattock observes, male authors could join London clubs at which they might meet other authors, editors, and publishers.[38] Women did not receive invitations to such publishers' dinners, nor were they able to join London clubs for most of the century. Like male authors, women could attend literary salons, large evening parties, and small "at homes." And some, like Oliphant, had personal relationships with publishers that extended to informal suppers, holiday visits, and even travel abroad.

Yet Oliphant, who had such friendships with the Blackwoods and the Blacketts, complained that the paternalistic relationship she fell into with the elder Blackwoods, fueled by a constant need for funds to sustain her household, meant she could never bargain for high payments. Such paternalism certainly had a gender component: "I took what was given me and was very grateful," she comments in her *Autobiography*.[39] Even so, in terms of successful financial negotiations with publishers, Oliphant compared herself not to male counterparts but to Dinah Mulock (later Craig). Mulock, whom Oliphant introduced to Hurst and Blackett, negotiated successfully over payments for *John Halifax*, a best-selling novel, and her subsequent fiction; "she made a spring thus quite over my head with the helping hand of my particular friend, leaving me a little rueful." Mulock was a publisher's terror, however: "it was Henry Blackett who turned pale at Miss Mulock's sturdy business-like stand for her money"[40] – a masculine trait Oliphant presumably chose not to acquire.

Thus, when we raise the question of publishers' impact on Victorian women's writing, we must consider various factors: the period in which women published and its economic realities, the generic preferences of the firm and its readers, the personalities of both author and publisher, and the changing literary forms that enabled (or disabled) both men and women to place their work advantageously. Women writers often faced obstacles, as both Alexis Easley ("Making a Debut," ch. 1) and Joanne Shattock ("Becoming a Professional Writer," ch. 2) document, but those of high achievement usually found the ways and means to establish productive author-publisher relations.

NOTES

1. Currer Bell [Charlotte Brontë], "Biographical Notice of Ellis and Acton Bell," rpt. in *Wuthering Heights*, ed. Hilda Marsden and Ian Jack (Oxford: Clarendon Press, 1976), p. 437.
2. Ibid.
3. For example, see letters to William Smith Williams of May 1, 1848, and March 19, 1850, in *The Letters of Charlotte Brontë*, ed. Margaret Smith (Oxford: Clarendon Press, 2000), vol. 2, pp. 57–60, 364–65.
4. Juliet Barker, *The Brontës* (New York: St. Martin's Press, 1994), p. 537.
5. Charlotte Brontë to George Smith, December 3, 1850, in *Letters*, vol. 2, pp. 522–23.
6. Helen C. Black, *Notable Women Authors of the Day* (London: Maclaren, 1893). I have used a modern reprint, ed. Troy J. Bassett and Catherine Pope (Brighton: Victorian Secrets, 2011), pp. 33–34.
7. Elisabeth Jay, *Mrs Oliphant, A Fiction to Herself: A Literary Life* (Oxford: Clarendon Press, 1995), p. 248.
8. Mrs. M. O. W. Oliphant, *Autobiography* (Edinburgh and London: William Blackwood and Sons, 1899), p. 70.
9. Jay, *Mrs Oliphant*, p. 247.
10. Letter from Christina G. Rossetti to Alexander Macmillan, [April 8, 1861], in *The Letters of Christina Rossetti*, ed. Antony H. Harrison (Charlottesville and London: University of Virginia Press, 1997–2004), vol. 1, p. 146.
11. See Anna Kimball Tuell, "Mrs. Meynell in Journalism," in *Mrs. Meynell and her Literary Generation* (New York: E. P. Dutton, 1925), pp. 32–42, for an account of Meynell's career as a journalist.
12. [J. M. Barrie], "A Publisher of Minor Poets: A Chat with Mr. John Lane," *The Sketch*, December 4, 1895, p. 6.

13. *The George Eliot Letters*, ed. Gordon S. Haight (New Haven: Yale University Press, 1955), vol. 2, p. 269.
14. Ibid., vol. 2, p. 272.
15. Ibid., vol. 2, pp. 273–74.
16. Ibid., vol. 2, pp. 276, 363–64. Emphasis in original.
17. Gordon Haight, *George Eliot: A Biography* (1968; New York: Viking Penguin, 1985), p. 212.
18. Qtd. in Rosemary Ashton, *George Eliot: A Life* (1996; London: Penguin, 1997), p. 214.
19. Haight, *George Eliot*, p. 278.
20. Qtd. in Robert L. Patten and David Finkelstein, "Editing Blackwood's; or, What Do Editors Do?" in *Print Culture and the Blackwood Tradition, 1805–1930* (Toronto: University of Toronto Press, 2006), p. 166.
21. *Eliot Letters*, vol. 4, p. 38.
22. Ashton, *George Eliot*, p. 313.
23. *Eliot Letters*, vol. 4, pp. 294–96.
24. Qtd. by Francis Espinasse, "John Blackwood," *Oxford Dictionary of National Biography* online.
25. David Finkelstein, *The House of Blackwood: Author-Publisher Relations in the Victorian Era* (University Park: Pennsylvania State University Press, 2002), p. 34, esp. Tables 1 and 2.
26. Letter from George Bentley to Mary Cholmondeley, August 17, 1886, qtd. in Percy Lubbock, *Mary Cholmondeley: A Sketch from Memory* (London: Jonathan Cape, 1922), p. 83.
27. The contract for "Deceivers Ever" (original title of *Sir Charles Danvers*), dated June 14, 1888, specifies the sale of copyright for £50, plus "£20 if 550 copies are sold in Library Edition, £20 if 650 copies are sold, and addl. £20 for each addl. 100 copies"; see Linda H. Peterson, *Becoming a Woman of Letters: Myths of Authorship and Facts of the Victorian Market* (Princeton: Princeton University Press, 2009), p. 211.
28. Contract for "Nemesis" (original title of *Diana Tempest*), September 2, 1892, quoted in ibid., p. 211.
29. Carolyn W. de la Oulton, "'The Shadow Which I Call Pain': Mary Cholmondeley and the Dilemma of Bodily Weakness," *Life Writing* 6:3 (2009), 303–12. For details of Bentley's support, see Oulton's biography, *"Let the Flowers Go": A Life of Mary Cholmondeley* (London: Pickering & Chatto, 2009), pp. 49–53.
30. Mary Cholmondeley to Macmillan, letters of January 29, 1899, and July 2, 1900, quoted in Peterson, *Becoming a Woman of Letters*, p. 212.
31. Gaye Tuchman and Nina E. Fortin, *Edging Women Out: Victorian Novelists, Publishers, and Social Change* (New Haven: Yale University Press, 1989), esp. chap. 9, "The Case of the Disappearing Lady Novelists," pp. 203–18.
32. Ibid., pp. 8–9.
33. Ibid., p. 5.
34. "The Fraserians; or, The Commencement of the Year Thirty-Five, A Fragment," *Fraser's Magazine* 11 (January 1835), 1–27. The illustration appears between pp. 2 and 3.

35. "Regina's Maids of Honour," *Fraser's Magazine* 13 (January 1836), 80. The illustration is inset opposite the text.
36. [Martin Garrett], "Mary Russell Mitford," *Oxford Dictionary of National Biography* online.
37. Peter J. Shillingsburg, *Pegasus in Harness: Victorian Publishing and W. M. Thackeray* (Charlottesville: University of Virginia Press, 1992), p. 69.
38. Joanne Shattock, "Professional Networking, Masculine and Feminine," *Victorian Periodicals Review* 44:2 (Summer 2011), 131–32.
39. Oliphant, *Autobiography*, pp. 84–85.
40. Ibid., pp. 83, 85.

4

BETH PALMER

Assuming the role of editor

From soliciting articles, managing a magazine's finances and employees, and overseeing production, to maintaining a house style, proof-reading articles, providing contributions, and corresponding with readers, an editor's responsibilities were complex and varied across different sectors of the press. The term "editor" itself only came to imply what this chapter addresses as its primary meaning – the conducting of a newspaper or periodical – early in the nineteenth century. Before 1800, an editor was someone who published or prepared the work of other writers, and such work is, of course, part of a newspaper or magazine editor's remit. After 1800, the meaning of editorship, always elastic, might encompass roles that included financial investment, social networking, and the use of business skills as well as literary acumen.

Throughout the nineteenth century, however, many of the qualities of good editorship were characterized as masculine. Books and articles advising young women journalists how to succeed in the industry almost universally assume that the editor of periodicals (and other publications) will be a man. In *Journalism for Women: A Practical Guide* (1898), Arnold Bennett suggests that young women writers should "resolve to see your editor face to face" because it will be more difficult for him to say no "especially to a woman."[1] Even the female writer Frances Power Cobbe, while encouraging women to take up journalism, makes the same assumption. She cautions that "the disappointment and worry to an editor of erratic attendance and imperfect work must be enough to disgust a man with female contributors once and forever."[2]

Even so, editing was in many ways well suited to the careers of women of letters in the Victorian period. Editing a magazine, unlike practicing a traditional profession – for instance, law and medicine, from which women were still chiefly excluded – could be carried out in domestic spaces or alongside familial duties. Rachel Beer (1858–1927), for example, often edited the *Sunday Times* (1821–) newspaper from her home in Mayfair in the mid-1890s, and Ellen Wood (1814–87) edited and wrote much of the *Argosy* (1865–1901) confined to her invalid setting. Editing could also be combined with other jobs, and working methods could be tailored to an individual woman's needs. One contributor was surprised at being summoned to see Charlotte Riddell (1832–1906) at her husband's shop where she was "engaged in making out invoices" for his business while conducting her editorial work for *St James's Magazine* (1861–1900).[3] Some female editors adopted more professional spaces for their work. Henrietta Stannard (1856–1911) produced *Golden Gates* (1892–95, renamed *Winter's Weekly*) from her office in Fleet Street, and the Langham Place Group had its own lively central London offices, which included a reading room and meeting spaces. Thinking about female editorship requires a relatively fluid understanding of professionalism in which the commercial and the social are interwoven.

If editors carried out multiple and shifting roles, how might we begin to further investigate female editorship in the Victorian period? What motivated women writers to assume editorial positions? How did women make and maintain networks of contributors – in the same way as men or differently – through family, friendship, and professional connections? Was the female editor, sometimes called an "editress," exposed to different expectations from her male counterparts? Was she more likely to work in a niche market of the press than to edit a magazine or newspaper aimed at a general readership? Perhaps most problematic for the scholar is a question that applies both to male and female editorships: how to uncover editorial practices that are often concealed beneath the finish of a published magazine or newspaper. Publisher's archives, editorial correspondence, and the visible work of editors (opening remarks, editorials, reviews, and answers to correspondents) all help the modern scholar reconstitute the work of the editor, but such sources are not always available. The editorial correspondence of a canonical male author such as Charles Dickens is much more likely to have been kept and catalogued than that of a little remembered female editor working in a specialist area of the press, such as Mary Anne Hearne (1834–1909) of the evangelical weekly *Sunday School Times* (1860–1925). Despite these difficulties, piecing together editorial activities, policies, and methods is worthwhile as it helps modern scholars understand a periodical's goals and ideological position, for which the editor is ultimately responsible. In attempting to address these questions, this chapter introduces some classifications of editorship – celebrity, political, and collaborative – that aim to give a sense of the multiple ways in which women navigated this significant and complex role in the literary landscape of nineteenth-century Britain.

Celebrity and author-editors

The Victorian period saw many celebrity writers take on editorships: Frederick Marryat with the *Metropolitan* (1831–50), Charles Dickens with *Household Words* (1850–59) and *All the Year Round* (1859–95), W. M. Thackeray with the *Cornhill* (1860–1975), and women such as Mary Elizabeth Braddon (1835–1915) with *Belgravia* (1867–99), Anna Maria Hall (1800–81) with *St James's Magazine* (1861–1900), and Florence Marryat (Frederick's daughter, 1833–99) with *London Society* (1872–98). In different ways, author-editors such as these bolstered their literary profile, decided what material would best complement their own work, and usually gained monetarily either directly through an editorial salary or by boosting the earnings from the serial (and later volume) editions of their novels.

The longest-serving novelist-editor of the nineteenth century was Charlotte Yonge (1823–1901), a woman who was not interested in celebrity for its own sake but for what it could do to help promote her Tractarian belief in the importance of the established Protestant church. She launched her *Monthly Packet* in 1851 and stayed in the editorial chair for thirty-nine years. When Yonge's early novel became a best seller on publication in 1853, she soon capitalized on her newfound fame by asserting that the *Packet* was edited by "the author of *The Heir of Redclyffe*" (Yonge officially revealed her name as editor in 1881, but readers would have known her identity much earlier). Yonge's celebrity was characterized by the creation of a direct and even intimate relationship between herself and her readers. Unlike many literary celebrities, she did not move to London or attend fashionable parties. Her life revolved around her writing and her parish duties, and she used her magazine to reach out to girls and young women across the country living similar lives. This sympathetic principle comes through clearly in the editorial introduction to the *Monthly Packet*:

> It has been said that every one forms their own character between the ages of fifteen and five-and-twenty, and this Magazine is meant to be in some degree a help to those who are thus forming it, not as a guide, since that is the part of deeper and graver books, but as a companion in times of recreation, which may help you to perceive how to bring your religious principles to bear upon your daily life, may show you the examples, both good and evil, of historical persons, and may tell you of the workings of God's providence both here and in other lands.[4]

By framing this highly companionate prefatory piece as an "Introductory Letter," Yonge encourages a sense of dialogue between reader and editor, a sense that would be confirmed by the "Notices to Correspondents" on the last page of each issue, which offers a monthly reminder that correspondence is valued and responded to. Features such as the long-running "Conversations on the Catechism" or "Aunt Louisa's Travels" continue the dialogic tone of a friend, mentor, or female relation. The first features a "Miss O" guiding, questioning, answering, and encouraging her pupils Helena, Audrey, and Mary in their religious enquiries; it is easy to imagine Yonge drawing on her own role as Sunday-school teacher while writing these features.

Within a short time of taking up her editorship, Yonge also assumed the role of literary mentor to many young women ambitious to become women of letters like her. She fostered a generation of contributors to the *Monthly Packet* by acting as "Mother Goose" for a young women's writing society and helping them produce their own manuscript magazine entitled *The Barnacle*. Christabel Coleridge was one of the "goslings" who developed into Yonge's protégée and later coeditor. She summarizes Yonge's qualities as an editor:

> I think her relation to us precisely exemplified that in which she stood to numberless other girls and young women who only knew her through her writings. The pleasure she took in all that pleased us, the guidance she gave without seeming to preach, the enthusiasm with which we regarded her, also inspired her readers and made them all her life a circle of friends.[5]

Key to her longevity was this sense that readers of the *Monthly Packet* felt as if they knew Yonge personally and were encouraged by the moral guidance and educational direction she offered. Aligning the magazine so closely with her own moral values and religious persuasions meant that the magazine, despite making some modernizing changes under new editorship, could survive only briefly without Yonge at the helm.

It was not just novelists but poets, too, who created celebrity through editorship or capitalized on their existing literary fame. Editorship of the expensive and lavishly illustrated early Victorian annuals was often reserved for literary celebrities, often female poets. Letitia Elizabeth Landon (1802–38), Caroline Norton (1808–77), Louisa Henrietta Sheridan (?–1841), and the Countess of Blessington (1789–1849) are notable examples. The Countess of Blessington had become famous when her memoir *Conversations with Lord Byron* was released in 1834, capitalizing on his notoriety and bringing her into the social and literary spotlight. She edited both *The Keepsake* (1827–56) and *The Book of Beauty* (1833–47) for several years and contributed widely to other periodical publications. The first *Book of Beauty* she edited in

1834 featured her own portrait as its frontispiece. This clever move by Charles Heath, her publisher, created a strong link between the title, the new editor, and an image of beautiful, feminine gentility, which catered to the aspirations of its mostly female readers. But the Countess of Blessington was not just a figurehead editor; she contributed much poetry to the annuals she edited, and she relied on the remuneration she received as editor to alleviate financial difficulties. The Countess of Blessington's celebrity status, along with her impeccable social skills, helped her acquire many sought-after writers. She entertained potential contributors personally at her dinners and soirées. The poet Thomas Moore found it hard to resist an invitation to contribute to one of her publications despite his horror of "*Albumizing, Annualizing*, and *Periodicalizing*": "When persons like you condescend *so* to ask, how are poor poets to refuse?"[6] Even when requesting contributors to make changes, she managed to soothe their egos. Frederick Marryat's acquiescence equates her genteel femininity with her editorial expertise: "you may alter it [his story] in any way you think fit, as you have a nicer sense of what a lady will object to, than a rough animal like me."[7] Her editorial influence extended to female writers also; fellow editors Anna Maria Hall and Letitia Elizabeth Landon attest their willingness to produce their best work for an editor who balances high professional standards with elegant sociability.[8]

Several women writers used the currency of their well-known names to link to their own magazines. *Mrs Ellis' Morning Call* (1850–52) provided further definition and exemplification of respectable female conduct, albeit in less didactic terms than publications such as *The Women of England* (1839) that had made Sarah Stickney Ellis (1799–1872) famous. Later in the century, the novelist Annie Swan (1859–1943) lent her name to the subtitle of *Woman at Home: Annie S. Swan's Magazine* (1893–1920), although her publication reflects more visibly than Ellis's the conflict inherent in a professional female editor advising women readers that domestic duties should surmount all others. The pulling power of an editor's name might trouble social conventions, too. Eliza Cook capitalized on her enormous popularity as a poet to launch *Eliza Cook's Journal* (1849–54) with the aim of educating and empowering men and women of the working classes. Henrietta Stannard, who served as the first president of the Society of Women Journalists, used her celebrity pseudonym as the writer John Strange Winter to raise issues of gender equality in *Winter's Weekly*. Strong ideological convictions were often a prerequisite for female editors in a competitive publishing world in which periodicals might struggle to survive without a truly committed editor.

Political editorships

Membership in a political or activist group often presented opportunities for women to extend their personal convictions through editorship. Groups campaigning for sanitary reform, suffrage, and educational or employment opportunities often founded their own publications to promulgate their activities. Clementina Black (1853–1922), for example, worked for the Women's Industrial Council, which in turn led her to become editor of its *Women's Industrial News* (1895–1919), a magazine reporting on conditions in women's work and campaigning for unionization, fair pay, and a minimum wage. Josephine Butler (1828–1906) took on several editorships associated with her reformist projects including the *Shield* (1870–1933) in connection with her campaign against the Contagious Diseases Act and *Dawn* (1888–96), the publication of the General Federation for the Abolition of the State Regulation of Vice. Editors of these kinds of magazines often enjoyed the advantage of working with like-minded individuals for a target audience whose preferences in their reading material could, to some extent, be predicted by their political bent. But editors of specialized political magazines also faced the challenges of small circulation and could rarely attract prestigious contributors with high fees, having instead to rely on the variable talents of their colleagues and friends. The editors of political magazines seldom came from literary or publishing backgrounds; they had to learn the working practices of editorship on the job, and they worked with the reward of reform rather than remuneration in mind. Lydia Becker's (1827–90) commitment to suffrage for women was expressed not only in her co-founding and editing of the *Women's Suffrage Journal* (1870–90) but also her frequent subsidies that kept the publication afloat.

Eliza Sharples (1803–52), perhaps the earliest politically active woman editor, was committed to conveying her radical ideas to the widest possible audience. To that end, the "Discourse[s]" on subjects such as "A View of the Existing Human Mind" that opened each issue of her *Isis* (1832) were also delivered as lectures at the Rotunda, an important meeting place for freethinkers of all kinds in London. Sharples's social, political, and religious reformism chimed precisely with those of her lover Richard Carlile, whose work she continued while he was imprisoned for publishing Thomas Paine's *The Age of Reason*. Another early political editor, Christian Isobel Johnstone (1781–1857), was much less likely to demonstrate her ideological commitments through ardent editorial polemics. Instead, when she took over editorship of the reformist *Tait's Edinburgh Magazine* (1832–61) in 1834, she expressed her convictions on class reform and gender equality by encouraging contributions from the artisan classes and from female writers such as Mary Russell Mitford and Eliza Meteyard.

The *Westminster Review* (1824–1919), another distinguished reformist publication, similarly benefited from the hard work of a female editor, Marian Evans (1819–80), before her career as the novelist George Eliot began. Evans did the majority of the editorial work between late 1851 and 1854, although her friend and publisher John Chapman was the official editor at mid-century. Working on the review, Evans associated with reformers and intellectuals during the early 1850s and sought contributions from such stars as Harriet Martineau, J. S. Mill, and the Italian political exile Giuseppe Mazzini, writing to a friend in January 1852, "We are trying Mazzini on Freedom V. Despotism."[9] These writers, and others like them, were in sympathy with the *Westminster*'s political perspective; all could have sold their contributions for greater remuneration to other publications but chose the *Westminster* because of its political goals. Evans herself worked for nothing while staying in Chapman's house on the Strand in London, something of a social hub for liberal intellectuals and women activists such as Barbara Leigh-Smith, who later helped found the Langham Place Group. Despite working without remuneration, Evans took the job very seriously, "stamping with rage" at typographical errors and offering Chapman detailed advice on all aspects of the periodical's production from its prospectus onward.[10] She did not, however, have control of the review's finances and sometimes found Chapman's disorganized business practices frustrating. Evans left the editorship in 1854 (to spend time in Germany with G. H. Lewes) but continued writing for the *Westminster* while her career as a novelist began to blossom. Editorship of a reformist magazine introduced the writer to people and ideas she may not otherwise have encountered.

Evans's experience put her in a position to proffer advice when members of the Langham Place Group began their own periodical publications. She suggested to Bessie Parkes, editor of the *English Woman's Journal* (1858–64), that "the more business you get into the Journal ... and the *less literature* the better."[11] The *English Woman's Journal* did contain some literary content, whereas its successors, the *Englishwoman's Review* (initially edited by Jessie Boucherett, 1866–1910) and the *Victoria Magazine* (edited by Emily Davies and Emily Faithfull, 1863–80), took oppositional opinions on the compatibility of entertainment and serious-minded reformism. Although none of these publications was the official journal of a specific reform organization, the Langham Place Group had links with the National Association for the Promotion of Social Sciences, the Society for the Promotion of the Employment of Women, and the Female Middle Class Emigration Society. Meetings and activities of these organizations were reported in Langham Place productions, particularly in the *Englishwoman's Review*, and because they shared offices, opportunities for personal interactions between activist readers and editors arose. "A Woman's Struggles: the True Account of an American Shorthand Writer" is prefaced by a headnote from the editor that gives a sense of an open and sympathetic editorial policy:

> [Its writer] called at this office, and in the course of conversation gave a rapid sketch of her early difficulties. We urged our visitor to allow us to publish it in the *Victoria Magazine*, believing it impossible to estimate the good sometimes achieved by the simple narrative of another person's persistent courage and ultimate success in some new business or profession.[12]

Emily Davies (1830–1921), at work on the *English Woman's Journal* in the 1860s, however, found it less easy to find contributions. Letters to colleagues express her anxieties about the journal's financial situation, which forced her to find a large percentage of the magazine's content from contributors willing to write without remuneration. Other such financial difficulties pressed on the editorial team of the *English Woman's Journal*; when it ceased publication, Davies worked instead on the *Victoria Magazine*, a vehicle that she and Emily Faithfull conceived as more likely to make a profit by giving its readers popular literature, as did the shilling monthlies with which they were competing.

This activist route had, by the end of the century, become a relatively well-trodden pathway into editorship for politicized women of the middle and upper classes – representing a trend of increasing importance for professional women. When Annie Besant (1847–1933) wrote to Charles Bradlaugh's *National Reformer* (1860–91) seeking further information on the National Secular Society after losing her Christian faith, she set herself on a trajectory toward political editorship. On their first meeting, Bradlaugh saw that Besant was a committed reformer and encouraged her writing for the magazine. In her autobiography, she tells us that from 1877 until Bradlaugh's death in 1891, she subedited "so as to free him from all the technical trouble and the weary reading of copy, and for part of this period was also co-editor."[13] Both Bradlaugh and Besant tied their publishing work to a dynamic activism that involved relentless speaking at institutions and lecture halls around the country. The two strands of her political career, she believed, worked together: "The written and the spoken word start forces none may measure, set working brain after brain, influence numbers unknown to the forthgiver of the word, work for good or for evil all down the stream of time."[14]

When Besant became a socialist in 1887, however, she created an ideological rift between herself and her coeditor and recognized that she would need to sacrifice her editorial role for the *Reformer* to avoid the "inconvenience and uncertainty that result from the divided editorial policy of this paper on the question of Socialism."[15] Besant continued to write for the *National Reformer*, but she developed another editorial outlet that, although published from the same offices, was under her sole charge and could therefore more fully reflect her changing political convictions. In its early issues, *Our Corner*, a 6d magazine, was less radical in tone than audiences might have expected from Besant. Its sixty or so pages of content and illustrations contained much that was similar to many of the nonpolitical family monthly magazines available in the 1880s; it even set out a series of domestic features such as the "Gardening Corner," "Chess Corner," and "Young Folks Corner," which addressed themselves to special interests within the family group. By the last two or three years of publication, however, Besant's socialism had crystallized, and this commitment comes across much more strongly as the editorial underpinning of the magazine. The general interest and domestic features disappear to be replaced by verbatim reports of socialist lectures by activists such as Sidney Webb, articles such as "Comtism from a Secularist Point of View" and "The Transition to Social Democracy," and prospectuses for the Fabian Society. The five-year run of the magazine tracks its editor's shifting political convictions, although Bradlaugh himself remained a stalwart contributor.

Collaborative editors

In many ways, any and every editor is a collaborative worker. Thinking about editorship (and the production of periodicals more generally) as a collaborative process enables us to reconsider the sense of hierarchy that is often implied by the idea of single editors and their stable of contributors. Yet marital and maternal relationships were the basis for many strong editorial partnerships during the nineteenth century. Margaret Gatty (1809–73) was editor of the juvenile periodical *Aunt Judy's Magazine* (1866–85), and her children, Juliana and Horatia, acted as contributors before assuming joint editorship at her death. Their first issue is touchingly prefaced by an endorsement of their mother's editorial principles, which they "have endeavoured to follow ... throughout these pages, in the service of those young readers whom she delighted to teach and to amuse."[16] Margaret and Beatrice de Courcy were another mother and daughter editorial partnership behind the *Ladies Cabinet of Fashion, Music and Romance* (1832–70), of which they were also the main contributors. One of the best-known editing teams of the nineteenth century was Samuel and Isabella Beeton (1836–65) who coedited the very successful *Englishwoman's Domestic Magazine* (1852–79) alongside their other publishing enterprises.

Some collaborations and networks seem rather nepotistic. For example, when Mary Cowden-Clark (1809–98) took up editorship of the *Musical Times* (1844–) in 1853, she was taking control of a journal founded by her brother, J. Alfred Novello. Her work was also closely connected to that of her husband, Charles Cowden-Clarke, who briefly edited the *Musical World*, published by Mary's father, the musician Vincent Novello. These sorts of familial arrangements were not unusual, and nepotism was a general feature of the press, regardless of gender. The long-running and influential *Blackwood's Magazine*, for example, passed its editorship down the male line throughout the century, precluding the possibility that the prolific and loyal contributor Margaret Oliphant be given editorial responsibility for a major, general-readership magazine that she sought. For one unconnected writer in *Blackwood's Magazine*, purporting to give "The Experiences of a Woman Journalist," the insularity of the press debarred her entry entirely. Every editor she approached "had relatives and friends and fellow-workers of their own, ready and willing to take anything they had to offer. Why should they bother about outsiders?"[17]

But collaborative editorship could also be a valuable means by which women entered into editorial positions and wielded literary control. Looking back on their literary lives after his wife's death, Samuel Carter Hall actively emphasizes the closely entwined nature of his work with Anna Maria Hall:

> It is not easy for me to separate that which concerns her from that which belongs to me. We were so thoroughly one in all our pursuits, occupations, pleasures, and labours ... producing our books not in the same room, but always under the same roof, communicating one with the other as to what should be or should not be done ... It is no wonder that I find it difficult to separate her from me or me from her.[18]

Both husband and wife held several editorial roles: they coedited the *Spirit and Manners of the Age* (1826–29, continuing as the *British Magazine*, 1830), and Anna Maria Hall controlled a number of annuals and periodicals as solo editor, including *Finden's Tableaux* (1837), the *Juvenile Forget Me Not* (1826–34), *Sharpe's London Magazine* (1845–70) in the 1850s, and *St James's Magazine* in the 1860s. Nonetheless, in his memoir Samuel Carter Hall somewhat patronizingly credits himself for finding his wife's talent and providing her with an outlet for much of her early writing in his many editorial projects. He also places himself as her ultimate editor, suggesting that "whatever she wrote she rarely read after it was written, leaving it entirely for me to prepare it for the printer and revise proofs, never thinking to question my judgement as to any erasure or addition I might make."[19]

Anna Maria Hall's own writing often seeks to place her husband as a significant authority at the expense of her own fame, although we do get the occasional glimpse of disharmony between the two. She tells us,

> I can also remember, how fearful my husband was that literature—its care, its claims, and its fame—would unfit me for the duties which every woman is bound to consider only next to those she owes her Maker. I daresay I was a little puffed up at first, but happily for myself, and for those who had near and dear claims upon my love and labour, I very soon held my responsibilities as an author second to my duties as a woman; they '*dovetailed*' charmingly, and I have never found the necessary change to domestic from literary care, though sometimes laborious, not only heartfelt, but pleasant.[20]

Anna Maria Hall's emphasis on her domesticity was not just a sop to please a husband anxious to assert his authority over their marital and professional lives. It was a strategic tactic in the publishing industry that highlighted her domesticity to readers to reassure them that her editorial priorities were compatible with those of wife and mother. In the introduction to the first volume of *Sharpe's London Magazine*, she not only affirms the excellence of the contributions and the magazine's good value but also states: "The Editor would entreat the attention of Parents to the fact that she watches every page with minute care, so that nothing can creep in that may not be read aloud in the domestic circle."[21] Here, and elsewhere in her editorial introductions, Anna Maria Hall places herself in a network of cooperative relations (with coeditors, contributors, publishers, and crucially readers). She does not wish to be seen as an editor functioning alone from the top.

Although Anna Maria Hall was not a supporter of women's rights, the content of her journals frequently undermines any anxiety we might notice about professional female authority. She frequently sought to represent female capability and cooperation in her magazines. For example, in her own novel *Can Wrong be Right?*, (serialized in *St James's Magazine*, 1861–62) the young heroine is beautiful, but her poor schoolmaster father refuses to let her rely on her feminine attractions, arguing,

> I would give every girl a trade, a pursuit—yes, I would to the highest lady give what she can proudly rest upon, and say, "By *this* I can live—*this* art can save me, if the world goes mad, as it has done often . . . by THIS I can stand, and save myself from the degradation of want or dependence."[22]

This message is replicated in nonfiction pieces such as "Something of What Florence Nightingale Has Done and Is Doing," which argues that for women, as for men, "The first great principle of nature is WORK."[23] Perhaps most importantly, Anna Maria Hall followed these principles in her encouragement of younger women authors and editors. She provided valuable training for Mary Elizabeth Braddon, who went on to edit the shilling monthly *Belgravia*, and for Charlotte Riddell, with whom she jointly edited *St James's* for the final year of her editorship before Riddell took full control and proprietorship in 1868.

Mary Howitt (1799–1888) took collaborative editorship even further than the Halls, coediting *Howitt's Journal* (1847–48) with her husband and involving their entire family in its production. Writing to her sister just before the first issue appeared, she describes the plurality of the magazine's production and the harmonious familial excitement it has engendered: "We are very, very busy, as on the 1st January comes out our *own Howitt's Journal* … we are all in high spirits; and it is perfectly cheering to see how warm and enthusiastic people are about our journal."[24] Husband and wife wrote and solicited contributions while also arranging production and distribution; their daughter Anna Mary provided some of the illustrations for *Howitt's*; and Mary Howitt used her regular feature "The Child's Corner" to chronicle the early lives of her own younger children. Linda Peterson sees these examples of collaboration as part of Howitt's attempt to "re-envision collaborative work and create a new kind of writing project that could encompass every family member."[25]

Conclusion

The historical evidence shows that it was, then, feasible for women of letters to inhabit the role of editor while shaping it to suit their own working practices, ethics, and ideological commitments. Women editors of the nineteenth century were strategic operators in a shifting landscape of annuals, periodicals, and newspapers. All competed for an expanding base of potential readers and needed to keep pace with developments in technology and communications that were changing the shape of the publishing industry. These women made choices about how best to use any status they had; how to express literary, political, or religious convictions to their readers; and how to go about the daily work of editing to ensure a publication's success (whether we attempt to gauge success in terms of sales, longevity, or influence). Irrespective of such measures, an editor's choices affected the ways in which texts and images in their publications were received and understood by their readers.

Editors used their magazines to help make abstract concepts or identities concrete to their readerships: what it was to be Tractarian in one's religious beliefs, what it was to abandon religion altogether, how one might turn political convictions into actions, or what being a leisured lady of the middle classes involved. But even with a periodical that had a coherent editorial policy and a relatively homogeneous readership, as with Yonge and her *Monthly Packet*, the periodical editor was always working within an ultimately miscellaneous format. For the modern scholar, the tensions and inconsistencies that sometimes spring from an editor's selections are as important as any attempts at uniformity; indeed, such ideological tensions are part of what makes periodicals interesting and worthy objects of study. As we have seen, editors always worked in networks and often occupied other literary positions, and the content they were editing linked outward from serial novels or individual poems to volume editions, from reviews to the books reviewed, and from the current issue to the next week's, month's, or year's. Exploring the work of a female editor will always open up new connections within the Victorian literary landscape and lead to unexpected avenues of research. As Besant suggested, editors spark interests and ideas; the best of them feed and shape those interests for their readers over periods of months and years, while simultaneously listening to what readers themselves want from the Victorian press.

NOTES

1. Arnold Bennett, *Journalism for Women: A Practical Guide* (London and New York: John Lane, The Bodley Head, 1898), p. 76.
2. Frances Power Cobbe, "Journalism as a Profession for Women," *Women's Penny Paper* 1 (1888), 5.
3. *Memoirs of Sir Wemyss Reid*, ed. Stuart Reid (London: Cassell & Co, 1905), p. 141.
4. Charlotte Yonge, "Introductory Letter," *The Monthly Packet of Evening Readings for Younger Members of the English Church* 1:1 (January 1851), i–ii.
5. Christabel Coleridge, *Charlotte Mary Yonge: Her Life and Letters* (London: Macmillan and Co., 1903), p. 203.
6. *The Literary Life and Correspondence of The Countess of Blessington*, 3 vols., ed. R. R. Madden (London: T. C. Newby, 1855), vol. 1, p. 296. Emphasis in original.
7. Ibid., vol. 3, p. 226.
8. Ibid., vol. 1, p. 229; vol. 2, pp. 304–5.
9. George Eliot to Sara Sophia Hennell, [January 21, 1852], *The George Eliot Letters*, 6 vols., ed. Gordon Haight (New Haven: Yale University Press, 1954) vol. 2, p. 5.
10. George Eliot to Sara Sophia Hennell, [September 1852], *George Eliot Letters*, vol. 2, p. 58.
11. George Eliot to Bessie Rayner Parkes, September 1, [1857], ibid., vol. 2, p. 379. Emphasis in original.
12. Anon., "A Woman's Struggles: the True Account of an American Shorthand Writer," *Victoria Magazine* 30 (December 1877), 126.
13. Annie Besant, *An Autobiography* (London: T. Fisher Unwin, 1893), p. 180.

14. Ibid., p. 189.
15. Qtd. in ibid., p. 320.
16. Juliana and Horatia Gatty, Dedication, *Aunt Judy's Magazine* (December 1874), n.p.
17. [Charlotte O'Conore Eccles], "The Experiences of a Woman Journalist," *Blackwood's Magazine* 153 (June 1893), 834.
18. S. C. Hall, *Retrospect of a Long Life: From 1815 to 1883*, 2 vols. (London: Richard Bentley & Son, 1883), vol. 2, pp. 421–22.
19. Ibid., vol. 2, p. 426.
20. Mrs. S. C. Hall, *Sketches of Irish Character* (London: Nattali & Bond, 1854), p. xvi. Emphasis in original.
21. A[nna]. M[aria]. Hall, "Preface," *Sharpe's London Magazine of Entertainment and Instruction for General Reading* 1–2 (1852–53), n.p.
22. Anna Maria Hall, *Can Wrong be Right? St James's Magazine* 1 (April 1861), 13. Emphasis in original.
23. "Something of What Florence Nightingale Has Done and Is Doing," *St James's Magazine* 1 (April 1861), 40.
24. Mary Howitt, *An Autobiography*, 2 vols. (London: W. Isbister, 1889), vol. 2, p. 41. Emphasis in original.
25. Linda H. Peterson, "Collaborative Life Writing as Ideology: The Auto/biographies of Mary Howitt and Her Family," *Prose Studies* 26 (2003), 180.

5
ALISON CHAPMAN
Achieving fame and canonicity

The literary canon was (and indeed is) not static but rather a series of uneven formations that retell the literary past using a variety of sources. Literary excellence was established, for example, by publications that asserted, directly or indirectly, the significance and worth of the author: biographies, memoirs, and correspondence; elegies and obituaries; anthologies and collected editions of literary works. Literary criticism also assessed excellence, whether in periodical reviews or books of literary criticism. Other cultural indicators of esteem included prizes, honors, memorials, and monuments. Determining exactly which women authors were considered canonical by the Victorians is difficult, but the process by which authors were canonized uncovers important information about what the Victorians prized about both literature and gender.

The Victorians deployed the term "canonical" to denote an "admitted" and "accepted" standard of literary value (*O.E.D.* 4). These values were not just those of aesthetics; rather, literary value accrued through other factors, such as appropriate politics, genre status, gender decorum, class affiliation, geographical identification, and national affiliation and patriotism. Increasingly, as the century progressed, canonical status for women was contingent on representations of personality, as the cult of celebrity was fueled through the explosion of print media and an insatiable appetite for access to the lives of famous writers. Victorian women certainly became acclaimed authors during their lifetimes, but often this acclaim was contingent on the writer's popular reception rather than her own significant interventions in literary culture. Professionalism and professional success, as with popularity in general, did not necessarily translate into lasting canonical status; indeed, canonization (as the term suggests) was ultimately a posthumous achievement. Thus for women writers, as for men, achieving literary status was often contingent on factors outside their control, including the posthumous assessment of biographers and critics mentioned earlier. Nonetheless, women writing as critics, reviewers, and biographers were invested in shaping a female literary tradition, and their efforts helped establish the canonicity of the prominent women writers who achieved status in the last fifty years of the century: Charlotte Brontë (1816–55), Elizabeth Barrett Browning (1806–61), George Eliot (1819–80), and Christina Rossetti (1830–94).

The Victorian marketplace and canon formation

What it meant to achieve acclaim was closely wrapped up in the production, circulation, and reception of literature, a business more hospitable to men than to women, based as it was in the public masculine sphere. Certainly, women's authorship increased with the expansion of the book trade, and many women successfully negotiated this masculine sphere in terms of literary professionalism, as Joanne Shattock's chapter (ch. 2) on "Becoming Professional" reveals. Yet achieving status in literary culture involved an accrual of value from external sources – through successful book publication, acclaim in literary reviews and criticism, and representation in high-profile anthologies and biographies – and, while women writers could often maximize their success in these modes in productive ways during their lifetimes, they could not control all the important markers of value.

For example, one of the distinctive markers of poetic status, the poet laureateship, was awarded on Wordsworth's death in 1850 to Alfred Tennyson, and then after Tennyson's death in 1892 to Alfred Austin (not considered a canonical poet even in his own day). Women poets were never serious contenders for this prestigious position, although Alice Meynell was nominated by Coventry Patmore in a *Saturday Review* column and Christina Rossetti was mooted as a possible successor to Tennyson. Jan Marsh, one of Rossetti's recent biographers, terms her "the lost laureate."[1] It was only in 2009 that Carol Ann Duffy was appointed the first woman poet laureate, a fact that illustrates the long history of the exclusion of women from the literary canon, or at least this particular canon of official public acclaim.

The Victorian literary establishment, and the very business of publishing, privileged male writers. The most influential literary periodicals were published and edited by men; the chief publishing houses were owned by men (Alexander Macmillan, William Blackwood, John Murray, the Chambers brothers, and others); and many of the publishers' readers of literature were male. Of course, there were exceptions. As Beth Palmer shows in ch. 4, women edited periodicals that helped shape literary taste, although often for a popular market (e.g., Mary Elizabeth Braddon's editorship of the *Belgravia* from 1867 to 1876). Some women, such as Charlotte Brontë unofficially for George Smith and Geraldine Jewsbury officially for Richard

Bentley, served as readers for publishing houses. And Emily Faithfull's female-run and female-operated Victoria Press was founded in 1860. Thus, women had opportunities to participate in public literary culture as writers, reviewers, and editors, but their activity in the business of literature did not necessarily translate into the cultural capital of literary canonicity.

Because overt engagement in business of any kind was associated with the masculine sphere of public life, women writers' superlative literary achievement often occluded acknowledgment of their professional activities. As Robert Southey famously advised Charlotte Brontë, "literature cannot be the business of a woman's life: & it ought not to be. The more she is engaged in her proper duties, the less leisure will she have for it, even as an accomplishment & a recreation."[2] Thus for women, despite their advances in forging models of literary professionalism, achieving canonical status was represented in this period as a feature of their success as *women* writers – that is, as writers whose gender largely conformed to a middle-class ideology of femininity and domesticity. To put it differently, the status of women as writers in the period was unremarkable, so long as propriety was not flouted.

Linked to separate spheres ideology, Victorians assumed that certain kinds of writing were natural for women, such as affective, lyrical poetry and novel writing, because both genres were seen to draw on women's apparently natural capacity for empathy. Victorians also acknowledged that writing itself was an activity open to all educated people; indeed, many popular periodicals (provincial newspapers and magazines such as *Atalanta*) relied on this belief to encourage and publish contributions from readers. But the notion of the "literary" – that is, an authoritative, acclaimed, and elevated standard of literature – was perceived as an entirely separate kind of writing, distinct from the amateur, ephemeral, or journalistic. Many of the genres in which women wrote did not meet this elevated standard.

There were some awkward moments when this evaluative distinction between writing and literature broke down – awkward in that they exposed the fragility of the distinction, despite energetic and voluminous attempts to assert the boundary of the literary. One case came in 1859 when the Burns Centenary prize of fifty guineas for the best poem on Robert Burns was awarded at a public celebration in the Crystal Palace in front of an audience of more than 14,000 people. A total of 621 poems had been submitted, within the stated length of 100 to 200 lines. The prize announcement was preceded by a concert, an unveiling of a new commemorative bust of Burns, and the display of relics associated with the poet. Implicitly, the winner of the best poem on Burns was associated with one of the most canonical poets of the previous generation, a venerated literary figure. The prize winner was announced, in front of an eager and rapt audience, as Isa Craig (1831–1903).

After her poem on Burns was recited by an organizer of the event, as reported in *The Scotsman* for January 27, 1859, the audience called for the poet to reveal herself in person to receive acclaim (and her prize money), but no one appeared.[3] In fact, according to *The Scotsman*, not only did Craig not appear that day, neither did she collect her check for fifty guineas, "from feelings either of timidity or poetic delicacy and pride." One implication of this report is that Craig did not attend out of delicacy at popular associations of the canonical Burns with his reputation for sexual and other indiscretions, but looming even larger in this account is the indelicacy of a female poet accepting honors at such a public civic event.

At mid-century, when few women won any public literary honors or acclaim, the Burns Centenary Prize was a telling moment – and contrary to the myth of the acclaimed woman poet in Germaine de Staël's 1807 novel *Corinne, Or Italy*. De Staël's fictional poet-heroine Corinne receives public praise when crowned as laureate in the Forum at Rome. But in England, the separate spheres ideology that kept women in the domestic realm became more dominant in the early Victorian period, making Corinne's own uncomfortable association of public acclaim and private unhappiness a more overt reason for disavowing public success. Women might win high-profile and lucrative literary prizes, but receiving acclaim in person and in public was indecorous. Barrett Browning's novel-poem *Aurora Leigh* (1856, date stamped 1857) registers this tension when the eponymous writer-heroine crowns herself privately in a garden with laurel leaves in a revision of Corinne's Forum scene but is embarrassed when her male cousin catches her in the act.[4] Later, when Aurora's book of poems becomes a critical and commercial success in England, she receives the news of its acclaim in a letter sent to her in Italy (7: 551–71), but she denies that women care "for the crowns and goals / And compliments on writing our good books" (7: 742–43). In both cases, Barrett Browning underlines the discomfort that women writers feel with critical and popular success.

Isa Craig, winner of the Burns prize, was in fact one of the most prolific Victorian poets, publishing along with her 1856 collection *Poems by Isa* a huge quantity of periodical poetry, as well as novels and journalism. She was well connected in literary circles, prominent in the Langham Place Group, and an activist for women's rights. Yet despite her official prize and her many publications in various print media and genres (including her editorship of *The Argosy* from its launch in 1865 and the prominent 1863 collection for the Victoria Press, *Poems: An Offering to Lancashire*), Craig was obviously not considered part of the Victorian literary canon. (Nor is she part of the teaching and research canon that we enjoy today.) Isa Craig, prolific, prizewinning, and successful as a professional writer, did not fit into the Parthenon of Victorian literary greats, partly because she was too much associated with mere professionalism and partly because her Scottish working-class origins made her hard to classify as a high-culture woman writer.

Beyond separate spheres ideology, another major feature of Victorian literary culture that affected women writers' status was the medium of publication. The print media in which most Victorians read poetry – the newspaper and periodical press – featured a large proportion of women authors writing in their own names, pseudonymously, or anonymously. For example, in one of the longest-running periodicals that published poetry, the middle-class magazine *Good Words*, around a third of poems published between 1860 and 1899 are known to be written by women (and this does not include the pseudonymous and unsigned poems for which the gender of the author is currently unknown).[5] Serial publication of fiction also dominated the periodical market as a prelude to book publication, often in three volumes for the circulating libraries. Yet publication in ephemeral print media was associated with lower-status, popular literature, whereas publication in book form was considered more distinguished. Nevertheless, serial and book print were closely related because many authors published in both forms and because the success of a book relied on the reviews and advertisements published in mass print media. Ironically, the process by which the canon was formed in the Victorian era involved, in large part, the popular periodical press, and yet the kinds of literary publications that were seen to be high status were invariably books.

Certain kinds of books, though, were valued over others because genre was also part of the hierarchy of status and achievement. Books of single-authored original poetry and novels published in book form were prized more highly than genres such as biography, memoir, children's fiction, travelogues, or popular forms of publication such as anthologies, even though these genres and other media helped shore up ideals of literary excellence. As print culture and the reading public continued to expand, poetry and fiction were increasingly categorized according to their status as literary objects. Poetry by women was frequently assessed as "poetess" poetry, a category that implied hyper-feminine lyric effusions and domestic affections, and a term often used interchangeably with "woman poet," as Susan Brown has argued.[6] Sensation fiction by prominent novelists such as Mary Elizabeth Braddon and Ellen Wood was dismissed as popular and journalistic, its emergence attributed to the "violent stimulation of serial publication."[7]

Although women poets experimented in a wide variety of forms, as did their male counterparts, their *oeuvre* was often evaluated not in terms of their innovations but for their achievements in "feminine" genres. At the end of the Victorian period, Elizabeth Barrett Browning was hailed, often along with Christina Rossetti, as the period's preeminent British woman poet. The poetry for which Barrett Browning was praised, however, in criticism, biographies, and reviews was her lyrical and semi-autobiographical *Sonnets from the Portuguese*, rather than her epic *Aurora Leigh*. Barrett Browning's political poetry (*Casa Guidi Windows* [1851] and *Poems before Congress* [1860]), which dominated the final decade of her career and garnered criticism for breaking the model of the poetess because of its outspoken support of a political cause, the Italian Risorgimento, was largely ignored in assessments of her status after her death – despite the fact that her revisions of what a woman poet could achieve were hugely influential on the poets who followed her. Moreover, a publication that helped cement her canonical status – Frederic G. Kenyon's two-volume 1897 edition of her *Letters* – excises many references to politics that dominated her letters after her move to Italy (a fact obvious when the edition is compared with the typescript in the British Library); Kenyon explains away any remaining political opinions she opines as a "hysterical" aberration caused by her illness.[8] In his introduction, Kenyon suggests that the correspondence illustrates her "character" rather than her "genius" (1: ix), and then goes on to assess her poetic worth as part of her biographical persona: "her best poetry is that which is most full of her personal emotions" (1: x). He includes her Italian poems as well as *Aurora Leigh* on these grounds, and of course also *Sonnets from the Portuguese*. Ironically, the canonical status of this sonnet cycle was created, in large part, by a forged edition that Henry Buxton Forman and Thomas Wise published after Barrett Browning's and Robert Browning's deaths, widely referred to as the "Reading" edition because of its purported private printing in Reading, England.

Women writers most commonly received acclaim posthumously, often as a worth enshrined in the language of homage and tribute and a value that, as with the case of Kenyon's assessment of Barrett Browning, was closely tied to gender conventions. Another example is afforded by the first major biography of Charlotte Brontë, written by her friend Elizabeth Gaskell (1810–65). Gaskell, for the first time, fleshed out the context of the Brontës' family life and its multiple tragedies, drawing heavily on Charlotte's unpublished correspondence. *The Life of Charlotte Brontë*, published in 1857 by Brontë's own publisher George Smith, suppressed many nonconventional details of Brontë's life that would have affronted middle-class Victorian morality (especially given the contemporary reviews of her work that accused her of coarseness); it aimed, as Gaskell explained to her publisher, to inspire readers to "honour the woman as much as they have admired the writer." As Linda

Peterson argues, Gaskell's biography aimed to reevaluate Brontë's genius within middle-class gender norms, in particular arguing that Brontë was not "unwomanly" (a charge flung at her from the critics) but rather that she possessed a genius compatible with her deep sense of feminine virtue, domesticity, and duty.[9] This representation of Brontë's literary value proved extremely attractive to contemporary readers.

Charlotte had herself deployed biography to secure her sisters' posthumous literary status in her "Biographical Notice of Ellis and Acton Bell" that prefaced the 1850 edition of Emily's *Wuthering Heights* and Anne's *Agnes Grey*. Charlotte's biographical account was the first to confirm definitely the writers' gender as female, as well as to attempt to absolve both women from the charge of coarseness – first by representing Emily as a strange, wild romantic figure inspired by the landscape of the moors, and then by presenting Anne as a dutiful, innocent, and sensitive Christian woman. Biographical representation of these women writers' lives was critical in securing their literary accomplishments and posthumous status. This often involved the suppression or retelling of controversy to satisfy dominant gender norms. Thus, what many critics registered as the uncomfortable strangeness of *Wuthering Heights*, its refusal to fit neatly into generic conventions, was explained as a product of Emily's romantic yet naïve character: "stronger than a man, simpler than a child, her nature stood alone."[10] By explaining Emily's novel in terms of its writer's personality and environment, Charlotte implies that her sister's writing was a reflection of her persona, a position reinforced with Charlotte's "Preface" to the 1850 edition of *Wuthering Heights*.

Biographies of George Eliot, another woman writer whom contemporaries praised for greatness, appeared shortly after her death, and these, too, made a bid to secure the writer's personal character and literary achievement. Mathilde Blind's account, in the *Eminent Women* series, appeared three years after Eliot's death in 1880, followed by the 1885 biography by John Cross, Eliot's husband, in *George Eliot's Life as Related in her Letters and Journals*; the latter was especially influential in shaping her posthumous persona because of his intimate access to its subject and her papers. Making a bid for canonical status, posthumous biographies of women writers often molded the writer's persona and her works into the form acceptable to Victorian literary culture. This came at a cost of full disclosure. Cross, in his pitch to confirm Eliot's genius, was eager to suppress details of her unconventional life, such as her long affair with the married George Henry Lewes. Contemporary readers, however, noticed his omissions; William Gladstone, for example, termed the biography "reticence in 3 volumes."[11] Moreover, Cross's dry account of George Eliot's life may have kept safe her acclaimed and highly moral place in Victorian fiction, but one consequence was to make her deeply unappealing for the next century until revisionist biographies uncovered her radicalism.

In the case of Christina Rossetti, such a conjunction of canonical literary worth with biographical representation established her as "Santa Christina," a great woman poet who was, as Tricia Lootens argues, sanctified even while living because of her self-abnegating retreat from the public sphere and her sage religious writing. Rossetti was represented as performing her canonicity – and, indeed, given the term's underlying religious connotations, she appeared to be sanctified even while publishing some of her most powerful later poetry (such as her 1893 *Verses*).[12] After Rossetti's death, this representation of her literary greatness, an estimate contingent on her saintliness, was affirmed by the Irish poet Katherine Tynan's hagiographical essay for *The Bookman* in January 1912, entitled "Santa Christina."[13] As Lorraine Janzen Kooistra points out, even the approach to producing books by Christina Rossetti changed after her death, when her portraits began to appear as frontispieces to signify her saintly beauty and to underscore the personal in her poetry.[14]

Rossetti's canonical status was further affirmed by a flourishing of posthumous essays, editions, biographies, and other memorials. For example, Henry Mackenzie Bell, who had sent his book of poems to Rossetti in October 1893, wrote a memorial poem just after Rossetti's death on December 29, 1894, "To Christina G. Rossetti (Greater as a Woman than even as a Poet)," and sent it to the *Literary World* for publication on January 4, 1895. Having smoothed the way and proved his hagiographical credentials, on February 8, 1895, Bell offered to write Christina's biography, and her brother William Michael accepted swiftly. With William Michael's help and approval, Bell's *Christina Rossetti: A Biographical and Critical Study* (1898) effectively became the official biography. This was just one of the biographical accounts that flooded the market with praise of Rossetti's piety and poetic achievements, but the speed with which Bell acted to memorialize her and his setting of womanly greatness above poetic genius represent a pattern intrinsic to the canonization of women writers. Literary status, conceived in this period as dependent on a writer's genius but given only to women whose lives could be taken to demonstrate their exemplarity, was nonetheless produced and sustained by the book market.

How Victorian women writers shaped the canon

From the middle of the nineteenth century, women writers became more prominent in contributing to the discourse of canon formation. To begin with, women wrote biographies and literary studies of other women writers, and publishers developed book series designed specifically to assess and promote literature by women. One example, the Eminent Women series, edited by John H. Ingram and published by W. H. Allen, matched a contemporary biographer with a deceased woman writer, and women frequently contributed to the series: Mathilde Blind wrote on George Eliot (1883), A. Mary F. Robinson on Emily Brontë (1889), Charlotte Yonge on Hannah More (1888), and Lucy Madox Brown Rossetti on Mary Shelley (1890). In her introduction to the Brontë volume, Robinson self-consciously refers to the process of deciding what books are worthy of attention. She begins her biographical study by declaring that contemporary popularity does not often predict literary greatness: "there are, perhaps, few tests of excellence so sure as the popular verdict on a work of art a hundred years after its accomplishment."[15] For more recent authors, however, battles must be fought and reputations staked: "these we reserve to them for whom the future is not yet secure, for whom a timely word may still be spoken, for whom we yet may feel that lancing out of enthusiasm only possible when the cast of fate is still unknown, and, as we fight, we fancy that the glory of our hero is in our hands."[16] Robinson pitches her book as a fight to secure the victory of recognition for her subject, whom she admits is not popular and has untypical writer's qualities. Brontë's claim to canonical status is made by virtue of her "different class," her "imagination of the rarest power" that is "fearless" and "passionate," "narrower, but more intense" than that of other writers."[17] Even for Robinson, however, the logic of canonical inclusion is gendered: Brontë's power as a writer depends on her exceptional difference, yet this artistic genius is nonetheless a product of her "high noble character" and her faithful record of her own experience. Indeed, Emily Brontë's character and writing are so intermeshed that the claim to achieving literary status in this biography depends overtly on conveying accurately her persona: "to represent her as she was would be her noblest and most fitting monument."[18]

Robinson's biography partly depended on her access to previously unpublished material, including Ellen Nussey's notes on Emily and Charlotte, as well as the Brontë family correspondence and literary manuscripts. Similarly, Blind's biography of George Eliot and Lucy Rossetti's on Mary Shelley in the same series drew overtly on unpublished material. Reaching the subjects through their papers was important at this time before letters and full editions were published. When Christina Rossetti was approached in April 1883 by Ingram to write a biography of Ann Radcliffe, Rossetti decided to decline after hunting fruitlessly for biographical material; she had already rejected a proposed volume on Elizabeth Barrett Browning (her preferred subject) because Robert Browning refused to give permission to view family documents. (Ingram himself wrote the volume on Barrett Browning.) The Eminent Women series suggests, by its very title, that a claim to literary distinctiveness and status is connected to gender. But the series also associates the women who wrote biographies with their precursors, and suggests that they were writing themselves into the canon when they participated in the formation of literary knowledge and women's literary history. Robinson identified herself with Brontë's Romanticism, Blind with Eliot's Darwinism, and Rossetti with Mary Shelley's place in a male artistic circle.

Other literary criticism, biographies, and histories that placed women writers in a prominent literary position similarly identified and categorized the writers primarily through their gender. Eva Hope's *Queens of Literature of the Victorian Era* (1886) offers chapters on Mary Somerville, Harriet Martineau, Elizabeth Barrett Browning, Charlotte Brontë, George Eliot, and Felicia Hemans as varied examples of "queenly" writers, or paragons of their gender, in relationship with the queenly example of Victoria herself. While this rhetorical move might seem deeply conventional and even patronizing, Hope in fact deployed the queenly metaphor to argue for her women writers' power and influence. For example, she concludes the chapter on Martineau by stating that "no woman, either before or since, has done so much for the people of England ... She made it possible for women to fill more exalted positions and do nobler work than before."[19] Thus, rather than merely illustrating gender ideals, the women writers' lives and works magnify and amplify the sphere of the woman writer.

Some books of criticism further implied that the claim for canonicity redefined the cultural expectations of women's writing. At the end of her introduction to the anthology *Women Poets of the Victorian Era* (1890), Elizabeth Sharp declares: "who shall predict what women shall do in the future? Daily, yearly, prejudices are being broken down, fetters are falling off; women are being ushered into knowledge and to experiences of life through wider doors."[20] The attested aim of Sharp's anthology is to "further emphasise the value of women's work in poetry" and to prove "a steady development of intellectual power, certainly not unaccompanied by artistic faculty – a fact which gives further sanction to the belief that finer still work will be produced in future by women writers."[21] Sharp dedicated the volume to the feminist writer and campaigner Mona Caird (1854–1932), "the most loyal and devoted advocate of the cause of woman" – a dedication that underlines the cultural work the volume does in promoting the excellence of a body of women's poetry defined by gender, and yet that aims to prove that the limitations of gender are being progressively dismantled.

Sharp's critical appraisal of women's poetry at the end of the century indicates the importance of anthologies in promoting a canon of Victorian women's writing, as well as the importance of women in their role as editors. Indeed, women had a long tradition of editing literature, beginning with the prolific editing of literary annuals by Letitia Elizabeth Landon, Mary Mitford, the Countess of Blessington, and others in the early Victorian period. Toward the end of the century, several anthologies defined the field as part of a wider attempt to articulate the achievement of poetry in the Victorian age – exemplified by Edmund Clarence Stedman's *Victorian Poets*, which had a generous selection of women poets, and Alfred H. Miles's *The Poets and the Poetry of the Century, Charles Kingsley to James Thomson*, which did not.[22] Women novelists, too, produced anthologies that consolidated their achievements in fiction – as in *Women Novelists of Queen Victoria's Reign* (1897), a collection of "appreciations" written by living novelists about the achievement of earlier women. The "Publishers' Note" underscores the aim of the collection to commemorate and canonize: "the eminence and permanence of the Brontës, George Eliot, and Mrs. Gaskell"; "the popularity of Mrs. Craik and Mrs. Henry Wood"; "Mrs. Crowe and Mrs. Clive [as] pioneers in domestic and 'sensational' ficton"; and so on.[23]

In addition, women played an active role as literary reviewers in periodicals and newspapers, an activity that often evaluated criteria for establishing literature's value and worth. Important examples include the unsigned essays by George Eliot for the *Westminster Review* (most famously her 1856 "Silly Novels by Lady Novelists") and Geraldine Jewsbury's and later Augusta Webster's reviews for the *Athenaeum* (see Joanne Wilkes's chapter [ch. 16] on reviewing for other examples).[24] The practice of anonymity in the press meant that women could write with the same authority as male reviewers, although it also meant that the capacity of women as literary critics, able publicly to evaluate and shape value and taste, was hidden. After the 1860s, the practice of anonymity, which had privileged the personality of the periodical above the identity of the writer, became less common. Nonetheless, women writers continued to publish reviews and essays about female contributions to the canon, often claiming the authority of their own gender to adjudicate the achievements of women's writing. Amy Levy's influential signed essay on Christina Rossetti for *Woman's World* (1888) was part of the magazine's promotion and publication under editor Oscar Wilde of contemporary women's poetry to demonstrate its artistry and spirit of the age to a middle- and upper-class female audience. Levy, who published five of her own poems in *Woman's World*, judges the artistry of Rossetti's poetry as "not great" but "good" but again asserts Rossetti's uniqueness as a poet, overtly aligning her with the poetry of her brother Dante Rossetti.[25] Levy's critique of Christina Rossetti seems to be heavily qualified, yet the fact that her precursor's poetry is given serious literary evaluation in comparison to other literary greats such as her brother (as well as the male poets Shelley and Coleridge) should be juxtaposed to the tendency (as the scholarship of Alexis Easley demonstrates) to celebrate women writers in the popular press as celebrities whose value rests on transient popularity.[26] As this chapter has noted, literary status and contemporary popularity are not the same. Wilde pointed to this irony when he termed the series "Men of Letters" (published by Macmillan) and "Great Writers" (published by Walter Scott) as "cheap criticisms" in "cheap books."[27]

The prominent activity in the last decades of the century to produce a literary canon of the age included the evaluative capacity of women as editors and critics, but this must be understood in the context of a mass of critical studies and anthologies that attempted to define the status of the literary. Some of those attempts, such as Miles's *Poets and the Poetry of the Century* (1891–97), which he terms "an Encyclopædia of Modern Poetry" (1: iii), devote only one out of ten volumes specifically to women poets (volume 7, "Joanna Baillie to Mathilde Blind"). One of the most ambitious projects to define literary worth, the voluminous series "English Men of Letters" edited by John Morley, and published from 1879 to 1942, issued the vast majority of its volumes on male writers throughout English literary history. Morley included three women writers: George Eliot, Jane Austen, and Christina Rossetti. Although women did not fit easily into the category "Men of Letters," a distinctly masculine term for the literary canon, they did achieve canonicity and recognition in this series. Nonetheless, in most Victorian discourses of literary acclaim, women writers were evaluated primarily in terms of their gender.

Women writers were well aware of the gender ideology that defined their work within norms of femininity and middle-class decorum. Since the feminist recovery of a canon of women's writing in the last decades of the twentieth century, critics have identified strategies by which women writers were able to achieve success by negotiating gender conventions and sometimes subverting them. Victorian women writers themselves registered the logic of gender and writing, by which women were assumed to write as women; for example, Barrett Browning termed *Aurora Leigh* "an autobiography of a poetess—(not me)"; Augusta Webster's essay "Poets and Personal Pronouns" asserts "as a rule, I does not mean I."[28] Pseudonyms that implied a male writer (George Eliot) or that were ambiguously gendered (Acton, Currer, and Ellis Bell) aimed to protect women writers from judgments of literary worth based on gender. One of the ironies of the digital revolution, which has made out-of-copyright Victorian texts widely available on the web, is a new reckoning of literary value that comes with this recovery, which now must take into account the fact that many women writers concealed or disguised their identities in ways that make a quantitative reassessment of Victorian women's writing extremely challenging, if not impossible. In the current critical reformations of Victorian literary histories, negotiating gender conventions continues to play a crucial if problematic role.

NOTES

1. Jan Marsh, *Christina Rossetti: A Literary Biography* (London: Pimlico, 1994), chap. 12.
2. Margaret Smith, ed., *The Letters of Charlotte Brontë*, 3 vols. (Oxford: Oxford University Press, 1995–2004), vol. 1, p. 166.
3. *The Scotsman*, January 27, 1859, reprinted in http://gerald-massey.org.uk/massey/cmc_burns_centenary.htm.
4. Elizabeth Barrett Browning, *Aurora Leigh*, ed. Margaret Reynolds (New York: W. W. Norton, 1996), book 2, lines 1–60.
5. These figures are taken from the *Database of Victorian Periodical Poetry*, ed. Alison Chapman, http://web.uvic.ca/~vicpoet/database-of-victorian-periodical-poetry/.
6. Susan Brown, "'The Victorian Poetess,'" in *The Cambridge Companion to Victorian Poetry*, ed. Joseph Bristow (Cambridge: Cambridge University Press, 2000), pp. 180–202.
7. The phrase is Margaret Oliphant's, qtd. in Joanne Shattock, ed., *Oxford Guide to British Women Writers* (Oxford: Oxford University Press, 1993), p. 383.
8. F. G. Kenyon, ed., *The Letters of Elizabeth Barrett Browning*, 2 vols. (London: Macmillan, 1897), vol. 2, p. 306.
9. Linda H. Peterson, "Elizabeth Gaskell's *The Life of Charlotte Brontë*," in *The Cambridge Companion to Elizabeth Gaskell*, ed. Jill L. Matus (Cambridge: Cambridge University Press, 2007), pp. 59–61. For Gaskell's defense of Brontë, see Elizabeth Gaskell, *The Life of Charlotte Brontë* (Harmondsworth: Penguin, 1975), p. 68.
10. Currer Bell [Charlotte Brontë], "Biographical Notice of Ellis and Acton Bell," in Emily Brontë, *Wuthering Heights* (London: Penguin, 1965), p. 35.
11. Cited in Nancy Henry, ed., *The Cambridge Introduction to George Eliot* (Cambridge: Cambridge University Press, 2008), p. 107.
12. Tricia Lootens, *Lost Saints: Silence, Gender, and Victorian Literary Canonization* (Charlottesville: University of Virginia Press, 1996), chap. 5, pp. 158–82.
13. Katharine Tynan, "Santa Christina," *The Bookman* 41 (January 1912), 185–90.
14. Lorraine Janzen Kooistra, *Christina Rossetti and Illustration: A Publishing History* (Athens: Ohio University Press, 2002), p. 175.
15. A. Mary F. Robinson, *Emily Brontë* (London: W. H. Allen, 1889), p. 1.
16. Ibid., pp. 1–2.
17. Ibid., p. 3.
18. Ibid., pp. 5, 7.

19. Eva Hope, *Queens of Literature of the Victorian Era* (London: Walter Scott, 1886), p. 101.
20. Elizabeth Sharp, *Women Poets of the Victorian Era* (London: Walter Scott, 1890), pp. xxxii–xxxiii.
21. Ibid., p. xxxiii.
22. E. C. Stedman, *Victorian Poets: Revised, and Extended, by a Supplementary Chapter, to the Fiftieth Year of the Period Under Review* (London: Chatto and Windus, 1887), [1875]; A. H. Miles, ed., *The Poets and the Poetry of the Century, Charles Kingsley to James Thomson* (London: Hutchison & Co, 1905).
23. *Women Novelists of Queen Victoria's Reign: A Book of Appreciations* (London: Hurst & Blackett, 1897), pp. viii–ix.
24. [George Eliot], "Silly Novels by Lady Novelists," *Westminster Review* 66 (October 1856), 442–61.
25. Amy Levy, "The Poetry of Christina Rossetti," *Woman's World*, 1 (February 1888), 178–89, p. 180.
26. Alexis Easley, *Literary Celebrity, Gender, and Victorian Authorship, 1850–1914* (Newark: University of Delaware Press, 2011).
27. Cited in Josephine Guy, "Authors and Authorship," in *The Cambridge Companion to English Literature 1830–1914*, ed. Joanne Shattock (Cambridge: Cambridge University Press, 2010), p. 17.
28. Barrett Browning to John Kenyon, [March 1855], in Kenyon, ed., vol. 2, p. 330; Augusta Webster, "Poets and Personal Pronouns," in *Portraits and Other Poems*, ed. Christine Sutphin (Peterborough: Broadview, 2000), pp. 369–70.

PART II

Victorian women writers' achievements: genres and modes

6

LINDA K. HUGHES

Poetry

The explosion of print that facilitated careers for Victorian women of letters also aided poets. Skilled poets could earn steady income from individual poems in periodicals when sales of poetry volumes were less certain. Many more women contributed occasional poems to magazines and newspapers for small fees or published without payment. As a result of anonymous work and poems signed only with initials, we do not know the entire range of Victorian women poets, who emerged from the working as well as middle and upper classes, from the colonies as well as Great Britain, and who wrote poems of political (including feminist) protest, religious verse, love poems, epics, sentimental lyrics, dramatic monologues, ballads, sonnets, humorous verse, children's verse, translations, and short and long narratives. This massive body of poetry tells us much about publishing history, and an impressive number of women produced intriguing work that is worth revisiting today. To highlight Victorian women's poetic achievement, however, this chapter focuses on three early-, mid-, and late-century figures who rose to prominence and influenced other poets and poetic tradition: Felicia Hemans (1793–1835), Elizabeth Barrett Browning (1806–61), and Christina Rossetti (1830–94). Questions were raised throughout the century whether women's poetry was inherently feminine or could transcend sex. Hemans, Barrett Browning, and Rossetti addressed this question and other women's issues in their poetry. They also demonstrated through their formal innovations and range that women poets mattered, and that all subsequent women poets would indeed have "grandmothers," as Barrett Browning claimed she did not.[1]

Felicia Hemans

Felicia Hemans's lasting impact is clear from other writers. Soon after her death, William Wordsworth (1770–1850) incorporated a stanza on Hemans in "Extempore Effusion upon the Death of James Hogg" when he revised the original version in the December 12, 1835, *Athenaeum*. Rather than grieving for contemporaries who preceded him in death, he adjured,

> Mourn rather for that holy Spirit,
> Sweet as the spring, as ocean deep;
> For Her who, ere her summer faded,
> Has sunk into a breathless sleep. (lines 37–40)[2]

Placing Hemans among Hogg (1770–1835), S. T. Coleridge (1772–1834), and Sir Walter Scott (1771–1832), Wordsworth associates her with feminine sweetness but also poetic depth. Three decades later, Elizabeth Gaskell (1812–65) recalled Hemans's stature in chap. 6 of *Wives and Daughters* (1864–66). When Mrs. Hamley reads Hemans's poetry to the visiting Molly Gibson, who is soon absorbed in it, and compares her son's poems to Hemans's, the narrator adds, "To be nearly as good as Mrs. Hemans' was saying as much to the young ladies of that day, as saying that poetry is nearly as good as Tennyson's would be in this."[3] A century later, American poet Elizabeth Bishop (1911–79) appropriated Hemans's "Casabianca" as an extended metaphor for erotic love in her identically titled poem.[4]

Maintaining steadfast decorum in content and technique, Hemans's nineteen volumes display imagination, ambition, and range. *Records of Woman* (1828), her most popular volume, captured women in moments of loss, abandonment, or piety but also reminded readers of female achievement exceeding domesticity, as in "Joan of Arc in Rheims" and "Properzia Rossi" (on the sixteenth-century Italian sculptor). Placing these figures amid unknowns such as "The Peasant Girl of the Rhone" or "Imelda" tacitly suggests that "Woman" encompasses strength and inventiveness as well as affective depth and fidelity. All these qualities appear in the opening poem "Arabella Stuart," about the noblewoman who had enterprisingly escaped imprisonment dressed as a man and commandeered a French ship to await her captive husband Seymour after his escape from the Tower. Suffering recapture before they can reunite, she mourns for the husband she will never see again and then slips into madness:

> Now, with fainting frame,
> With soul just lingering on the flight begun,
> To bind for thee its last dim thoughts in one,
> I bless thee! (lines 233–6)[5]

Both the popularity and technical excellence of *Records of Woman* legitimized a focus on women by women poets. If earlier work had sung of women's lives, an entire volume devoted to the topic implied women's importance to history and helped pave the way for Barrett Browning's *Aurora Leigh*, a fictional autobiography, three decades later.

The title poem of Hemans's *The Forest Sanctuary* (1825)[6] demonstrates her ability to represent male as well as female subjectivity and her confidence in addressing political and religious issues. This two-part monologue set in the forests of sixteenth-century North America involves a Spanish conquistador who converts to Protestantism after seeing the Protestant comrade who saved his life in Peru burned at the stake during the Spanish Inquisition. After escaping prison, the speaker flees with his family to Peru and, after war erupts there, onward to North America with his surviving son. The poem solidifies English national identity since Protestant England escaped the threat of Philip of Spain and the Inquisition when the Spanish Armada was destroyed, but the poem is also notable for addressing the issues of religious freedom and tolerance, male domesticity, colonial conquest, and troubled marriage. This last arises when Leonor, the speaker's wife, reluctantly deems him a heretic from her own Catholic faith. Seeing in a "glance" or "word – less, less, the *cadence* of a word" her inward thoughts (2.370, 373), he is tortured by his wife's anguish and concludes, "Alas! for those that love, and may not blend in prayer! / We could not pray together midst the deep" (2.421–22). Hemans further complicates this passage by inserting into the speaker's Protestant utterance the Catholic evening prayer that draws him to his boyhood faith, a means of replicating textually the diverse orientations and religious conflict suffered by husband and wife. The future poet and novelist of troubled marriage George Eliot (1819–80) understandably found the poem "Exquisite."[7] Hemans's elevated treatment of faith, doubt, and religious oppression and freedom was a precedent for the ambitious religious poetry of Barrett Browning, especially *The Seraphim* (1838) and *A Drama of Exile* (1844), which respectively represented the Crucifixion from the standpoint of observing angels and rewrote Milton's story of Eve. Hemans's own ambition is announced by her reinvention of Spenserian stanzas – with an ababccbdd rhyme scheme rather than ababbcbcc – just as Barrett Browning and Rossetti would invent a range of new stanzas and rhyme schemes in turn.

The Forest Sanctuary also anticipates Alfred Tennyson (1809–92), whose mother read Hemans with delight, in the motif of chains (the central metaphor of Tennyson's "Columbus" [1880]) or the burial of Leonor at sea. The sound of a body entering water accompanied by a "flash" (Hemans, 2.539–42) informs Tennyson's moving stanza on the burial of his son at sea in "To the Marquis of Dufferin and Ava" (1889, lines 41–44).[8] And Hemans's "A Spirit's Return" (which the *Athenaeum* pronounced her finest poem[9]) may anticipate Section 95 of *In Memoriam* in concerning a suddenly bereaved woman who ceaselessly mourns and contemplates her relation to the dead until one calm summer night her sole "prayer ... 'Awake, appear, reply!'" is answered by his presence – although in Hemans's poem the return is literalized into an apparition that speaks and then is gone forever.[10]

Today Hemans stands as a major Romantic poet and popular figure among Victorians.[11] Yet her decorum made her susceptible to reification as a sweetly feminine "poetess" (in the invidious sense of an intellectually limited, merely emotional singer) from 1847 onward, beginning with George Gilfillan's assessment.[12] Even William Michael Rossetti, brother to Christina and sympathetic to women poets, accorded Hemans only contingent merit. He praised the "beauty" and "aptitude and delicacy in versification" of her poems but added,

> "Her skill ... hardly rises into the loftier region of art ... [Her poetry] leaves a certain artificial impression, rather perhaps through a cloying flow of 'right-minded' perceptions of moral and material beauty than through any other effect ... the atmosphere of her verse is by no means bracing."[13]

Elizabeth Barrett Browning

Victorians found more "bracing" poetry in the work of Barrett Browning. At her death, the *London Review* averred that she "combines all the sweetness of Mrs. Hemans and the depth of Tennyson, with occasional bursts of dramatic grandeur that remind of Shakspeare."[14] Earlier John Ruskin (1819–1900) pronounced *Aurora Leigh* (1856) "the greatest poem which the century has produced in any language."[15] If by 1932, Barrett Browning usually resided in the "servants' quarters" of literature along with Hemans and Eliza Cook (1818–89), Virginia Woolf contended of *Aurora Leigh* that "Speed and energy, forthrightness and complete self-confidence – these are the qualities that hold us enthralled." Granting Barrett Browning's "novel-poem" the palm over many Victorian novels, Woolf concluded that *Aurora Leigh* is "a book that still lives and breathes and has its being."[16]

Aurora Leigh is a central achievement in Victorian poetry. A generic hybrid that encompasses epic (in nine books and almost 11,000 lines), the domestic novel, Spasmodism (mid-century long narratives centered in poets' subjectivities), and a poetic manifesto, the poem draws on the novel *Corinne; or, Italy* (1807) by Mme. De Staël (1766–1817), the poetry of Letitia Landon (1802–1838), and Wordsworth's *Prelude* (1850), as well as Barrett Browning's own earlier verse.[17] Its form modulates from retrospective journal to present-tense dramatic utterance and incorporates not only a novelistic plot but also striking metaphoric patterns and lyric expression. It concerns an Anglo-Italian orphan brought from Italy to England to live with her paternal aunt, who tries to shape Aurora into a conventional Englishwoman, and Aurora's relations with her cousin Romney Leigh, a social reformer, and Marian Erle, the young working-class woman whom Romney determines to marry after Aurora refuses him on her twentieth birthday. Above all, the poem is about Aurora's life as a poet and her insight into the relation of spiritual to material existence that a poet's cosmic vision grants her: "O life, O poetry, / — Which means life in life! cognisant of life / Beyond this blood-beat" (1.915–17).[18]

Aurora Leigh is explicitly the story of a woman, and a woman who must manage a career as well as erotic, domestic, and social relations. If the story looks back to Hemans's *Records of Woman*, Aurora's dilemmas also illuminate *Aurora Leigh*'s renewed importance (after four decades' neglect) during second-wave feminism in the 1970s. Even Victorians recognized the work's feminist elements. In 1861, William H. Smith observed that Aurora "vindicates for herself and for her sex the right to stand apart, lyre in hand, an independent and earnest artist."[19] And in donating her copy to the Library of Congress, U.S. suffragist Susan B. Anthony wrote, "I have always cherished [*Aurora Leigh*] above all other books."[20] Like its generic and formal features, the poem's feminism is dynamic, a point I want to trace through Aurora's adoption of multiple roles.

As a young woman, Aurora is a feminist rebel chafing against her aunt's campaign of feminization (which teaches women's "Potential faculty in everything / Of abdicating power in it" [1.441–42]) and repudiating relative status when Romney proposes:

> You want a helpmate, not a mistress, sir,
> A wife to help your ends,—in her no end! . . .
> You misconceive the question like a man,
> Who sees a woman as the complement
> Of his sex merely . . .
> I too have my vocation,—work to do.

(2.402–3, 434–36, 455)

Next, Aurora becomes a single woman pursuing a career in the city, facing the challenges of fickle critics ("My critic Hammond flatters prettily" while "My critic Belfair wants another book / Entirely different" [3.66, 368–69]), too little income ("[I] scarce have money for my needs" [3.57]), and the drudgery of a "day job" in journalism that supports work on her craft at night: "I stood up straight and worked / My veritable work" and "life, in deepening with me, deepened all / The course I took, the work I did" (3.327–28, 334–35).

After her encounters with the overtly sexual Lady Waldemar and submissive Marian Erle (possible female alternatives) and the trauma of Romney's aborted wedding to Marian, Aurora leaves for Paris where she encounters

Marian, now a single mother after being raped through the machinations of Lady Waldemar's corrupt maid. At first censuring Marian, Aurora ultimately embraces her and her child, and Aurora's next living arrangement is in a female-headed household composed of two women and a baby:

> ye are my own
> From henceforth. I am lonely in the world,
> And thou art lonely, and the child is half
> An orphan. Come,—and henceforth thou and I
> Being still together will not miss a friend,
> Nor he a father, since two mothers shall
> Make that up to him.   (7.119–25)

Their roles in Tuscany are consistent with lesbian and other nontraditional households, but the poem also validates freely chosen heterosexual unions after Aurora gradually realizes her long-standing love for Romney. When he appears in Tuscany, now blind from a fire in his phalanstery, he first dutifully offers marriage to Marian. But she, taking a page from the young Aurora's book, spurns him for an autonomous life as single mother: "Here's a hand shall keep / For ever clean without a marriage-ring, / To tend my boy" (9.431–33). Nor is the heterosexual happy ending entirely conventional, since Aurora is first to declare her love and claims a man's customary prerogative to make a declaration before receiving a reply: "when a woman says she loves a man, / The man must hear her, though he love her not, / Which .. hush! .. he has leave to answer in his turn" (9.613–15). After their passionate embrace and "ecstatic" kiss (9.721–22), the poem ends in happy erotic union with Aurora's career and cosmic vision intact, as the concluding lines on the New Jerusalem attest: "'Jasper first,' I said, ... The rest in order, – last, an amethyst'" (9.962, 964). The poem culminates in heterosexual union, but this does not negate earlier phases of existence that have created the mature poet at the end. Read in these terms, *Aurora Leigh* offers a model consistent with twenty-first-century feminism's insistence on multiple female choices and opportunities.

Readers who know only *Aurora Leigh*, however, miss the full range of Barrett Browning's poetic production. Supported by her Christian faith and Romantic conceptions of the visionary poet, Barrett Browning confidently addressed social issues in several formally inventive works: "The Cry of the Children" (1843; revised 1844), which critiqued child labor, exposed Britain's Christian hypocrisy, and evoked through meter and repetition the subjective experience of being pent in a factory; "Runaway Slave at Pilgrim's Point" (1848; revised 1850), a transatlantic abolitionist poem that confronted Christian and U.S. hypocrisy in countenancing slavery; and *Casa*

Guidi Windows (1851), a long narrative in which Barrett Browning advocates as poet, mother, and Englishwoman for the Italian Risorgimento (a struggle for autonomous rule). Her early ballads are closest to the work of poetess precursors, especially since several appeared in literary annuals. But even as she adopted poetess conventions, Barrett Browning stretched them almost to breaking. In "The Romaunt of the Page" (1839; revised 1844), for example, a wife cross-dresses as a page and sacrifices herself in battle for her unappreciative husband – a comment on the institution of marriage as well as women's gender roles. Though the single line "How do I love thee? Let me count the ways" (43.1) remains best known (and often parodied), *Sonnets from the Portuguese* (1850) is complex and intellectually challenging, merging meditative sonnets on love, death, and God with an amatory sonnet sequence.[21]

Her lyrics remain Barrett Browning's least studied works. "A Reed" (1846; revised 1850), given in full here, is seldom discussed but demonstrates her importance as a lyric poet:

>   I
> I am no trumpet, but a reed:
> No flattering breath shall from me lead
>   A silver sound, a hollow sound.
> I will not ring, for priest or king,
> One blast that in re-echoing
>   Would leave a bondsman faster bound.
>
>   II
> I am no trumpet, but a reed,—
> A broken reed, the wind indeed
>   Left flat upon a dismal shore;
> Yet if a little maid, or child,
> Should sigh within it, earnest-mild,
>   This reed will answer evermore.
>
>   III
> I am no trumpet, but a reed.
> Go, tell the fishers, as they spread
>   Their nets along the river's edge,
> I will not tear their nets at all,
> Nor pierce their hands, if they should fall;
>   Then let them leave me in the sedge.[22]

Adopting a sextilla or Spanish sestet (aabccb), Barrett Browning enhances the musical associations of her title in a refrain that pairs a trumpet and a reed. The trumpet, instrument of choice for martial and courtly settings, pointedly contrasts the quieter reed that is easily broken. The juxtaposition suggests a gendered dyad of loud, public masculinity versus retiring feminine modesty, especially since the poet-speaker ends up a broken reed asking to be left "in the sedge" (a mass of marshy plants).

Yet the reed-poet is markedly assertive in the first stanza, expressing defiance of cooptation by established powers of the church and state. In fact, this lyric is another artistic credo, and (like her social protest poems) it refuses to be an instrument of oppression. As the second stanza indicates, perhaps with a glance toward Barrett Browning's earlier "broken" state of invalidism, the reed is activated by the lowly and the young, to whose sighs this instrument perpetually reverberates. In keeping with these loyalties, the last stanza disavows the harmful effects of violence and destruction.

The complex tissue of allusions and wordplay in the poem as well as what seems at first the odd non sequitur of being left in the sedge further complicate the initial impression of feminine modesty. A reed signifies not only a musical instrument or plant but also a pen, linking the poet to the age of print and to poetry that outlasts transient sound. The "broken reed" of stanza 2 alludes not merely to the natural phenomenon of windblown reeds but also to Isaiah 36:6–7, which contrasts false power with that derived from God: "thou trustest in the staff of this broken reed, on Egypt; whereon if a man lean, it will go into his hand, and pierce it." This allusion carries into the third stanza, but the poet's broken reed abjures violence and will not pierce the hand. In this allusive context, the fishers spreading their nets recall Christ's disciples, "fishers of men" (Matthew 4:19). The last stanza, then, announces poetry firmly allied with Christianity: Christ's followers will not be hurt in leaning on this reed, which can support them. Leaving this poetry "in the sedge," through a last play on words, simultaneously suggests a place among the discarded and overlooked on earth and a poet established in a seat of power. For an older meaning of "sedge" derived from the Italian *seggia* is a seat or assembly hall. The last line, read thus, offers a contrasting hall to that of kings and priests in stanza 1 and affirms that alignment with the lowly, the powerless, and the faithful is also the means to a lasting oppositional poetics of power. Musical and accessible, "The Reed," like *Aurora Leigh*, offers multiple possible subject positions and a poetic credo – in the compass of three lyric stanzas.

Christina Rossetti

At Barrett Browning's death, her poetic solecisms as well as powers were noted. By century's end, her indifference to "rules," her overt political advocacy, and aestheticism's increasing emphasis on chiseled form and subordination of morality conspired to bring her achievement into question. Robert Browning became the preeminent Victorian poet among aesthetes and Modernists, and rather than Barrett Browning, Christina Rossetti became the foremost woman poet. As poet and literary journalist Alice Law (fl. 1894–1928) concluded shortly after Rossetti's death,

> It is commonly remarked that Mrs. Browning is the greater poet of the two by reason of her wider sympathy and more extended vision. But ... the slipshod carelessness and frequent pedestrianism of much of her work seriously detracts from Mrs. Browning's artistic reputation ... Miss Rossetti, on the other hand, though rarely posing as teacher, philosopher, or moralist, is yet always a consummate artist.[23]

Virginia Woolf confirmed this persisting judgment in the twentieth century: "One has only to compare [Barrett Browning's] reputation with Christina Rossetti's to trace her decline. Christina Rossetti mounts irresistibly to the first place among English women poets."[24] Nor has Rossetti's poetic stature survived relative only to women. Poet Philip Larkin (1922–85) kept Rossetti's poems at his desk, and in 1993 Isobel Armstrong displaced Matthew Arnold to name Tennyson, Browning, and Rossetti as the three great Victorian poets.[25]

Both Hemans and Barrett Browning influenced Rossetti,[26] but Rossetti is distinctive in fusing exquisite technique and expression with striking impersonality and reserve. The resulting instability of meaning, a common reference point in scholarly commentary today, was understood in 1895. When she first encountered Rossetti's work, according to Alice Law,

> Its beauty danced ever before me, but, like the phantom of her own *Fata Morgana*, it eluded capture. The absence of all harsher and more rugged qualities, of all topical didacticism, of any rigid philosophical system on which we can lay hold, their seeming artless, yet aesthetic and finished perfection, all these combine to give the poems an air of elevated inaccessibility which renders critical approach difficult.[27]

Nearly a century later, Jerome McGann underscored Rossetti's elusive meanings and inaccessible (or "alienated") stance that challenge while intriguing readers.[28] The compatibility of these qualities with the aloof detachment of Modernism is one factor in Rossetti's sustained prestige.

Studying Rossetti alongside other Victorian women poets, conversely, illuminates Rossetti's vibrant engagement with women's issues and religion. Both inform her best-known poem *Goblin Market* (1862),[29] which has been interpreted in relation to religious salvation, domesticity, fallen women, drug addiction, same-sex desire, and the Victorian commodity market. Rossetti's recourse to a fairy-tale register begs for interpretation and a moral, but, like the goblin fruits themselves, no single interpretation ever fully satisfies readers after a first "taste" of this memorable work. "Morning and evening / Maids heard the goblins cry" (lines 1–2): "Maids" looks generic but specifies young virgins, whereas the goblin market remains multiplicitous in meaning, from a site of satanic tempters to nightmarish country markets, the Victorian commodity market, or the fleshly market of prostitutes.

The poem's larger tale is clear enough. A brotherhood of goblins tempts sisters Laura and Lizzie with rarely delectable fruits. Laura succumbs, and Lizzie rescues her sister from early death by undergoing the goblins' assault and restoring Laura to health and wholesome life. The poem's conclusion then celebrates sisterhood ("there is no friend like a sister / . . . To fetch one if one goes astray" [lines 562, 565]) and the domestic life it secures. Fruits and a fall suggest Eve and the Garden of Eden, but here the redeemer of the fallen is not Christ but a girl's sister, nor is there any expulsion of the fallen from a prelapsarian world. Laura is instead fully restored to innocence and marriageability.

Significantly, Laura's restoration depends not on spiritual conversion but on the linguistic inversions Lizzie effects in the text. Lizzie is as much a figure of the poet and reader (who likewise adjudicate textual meaning) as of Christ and loving sister, foregrounding the literariness of Rossetti's tale. At the outset of the poem, both sisters lie "Crouching close together / . . . With tingling cheeks and finger tips" (line 36), their tingling a register of both fear and sexual arousal. Laura, who listens to the "iterated jingle" of fruit cries (line 233), becomes infected with the goblins' phallic sexuality and "Prick[ed] up" and "reared her glossy head" (lines 41, 52). Lizzie must then set off to remedy her sister's fall and endure physical attack. Lizzie neutralizes Laura's earlier "Pricking up her golden head" as she returns home from her ordeal: "Nor was she pricked by fear" (line 460). Lizzie's heroic efforts likewise transform the goblins' "iterated jingle" into Lizzie's self-possession and delight on hearing "her penny jingle / Bouncing in her purse" (lines 452–53). And the earlier "tingle" of desire (line 39) becomes the "smart, ache, tingle" of Lizzie's salvific wounds (line 447). Lizzie's most powerful inversion, however, is her transformation of gobbled fruit and goblin "hugs" (line 348) into a eucharistic feast and the life-giving embrace to which she invites her sister:

> Hug me, kiss me, suck my juices
> Squeezed from goblin fruits for you,
> Goblin pulp and goblin dew.
> Eat me, drink me, love me. (lines 468–71)

As savior-poet, Lizzie cancels prior resonances of words and sets new meanings against old, just as she provides homeopathic domestic care of Laura, using poisonous goblin fruit to cure its earlier effects. The fruit turns "wormwood" in Laura's mouth (line 494), and she writhes, leaps, sings, and rips a dress (lines 496–97), reminiscent of Lizzie's experience during the goblins' assault. By means of these transformations, Lizzie brings Laura "out of death" (line 524), and Laura awakens whole and hale the next morning while "early reapers plodded to the place / Of golden sheaves" (lines 531–32), a sly allusion to Tennyson's "The Lady of Shalott" and its irreversible feminine fall.

Key words that can equally narrate a fall or rebirth, however, suggest these states' proximity and thereby an important theological point. Laura's recovered innocence defies the logic of biblical original sin, time's irreversibility, and Victorian customs regarding fallen women. But this reversibility also enforces the teaching that even innocent girls are defined by their fallen human nature: the boundary between human innocence and fallenness has always already been breached according to the doctrine of original sin. Hence, the fallen (whether sisters, sinners, or prostitutes) cannot with consistency be shunned or ignored.

Goblin Market offers readers pleasure through luscious imagery and sounds, inventive rhythms, and its intriguing story. In contrast, Rossetti's well-known "Song" ("When I am dead, my dearest," 1862)[30] shuts down story and shuts out easy sympathies aside from delight in pure diction and form. An exemplar of Rossetti's "alienated" perspective, the sixteen-line "Song" is an anti-love lyric that spurns lyric's customary mainspring, the expression of feeling:

> When I am dead, my dearest,
>   Sing no sad songs for me;
> Plant thou no roses at my head,
>   Nor shady cypress tree:
> Be the green grass above me
>   With showers and dewdrops wet;
> And if thou wilt, remember,
>   And if thou wilt, forget.   (lines 1–8)

Setting aside heterosexual romance, the lyric instead foregrounds an alienated female voice that sings of the body's insensibility in death.

The text's significance is further clarified in relation to other Victorian women's poetry. "Song" is the antiphonal voice of Rossetti's contemporaneous "A Birthday" ("my love is come to me" [lines 8, 16) and "Remember" ("Remember me when I am gone away, / Gone far away into the silent land" [lines 1–2]).³¹ It forms an additional intertextual relationship with Letitia Landon's "Night at Sea" (1839), notable for its refrain "My friends, my absent friends! / Do you think of me, as I think of you?" (line 10 ff.),³² and "L.E.L.'s Last Question" (1839) by Barrett Browning – so called because the nine stanzas respond to Landon's posthumously published "Night at Sea."³³ In refusing remembrance, "Song" contests Landon's refrain, and while it is congruent with Barrett Browning's outlook in "L.E.L.'s Last Question" – "when her questioned friends in agony / Made passionate response, 'We think of thee,' / Her place was in the dust, too deep to hear" (lines 33–35) – Rossetti's lyric contests Barrett Browning's preferred medium of direct statement: "Not much, and yet too much, / Is this 'Think of me as I think of you'"; "HE ... drew / All life from dust, and for all, tasted death" (lines 55–56, 60–61). "Song" eludes both yearning for loving remembrance and theological statement, effacing all human sensibility in the imagined grave and leaving open whether aloof detachment from human connection is a matter of chance or a boon ("Haply I may remember, / And haply may forget" [lines 15–16]).

In the later *Pageant and Other Poems* (1881), Rossetti more explicitly signals indebtedness to Barrett Browning while diverging from her example once more. "Monna Innominata: A Sonnet of Sonnets" imagines the poetic utterance of an unnamed early modern women poet.³⁴ Rossetti's headnote, tartly commenting on the "scant ... attractiveness" of Dante's Beatrice and Petrarch's Laura, continues:

> Had such a lady spoken for herself, the portrait left us might have appeared more tender, if less dignified ... Or had the Great Poetess of our own day and nation only been unhappy instead of happy, her circumstances would have invited her to bequeath to us, in lieu of the "Portuguese Sonnets," an inimitable "donna innominata" drawn not from fancy but from feeling, and worthy to occupy a niche beside Beatrice and Laura.³⁵

Rossetti's fourteenth sonnet thus ends, like "Song," by erasing the expression of love:

> Youth gone and beauty gone, what doth remain?
>   The longing of a heart pent up forlorn,
>   A silent heart whose silence loves and longs;
>   The silence of a heart which sang its songs
>   While youth and beauty made a summer morn,
> Silence of love that cannot sing again.   (14.9–14)

Devotional lyrics are integral to Rossetti's oeuvre, as with many Victorian women poets for whom religious verse and hymns were a major outlet.[36] Rossetti's 1862 and 1866 volumes included devotional lyrics such as "A Better Resurrection" and "Weary in Well-Doing";[37] others were published individually in magazines or anthologies; and *Verses* (1893), issued by the Society for Promoting Christian Knowledge, was composed entirely of devotional lyrics. "Paradise: in a Symbol" (1869) appeared in Orby Shipley's *Lyra Messianica*.[38] Rossetti contributed four poems to the first edition, along with six other women poets including her friends Dora Greenwell (1821–82) and Adelaide Anne Procter (1825–64). "Paradise," added to the second edition, shares the distinctive lyric qualities of Rossetti's secular poems:

> Golden-winged, silver-winged
>   Winged with flashing flame,
> Such a flight of birds I saw,
>   Birds without a name:
> Singing songs in their own tongue
>   (Song of songs) they came.   (lines 1–6)

Here, however, the alienated perspective (the birds' incommunicable names and song) has a religious function, marking off paradisal birds – the symbol of ascended souls – from terrestrial auditors.

The untitled prefatory poem of *Annus Domini: A Prayer for Each Day of the Year* (1874),[39] Rossetti's first volume of devotional prose, cannot be compared in originality to "Carrion Comfort" by Gerard Manley Hopkins (1844–89).[40] But it is intriguing that the poems share the situation of a believer wrestling with and against the Lord each desires:

> Alas, my Lord,
> How should I wrestle all the livelong night
> With Thee my God, my Strength and my Delight?
>
> How can it need
> So agonized an effort and a strain
> To make Thy Face of Mercy shine again?
>
> How can it need
> Such wringing out of breathless prayer to move
> Thee to Thy wonted Love, when Thou art Love?   (lines 1–9)[41]

Rossetti's lyric anticipates not only the language of wrestling and wringing in Hopkins ("why wouldst thou rude on me / Thy wring-world right foot rock?"; "that year / ... I wretch lay wrestling with (my God!) my God" [lines 5–6, 13–14]) but also the spiritual revelation that the believer's antagonist and beloved Lord are the same. Rossetti's diction and rhythm are decorous relative to Hopkins's, but this should not blind us to her imaginative daring and inventive technique in "Alas my Lord."

The poem opens as a lyric, one ostensibly addressed to the Lord but really an internal dialogue, as signaled by "I" and the speaker's conflicted situation. The female poet's transgressive wrestling with God is enforced by the "breathless prayer" that implies at once anticipation, aspiration, and breathlessness from physical struggle. Equally transgressive are succeeding stanzas that unfold a cavalcade of biblical patriarchs who stand as precursors, potentially implying the speaker's equality with them, especially Jacob, who was blessed after wrestling with God (Genesis 32:24–30): "Yet Jacob did / So hold Thee by the clenched hand of prayer / That he prevailed, and Thou didst bless him there" (lines 13–15). The cavalcade ends in the supreme exemplar, Christ. If the speaker remains self-regarding – "Alas for him / Who faints, despite Thy Pattern, King of Saints: / Alas, alas, for me, the one that faints" (lines 31–33) – the speaker now "faints" rather than wrestling. Christ's efficacy as savior is then immediately enacted in the final stanzas, when the lyric "I" becomes lost in communal prayer:

> Lord, give us strength
> To hold Thee fast, until we hear Thy Voice
> Which Thine own know, who hearing It rejoice.
>
> Lord, give us strength
> To hold Thee fast until we see Thy Face,
> Full Fountain of all Rapture and all Grace.
>
> But when our strength
> Shall be made weakness, and our bodies clay,
> Hold Thou us fast, and give us sleep till day.　　(lines 34–42)

The vague referent of "it" in "How can it need" (lines 4, 7) signals the speaker's inability or unwillingness to face and rectify her situation; "It" in the last triad of stanzas is specific, identifying Christ's voice that is recognized by true followers. Rossetti's shift from self-regarding lyric to communal prayer models the turn to prayer that her book is designed to foster. Yet this performative religious lyric is inseparable from her testing and revising of women's roles.

The works of Hemans, Barrett Browning, and Rossetti represent only a small portion of memorable poems by Victorian women, and only a few of their poems are discussed here. If these nonetheless suggest how absorbing, challenging, and inventive Victorian women's poetry can be, they register the achievement of Victorian women and the rich abundance of other poems awaiting exploration.

NOTES

1. Elizabeth Barrett to Henry Fothergill Chorley, January 7, 1845, *The Brownings' Correspondence*, 21 vols., ed. Philip Kelley and Scott Lewis (Winfield: Wedgestone Press, 1992), vol. 10, p. 13.
2. *Poems of William Wordsworth, Volume 3: Collected Reading Texts from The Cornell Wordsworth*, ed. Curtis Jared (Penrith: Humanities-Ebooks, LLP, 2009), p. 724.
3. Elizabeth Gaskell, *Wives and Daughters*, ed. Frank G. Smith (Harmondsworth: Penguin, 1975), p. 97.
4. Elizabeth Bishop, *The Complete Poems: 1927–1979* (New York: Farrar Straus Giroux, 1983), p. 5.
5. "Arabella Stuart," *Felicia Hemans: Selected Poems, Prose, and Letters*, ed. Gary Kelly (Peterborough: Broadview Press, 2002), pp. 307–17.
6. *The Forest Sanctuary*, in ibid., pp. 227–89.
7. *The George Eliot Letters*, ed. Gordon S. Haight, 9 vols. (New Haven: Yale University Press, 1954–1978), vol. 1, p. 72.
8. Alfred Tennyson, "To the Marquis of Dufferin and Ava," in *The Poems of Tennyson*, ed. Christopher Ricks, 3 vols. (Berkeley: University of California Press, 1987), vol. 3, pp. 198–201.
9. "Mrs. Hemans," *Athenaeum* 395 (May 23, 1835), 392.
10. *The Poetical Works of Mrs. Felicia Hemans*, ed. with a Memoir by William Michael Rossetti (London: Ward & Lock, 1879), p. 198.
11. Andrew Stauffer, "Hemans by the Book," *European Romantic Review* 22:.3 (2011), 374–76.
12. George Gilfillan, "Female Authors – Mrs. Hemans," *Tait's Edinburgh Magazine* 14 (June 1847), 359–63.
13. William Michael Rossetti, "Prefatory Notice," *Poetical Works of Mrs. Felicia Hemans*, pp. xxvi–xxvii.
14. "Elizabeth Barrett Browning," *London Review* 16 (July 13, 1861), 41.
15. John Ruskin, *The Works of John Ruskin*, ed. E. T. Cook and Alexander Wedderburn, 39 vols. (New York: Longmans Green, 1903–12), vol. 15, p. 227.
16. Virginia Woolf, "Aurora Leigh," *The Second Common Reader* (1932), in *Aurora Leigh*, ed. Margaret Reynolds (New York: W. W. Norton, 1996), pp. 439–40, 446.
17. Linda Peterson, "Rewriting A History of the Lyre: Letitia Landon, Elizabeth Barrett Browning, and the (Re)Construction of the Nineteenth-Century Woman Poet," in *Women's Poetry, Late-Romantic to Late Victorian: Gender and Genre, 1830–1900*, ed. Isobel Armstrong and Virginia Blain (Basingstoke: Macmillan, 1999), pp. 115–32; Marjorie Stone and Beverly Taylor, "Introduction," *Elizabeth Browning: Selected Poems* (Peterborough: Broadview Press, 2009), pp. 35–36.

18. *Aurora Leigh, The Works of Elizabeth Barrett Browning*, ed. Sandra Donaldson et al., 5 vols. (London: Pickering & Chatto, 2010), vol. 3, pp. 3–317.
19. William Henry Smith, "Poems [by Elizabeth Barrett Browning]," *British Quarterly Review*, 68 (October 1861), 368.
20. Qtd. in *Aurora Leigh*, ed. Reynolds, p. viii.
21. *Sonnets from the Portuguese*, in *Works of Elizabeth Barrett Browning*, vol. 2, pp. 442–80.
22. "A Reed," *Works of Elizabeth Barrett Browning*, vol. 2, p. 369.
23. Alice Law, "The Poetry of Christina Rossetti," *Westminster Review* 143 (January 1895), 452.
24. Woolf, "Aurora Leigh," p. 439.
25. Constance Hassett, "Christina Rossetti: Ravens, Cockatoos, and Range," in *The Oxford Handbook of Victorian Poetry*, ed. Matthew Bevis (Oxford: Oxford University Press, 2013), p. 445; Isobel Armstrong, *Victorian Poetry: Poetry, Poetics, Politics* (London: Routledge, 1993), p. 8.
26. Constance Hassett, *Christina Rossetti: The Patience of Style* (Charlottesville: University of Virginia Press, 2005), pp. 65–71, 98–99; Marjorie Stone, "Sisters in Art: Christina Rossetti and Elizabeth Barrett Browning," *Victorian Poetry*, 32:3–4 (Autumn/Winter 1994), 339–64.
27. Law, "The Poetry of Christina Rossetti," p. 444.
28. Jerome McGann, "Christina Rossetti's Poems: A New Edition and a Revaluation," *Victorian Studies* 23 (1980), 237–54.
29. *Goblin Market*, in *The Complete Poems of Christina Rossetti: A Variorum Edition*, ed. R. W. Crump, 3 vols. (Baton Rouge: Louisiana State University Press, 1986), vol. 1, pp. 11–26.
30. Ibid., vol. 1, p. 58.
31. Ibid., vol. 1, pp. 36–377.
32. *Letitia Elizabeth Landon: Selected Writings*, ed. Jerome McGann and Daniel Riess (Peterborough: Broadview Press, 1997), pp. 205–8.
33. "L.E.L.'s Last Question," *Works of Elizabeth Barrett Browning*, vol. 1, pp. 544–66.
34. "Monna Innominata," *Complete Poems of Christina Rossetti*, vol. 2, pp. 86–93.
35. Ibid., vol. 2, p. 86.
36. F. Elizabeth Gray, *Christian and Lyric Tradition in Victorian Women's Poetry* (New York: Routledge, 2010), pp. 5–6.
37. "Song," *The Complete Poems of Christina Rossetti*, vol., 1, pp. 68, 182.
38. "Paradise: in a Symbol," ibid., vol. 3, pp. 42–43.
39. Christina Rossetti, *Annus Domini: A Prayer for Each Day of the Year, Founded on a Text of Holy Scripture* (London: James Parker & Co., 1874).
40. "[Carrion Comfort]," *Gerard Manley Hopkins: The Major Works*, ed. Catherine Phillips (Oxford: Oxford University Press, 2002), p. 168.
41. "Alas, my Lord," *Complete Poems of Christina Rossetti*, vol. 3, pp. 44–45.

7

ELLA DZELZAINIS

Silver-fork, industrial, and Gothic fiction

Splicing together literary genres and modes as diverse as melodrama, satire, realism, factual reportage, and the Gothic, the early Victorian novel is characterized by its formal hybridity. Women writers were often in the vanguard of this technical experimentation, whether their novels proved ephemeral or canonical. Catherine Gore, for example, worked innovatively with the conventions of the silver-fork novel in the now obscure *Cecil* (1841) and inspired William Thackeray's part parody, part homage in *Vanity Fair* (1847). By fusing fiction with economic theory, Harriet Martineau's now little-read *Illustrations of Political Economy* (1832–34) prompted the industrial novel, one of whose most successful practitioners is Elizabeth Gaskell. Charlotte Brontë is justly celebrated for incorporating elements of the eighteenth-century Gothic into the domestic realism of *Jane Eyre* (1847) and *Villette* (1853), novels central to the Victorian literary canon. Women's formal creativity ran in tandem with their recognition of the novel as a vehicle through which they could legitimately engage with public questions. Writing in a period of political transition – the long, slow march from aristocratic to democratic government – early Victorian women authors used fiction to discuss not just class politics but also what was usually referred to as the "woman question": that is, the state (or lack) of women's access to social, legal, and political self-determination. In this regard, women novelists required their readers to extrapolate political and social meanings from stories of domestic life and courtship. Contemporary responses to the novels suggest that many obliged. Accordingly, this chapter sketches out some of the ways in which this method of writing and reading could transmute the seemingly private into public questions.

Silver-fork novels

The prevalence of this extrapolatory mode of reading is confirmed in a survey of literary trends included in *England and the English* (1833), written by the popular novelist and independent Radical Member of Parliament, Edward Bulwer Lytton. Bulwer (as he was usually known) made bold claims for the political influence of the fashionable or silver-fork novel, a body of fiction that pored over the manners and mores of the aristocracy in minute detail. In the process of parading the "frivolity, the ridiculous disdain of truth, nature, and mankind, the self-consequence and absurdity" and engendering in the reader "mingled indignation and disgust," this immensely popular literary school had "been converting the multitude" to the democratic cause and creating the "change in feeling" necessary for the passage of the 1832 Reform Act, which widened the electoral franchise to include more men of the middle class.[1] In other words, the silver-fork novel had revealed the aristocracy to the people, whose contempt at the spectacle had led directly to the clipping of aristocratic power. As the author of *Pelham* (1828), one of the most popular of the early silver-fork novels, Bulwer had a vested interest in staking this claim for the subgenre's sociopolitical influence. As we shall see, it is unlikely that he would have staked it quite so cheerfully six years later, when his estranged wife, Rosina, published *Cheveley; or, the Man of Honour* (1839), a silver-fork *roman à clef* in which the aristocratic brute of a husband is Bulwer himself in thin disguise.

Written for the most part by men and women either in or on the fringes of the aristocracy, the silver-fork novel was at its popular height between the mid-1820s and the early 1840s, from the parliamentary run-up to the Reform Act until the defeat of Lord Melbourne's post-Reform Whig government. Scholars have associated the ephemerality of this once popular but now little-read literature with the passing of the political climate that produced it, but it has recently become the subject of renewed critical scrutiny. Male silver-fork authors turned their attention elsewhere after 1832, but its best-known female practitioners – Marguerite, Countess of Blessington; Lady Rosina Bulwer Lytton; and, most prolific and significant of all, the upper-middle-class Mrs. Catherine Gore – continued to write in this genre. The term "silver-fork" was a critical one, coined in 1827 by William Hazlitt in a review of fashionable novels by Benjamin Disraeli and Theodore Hook. In its fawning over the exclusivity of patrician tastes, he protested, the genre was pro-aristocratic and anti-reform: to the authors of such works, as long as "a few select persons eat fish with silver forks," it was "a circumstance of no consequence if a whole country starves."[2] In a comment that negotiates Hazlitt's and Bulwer's contrasting interpretations, Winifred Hughes notes the subgenre's "radical instability of tone."[3] One of the pleasures of the silver-fork novel was that it could feed aspiration, functioning as an etiquette guide for an arriviste middle-class readership. At the same time, its revelation of aristocratic corruption meant it could be read as satire, justifying the accretion of middle-class power that continued through the century. These two positions need not be mutually exclusive: readers could revel in the spectacle of aristocratic luxury while condemning the system that perpetuated it.

April Kendra uses gender to identify two strands within the silver-fork school: the "dandy novel" with its "hero-centred" bildungsroman structure, written by the likes of Bulwer and Disraeli, and the female-authored "society novel," which was more likely to offer multiple shifts of narrative focus and an emphasis on family and community that later became typical of nineteenth-century domestic realism. To make her case that "the true hero of the society novel is society itself," she discusses Catherine Gore's *The Hamiltons* (1834), showing how the novel conveys the impact of the Reform Bill on a community as well as on the heroine and supports the principle of political change while acknowledging its difficulties.[4] In practice, Kendra's gendered subdivision of silver-fork fiction, a move made to recuperate the neglected female writer, is troubled by Gore's own dandy novel *Cecil, or the Adventures of a Coxcomb* (1841), discussed later. The definition also risks underplaying the often melodramatic excesses of the subgenre's plots, characters, and affective register, as well as its unabashed delight in detailing the accoutrements of wealth. But her larger point – that in the hands of writers such as Gore, the silver-fork novel could champion domestic and community values and sought to extend them to the public realm – remains a suggestively useful one. It helps locate the female silver-fork novel as a transitional form between the novel of manners as practiced by Jane Austen and the emergence of the Victorian realist novel, whether the domestic realism of works such as Harriet Martineau's *Deerbrook* (1838) and Elizabeth Gaskell's *Cranford* (1851), with their depictions of the quotidian lives of doctors, governesses, and spinsters, or the high realism of George Eliot's broader social canvas, most famously in *Middlemarch* (1871–72).

A distinctive quality of a number of silver-fork novels by women was their folding of gender into class critique. Exposing patriarchal as well as aristocratic structures, the novels offer an early and powerful articulation of a prototypically Victorian set of concerns about the inequities of women's lot – concerns more usually associated with the industrial subgenre and the work of the Brontë sisters. Lady Blessington's highly melodramatic epistolary novel *The Victims of Society* (1837), for example, tells a story of ruined innocence while protesting against the sexual double standard and women's humiliations in the aristocratic marriage market. For its heroine Caroline Montressor, who proves to be both villain and victim of aristocratic society, the sight of young debutantes being presented at court reminds her of "the horses, mules, and asses, in Italy, decked in plumes and tinsel, on the *fête* of

St. Anthony, and led to be blessed by that patron of animals, preparatory to the exhibition for sale."[5] She also makes explicit the link between social and political reform in the novel, describing fashionable society as "that unreformed borough."[6] Its rotten rituals have codified women's subordination – and the fact that neither she nor her former friend, the virtuous Lady Augusta Annandale, escapes alive underscores the need for political and social change. In *Cheveley*, Lady Rosina Bulwer Lytton portrays her husband Edward in the character of Lord De Clifford, a wife-beating adulterer who stands successfully as an MP. Making charges throughout the novel that allude to events in her own marriage, Lady Lytton rages against male privilege, including the expectation that women should "devote their lives to ... their children, without ever being able to obtain one single conventional or legal right over them" (I, 276). She also insists on the indivisibility of the public and the private, tying the two spheres together through the language of politics: "in private life," De Clifford is a "tyrannical autocrat" (I, 88); in his liberal politics, he is a power-seeking "hypocrite" – for there is "no tyrant like a democrat" (I, 183). In Rosina's analysis, domestic abuse is inseparable from political abuse. The novel ends with a revenge fantasy as De Clifford's moral transgressions are publicly exposed and his head is smashed in a riding accident, leaving his wife free to remarry for love.

A less personal analysis of aristocratic male privilege appeared two years later in Gore's final fashionable novel *Cecil*, which develops a link between the cavalier treatment of women and a disregard for the poor. Its publication in the dying days of the Melbourne government (1835–41) marked the end of silver-fork fiction's popularity, with the final blow dealt by Thackeray's part-parody, part-homage in *Vanity Fair* (1847). Writing anonymously, and in a wittily confident piece of gender ventriloquism, Gore assumes the voice of Cecil Danby, who while legally the younger son of Lord Ormington is in fact the result of his mother's adulterous liaison. Perfectly content in his narcissism – "the leading trait of my character has its origin in the first glimpse I caught of myself, at twelve months old, in the swing-glass of my mother's dressing-room. I looked and became a coxcomb for life!" (I, 1) – Cecil reveals an aristocratic solipsism that reduces the lives of others, especially women and the lower orders, to an aesthetics of surface.[7] He treats his many women as merely decorative objects and also refuses epochal and political change, clinging on to the memory of a "gilded" (I, 223) Regency while sneering at the "money-making" (I, 186) habits of the Victorian middle class and rejecting the pro-reform "mass" on account of its dreariness: "a popular assemblage in England, is the dullest-looking thing in nature. Its dinginess seems arrayed in sackcloth and ashes; diversified here and there by the diabolism of a chimney sweep" (III, 3). In her capacity as a cross-dressing, middle-class author, Gore ensures her representative aristocrat self-condemns through his denial of the subjectivity of his social subordinates.

The moral delinquency of Cecil's contempt for the dull and dingy masses – as well as the force of Gore's critique – emerges fully when placed in historical and literary context. The novel was published at the start of the "Hungry Forties," a decade when cycles of economic boom and bust caused widespread working-class suffering, particularly in the northern industrial towns, and led to popular unrest.

Industrial novels

The chief literary response to this period of social and political turmoil was the industrial novel, a literature of class mediation, if also of vicious political factionalism, that sought to convey the realities of working-class life to the more privileged classes to procure sympathy and sociopolitical change. Middle-class women authors were in the vanguard of this literary innovation, which placed the poor center stage. Industrial fiction was marked from its inception as a genre of the novel in which women could engage either explicitly or implicitly with political debate over England's future as it shifted from an agricultural to a commercial and manufacturing economy. One of the consequences was that industrial fiction became a forum in which women were represented both as victims and as agents of change. The canonical industrial novels – including Disraeli's *Sybil* (1845), Charles Kingsley's *Alton Locke* (1850), Charles Dickens's *Hard Times* (1854), and Elizabeth Gaskell's *Mary Barton* (1848) and *North and South* (1855) – appeared from the mid-1840s to the mid-1850s, but the origins of the genre can be traced back much earlier to the publication of Harriet Martineau's *Illustrations of Political Economy* (1832–34). Martineau wrote her twenty-five-part series of short tales to disseminate the basic tenets of early-nineteenth-century political economy, ignorance of which she believed hampered social progress. The first two industrial novels, Frances Trollope's *The Life and Adventures of Michael Armstrong, the Factory Boy* (1840) and Charlotte Elizabeth Tonna's *Helen Fleetwood* (1841), were written in support of a Ten Hours Bill to limit child factory labor, and each can be read as a response to the formal experimentation in Martineau's stories, as well as Tory repudiations of her pro-democratic enthusiasm for industrial society.

In composing her series, Martineau drew extensively on nonfictional material, ranging from seminal economic works such as Adam Smith's *Wealth of Nations* (1776) and T. R. Malthus's *Essay on the Principle of Population* (1798) to parliamentary reports on fisheries and travel books on South Africa and the West Indies. In using the fictional form to reify the abstractions of political economy, Martineau intended to reach an audience of men, women, and children of all classes. Her innovative suturing of economics and literature proved a publishing sensation. Martineau referred to her characters as "embodied principles," with the series performing its tutelary work through a formal mixture of domestic realism, dialogue (or pseudo-dialogue: there is no mistaking whose view Martineau thinks correct), and allegory, often all in the same story.[8] "Weal and Woe in Garveloch" is a prime example. Set on a remote Scottish island, the tale describes the starvation that ensues in a once-thriving fishing community when the herring harvest fails and the population outstrips the food supply. Deft realist touches lie in moments that describe the scene of labor: the sights and sounds on the shoreline as the heroine, Ella, and her children salt and pack herrings and of the widow Katie Cuthbert netmaking at home while singing lullabies to her baby. Martineau propagandizes through the conversations between Ella and Katie, working-class matrons who both recognize the need for sexual restraint: it is overpopulation that creates working-class hunger in times of economic downturn. In allegorical terms, Garveloch is England writ small.

Submerged throughout Martineau's series is an implicit advocacy of a set of radical-liberal, dissenting, and feminist principles for future change – including universal franchise for men and women of all classes, the disestablishment of the Anglican Church, and an assertion of women's rational capacities and right to personal autonomy – that can be extrapolated only through an allegorical reading of what one contemporary critic deemed her "miniature models."[9] Her gender politics were not lost on her Tory opponents, who were quick to compare her to "Mother Woolstonecroft[sic]."[10] But the requirement to read on a symbolic as well as realist plane to comprehend Martineau's full engagement with political questions suggests continuities in methodology and interpretation between the silver-fork novel and the *Illustrations*, even if the latter was more overtly ideologically driven and experimental. So, too, does Martineau's use of a narrative mode that links the private subject with public affairs, in this case via a coupling of domestic and political economy. A crucial difference, of course, is that the tales are centrally engaged with life outside the aristocracy. Cumulatively, the individual stories add up to a paean to the values of the industrial and commercial middle class, with women characters of all social backgrounds often most quick to recognize the benefits of political economic understanding for nations as well as individuals. But there is a consistent engagement with working-class subjectivity through sympathetic characterization – many of the stories, such as "Cousin Marshall" and "A Manchester Strike," have ethically and intellectually admirable working-class heroes and heroines – even if Martineau's inflexibly dogmatic solution to their misery is to behave more like the middle class.

Given the success of the *Illustrations* as a fictional experiment in propaganda, it is not surprising that Tonna and Trollope built on Martineau's achievement by using serial narrative as a means to propagandize on behalf of child factory labor and, in doing so, launched the industrial novel. As its name suggests, the ultimate goal of the Ten Hours Movement was to secure a ten-hour working day for all factory workers, though for tactical reasons it began with children. Both novels commenced monthly serialization in 1839, with Trollope's *Michael Armstrong* appearing in shilling parts and Tonna's *Helen Fleetwood* in the ultra-Evangelical *Christian Lady's Magazine*, which Tonna edited. While they drew on very different literary genres and modes –Trollope waltzes freely (and controversially) through caricature, comedy, Gothic, pastoral, and romance; Tonna's domestic realism is inflected with an unrelenting religious determinism – both women used written and oral testimony to inform their novels. Questions about the gendering of knowledge become central in the novels, as each author seeks to legitimize women's engagement in industrial questions through a process of mediation between female author, middle- and upper--class reader, and working-class subject.

Although *Michael Armstrong* follows the fortunes of its hero from exploited factory child to suffering apprentice in Deep Valley Mill and from thence to gentrified romantic lead, much of the story follows the investigations of the heroine, factory heiress Mary Brotherton. As Rosemarie Bodenheimer suggests, in the novel Trollope "reveals a social sensibility that is simultaneously paternalist and anti-patriarchal."[11] The working poor (represented as actual and symbolic children) are shown to be victims in need of care and protection from their social superiors, while descriptions of Mary's determined investigation into the horrors of the factory system, made despite a male conspiracy to thwart her, positions her as a knight-like female paternalist who must "unmask the guilty secrets of the patriarchs."[12] In the process, Trollope mandates women's pursuit of industrial knowledge, framing it as both a social duty and a duty to the self. Throughout, she reiterates the need for the legislative intervention of a Ten Hours Bill, in view of which the apparent celebration of individual philanthropy at the end of the novel is something of a surprise: Michael is married to Fanny (a factory apprentice rescued by Mary); Mary is married to Edward, Michael's brother; and both couples are ensconced in Mary's newly purchased castle on the Rhône. However, Trollope's preface to the 1840 bound edition explains how recent "scenes of outrage and lawless violence" (rioting in the factory districts) had sullied the cause and so the planned further numbers in which Michael joined the Ten Hours Movement would not be written.[13]

Consideration of an *Athenaeum* review, published after six parts of the novel had appeared, suggests more complicated motives. The unsigned review was by Sydney Owenson, Lady Morgan, who grounded her objections to *Michael Armstrong* in the material and formal qualities of the work. The popularizing publication in cheap shilling parts, the use of inflammatory illustrations (the worst of which showed ravenous apprentices wolfing turnip peelings from a pig trough), and the writing of a tale slating the manufacturing class: all these aspects meant Trollope was "scattering firebrands among the people" at a time of political unrest, particularly by Chartists protesting against working-class exclusion from the franchise.[14] Trollope's narrative method was also at fault: "she embodies her notion of the manufacturers in a fictitious personage—a sort of moral scape-goat, laden with all the sin and all the error with which they may, in justice or injustice, be chargeable" (588). Morgan quotes passages in which Sir Matthew speaks with the anomic brio of a pantomime villain, while, in contrast, Michael is a "regular tract-drawn 'good boy'" (589). The result is a "miserable farce, equalled only by the worst comedies of the quondam German-English school" (589). In Morgan's view, Trollope's use of the comic, the sensational, and the grotesque rendered her novel "worthless" to the Ten Hours cause (590). Nonetheless, reflecting on the movement a decade after the 1847 Ten Hours Bill was passed, Samuel Kydd, one of its stalwarts, described *Michael Armstrong* as "much abused" but "useful."[15] Selling well, the novel's lowbrow mix of literary modes galvanized popular radical feeling, even as it caused outrage among sectors of the social and political elite. In short, as an instrument of class mediation the novel had failed spectacularly. A renowned anti-democrat since opposing the 1832 Reform Bill in her preface to *Domestic Manners of the Americans* that same year, Trollope most likely abandoned her narrative experiment once she realized that her haphazard stitching together of a patchwork of literary techniques had created a political monster.

In contrast, Tonna's handling of fictional modes in *Helen Fleetwood* offers little room for misinterpretation. The novel gives a graduated portrayal of the moral, physical, and spiritual disintegration of a devout rural family once poverty compels its younger members to work in a factory in the town of M. (most likely Manchester). As a pre-Millenarian Evangelical, Tonna construes the factory in apocalyptic terms and is explicit in her visceral opposition to Martineau's social and political beliefs elsewhere in her writing. Governed by laissez-faire principles and man's covetousness, the factory system is the work of Satan – a "diabolical child-market" or "pandemonium" that inexorably destroys those within it and whose perpetuation would lead to England's destruction.[16] The language here refuses the figurative: for Tonna, every mill really is the Devil's domain. Her religious schema produces a highly deterministic plot; in many ways, only the amplitude of character, scene, and incident lifts the novel above a religious tract. *Helen Fleetwood* could not be further removed from *Michael Armstrong* in its literary method, but it too berates men as failed patriarchs, while advocating social paternalism, and urges women to petition men to vote for candidates supporting a Ten Hours Bill.

Tonna developed this analysis further in *The Wrongs of Woman* (1843–44), four interconnected stories that delineate in painful detail the physical, moral, and spiritual sufferings of female labor (pin-headers, seamstresses, lace makers, and factory women) under the laissez-faire system. In their demand for the return of working women and girls to the domestic hearth, the stories express a fierce separate spheres ideology that makes clear Tonna's opposition to any claims to female equality with men. Ostensibly, this seems at odds with her advocacy of women's political activism in *Helen Fleetwood* and also with her own career. But throughout her writing, Tonna supplies scriptural sanction for her own and other right-minded Christian women's outspokenness. As with the biblical Deborah, imminent crisis licensed female engagement in the public sphere, even if as daughters, wives, and mothers, their proper place was subordinate to man and as a helpmeet in the home. If men were manly and governments were properly paternalistic, then women would not be forced to fill the void created by the dereliction of patriarchal duty.

As precursors of the canonical industrial novel, the works of Martineau, Trollope, and Tonna benefited from the advent of feminist literary criticism in the 1970s, which set about recuperating long-neglected fiction by women. A further beneficiary of this feminist turn was Elizabeth Gaskell, although her critical renaissance had begun earlier with the Marxist literary critics of the 1950s and 1960s, who praised the intensity of her portrayals of working-class poverty in *Mary Barton* (1848) and *North and South* (1855), while lamenting her lack of systemic analysis. The title of *Mary Barton* is somewhat misleading: as Gaskell stated, it was Mary's Chartist and trades unionist father, John, who was really "my hero, *the* person with whom all my sympathies went, with whom I tried to identify myself at the time."[17] In the novel, Gaskell details the social and political injustices – the starvation of his dying child, the rejection of the 1842 Chartist petition, the employers' refusal to pay adequate wages – that lead Barton to murder his employer's son. For Raymond Williams, Barton's murder of Henry Carson is the moment when Gaskell loses control of her novel. The violence is historically unrepresentative, Williams argues, and her loss of political nerve is revealed through a shift in genres, with realism giving way to melodrama. Indeed, the melodramatic tropes in *Mary Barton* are multiple: the pure heroine defying convention to save her lover, the courtroom spectacle, a jolly Jack Tar last-minute reprieve, the tale of the seduced woman. In this analysis, the public sphere (the story of John's politicization) is held separate from the private (Mary's romance).[18] Subsequent readings have questioned this disconnection by noting, for example, how in his plea for "a bit o' fire for the old granny ... and for victuals for the childer," John's political anger stems from domestic feeling or by reconsidering the relationship between realism and melodrama in the novel.[19] For if, as Peter Brooks argues, melodrama is an "intense emotional and ethical" genre whose purpose is to "recognize and confront evil, to combat and expel it, to purge the social order," then the sympathy Gaskell has evoked through realism is still carried forward in *Mary Barton*.[20] Sympathy's affective weight is now borne by the more popular melodramatic mode, with public and private domains merging in a flood of feeling.

Although Gaskell's dissenting faith pervades the novel (like Martineau, her background was Unitarian) and her middle-class liberalism informs her plea for class reconciliation, a striking aspect of *Mary Barton* is, as Marjorie Stone argues, its "polyphony of voices."[21] The novel was published anonymously and the educated narrative voice, with its direct addresses to the reader, is joined and often subverted by other textual voices that cross class and gender: in the working-class poetry and song used as chapter epigraphs, in the female characters who air conflicting views on factory legislation for women and children, through the use of dialect, and so on. The novel engages a set of dialogic literary strategies that, in its acceptance of difference and uncertainty, opens up considerable methodological distance between Gaskell and authors such as Martineau and Tonna, who, while politically opposed, deployed the same weapons of didacticism and ideologically determined plots. But in *North and South*, Gaskell conducts a much cooler analysis of the relation between employer and employed – and of women's role in a society transitioning into a fully fledged industrial economy – that places her much closer to Martineau than to her immediate female predecessors.

In *North and South*, the debate over industrialization is primarily aired through a series of triangulated discussions involving the upper-middle-class heroine, Margaret Hale. As a southern newcomer to Milton Northern (Manchester again), Margaret's prejudices about trade and manufacturing are dismantled by forthright exchanges with the factory worker Nicholas Higgins, and even more combative ones with the factory owner John Thornton, to whom Margaret is betrothed by the end. Critics of the novel have long been concerned to understand the uneasy relation between the industrial and romance plots, with the impending marriage generally interpreted as one of symbolic compromise: as a marriage of north to south, of trade to gentry, or of masculine commerce to feminine philanthropy (the latter often framed in terms of Margaret's womanly influence on Thornton). An alternative reading of this marital union, one that links Gaskell's liberal endorsement of industrial progress to gender equality, would be to see it as marking a turn toward democracy more than a compromise – that is, as a step further into the new political epoch that Cecil, Gore's aristocrat, refused to countenance. With Margaret having eschewed the chivalric self-fashioning of a feudal queen and Thornton no longer treating his workers like large children, the couple are finally fit to face an egalitarian future together in a capitalist economy. Nonetheless, for all its optimism about industrial progress, the ending still reverberates with the gender conventions that Victorian women in search of a wider sphere of action had to negotiate. The lovers' embrace deliberately echoes that in the riot scene, when Margaret drapes her body protectively around Thornton's, only for her to be injured by a missile thrown from the crowd. This highly public wounding has been interpreted in several ways, including as a symbolic defloration signifying the transgressive nature of women's intervention in workplace affairs or, alternatively, as a displacement of Gaskell's own anxieties about the self-exposure entailed by female authorship (particularly after the controversy caused by the 1853 publication of *Ruth*, with its fallen woman heroine).

Reviewing the novel in 1855, Margaret Oliphant described the combative romance between Margaret and Thornton as a ripple from the stones first cast in the water by Charlotte Brontë with *Jane Eyre* (1847) and later *Villette* (1853). As a heroine, Jane – with her claims to equality, her rage at women's subordination, and her fierce battles with Rochester – was a revolutionary: "this furious love-making," Oliphant declares, "was but the 'Rights of Woman' in a new aspect" and "a mere vulgar boiling over of the political cauldron, which tosses your French monarch into chaos and makes a new one in his stead."[22] In staging this comparison between *Jane Eyre*, *Villette*, and *North and South*, Oliphant raises to the surface the proto-feminist politics inherent in each novel's engagement with the circumscriptions of Victorian women's lives. The final section considers the way in which Charlotte Brontë and her sisters, Emily and Anne, used the gothic as a literary mode with which to explore the less reachable, more deeply interiorized aspects of women's experience in their novels.

Domestic Gothic novels

Eschewing the terror to be found in the remote castles and supernatural paraphernalia of eighteenth-century Gothic fiction, such as Horace Walpole's *The Castle of Otranto* (1764) and Ann Radcliffe's *The Mysteries of Udolpho* (1794), the Brontës instead domesticate the Gothic by using it as a mode to explore the subjective experience of femininity. For their Victorian heroines, the place of terror is closer at hand: in the family, the home, and the social, economic, and legal conventions that govern women's daily life in a patriarchal culture. Consequently, the Brontës' works have been seen as a bridge between early Gothic literature and the sensation novels of the 1860s (though one should note, too, that the industrial novel puts its own spin on the Gothic, with the factory framed as a cannibalistic and sexualized locus of violence and terror for Trollope's and Tonna's child victims).

In the Brontës' novels, the home could be a site of horror as a literal prison: the physical confinement of the young Jane in the Red Room and of Bertha in the attic in *Jane Eyre*, for example, or Isabella's incarceration by her husband, Heathcliff, in Emily Brontë's *Wuthering Heights* (1847). Alternatively, it could be the space where the laws of coverture, through which women's legal identity was subsumed into that of their husband's on marriage, bore down oppressively on them. In Anne Brontë's *The Tenant of Wildfell Hall* (1848), as the marriage between the heroine, Helen, and the increasingly dissipated Arthur Huntingdon breaks down, her husband exerts his patriarchal rights by burning her painting materials and denying her access to money: actions to remind Helen of her status as chattel and to enforce compliance. Eventually, she flees the marital home with her son, living secretly under an assumed name to prevent her alcoholic tyrant of a husband from exercising his legal right to sole custody of their child. As events in Rosina Bulwer Lytton's own life testify, this fictional account of the law as an instrument of terror for mothers was not merely a flight of fancy.

Each of these vignettes performs its own interrogation of the Victorian cult of domesticity. If the home was meant to be a feminine domain providing sanctuary from the depredations of the public, masculine sphere, then narratives using the Gothic mode to convey women's subjective experience of physical and emotional fear within it exposed the separate spheres ideology for what it was: not necessarily a lived practice but an ideal – and one predicated on women's willingness to internalize its values and discipline themselves accordingly. In this light, there is perhaps no more sickeningly Gothic moment in Charlotte Brontë's *oeuvre* than six-year-old Paulina Home's eagerness to perform the feminine domestic role, despite (or perhaps, masochistically, because of) the self-mutilation it demands. In chap. 2 of *Villette* (1853), we witness her hemming a handkerchief: "pricking herself ever and anon, marking the cambric with a track of minute red dots; occasionally starting when the perverse weapon – swerving from her control – inflicted a deeper stab than usual; but still silent, diligent, absorbed, womanly."[23] Elsewhere in the novel, Brontë engages with the Gothic in a way that is similarly knowing but ostensibly more playful. The mode is made to perform double duty when the hauntings of the spectral nun turn out to be an ironic disguise used by Ginevra Fanshawe's secret male visitor. Yet, simultaneously, when the illicit couple play a practical joke on Lucy and she finds what she thinks is the nun in her bed, she tears what turns out to be only a costume to pieces, symbolically rejecting what the nun's habit represents – the confinement of the cloister and the suppression of desire.

Charlotte Bronte's identification of femininity with multiple forms of violence – whether the self-inflicted wounds required by domestic conformity, frustrated rage at women's limited sphere of action, or the vehemence of women's sexual feelings – permeates her work, but arguably in none more so than *Jane Eyre* (1847). Much has been written on the Gothic tropes in this novel, particularly since the publication of Gilbert and Gubar's *The Madwoman in the Attic* (1979). This seminal study put firmly into critical play the idea that Rochester's mad, sexually voracious, and animalistic wife, Bertha, functions in the novel as Jane's Gothic double, a psychic repository for her unacceptable feelings of social rebellion and passionate desire. Yet, Jane's most famous statement of women's frustration at their constricted lives is a classic statement of the kind of liberal, rational feminism espoused by Mary Wollstonecraft and, following her, Harriet Martineau: "women feel just as much as men feel; they need exercise for their faculties and a field for their efforts as much as their brothers do ... and it is narrow-minded in their more privileged fellow-creatures to say that they ought to confine themselves to making puddings and knitting stockings, to playing on the piano and embroidering bags."[24] The rational meshes with the Gothic here in complex ways. For if, as Peter Brooks suggests, the Gothic is a post-Enlightenment mode that "stands most clearly in reaction to desacralization and the pretensions of rationalism," then the use of its tropes in *Jane Eyre* enriches Brontë's proto-feminism by demanding recognition of women's experience of intense bodily and emotional feelings that lie beyond "the daylight self and the self-sufficient mind."[25] It took till the 1850s for organized political (or "first wave") feminism to get under way. But *Jane Eyre*'s vivid imbrication of gender and genre clarifies the formative contribution of literature to the movement, confirming the ways in which its discursive parameters were being drawn in the experimental fiction of early Victorian women.

NOTES

1. Edward Bulwer Lytton, *England and the English*, 2 vols. (New York: J & J Harper, 1833), vol. 2, p. 74.
2. [William Hazlitt], "The Dandy School," *Examiner* (November 18, 1827), 721–23, p. 722.

3. Winifred Hughes, "Silver Fork Writers and Readers: Social Contexts of a Best Seller," *NOVEL: A Forum on Fiction* 25 (1992), 328–47, p. 329.
4. April Kendra, "Gendering the Silver Fork: Catherine Gore and the Society Novel," *Women's Writing* 11 (2004), 25–37, pp. 27, 35.
5. Countess of Blessington, *The Victims of Society* (Paris: Baudry, 1837), p. 19.
6. Ibid., p. 119.
7. Catherine Gore, *Cecil, or the Adventures of a Coxcomb*, 2nd edn., 3 vols. (London: Bentley, 1843; first published 1841), vol. 1, p. 1. References are in parentheses in the text.
8. Harriet Martineau, *Autobiography*, ed. by Linda H. Peterson (Peterborough, Ontario: Broadview, 2006), p. 159.
9. [William Empson], "Mrs Marcet – Miss Martineau," *Edinburgh Review* 57 (April 1833), 1–39, p. 7.
10. [William Maginn], "Gallery of Literary Characters. No. XLII. Miss Harriet Martineau," *Fraser's Magazine* 8 (November 1833), 576.
11. Rosemarie Bodenheimer, *The Politics of Story in Victorian Social Fiction* (Ithaca, NY: Cornell University Press, 1988), p. 25.
12. Ibid.
13. Frances Trollope, *The Life and Adventures of Michael Armstrong, the Factory Boy*, facsimile edn. (London: Frank Cass, 1968; first published 1840), p. iv.
14. [Sydney Owenson, Lady Morgan], "*The Life and Adventure of Michael Armstrong, the Factory Boy*," *Athenaeum* 615 (August 10, 1839), 587–590, p. 588. Further quotations are in parentheses in the text.
15. "Alfred" [Samuel Kydd], *The History of the Factory Movement from the Year 1802 to the Enactment of the Ten Hours' Bill in 1847*, 2 vols. (London: Simpkin, 1857), vol. 2, p. 295.
16. Charlotte Elizabeth Tonna, *Helen Fleetwood* (London: Seeley and Burnside, 1841), pp. 51, 52.
17. Elizabeth Gaskell to Mrs Greg, [?Early 1849], in *The Letters of Mrs. Gaskell*, ed. J. A. V. Chappell and Arthur Pollard (Manchester: Manchester University Press, 1997), p. 74. Emphasis in original.
18. Raymond Williams, *Culture and Society, 1780–1950* (London: Chatto & Windus, 1958), pp. 87–91.
19. Elizabeth Gaskell, *Mary Barton*, ed. Thomas Recchio (New York: Norton, 2008), p. 166.
20. Peter Brooks, *The Melodramatic Imagination: Balzac, Henry James, Melodrama, and the Mode of Excess* (New Haven and London: Yale University Press, 1995), pp. 12, 13.
21. Marjorie Stone, "Bakhtinian Polyphony in *Mary Barton*; Class, Gender, and the Textual Voice," *Dickens Studies Annual* 20 (1991), 175–200, p. 196.
22. [Margaret Oliphant], "Modern Novelists – Great and Small," *Blackwood's Edinburgh Magazine* 77 (May 1855), 554–68, p. 557.
23. Charlotte Brontë, *Villette* (Oxford: Oxford University Press, 1998), pp. 18–19.
24. Charlotte Brontë, *Jane Eyre* (Oxford: Oxford University Press, 2000), p. 109.
25. Brooks, *Melodramatic Imagination*, p. 17.

8

DEIRDRE D'ALBERTIS

The realist novel

> So I am content to tell my simple story, without trying to make things seem better than they were; dreading nothing, indeed, but falsity, which, in spite of one's best efforts, there is reason to dread. Falsehood is so easy, truth so difficult.
>
> George Eliot, *Adam Bede* (1859)

From the moment people began to write them, novels have confronted the impossibility of capturing something evanescent yet essential about "the real world." To this day, literary "realism" gestures toward a heterogeneous host of concepts and values: from mimesis, verisimilitude, empiricism, and the natural, to historical representation, moral vision, and the production of sympathy. In its aesthetic sense, the word first appeared in German philosophical and literary discourse toward the end of the eighteenth century, while the French initially employed it in the nineteenth century to debate pictorial conventions.[1] Early English novelists such as Defoe and Richardson grappled with the novelty of this new form of writing, and each successive generation of practitioners aspired (as did their predecessors) to represent nothing less than life itself. Surprisingly few writers in the English tradition referred directly to, much less theorized, realism until the great work of mid-Victorian fiction was underway. Only then does the novel become a focal point for thinking about what Roland Barthes would later term "the Reality Effect."[2]

The work of a single novelist, George Eliot (1819–80), changed all of that. As the cited passage from *Adam Bede* makes clear, self-conscious discourse about the formal features of realism appear from the 1850s on in Eliot's work, which calls for "simple story," rejection of idealizing tendencies, and arduous fidelity to truth. Yet, as the narrator of *Adam Bede* admits, "falsehood is so easy, truth so difficult." The project of the realist novel is attended by "reason to dread" because of an absolute imperative to represent truth. But whose truth? And to what end?

In her greatest novel *Middlemarch* (1871–72), written at the height of her creative powers, Eliot addressed these questions head-on. The well-known opening of Book III, chap. 27 offers a "parable" that stresses the radical limitation of individual perspective and by implication the difficulty for the novelist in accessing truth:

> Your pier-glass ... will be minutely and multitudinously scratched in all directions; but place now against it a lighted candle as a centre of illumination and lo! the scratches will seem to arrange themselves in a fine series of concentric circles round that little sun. It is demonstrable that the scratches are going everywhere impartially, and it is only your candle which produces the flattering illusion of a concentric arrangement, its light falling with an exclusive optical selection.[3]

Eliot's narrator explicates for the reader this extended conceit: "the scratches are events, and the candle is the egotism of any person now absent."[4] Eliot's linkage of narrative point of view with a complex modeling of realism highlights the "flattering illusion of concentric arrangement." Consequences of interpretation, furthermore, materially alter narrative possibility. "The question of whether an event is the 'same' event for different parties," Elizabeth Ermath notes in her analysis of "invisible community" in Eliot's fiction, "or of whether a character is the 'same' from one time to another becomes urgent" in *Middlemarch*.[5] It is the duty of the novelist to escape the distortions of singular vision and to investigate hitherto obscure points of view, for instance, the "egotism" of a Rosamund Vincy, who (like every other man and woman) sees things from her own perspective, endowed with "a Providence of her own" (167). Eliot's persistent skepticism about privileging any one perspective at the expense of others is felt equally at the level of characterization and form. Whether heroine or hero, protagonist or antagonist, primary or secondary character, there is to be no fixed point in this novel against which any other is measured or judged. At one point, the narrator asks:

> But why always Dorothea? Was her point of view the only one possible with regard to this marriage? I protest against all our interest, all our effort at understanding being given to the young skins that look blooming in spite of trouble; for these too will get faded, and will know the older and more eating griefs which we are helping to neglect. (175)

Focalization through the consciousness of multiple and divergent minds is central to the novel, not least because we know that Eliot created *Middlemarch* (a novel she subtitled a "Study of Provincial Life") deliberately by joining together two stories begun separately, one about an ambitious outsider embarking on a medical career and the other, "Miss Brooke," which shapes the opening of the book as a whole.

In an introductory "Prelude" to *Middlemarch*, Eliot establishes the specific and limiting frame for her experiment in narrative form. Hailing her readers as those who "care much to know the history of man," the narrator shifts to interrogate the private actions of women in the present day: "later-born Theresas ... helped by no coherent social faith and order ... their ardour alternat[ing] between a vague ideal and the common yearning of womanhood" (3). This Victorian Saint Theresa, "foundress of nothing," is presented as a key to understanding *Middlemarch*'s "history of man." If the modern individual along with the invention of literary interiority were produced by domestic ideology and the rise of the novel, as Nancy Armstrong has influentially argued, what is produced by a form no longer identified with the fate of any one character?[6] Eliot introduces gender not in the service of a history of subjectivity but rather to advance an account of what Pierre Bourdieu would later describe as *habitus*, a complex set of expectations or values associated with particular social groups: "some have felt that these blundering lives are due to the inconvenient indefiniteness with which the Supreme Power has fashioned the natures of women," yet "the limits of variation are really much wider than any one would imagine from the sameness of women's coiffure and the favourite love-stories in prose and verse" (3). Eliot takes as given Dorothea Brooke's failure first as a would-be activist on behalf of the poor and then as a literary helpmeet. Her case announces and makes legible the struggles of others. In fact, the novel as a whole can be read as the aggregate experience of grand narrativizers whose doomed plots unravel because of limited perspective, a phenomenon central to Eliot's investigation of realism, from Casaubon's abortive attempt to devise a scholarly Key to All Mythologies to Lydgate's abandoned research inquiry into the "primitive tissue" of life. Nearly all the characters are motivated by some impossibly grand idea, scheme, or illusion. A somber mood of muted disappointment, a resigned acceptance of things as they are, hangs over the sprawling narrative's conclusion. Perhaps that is why Virginia Woolf referred to *Middlemarch* as a "magnificent book which with all its imperfections is one of the few English novels written for grown-up people."[7] Eliot's novel follows the human will to power as it is expressed negatively through rejection or refusal as often as it is in acts of creation or affirmation.

George Eliot did not arrive at the mature vision of *Middlemarch* overnight, nor did she see the condition of women as integral to the work of realism until she was well established in her career as a novelist. In what follows, I trace the development of her aesthetic vision, her early rejection of women's literary culture, and her absorption of some of its forms and concerns, before turning to the impact of, and response to, her realist practice on the work of two contemporary woman writers, Elizabeth Gaskell (1810–65) and Margaret Oliphant (1828–97), as well as those who came after.

Old women scraping carrots and silly lady novelists

In chap. 17 of *Adam Bede* (1859), her first full-length novel, Eliot's narrator directly addresses the reader in a section entitled "In Which the Story Pauses a Little," countering presumed resistance to its rustic subject matter:

> Do not impose on us any aesthetic rules which shall banish from the region of Art those old women scraping carrots with work-worn hands, those heavy clowns taking holidays in a dingy pot-house, those rounded backs and stupid weather-beaten faces that have bent over their spade and done the rough work of the world—those homes with their tin pans, their brown pitchers, their rough curs, and their clusters of onions. In this world there are so many of these common coarse people, who have no picturesque sentimental wretchedness! It is so needful we should remember their existence, else we may happen to leave them quite out of our religion and philosophy, and frame lofty theories which only fit a world of extremes. Therefore let Art always remind us of them.[8]

Eliot dwells frankly on the plainness and obscurity of her characters and their milieu, noting "it is for this rare, precious quality of truthfulness that I delight in many Dutch paintings, which lofty-minded people despise" (158). Drawn to early modern Dutch painting for what she calls "faithful pictures of a monotonous homely existence," as critics Ruth Bernard Yeazell and Rebecca Gould have demonstrated, Eliot here articulates a kindred vision through her own novelistic practice.[9] The "homely" lexicon she derives from northern European visual culture is stark and uncompromising, featuring "work-worn hands," "rounded backs," and "stupid weather-beaten faces." This world without "picturesque sentimental wretchedness" is "heavy," "dingy," "brown," "rough," "common," and "coarse."

Eliot's treatment of literary realism enacts a double vision, attending both to the neglected surfaces of the world and to underlying truths they body forth, signaling a divided consciousness integral to subsequent discussions of the term. Thus it is that while some critics focus on the materiality of realism – its concern with objects – others concentrate on subjects – its address to the reader, the production of affective response or mental states toward a specific end.[10] "*Real*, from the beginning, has had this shifting double sense," writes Raymond Williams in *Keywords*, "from rw *res*, L – thing. Its earlier English uses ... were in matters of law and property, to denote something actually existing."[11] He elaborates: "'Let's be realistic' probably more often means 'let us accept the limits of this situation (*limits* meaning *hard facts*, often of power or money in their existing and established forms) than 'let us look at the whole truth of this situation' (which can allow that an existing *reality* is changeable or is changing)" (259). Realism of objects, on the one hand, leads Eliot to an apotheosis of everyday life, participating in a powerful current in English letters that courses through the work of writers as diverse as Charles Dickens, William Thackeray, and Anthony Trollope. The realism of subjects, on the other hand, as Williams maintains, impels the novelist to represent "the many real forces—from inner feelings to underlying social and historical movements—which are either not accessible to ordinary observation or which are imperfectly or not at all represented in how things appear, so that a *realism* 'of the surface' can quite miss important realities" (260). The latter form of realism leads ideally to cultivation of sympathy and true vision or awareness, "so that ye may have / Clear images before your gladdened eyes / Of nature's unambitious underwood / And flowers that prosper in the shade," to quote the epigraph from Wordsworth that appears at the beginning of *Adam Bede*. Eliot aims at both kinds of realism.

Prior to her fictional debut with *Scenes of Clerical Life* (1857), Eliot assembled a veritable blueprint for her approach to literary realism. From the platform of an editorial position at *The Westminster Review*, the already accomplished translator and reviewer articulated an ambitious program for the contemporary novel, alluding to realist aesthetics in her review of Ruskin's *Modern Painters* III (April 1856), expanding on the concept in an essay entitled "The Natural History of German Life" (July 1856), and trenchantly guarding against inferior practitioners in "Silly Novels by Lady Novelists" (October 1856).[12]

Initially, Eliot explores truth of representation as a sociological proposition. Reviewing cultural historian Wilhelm Heinrich von Riehl's writings, Eliot argues in "The Natural History of German Life" for heightened awareness of a generative link between artistic representation and social science: "how little the real characteristics of the working-classes are known to those who are outside them, how little their natural history has been studied, is sufficiently disclosed by our Art as well as by our political and social theories."[13] Eliot blames the distorting "influence of idyllic literature" for the perpetuation of conventional images, even as she calls for greater fidelity to the conditions of agricultural and provincial life: "the thing for mankind to know is, not what are the motives and influences which the moralist thinks *ought* to act on the labourer or the artisan, but what are the motives and influences which *do* act on him."[14] Literature and painting bear a special burden when it comes to representing rural laborers, for "art is the nearest thing to life"; "it is a mode of amplifying experience and extending our contact with our fellow men, beyond the bounds of our personal lot." For this reason, "it is serious that our sympathy with ... the life of our more heavily-laden fellow-men, should be perverted, and turned towards a false object instead of the true one."[15] Following Wordsworth's critique of artifice in poetry, Eliot defines as "sacred" the "task" of representing "true" objects so as not to "pervert" but rightly to train "our sympathy." "A real knowledge of the People," Eliot goes on to argue, must be grounded in study of "the natural history of our social classes." Social science alone is not enough; the natural historian's (and by extension the realist novelist's) observations are presented here as an invaluable "aid to the social and political reformer."[16]

Contemporary identification of representation with reform empowered Eliot to assume this particular stance toward truth. Critic Amanda Claybaugh has usefully explained the primary distinction between the Anglo-American realist novel and its Continental counterpart in the nineteenth century as one based not simply on content or subject matter (although that distinction exists and is important) but rather on an authorizing commitment to "purpose" or social reform. It is precisely this reformist strain in the English novel, she observes, with which Eliot ambivalently contended throughout her career. "Female novelists struggled with the presumption that the novel was a public genre and thus the proper domain of men," writes Claybaugh, "reform, however, provided a plausible justification for a woman's entrance into print."[17] Although *Middlemarch* places reform at the very heart of its represented concerns (its action unfolds in the years prior to the First Reform Bill in 1832), Eliot herself was disinclined to agitate personally for the enfranchisement of the working classes or the advancement of women's rights, two great reform movements of the day.

For this and other reasons, Eliot sought aggressively to disassociate herself from reform efforts aligned with the "domestic realism" of most women writers. In the popular imagination, Marian Evans wrote under the male pseudonym of George Eliot to escape the discrimination attendant on Victorian gender ideology in a male-dominated literary marketplace. As Rosemary Ashton has demonstrated, however, such a view fails to account for the fact that women had been publishing prolifically and unapologetically under their own names since the beginning of the century.[18] Eliot's literary persona was formed consciously in opposition to this phenomenon. Figures as dissimilar as Mrs. Gore, Susan Ferrier, Hannah More, Elizabeth Sewell, and Charlotte Yonge, according to literary historian Vineta Colby, helped produce the flourishing domestic fiction against which Eliot reacted, even as her own work was anticipated and informed by it.[19]

In "Silly Novels by Lady Novelists," published anonymously as were her other *Westminster Review* essays, Eliot castigates "a genus with many species" unified only by the "quality of silliness that predominates in them—the frothy, the prosy, the pious, or the pedantic."[20] With considerable drollness, she reviews a wide range of literary works by women writers, outlining in the process a negative taxonomy of generic conventions. Although she mocks "mind-and-millinery," "white neck-cloth," and "modern-antique" novels as irredeemably trivial, Eliot reserves special scorn for the pseudo-learning and philosophizing found in "the most pitiable of all silly novels," the "oracular" texts she lampoons: "as a general rule, the ability of a lady novelist to describe actual life and her fellow-men is in inverse proportion to her confident eloquence about God and the other world, and the means by which she usually chooses to conduct you to true ideas of the invisible is a totally false picture of the visible."[21] Eliot's critique encompasses novels of high society, clerical novels, romantic fictions, novels of ideas, and reformist tracts, all of which she asserts will confirm male suspicions that women are not worth educating and incapable of genuine learning. Most seriously, "silly novels by lady novelists" falsify the very objects they purport to represent, producing a "driveling kind of dialogue, and equally driveling narrative, which like a bad drawing, represents nothing."[22] It is not the case, Eliot insists, that no woman has ever been capable of describing "actual life and her fellow-men." "Why can we not have pictures of religious life among the industrial classes in England," she asks midway through this catalogue of feminine fatuity, "as interesting as Mrs. Stowe's pictures of religious life among the negroes?"[23] Yet even Stowe's excellence, she stresses, is derived from gender-specific virtues: "women can produce novels not only fine, but among the very finest – novels too, that have a precious speciality, lying quite apart from masculine aptitudes and experience."[24] If "lady novelists" are cynically praised or "puffed" by the press for their substandard efforts, the few exceptions who show they "have genius or effective talent" paradoxically forfeit the critical immunity of their sex: "Harriet Martineau, Currer Bell, and Mrs. Gaskell have been treated as cavalierly as if they had been men."[25] Jocose and entertaining as it is, "Silly Novels" delivers both an indictment of amateurism and a manifesto for what was to become Eliot's trademark moral realism:

> For it must be plain to every one who looks impartially and extensively into feminine literature, that its greatest deficiencies are due hardly more to the want of intellectual power than to the want of those moral qualities that contribute to literary excellence—patient diligence, a sense of the responsibility involved in publication, and an appreciation of the sacredness of the writer's art.[26]

How did George Eliot's contemporaries, particularly fellow women writers, respond to her advocacy of this higher form of realism? Charlotte Brontë died in 1855, too soon to read either the *Westminster Review* pieces or Eliot's early fiction. But did Martineau and Gaskell, whom Eliot praised in contrast to the "lady novelists" she so disparaged, see their work as compatible with hers? More broadly speaking, was hers an example to be emulated, resented, or both?

"You are an Electric telegraph something or other"

The publication of *Adam Bede* was met by considerable controversy as well as acclaim. Theories about the anonymous author's identity were debated energetically, even urgently, as in this 1859 letter from Elizabeth Gaskell to Harriet Martineau:

> And after all one gets into a desponding state of mind about writing at all, after 'Adam Bede,' and 'Janet's Repentance' choose (as the Lancashire people say,) whoever wrote them. You heard truly that I have stuck out that I believed a *man* wrote them. I am shaken now, and should like much to receive your evidence.[27]

The exchange between Gaskell and Martineau is telling. In the late 1850s, both women were at the top of their game, so to speak, commanding professional respect and public esteem. Both, like Eliot, wrote realist novels representing contemporary economic, social, and political concerns. Martineau, the older writer, was as famous for her translations of Comte and her *Illustrations of Political Economy* (1832–34) as for her novel *Deerbrook* (1838); Gaskell was the celebrated author of such social problem novels as *Mary Barton* (1848), *Ruth* (1853), and *North and South* (1855) as well as *The Life of Charlotte Brontë* (1857), one of the century's most influential critical biographies. As we know, Eliot thought well of both women, remarking of Martineau in 1852 that she is "the only English woman that possesses thoroughly the art of writing."[28] A woman writer herself, why would Gaskell cling to the theory that George Eliot must be a male author, much less fall into "a desponding state of mind about writing at all" when contemplating her peer's earliest attempts at realism?

Disturbing certainly to Gaskell was the younger woman's private life. Still obsessing over Eliot's true identity, having by then learned of Marian Evans's unconventional ménage with George Henry Lewes, she declared in a private letter to her publisher George Smith that *Adam Bede* "is a noble grand book, whoever wrote it,—but Miss Evans' life taken at the best construction does so jar against the beautiful book that one cannot help hoping against hope" that a local Warwickshire man Joseph Liggins was in fact was its author.[29] Behind her concern with social propriety, however, was the more pressing matter of reception, a basic confusion that might arise between Gaskell's own work and Eliot's. Best known for industrial fiction, or what Amanda Claybaugh classifies as "novels of purpose" representing class strife and the plight of "fallen women," Gaskell was also associated by the reading public with such carefully observed sketches of provincial life as *Cranford*

(1851–53). Earlier in the year, she playfully wrote directly to "Mr. 'Gilbert' Eliot," whose identity was still shrouded in secrecy: "Since I came up from Manchester to London I have had the greatest compliment paid me I ever had in my life, I have been suspected of having written Adam Bede." She goes on to admit: "Well! If I had written Amos Barton, Janet's Repentance & Adam Bede I should neither be nor have not to hold with pride & delight in myself—so I think it is very well I have not."[30] Despite the light tone, "Mrs. Gaskell" may well have feared the possibility of being critically eclipsed or even displaced by "George Eliot."

Gaskell's ideas about realism (expressed in private communications to family and friends rather than in the quarterly reviews) overlapped with Eliot's insofar as both sought ethically and formally to reinvent narrative perspective. But where Eliot invoked the representational fidelity of Dutch art, Gaskell preferred mechanical metaphors of registering and recording the world around her. "You must observe what is *out* of you, instead of examining what is *in* you," she exhorts Marianne Gaskell in response to her daughter's novice attempts at fiction: "Just read a few pages of De Foe &c—and you will see the healthy way in which he sets *objects* not *feelings* before you. I am sure the right way is this. You are an Electric telegraph something or other." Gaskell eschews self-conscious authorial subjectivity in favor of setting "*objects* not *feelings*" ("a weakening of the art which has crept in of late years") squarely before the reader. "Work hard at this till it becomes a reality to you," she insists,

> a thing you have to recollect & describe & report fully & accurately as it struck you ... Don't intrude yourself into your descriptions. If you but think eagerly of your story till *you see it in action*, words, good simple strong words, will come,—just as if you saw an accident in the street that impressed you strongly."[31]

Endorsing communicative action rather than expressionist vision, Gaskell invokes an alternative model of realism as reportage, recording life as "an accident in the street."

Throughout her *oeuvre*, Gaskell stages again and again this definition of realism as consonant with a bracing movement out of doors, from self-absorption to external observation, as in *North and South*: "Margaret went out heavily and unwillingly enough. But the length of a street—yes, the air of a Milton street—cheered her young blood before she reached her first turning ... She began to take notice, instead of having her thoughts turned so exclusively inward."[32] In the preface to her first novel, *Mary Barton*, Gaskell explicitly thematizes the encounter in the street as a point of origin for her own literary production:

> Three years ago I became anxious (from circumstances that need not be more fully alluded to) to employ myself in writing a work of fiction. Living in Manchester ... I bethought me how deep might be the romance in the lives of some of those who elbowed me daily in the busy streets of the town in which I resided. I had always felt a deep sympathy with the care-worn men, who looked as if doomed to struggle through their lives.[33]

Training an ever-observant eye on these careworn men, Gaskell's industrial fiction becomes hybridized when joined to a marriage plot worthy of Jane Austen in *North and South*. Her work builds on narrative forms questioned by Eliot as too closely allied with an inferior tradition of domestic realism. Navigating between seemingly incommensurate domains of private and public life, Gaskell's narrator (like Eliot's) confronts "that most difficult problem for women, how much was to be utterly merged in obedience to [male] authority, and how much might be set apart for freedom in working" (508).

Ultimately, both Eliot and Gaskell mobilize and interrogate gender ideology in forwarding an ethics of reading made concrete by both the form and content of the realist novel. Observation and interpretation are explicitly thematized in the latter's work as dramatically limited according to perspective. Vision as well as action are shown always to be informed by these limits. The heroine of *North and South*, Margaret Hale, literally hesitates on the threshold between domestic and economic spheres, bearing witness to an angry mob outside industrialist John Thornton's mill:

> She threw the window wide open. Many in the crowd were mere boys; cruel and thoughtless,—cruel because they were thoughtless; some were men, gaunt as wolves and mad for prey. She knew how it was; they were like Boucher,—with starving children at home—relying on ultimate success in their efforts to get higher wages, and enraged beyond measure at discovering that Irishmen were to be brought in to rob their little ones of bread. Margaret knew it all; she read it in Boucher's face, forlornly desperate and livid with rage. (233)

Although this moment is typically read as crucial in revealing a central character's lack of self-awareness (and the problem of being read inaccurately by others), the passage also exemplifies a form of realist perception that is entirely astute in terms of what Margaret Hale sees unfolding in front of her. It is tempting to read forward from this moment (*North and South* was published in 1855) to the powerful conclusion of chap. 80 in Eliot's *Middlemarch*, as Dorothea Brooke transcends her own bitterness and pain to witness fully what is outside of herself perhaps for the first time in her life:

> She opened her curtains, and looked out towards the bit of road that lay in view, with fields beyond, outside the entrance-gates. On the road there was a man with a bundle on his back and a woman carrying her baby; in the field she

could see figures moving—perhaps the shepherd with his dog. Far off in the bending sky was the pearly light; and she felt the largeness of the world and the manifold waking of men to labour and endurance. She was a part of that involuntary, palpitating life, and could neither look out on it from her luxurious shelter as a mere spectator, nor hide her eyes in selfish complaining. (486)

It is equally compelling to place passages from Eliot's earlier fiction side by side with such late works by Gaskell as "Cousin Phillis" (1863–64), *Sylvia's Lovers* (1863), and *Wives and Daughters* (1865). The play of influence in terms of realist vision was mutual. As *Cornhill* editor Frederick Greenwood wrote in the conclusion he appended to serial publication of her final, unfinished masterpiece, "it is clear in this novel ... that Mrs. Gaskell had within these five years started upon a new career with all the freshness of youth, and with a mind which seemed to have put off its clay and to have been born again."[34] The subtitle to *Wives and Daughters*, "An Every-Day Story," reveals just how profoundly Gaskell felt the "noble," "grand," and "beautiful" example of *Scenes of Clerical Life* and *Adam Bede*, drawing on Eliot's vision of realism during this last, most fertile stage of her writing life.

The prodigious work of another close contemporary Margaret Oliphant flourished also under explicit privileging of "An Every-Day Story." In many ways, Oliphant was even more insistent than either Eliot or Gaskell on championing the dignity inherent in a realism of "ordinary" life, crafting in her popular *Chronicles of Carlingford* (1861–76) novels that helped expand the conceptual domain of realist writing. If we look to Eliot's published essays or novels and to Gaskell's private letters to divine in each case a governing account of the realist novel, we can do no better than turn to the opening of Oliphant's strange and beautiful autobiography to understand her particular, anti-theoretical relation to realism: "I have been tempted to begin writing by George Eliot's life ... I always avoid considering formally what my own mind is worth. I have never had any theory on the subject. I have written because it gave me pleasure, because it came natural to me, because it was like talking or breathing."[35] Invoking offhand remarks about Trollope's resolutely business like approach to novel writing in his own autobiography, Oliphant's retrospective account suggests an equally robust immersion in writing as living, or living as writing unmediated by critical manifestos or contemplative asides. As a critic, not surprisingly, Oliphant preferred the early work of George Eliot to late novels such as *Daniel Deronda* for the same reason:

> Her true inspiration had nothing to do with ... artificial and fantastic embodiments of new philosophy [found in the late novels] ... It is very likely that it was a most sincere attempt on her part to improve upon the greater simplicity of the

earlier method, in which the natural humility of genius has some share, as well as the increasing profundity of metaphysical studies, and the narrowing out of all true contact of life from the curious society of worshippers which had gathered round her, and kept her closely encircled, apart from the free air and natural atmosphere to which she had been born.[36]

The flaw in Eliot's realism, according to Oliphant, is its increasing reliance on theory, seen as "a narrowing out of all true contact of life" and a loss of "free air and natural atmosphere" that she associates with Marian Evans's provincial origins.

Subsequent generations of writers both acknowledged and fretted over Eliot's influence in shaping the realist novel well into the early twentieth century in England and America, ranging from Eliza Lynn Linton's rather peevish commentary in *Women Novelists of Queen Victoria's Reign* (1897) to Henry James's deeply appreciative if nonetheless challenging attempt to reimagine her legacy. James writes as early as 1873 of *Middlemarch*:

> There is nothing more powerfully real than these scenes in all English fiction, and nothing certainly more *intelligent* ... The author has desired to be strictly real and to adhere to the facts of the common lot, and she has given us a powerful version of that typical human drama, the struggles of an ambitious soul with sordid disappointments and vulgar embarrassments.

Even so, he concludes, "it sets a limit, we think, to the development of the old-fashioned English novel ... If we write novels so, how shall we write History?"[37]

New Women writers George Egerton, Mona Caird, Mary Cholmondeley, and Olive Schreiner, as Elaine Showalter has shown,[38] also struggled to establish an independent vision of the novel free from "Queen George's" at-times oppressive example, while reinventing the realist imperative at the heart of her work, even as that tradition may be said to have been continued and debated by contemporary writers as varied as Doris Lessing, Margaret Drabble, and A. S. Byatt.

NOTES

1. "Realism, n." *Oxford English Dictionary Online*, Oxford University Press, Web July 2014; Pam Morris, *Realism* (London: Routledge, 2003); Amanda Claybaugh, *The Novel of Purpose: Literature and Social Reform in the Anglo-American World* (Ithaca: Cornell University Press, 2007), p. 37.
2. Roland Barthes, "The Reality Effect," *The Rustle of Language*, trans. Richard Howard (Oxford: Blackwell, 1986), pp. 141–48.
3. George Eliot, *Middlemarch*, ed. Bert G. Hornback (New York: W. W. Norton, 2000) pp. 166–67.
4. Ibid., p. 166.

5. Elizabeth Deeds Ermath, *Realism and Consensus in the English Novel* (Princeton: Princeton University Press, 1983), p. 248.
6. Nancy Armstrong, *Desire and Domestic Fiction: A Political History of the Novel* (New York: Oxford University Press, 1987), p. 43.
7. Virginia Woolf, "George Eliot," *The Essays of Virginia Woolf*, ed. Andrew McNeillie (London: Hogarth Press, 1994).
8. George Eliot, *Adam Bede*, ed. Carol A. Martin (Oxford: Oxford University Press, 2008), p. 258.
9. Ruth Bernard Yeazell, *Art of the Everyday: Dutch Painting and the Realist Novel* (Princeton: Princeton University Press, 2008), and Rebecca Gould, "*Adam Bede*'s Dutch Realism and the Novelist's Point of View," *Philosophy and Literature* 36:2 (October 2012), 404–23.
10. Caroline Levine observes this same distinction between a realism of objects and subjects in her "Victorian Realism," *The Cambridge Companion to the Victorian Novel*, 2nd edn., ed. Deirdre David (Cambridge: Cambridge University Press, 2013).
11. Raymond Williams, "Realism," *Keywords: A Vocabulary of Culture and Society*, rev. edn. (New York: Oxford University Press, 1983), p. 258.
12. "The Natural History of German Life," *Westminster Review* 66 (July 1856), 51–79, and "Silly Novels by Lady Novelists," *Westminster Review* 66 (October 1856), 442–61, reprinted in Thomas Pinney, ed., *Essays of George Eliot* (New York: Columbia University Press, 1963), pp. 266–399, 300–24.
13. Pinney, ed., *Essays of George Eliot*, p. 268.
14. Ibid., p. 271. Emphasis in original.
15. Ibid.
16. Ibid., p. 272.
17. Claybaugh, *The Novel of Purpose*, p. 48.
18. Rosemary Ashton, "Evans, Marianne [George Eliot] (1819–1880)," *Oxford Dictionary of National Biography*, Oxford University Press, 2004; online edn., May 2008 [www.oxforddnb.com/view/article/6794].
19. Vineta Colby, *Yesterday's Woman: Domestic Realism in the English Novel* (Princeton: Princeton University Press, 1974).
20. Pinney, ed., *Essays of George Eliot*, p. 301.
21. Ibid., p. 311.
22. Ibid., p. 320.
23. Ibid., p. 319.
24. Ibid., p. 324.
25. Ibid., p. 323.
26. Ibid.
27. Elizabeth Gaskell to Harriet Martineau, [?Late October 1859], #444b, *The Letters of Mrs. Gaskell*, ed. J. A. V. Chapple and Arthur Pollard (Cambridge, MA: Harvard University Press, 1967), p. 903. Emphasis in original.
28. "G. Eliot to Mr. and Mrs. C. Bray and S.S. Hennell," qtd. in Deirdre David, *Intellectual Women and Victorian Patriarchy: Harriet Martineau, Elizabeth Barrett Browning, George Eliot* (Ithaca: Cornell University Press, 1987), p. 29.
29. Elizabeth Gaskell to George Smith, August 4 [1859] #438, *Letters of Mrs. Gaskell*, p. 566.
30. Elizabeth Gaskell to George Eliot, June 3 [1859] #431, ibid., p. 559.

31. Elizabeth Gaskell to Marianne Gaskell [After March 15, 1859] #420, ibid., pp. 541–42. Emphasis in original.
32. Elizabeth Gaskell, *North and South* (1855), ed. Dorothy Collins with an introduction by Martin Dodsworth (Harmondsworth: Penguin Books, 1970), p. 180.
33. Elizabeth Gaskell, *Mary Barton* (1848), ed. Edgar Wright (Oxford: Oxford University Press, 1987), p. xxxv.
34. Frederick Greenwood, "Conclusion," included in Elizabeth Gaskell, *Wives and Daughters*, ed. Frank Glover Smith (London: Penguin Books, 1985), p. 707.
35. Margaret Oliphant, *The Autobiography of Margaret Oliphant*, ed. Elisabeth Jay (Oxford: Oxford University Press, 1990), p. 14.
36. Margaret Oliphant, *The Victorian Age of English Literature* (New York: Lovell, Coryell & Company, 1892), vol. 2, p. 470.
37. "Henry James on *Middlemarch*," originally published in *Galaxy*, March 1873, in *The Complete Review Quarterly* III.2 (May 2002), www.complete-review.com/quarterly/vol3/issue2/jameshmm.htm. Emphasis in original.
38. Elaine Showalter, *Sexual Anarchy: Gender and Culture at the Fin de Siècle* (New York: Viking, 1990).

9

LYN PYKETT

Sensation and New Woman fiction

Although not exclusively the preserve of female writers (or readers), both the sensation novel of the 1860s and 1870s and the New Woman fiction of the 1880s and 1890s figured prominently in the late-twentieth-century recovery and reassessment of the work of the forgotten or undervalued women writers of the nineteenth century. These genres have continued to be explored in increasing depth and detail by twenty-first-century students of women's writing. Before the feminist-inspired recovery project, Wilkie Collins (1824–89) was perhaps the only sensation novelist considered worthy of critical attention, and the figure of the late-nineteenth-century modern woman styled by her contemporaries as the "New Woman" was most familiar in the pages of male novelists such as Thomas Hardy (e.g., his portrait of Sue Bridehead in *Jude The Obscure*, serialized in *Harper's New Monthly Magazine*, December 1894–November 1895), George Gissing (especially *The Odd Women*, 1893), George Moore (*A Drama in Muslin*, 1886, and *Esther Waters*, 1894), and Grant Allen (most notably, *The Woman Who Did*, 1895). As a result of the recovery project, Mary Elizabeth Braddon (1835–1915), Mrs. Henry (Ellen) Wood (1814–87), Rhoda Broughton (1840–1920), Ouida (the pen name of Maria Louise Ramé, 1839–1908), Charlotte Riddell (1832–1906), and Florence Marryat (1833–99) have all been extensively discussed as sensation novelists, although most of them wrote other kinds of fiction in their long careers as professional writers. Even Margaret Oliphant (1828–97), better known as a fierce critic of sensationalism, has been recognized as contributing to the genre with her 1863 novel *Salem Chapel*. Those whose novels and short stories have been classified as New Woman fiction include such diverse writers as Olive Schreiner (1855–1920), Sarah Grand (Frances Elizabeth Bellenden Clarke, 1854–1943), George Egerton (Mary Chavelita Dunne, 1859–1945), Mona Caird (1854–1932), Menie Muriel Dowie (1867–1945), Mary Cholmondeley (1859–1925), Ella Darcy (1851?–1937), Ella Hepworth Dixon (1857–1932), Netta Syrrett (1865–1943), and Iota (Kathleen Caffyn, 1855–1926).

Described by contemporary reviewers as "fast" novels, "crime novels," "newspaper novels," and "bigamy" novels, sensation novels were usually tales of modern life in domestic settings. They combined realism and melodrama in complicated plots involving secrecy, mystery, suspense, horror, duplicity, disguise, and crime and its detection. Blackmail, forged wills, bigamy, adultery, and other crimes within or against the family figured prominently. The New Woman fiction, as one authoritative contemporary reviewer put it, was "written by a woman, about women, from the standpoint of a woman" and demonstrated that "Woman at last has found Woman interesting to herself, and ... has studied her, painted her and analysed her as if she had an independent existence and ... a soul of her own."[1] At first sight, nothing could appear to be more different from the shocking, racy, plot-driven sensation novel, which came to prominence in the 1860s, and those "modern women's books of the introspective type"[2] that came to be associated with the "New Woman," as she was named in the 1890s. It was certainly the differences between the two types of fiction that Elaine Showalter emphasized in her groundbreaking contribution to the hidden history of women's writing *A Literature of Their Own*, in which she opposed the "portentous anthems of the feminists" to the "high spirits and comic exuberance of the [female] sensationalists" and lamented that it was "unfortunate" that the "feminist rebellion" of the 1880s and 1890s should have occurred "just as the literature of the sensationalists was opening up genuinely radical and experimental possibilities in feminine domestic realism."[3] In *The Woman Reader*, Kate Flint, too, emphasized formal and thematic differences, arguing that while sensation novelists aimed to thrill and keep their readers guessing, New Woman writers adopted the form of the bildungsroman (the novel of growth and development) and, taking their cue from nineteenth-century women's autobiography, tended to focus on a woman's life as a painful learning process in which she struggled to develop "self-generated and rationally arrived at" principles in the face of dominant social beliefs.[4] However, despite the many important differences of tone and technique, the women's sensation novel and the New Woman fiction have many shared concerns and preoccupations, and they often deploy similar rhetorical strategies.

Perhaps the most important link between the women's sensation novel and the New Woman fiction (in both novel and short story form) was that they both put female characters at their center, focusing closely on women's experiences, the particular circumstances of their lives, and the relationship of these particularities to contemporary generalizations or beliefs about woman's nature and the way it shaped women's role in the family and society. Both forms of fiction were, in part, the product of and, in many cases also self-conscious interventions in, the campaigns and debates around the "Woman Question," which gained new force in the mid-1850s and became fiercer in the following decades. In the mid-1850s, the first (failed) campaign for the reform of the property rights of married women and the debates that led to the passing of the Divorce Act of 1857 threw the spotlight on women's roles and rights within marriage and the family into the mainstream newspaper and periodical press as well as feminist periodicals such as the *English Woman's Journal* (1858–64), the *Alexandra Magazine* (1864–65), the *Victoria Magazine* (1863–80), and the *Englishwoman's Review* (1866–1910). These latter periodicals also campaigned for improved educational and employment opportunities for women, physical education for girls, and more sensible, less restrictive forms of female dress. In the 1880s and 1890s, there were renewed campaigns for women's access to the professions and the right to vote, further attempts to reform the divorce laws, and vigorous debates about the nature of marriage. An important catalyst for these debates was Mona Caird's essay in the *Westminster Review* in 1888, which claimed that marriage was a relatively recent institution and one particularly unsatisfactory from a woman's point of view. Caird focused on marriage as a social institution with an evolving history. Modern marriage, she argued, arose during the Reformation, a product of the rise of "commerce, competition, the great *bourgeois* class, and ... 'Respectability'"[5] in that period. It was based on and perpetuated false views of woman's nature and was "a peculiar medley of sensuality and decorum" in which "women were bought and sold as if they were cattle, and were educated, at the same time, to strict ideas of purity and duty."[6] Caird offered an alternative vision of marriage as a free and equal union. The *Daily Telegraph* responded to Caird's conclusion that "the present form of marriage" is a "vexatious failure"[7] by inviting letters on the question of "Is Marriage a Failure?" – 27,000 letters were received. Caird kept the debate going in further *Westminster Review* essays, which appeared from time to time until 1894 when she made a further splash by issuing them as a collection entitled *The Morality of Marriage and Other Essays on the Status and Destiny of Woman*. "The marriage problem" was further explored in a great deal of fiction and drama throughout the 1880s and into the 1890s. Throughout the period covered by this chapter, numerous attacks also appeared in the press on those women who questioned marriage or expressed discontent with, or sought to break out of, traditionally prescribed gender roles. Among the most famous examples are Eliza Lynn Linton's 1868 essay "The Girl of the Period," her 1891 essay on "The Revolt Against Matrimony," and her attacks on the "shrieking sisterhood" in "The Wild Women: As Politicians" and "The Wild Women: As Social Insurgents" (1891).[8]

Concerns and anxieties about the nature and limitations of women's role within the family; the limited opportunities available to middle-class women outside of the family; the economic and emotional dynamics of marriage and its unequal power relations under the current state of the laws governing marriage, inheritance, and women's property rights; the desirability (or otherwise) of divorce, and the circumstances under which it might be obtained; the rights of the divorced woman (particularly in relation to the custody of her children); the operations of the sexual double standard (in which chastity before marriage and sexual fidelity after it were expected of women but not of men) – various combinations of these issues underlie the plots of most sensation novels and New Woman novels. For example, two of the earliest (and best-selling) sensation novels, *Lady Audley's Secret* (first serialized from July 1861 and published in volume form in October 1862) and *East Lynne* (serialized from January 1860 and issued in volume form in September 1861), have heroines (Lucy Audley and Isabel Vane) who are propelled into marriage by the pressure of their unfortunate financial and parental circumstances and who are subsequently misunderstood, infantilized, and abandoned or neglected by their respective husbands. These marital discontents lead Lucy to make a second, bigamous marriage and make Isabel vulnerable to the lures of a seducer and become an adulteress, actions resulting in both women being separated from their children. Lucy – the more transgressive heroine, a criminal who becomes violent when cornered – defends her conduct in terms that expose the limited opportunities available to women and the realities of the marriage market: "I had learnt that which in some indefinite manner or other every schoolgirl learns sooner or later—I learned that my ultimate fate in life depended upon my marriage, and I concluded that if I was indeed prettier than my schoolfellows, I ought to marry better than any of them."[9] Both novels focus on marriage and the marital home as places of insecurity, doubt, and danger, rather than as the sanctuary envisaged by domestic ideology. For different reasons, neither heroine is "at home" in her marital home, and each of them is depicted as being disruptive of domestic tranquillity through her wishes and desires as well as her actions. Both novels explore the nineteenth-century stereotypes of the angel in the house and the fallen woman by presenting their heroines in both guises. Wood shows with much pathos the dangerous ease with which her vulnerable angel falls, and Braddon satirically demonstrates how effectively an unscrupulous woman can adopt the disguise or perform the masquerade of the domestic angel to achieve her own ends.

Like the female sensation novelists, the marriage problem and New Woman writers of the 1880s and 1890s also scrutinized rather minutely women's roles in marriage and the family. As W. T. Stead observed in 1894, "In almost every case the novels of the modern woman are preoccupied with questions of sex ... marriage ... maternity."[10] Many contemporary reviewers were disconcerted by what they saw as the negativity of this preoccupation. Margaret Oliphant, a prominent critic of the sensation novel in the 1860s, later attacked the role of New Woman writers and their female readers (as well as male novelists such as Hardy) in creating what she called "The Anti-Marriage League."[11] Hugh Stutfield, another prominent critic of what he saw as degenerative trends in late-nineteenth-century fiction, deplored the modern tendency to depict the "horrors of marriage from the feminine point of view."[12] One novel he might have had in mind is Mona Caird's *The Daughters of Danaus* (1894), a powerfully rendered narrative whose spirited central character, Hadria, is trapped in a stifling loveless marriage as a result of the pressures and machinations of her mother and sister and their appeals to conventional views of femininity. Hadria's experience leads her to wonder why marriage did not make all women openly and actively wicked: "If ever there was an arrangement by which every evil instinct and every spark of the devil was likely to be aroused ... surely the customs and traditions that clustered around this estate constituted that dangerous combination."[13] Marriage, as Hadria envisions it here, seems to provide the conditions for producing a sensation heroine, and indeed Caird's novel focuses feelingly on the consequences and effects of this "dangerous combination" and on the feelings and sensations of her heroine, just as the sensation novelist does.

Sarah Grand is another New Woman novelist who used sensationalism to focus on the plight of women trapped in degrading marriages. Among the various life stories explored in *The Heavenly Twins* (1893) are those of the high-principled and independently minded Evadne and the innocent and sexually pure Edith, each of whom is damaged by marriage to a sexually debauched but socially respectable man. Having failed to heed Evadne's warnings about the sexual history of her fiancé, the eminent doctor Mosley Mentieth, Edith goes into a decline and dies of a syphilitic brain fever, after giving birth to his sickly syphilitic child. There is an even more detailed dramatization of the emotional pressures of Evadne's refusal to consummate her marriage following her discovery of the truth of her own husband's sexual history on her wedding day. Grand's *The Beth Book* (1897) offers a similarly detailed depiction of the confinement and daily degradation of its free-spirited heroine, a woman of intense feeling, in her marriage to a coarsely sensual and brutal adulterer. His professional duties include overseeing a "Lock hospital" in which suspected prostitutes were held and subjected to invasive medical examinations under the terms of the Contagious Diseases Acts, which dated from 1864 and were the focus of feminist campaigns until their repeal some twenty years later.

Partly because of the way in which they treated such controversial subjects, the women's sensation novel and the New Woman fiction created something of a sensation – in terms of sales and in the critical and moral debates (as well as parodies) they generated in the periodical press. Indeed, as literary categories the sensation novel and the New Woman fiction were to a great extent press inventions or constructs. One of the reasons that these novels caused a sensation was their treatment of sex. Reviewers of sensation novels, particularly those by female authors, accused them of dwelling too closely on women's sexual feelings. Margaret Oliphant, for example, complained of the tendency of sensation novelists such as Braddon and (especially) Rhoda Broughton to create heroines who are "driven wild with love for the man who leads them into desperation ... who give and receive burning kisses ... and live in a voluptuous dream" in which the dreaming maiden longs "for flesh and muscles, for strong arms that seize her, and warm breath that thrills her through, and a host of other physical attractions."[14] In the 1890s, the New Woman fiction was also often attacked for its frank discussion of women's sexuality. A good example of such an attack is Hugh Stutfield's condemnation of the prevalence in New Woman fiction of the "emancipated woman," who

> loves to show her independence by dealing freely with the relations of the sexes. Hence all the prating of passion, animalism, the "natural workings of sex", and so forth, with which we are nauseated. Most of the characters in these books seem to be erotomaniacs. Some are "amorous sensitives"; others are apparently sexless, and are at pains to explain this to the reader. Here and there a girl indulges in what would be styled, in another sphere, "straight talks to young men".[15]

A great deal of anxiety surfaces in both the 1860s and the 1890s about the effects on readers of this perceived preoccupation with sex. For example, readers of sensation fiction were said to be in serious moral danger from the "utter unrestraint" with which the heroines of such novels were "allowed to expatiate and develop their stormy, passionate characters."[16] More sensationally, it was suggested that the erotic descriptions in George Egerton's short story collection *Keynotes* (1893) were likely induce a state in which a young man "either goes off and has a woman or it is bad for his health (and possibly worse for his morals) if he doesn't."[17] In fact, George Egerton's frank treatment of female sexuality is rather exceptional; many New Woman writers were "social purity" feminists, who sought to attack the double standard and reform male sexual behavior.

If, as contemporary critics argued, sensation novels worked by producing a reading experience in the body – "preaching to the nerves"[18] – both sensation novels and New Woman fiction tended to dwell on the "nervous" experience of their heroines. Both forms of fiction regularly depict highly strung and/or independently minded female characters who break down under the pressure of either indulging or repressing their feelings or as a result of their struggles to break out of the confines of domestic existence or the traditional concept of femininity. Lady Audley goes mad (or, perhaps, takes refuge in a fiction of madness); Isabel Vane's health breaks down under the pressure of her "sin" (and a railway accident does the rest); and Nell Lestrange, heroine of Rhoda Broughton's *Cometh up as a Flower* (1867), literally wastes away and dies in the confines of her loveless marriage to an older man, having failed either to marry or elope with the handsome young soldier whom she loves. In *The Heavenly Twins*, Evadne Frayling-Colquhoun, who at nineteen "looked out of narrow eyes at an untried world inquiringly" and who "wanted to know ... to see ... deep down into the sacred heart of things," suffers a serious physical and psychological breakdown and attempts suicide, before being treated by Dr. Galbraith for what he describes as a hysterical illness brought on by an "unwholesome form of self-repression."[19]

New Woman fiction is full of such inquiring women as Evadne, many of whom aspire to be artists. Indeed, New Woman writers frequently used the figure of the female artist to explore female subjectivity and desire, including a woman's desire to be an active agent in her own life and in society and to examine the forces that threatened or blocked them: social and cultural institutions such as marriage and motherhood, education, what we now call the culture industry, and conventional ideas about gender roles – what Mona Caird describes as "the numerous contradictory dogmas" about "'woman's nature,'" including the dogma that motherhood was woman's true vocation.[20] Several New Woman novels explore the conflict between the conventional view of a woman's vocation as one of self-sacrifice and the self-expressive vocation of the artist – not to mention the sheer labor required to fulfill that vocation. For example, Mary Cholmondeley's *Red Pottage* (1899) shows in some detail how the novelist Hester Gresley destroys her health by rising at 5 a.m. so that she can write without interruption from the domestic and social round of the household. Mona Caird focuses on Hadria Fullerton's difficulties in negotiating the conflicting demands of her vocation as a musician and the domestic ideal: her "greatest effort had to be given, not to the work itself, but to win an opportunity to pursue it," given her mother's belief that "it was not good for a girl to be selfishly preoccupied." On those occasions on which Hadria yielded to this view, "her mood and her work were destroyed"; if, on the other hand, she resisted conventional social pressures, her mood and work "were equally destroyed, through the nervous disturbance and the intense depression which followed the winning of liberty too dearly bought." Like Hester, Hadria, "unable to command any certain part of the day, began to sit up at night," with predictable consequences for her health; "the injury was insidious but serious."[21] The heroine of Grand's *The Beth Book* also suffers temporary breakdowns as a result of similar obstacles and frustrations that she encounters in her attempts to articulate her "genius," first as a writer and subsequently as a speaker and activist.

The apparent incompatibility of the demands of marriage and maternity versus those of an artistic vocation or professional career is a common trope in New Woman fiction. Hadria Fullerton, who ultimately must choose between fulfilling her musical ambitions and her role as wife and mother, has before her the not entirely happy example of Valeria Du Prel, who has had to avoid both marriage and motherhood to achieve success as a novelist. In *Red Pottage*, Hester Gresley apparently sublimates her marital and maternal desires in writing her novels, which she describes in terms a woman more often uses for her lover or a mother her child. Discussing her own career in 1932, George Egerton asserted that "Art is a jealous and arbitrary mistress and brooks no rival... Marriage, Motherhood and Writing are each a whole time job."[22] In her various collections of short stories – especially *Keynotes* (1893) and *Discords* (1894) – and also her novel *The Wheel of God* (1898) Egerton shocked her contemporary audience with her frank depiction of the complexities of women's psychological and emotional needs, sexual desires, and professional ambitions by offering portraits both of women who wrote and worked for a living and regarded marriage and motherhood as choices and of those who were entrapped in economic and emotional dependence in marriage and motherhood. For example, "Wedlock" (in *Discords*) juxtaposes the lives of a professional woman writer and her landlady Susan, who has married a cruelly controlling widower who simply wants someone to look after his children, in the illusory hope that this marriage would enable her to be reunited with her own (illegitimate) daughter whom she had been unable to support herself and had sent to live with her sister. United temporarily under the same roof, the writer and her landlady suffer separately: the latter coarsened by the alcohol to which she resorts to dull her senses against the pain of her maternal deprivation and marital sufferings, and the writer rendered supersensitive by overwork, lack of food, and "the agony of a barren period"... "nervous, overwrought, every one of her fingers seems as if it had a burning nerve-knot in its tip."[23] The writer is painfully isolated by her writing. Writing "for money... because she must, because it is the tool given her wherewith to carve her way," she needs to create a quiet space for her labors that cuts her off from the world, but as she walks in the crowded streets escaping her desk and the tensions of her lodging house, her "loneliness strikes doubly home to her, and she resolves to join a woman's club; anything to escape it."[24] She listens to the landlady's story and gives her advice, but she experiences the landlady's struggles either as background noise that hinders her writing or (somewhat guiltily) as "material" for it, and she leaves before the sensational denouement in which the landlady kills her stepchildren. It is as though the writer has stepped into – and then quietly steps out of – a sensation novel rewritten by George Moore.

Like several of the women labeled as New Woman writers, Egerton (who was embarrassed by the New Woman tag) was a formal innovator who, like Olive Schreiner in her novel *The Story of an African Farm* (1883) and her short story collection *Dreams* (1891), experimented with new ways of rendering the inner lives of her characters through a series of psychological moments or dreamlike passages. Although many New Woman writers continued to work within and rework the conventions of the nineteenth-century realist novel, some of them, such as Egerton, also sought new forms in which to tell a new story – the story of the modern woman. In many cases, they experimented with the form of the short story for which demand was growing as a result of changes in the publishing industry at the *fin de siècle*. In the 1860s, the sensation novel flourished in response to an expanding and diversifying reading public, a rapid increase in the number of family magazines, the dominance of circulating libraries such as Mudie's, and the rise of railway reading, all of which led to a demand for serialized fiction that could be reissued in three volumes for library lending or as one-volume yellowbacks for sale at railway bookstalls. By the 1880s and 1890s, the marketing model of the big circulating libraries and the power of their owners to impose their tastes and morals on their readers (and authors) were increasingly challenged, leading to the collapse of the three-volume novel by the second half of the 1890s. Railways continued to be an important shaping force in the publishing industry, providing a speedy distribution network for the growing number of magazines that published the shorter fiction that was attractive to railway travelers and other readers in a high-speed modern culture. In the 1890s, as H. G. Wells later observed, "Short stories broke out everywhere"[25] in such different magazines as the *Strand*, the *Black and White Magazine*, and the *Yellow Book*. If sensation novels met the demand for something "hot and strong for the journey"[26] and were associated with the formation of the modern nervous subject of a new high-speed technological age at mid-century, the New Woman fiction, particularly in its short story form, was "a kind of writing perfectly adapted to our over-driven generation"[27] at the *fin de siècle*. The increased demand for short stories in the 1890s also created a new opening for women writers, many of whom, like Egerton, used the form as the vehicle for experimentation. It is, perhaps, this experimentalism – in form, plotting, and characterization – that ultimately distinguishes the New Woman fiction from sensation fiction. However, there are also important continuities of form, not least in the persistence of sensation as a mode or language of representation. For example, a key feature of the scenes of crisis and transformation that figure so prominently in New Woman novels and stories is the use of a sensational language that is rooted in the sensation novel's representation of desire as a dangerous force that threatens the coherence of the individual.[28] New Woman writers often used the language of sensation to narrate those decisive moments in their plots of self-discovery when a female character has to battle with external, often irrational forces, such as dominant social beliefs, romantic feelings, or sexual desire.

The female sensationalists and the New Woman writers were both, in their different ways, concerned with the question, "What does a woman want?" In addressing this question, many sensation novels modernized late-eighteenth-century and early-nineteenth-century forms of the Gothic mystery. In the 1880s and 1890s, the sensation novel's "woman with a secret" was replaced by "the enigma of woman" in novels and stories, some of which anticipate the modern psychological novel and modernist experimentation with form.

NOTES

1. W. T. Stead, "The Novel of the Modern Woman," *Review of Reviews* 10 (1894), 64–74, p. 64.
2. Hugh Stutfield, "The Psychology of Feminism," *Blackwood's Magazine* 161 (1897), 104.
3. Elaine Showalter, *A Literature of Their Own: British Women Novelists from Brontë to Lessing* (London: Virago, 1977), p. 181.
4. Kate Flint, *The Woman Reader, 1837–1914* (Oxford: Clarendon Press, 1993), pp. 294–95.
5. Mona Caird, "Marriage," *Westminster Review* 130 (1888), 186. Emphasis in original.
6. Ibid., p. 191.
7. Ibid., p. 197.
8. Eliza Lynn Linton, "The Girl of the Period," *Saturday Review*, 25 (March 14, 1868), 776–77; "The Revolt Against Matrimony," *Forum* 10 (1891), 585–630; "The Wild Women: As Politicians," *The Nineteenth Century* 30 (1891), 79–88; and "The Wild Women: As Social Insurgents," *The Nineteenth Century* 31(1891), 596–605.
9. Mary Elizabeth Braddon, *Lady Audley's Secret*, ed. Lyn Pykett (Oxford: Oxford University Press, 2012), p. 298.
10. Stead, "Novel of the Modern Woman," p. 65.
11. Margaret Oliphant, "The Anti-Marriage League," *Blackwood's Magazine*, 157 (1896), 135–49.
12. Hugh Stutfield, "Tommyrotics," *Blackwood's Magazine* 157 (1895), 835–36.

13. Mona Caird, *The Daughters of Danaus* (London: Bliss, Sands, Foster, 1894), p. 168.
14. Margaret Oliphant, "Novels," *Blackwood's Magazine* 102 (1867), 259.
15. Stutfield, "Tommyrotics," p. 836.
16. "Our Female Sensation Novelists," *Christian Remembrancer* 46 (1863), 212.
17. T. P. Gill, qtd. in Terence de Vere White, *A Leaf from the Yellow Book: The Correspondence of George Egerton* (London: The Richards Press, 1958), p. 23.
18. Henry Mansel, "Sensation Novels," *Quarterly Review* 113 (1863), 481.
19. Sarah Grand, *The Heavenly Twins* (Ann Arbor: University of Michigan Press, 1992), pp. 3 and 645–46.
20. Caird, "Marriage," p. 186.
21. Caird, *Daughters of Danaus*, p. 109.
22. George Egerton, "A Keynote to Keynotes," in *Ten Contemporaries: Notes Towards the Definitive Biography*, John Gawsworth (London: Benn, 1932), pp. 59–60.
23. George Egerton, "Wedlock," in *Keynotes and Discords*, ed. Sally Ledger (Birmingham: University of Birmingham Press, 2003), p. 123
24. Egerton, "Wedlock," pp. 123, 126.
25. H. G. Wells, Preface to *The Country of the Blind and Other Stories* (London: Nelson, 1911), p. v.
26. Mansel, "Sensation Novels," p. 485.
27. Bliss Perry, "The Short Story," *Atlantic Monthly* 90 (1902), 250.
28. Lisa Hager, "Embodying Agency: Ouida's Sensational Shaping of the British New Woman," *Woman's Writing* 20 (2013), 236.

10

KATHERINE NEWEY

Drama and theater

Invisible women

Victorian women writers' invisibility was never more pronounced than in the theater: it was generally assumed that women were not playwrights. To be a woman and to be a playwright potentially meant to be unsexed but paradoxically beleaguered by heavily gendered expectations. At the beginning of the nineteenth century, and despite the growing involvement of women in public life through politics and literature in the aftermath of the French Revolution, it was still generally assumed that women lacked the life experience, education, and temperament to engage with the drama, particularly tragedy. Lord Byron wrote, "When Voltaire was asked why no woman has ever written even a tolerable tragedy? 'Ah (said the Patriarch) the composition of a tragedy requires *testicles*'.—If this be true Lord knows what Joanna Baillie does—I suppose she borrows them."[1] Byron admired Joanna Baillie (1762–1851); indeed, she was broadly held to be the leading playwright (male or female) of her generation. Although her work *Plays on the Passions* (two volumes published in 1798 and 1802) remained largely a project of dramatic literature and closet drama, her scheme for a thorough exploration of the emotions was highly influential across the nineteenth century, arguably precisely because they were *not* performed.

This paradox characterizes the position of women's playwriting in the nineteenth century: praised for nonperformance and absence from the physical stage, roundly criticized in highly gendered (and often misogynist) terms when women playwrights' words were embodied on the stage. Byron's comment wryly summarizes both the anti-female nature of critical conceptions of the playwright – notably referring to biological sex, as much as socially constructed gender – and typifies the kind of sexualized language that formed the *habitus* of the theater profession. These concerns – the physical presence of women in the theater, the conceptualization of the playwright, and the position of theater in British culture and society – were of crucial importance for women who wanted to write plays, even more so for women who wanted to see their plays produced and performed in public.

The issue of production was fraught. The spaces and the practices of the playwright's profession were coded as masculine. Making work, getting work, and creating a career happened through structures of public sociability in ways that were generally not available to women, particularly educated women of the middle and upper classes. The networks of the theater industry were situated mostly in the *demi-monde* of London's Bohemia of cramped theater manager's offices, dingy backstage green rooms, and men's clubs, and in the rowdiness of the pit and newspaper and periodical offices. These were spaces loaded with potential and actual danger for women wishing to preserve their bodily integrity and respectability. Until the last decades of the century, involvement in the theater could damage the character or respectability of a middle-class woman. Furthermore, writing for the theater involved an overt public presence, visible as work in a way that writing novels, for example, did not.

The experiences of Mary Russell Mitford (1787–1855) can stand for many women writers' experiences. Mitford lived in the countryside outside Reading, and her trips to London had to be carefully organized to accommodate both her status as a respectable single woman and her carefully concealed poverty. The managers of the London Theatres Royal with whom she hoped to place her poetic tragedies casually invited her to see them to discuss her manuscripts. But Mitford's visits to London could not be casual; as she wrote to one of her mentors, Sir William Elford:

> I am but just returned from town, whither I have been led by one of the evil consequences of dramatic authorship—that is to say, a false report— ... and really my soul sickens within me when I think of the turmoil and tumult I have undergone, and am to undergo ... I am tossed about between him [Charles Kemble] and [William] Macready like a cricket-ball—affronting both parties and suspected by both, because I will not come to a deadly rupture with either. Only imagine what a state this is, for one who values peace and quietness beyond every other blessing of life! ... But I would rather serve in a shop—rather scour floors—rather nurse children, than undergo these tremendous and interminable disputes, and this unwomanly publicity.[2]

Mitford's expressions of frustration are undoubtedly extreme and ambivalent. In the light of her troubles with fickle theater managers, her friends pressed her to write fiction. But she resisted, writing to William Harness: "You are the only friend whose advice agrees with my strong internal feeling respecting the drama. Everybody else says, Write novels—write prose! So that my perseverance passes for perverseness and obstinacy, which is very discouraging."[3]

Mitford's letters vividly communicate the tension between the attractions of the theater for women writers and the necessity for careful negotiation of the conditions and practices of the industry. While complaints about the difficulties of dealing with theater managers and star actors were made regularly by many aspirant playwrights throughout the century, women faced specific difficulties in working within the constraints of the respectable femininity and the propriety of the "lady." A single, non-metropolitan woman such as Mitford, not part of a theatrical family, needed alternative networks. Mitford could not rely on the advice of theater managers, so she sought reassurance and knowledge from a range of mostly male mentors who moved more freely in urban literary circles. She did not have the easy sociability of club membership or professional associations such as the Garrick Club (founded in 1831, and still offering membership only to men at the time of this writing) or the Dramatic Authors Society (founded in 1833), which admitted women only as honorary members.

Visibility

Mitford was a successful playwright by any measure: she wrote eight full-length plays and had five of them performed in the Theatres Royal at Covent Garden and Drury Lane. Like Mitford, despite obstacles, many women wrote plays and had them produced. Over the nineteenth century, some 500 women wrote more than 1,200 plays, across all genres, and for a variety of theatrical contexts. Women's dramatic writing comprised approximately 12 percent of the plays written in the nineteenth century. While these figures represent neither the majority of dramatic writing nor the majority of women's writing, women writers' engagements with theater and drama were nevertheless significant. The range of theater writing undertaken by women was wide and challenged both notions of what was appropriate for women to write and what constituted dramatic literature and writing for the theater and performance. While it has generally been assumed that women wrote mostly for the closet, producing reading texts without the expectation of public performance, an examination of the evidence shows that this was not the case. The attractions of public notice, the immediate and direct communication with an engaged and present audience, and the possibilities of writing big multivocal stories in moving language were as potent for women writers in the nineteenth century as for many other writers in English since the establishment of public theaters in the sixteenth century.

In these respects, perhaps we might wish to argue that women playwrights do not need to be treated as a separate class. Women wrote for the established Theatres Royal, producing comedies and historical verse tragedies; they wrote farces and comedies for the smaller theaters; and they wrote melodramas, comedies, and pantomimes for East End and working-class theaters. Women authors wrote plays for children, and they were the first translators of *avant-garde* European authors such as Henrik Ibsen and Gerhardt Hauptmann. Plays by women won three high-profile competitions across the century. The easy assumptions about the nature of both theater writing and women's writing, which relegate women's theater writing to the closet as a place of no power or influence, are overturned once we start looking for women playwrights and examine the theater and drama of the nineteenth century through the lens of the woman writer. The search for women playwrights offers an opportunity to widen our scope in the study of women's writing and to widen our understanding of theatrical performance and dramatic writing.

Female exceptionalism

While women generally wanted to be considered on an equal footing with male playwrights, they could not participate on equal terms. Misconceptions about their very existence, and about the kinds of dramatic writing they undertook, were among the obstacles women faced in making their dramatic writing visible. They were regularly marked out for their sex by others, and gendered judgments were made of them and their plays. In reviews of new plays and discussions about playwriting, the presence of a "lady playwright" was a matter of surprise or incredulity. Where women playwrights overcame their invisibility, they were usually cast as exceptional – not exceptionally talented, but always exceptional in their position as women who wrote plays. Each prominent woman playwright was treated as *sui generis*, one of a kind, and so across the nineteenth century this pattern of cultural forgetting served to identify the public stage as a masculine domain.

The example of women prizewinners in play competitions demonstrates the dilemma for women seeking public recognition as playwrights. Women won three prominent playwriting competitions held in 1843, 1901, and 1913. Each competition was sponsored by a theater manager eager to counter criticisms of the industry's lack of support for new writing and the accusation that only playwrights from a small clique favored by theater managers had a chance to have their work performed. Each competition was presented as an attempt to revive the national dramatic literature and was widely advertised and publicly speculated over. The numerous entries were judged anonymously, with the winning plays offered the prize of a public performance or reading. The success of female playwrights each time appeared to position women playwrights at the center of the revival of the dramatic literature in English, by recognizing their craft, originality, and dramatic qualities. Yet each time, the public announcement of a female winner prompted extended and adverse critical commentary on the sex of the writer and the likely limited quality of the entries. In 1843 and 1901, the play produced by the winning playwright was the last she wrote for public performance. These competitions point to the perils of exceptionalism for women in the theater, particularly those who had the temerity to beat men in a field they considered their own.

The winner of £500 prize offered by Benjamin Webster (manager of the Theatre Royal, Haymarket) for a modern comedy was announced in 1844 as "a lady, and one who is by no means unknown to literary fame" (*The Times*, May 21, 1844, 5). The "lady" was Catherine Gore (1798–1861), a prolific novelist, best known for her silver-fork novels about contemporary fashionable life. Subsequent discussion of the winning play was conducted in highly gendered terms, critical not only of female victory but also of female presence in the competition at all. Gore's win was held to be "remarkable" (*Spectator*, May 25, 1844, 492), although it was regretted that none of the "favourites have been in the field" (*Illustrated London News*, June 1, 1844, 356), underlining the assumption that if a woman had won the prize, the competition must have been weak. The first-night performance of the play *Quid Pro Quo* was booed and received universally bad reviews. The response, Gore suggested in her preface to the printed play, was orchestrated by a claque of disgruntled writers.[4] Perhaps the most devastating critique of the competition and the winning play was made by George Henry Lewes in the *Westminster Review*:

> If we should have the misfortune to pain Mrs Gore, we would bid her remember that there are ninety-six authors whose self-love has been wounded, whose time has been wasted; some, whose hopes ... have been disappointed by the awarding of the prize: ninety-six angry men who need consolation, and who, we cannot but think, deserve it.[5]

His assumption that Mrs. Gore intruded on masculine territory resonates well beyond the storm in a teacup of one playwriting competition.

Netta Syrett's (1865–1943) experience as winner of the Playgoers' Club competition for new plays in 1901 paralleled that of Gore, with added controversy about the connections between Syrett's own life and the world she created in her play *The Finding of Nancy*. Syrett's play took as its central conflict the choice protagonist Nancy has to make between a relationship outside of marriage or the life of low-paid work as a single respectable woman:

> I see life with all its colour and glitter sweeping on without me like some great full river, while I am caught in a little stagnant backwater, held fast by the weeds ... for the modern young woman who works for a living wage, and has the misfortune to be a lady, there is no chance of any kind. Not even of going to the devil.[6]

Clement Scott's review in the *Daily Telegraph* insinuated that Nancy's decision to live with her lover as his wife was based on Syrett's own experience: "Miss Netta Syrett ... can write out a situation which grips the heart with its painful actuality ... Sometimes, ... the unconventional strikes home, because it is real and because 'it has been lived.'"[7] The play had only one performance at a matinée (May 8, 1902), and Syrett notes in her autobiography, *The Sheltering Tree* (1939), that she lost a well-paid teaching job because of the gossip generated by the play. Like Gore, Syrett wrote no more plays for the mainstream London theater.

Seventy years after Catherine Gore's Pyrrhic victory at the Haymarket theater, another woman won another playwriting prize with another unperformed comedy. In 1913, Violet Pearn (1880–1947) won a national competition with her play *The Minotaur*, amid acerbic comments about the propensity of women to win such competitions. When taxed by the *Morning Post* with the observation that although women win playwriting prizes, they write comedy, not tragedy, Pearn responded with a letter to the paper declaring that "Possibly women are supposed to excel in the more difficult art [comedy] because, as all the world knows, the circumstances of their lives keep them remote from tragic events."[8] And thus, Pearn brought the debate about women's position as playwrights full circle back to Byron's joke about what females lack.

The National Drama

These playwriting competitions were testament to the ongoing anxieties about the status and quality of dramatic literature in the nineteenth century, which complicated the position of women writers within the field. The idea of the drama as an institution of national significance and influence was an important one. British drama (often referred to as the "National Drama") was held to be a defining feature of British culture, in particular through the inheritance of Shakespeare's work. Contemporary dramatic literature was thought to be in decline, unworthy of the heritage of Shakespeare and his contemporaries in tragedy, or of Sheridan and his contemporaries in comedy.

Yet, rather than seeing the results of these competitions as evidence of vitality and growth in English playwriting, the victories of women led critics to express further concern about the decline of the drama. Women winners added further proof to the argument of serious decline: if women could win in open competition, then dramatic writing must be generally weak.

Part of the debate over the National Drama focused on the contrast between the aesthetic ideals of English dramatic literature and the day-to-day practices of the theater as an industry. The theater was at the center of a series of conflicts over the ways in which art could and should be sustained in the rapid changes of industrial modernity. To stay solvent, theaters had to cater to new and expanding audiences, particularly in London and the new industrial centers of Birmingham, Manchester, and Leeds. These new audiences, while plentiful, were neither stable nor conventional in their tastes. To feed hungry audiences, managers, writers, and actors participated in a hugely creative and productive industry that invented new genres such as melodrama, the sensation play, domestic drama and comedy, ballet, and pantomime, as well as remaking farce, light opera, and comedy to suit new urban mass audiences. Rather than recognizing the innovation and modernity of such dramatic writing and theatrical performance, critical discussion focused on such inventiveness and popularity as a sign of the decline of British drama; specific reference was made throughout the century to the difficulties of squaring art and commerce. In this context, women playwrights suffered a double invisibility: neglect that was the result of high culture's attitude to the theater and invisibility in the public record characteristic of the treatment of women in cultural history in general.

Family networks

Overlooking or forgetting the work of women playwrights is a choice we modern scholars make, albeit unwillingly. However, women playwrights become visible if we know how to look for them, particularly in the organization of the theater profession. The mainstream of the nineteenth-century theater was resolutely commercial, organized through interconnecting networks and alliances. Charles Dickens's part-satirical portrait of the Crummles's theater company in *Nicholas Nickleby* (1838–39) suggests the way in which the structures and working practices of theater companies combined domestic relationships with professional networks. Those women who were most successful and prolific in the commercial theater of the nineteenth century were usually part of these networks, but their presence could be obscured by their familial roles as daughters and wives or as performers in theater companies that were themselves organized as quasi-families. Playwrights such as Marie Bancroft (née Wilton, 1839–1921), Aimée (Mrs. Oscar) Beringer (1856–1936), Caroline Boaden (fl. 1825–39), Mary Elizabeth Braddon (1835–1915), Adelaide (Mrs. Charles) Calvert (1836–1921), Elizabeth (Mrs. George) Conquest (fl. 1852–58), Eliza (Mrs. T. P.) Cooke (fl. 1842), Catherine Crowe (1803–76), Mrs. Denvil (fl. 1833–54), Mary (Mrs. Joseph) Ebsworth (1794–1881), Marie-Therese Kemble (née de Camp, 1777–1838), Sarah Lane (1822–99), Maria Lovell (née Lacy, 1803–77), Mrs. Herman Merivale (fl. 1873–88), Elizabeth (Mrs. Alfred) Phillips (fl. 1839–51), Eliza Planché (née St. George, 1796–1846), Elizabeth Polack (fl. 1830–38), Melinda (Mrs. Henry) Young (fl. 1861–67), and Margaret (Mrs. C. Baron) Wilson (1797–1846) all worked in the theater, often in partnership with husbands, fathers, or brothers, and each had plays produced. At the very top of the profession, the theatrical dynasty of the Kembles stretched across several generations, from the late eighteenth and early nineteenth centuries into the 1860s, as much through the work of Sarah Siddons and her niece Fanny Kemble as through the star tragedians and managers John Phillip Kemble and Charles Kemble. Fanny Kemble (1809–93) continued in the footsteps of her mother, Marie-Therese Kemble, as a writer and performer. This negotiation within professional families demonstrates a principal way in which women developed their careers within otherwise apparently restrictive Victorian legal codes and social expectations.

Mary Ebsworth provides an example of a way a woman could use family networks. She worked as an actress and wrote several comedies for the minor theaters (those other than the Theatres Royal of Drury Lane and Covent Garden). She was the daughter of Robert Fairbrother, who was a member of the Glovers' Company and a pantomimist and teacher of fencing. Fairbrother was a friend of Sheridan, and Ebsworth's mother had connections with Joseph Grimaldi, the clown. One of Ebsworth's brothers, Samuel, was a theatrical publisher; her other brother, Benjamin, worked in production roles (prompter and stage manager) in various London theaters. Mary married the playwright and musician Joseph Ebsworth in 1817, and their eldest daughter, Emilie, also married in the theater, to Samuel Cowell, a comedian. Mary Ebsworth worked closely with her husband on plays and translations, as well as producing four successful plays of her own.

Other theatrical professionals, such as Madame Vestris (1797–1856), Elizabeth Planché, Mrs. T. P. Cooke, and Mrs. Alfred Phillips, had successes with plays written for themselves and their husbands or their husbands' theater companies, while Jane Scott (1779–1839) wrote and produced around fifteen plays in a theater her father owned specifically for her to manage. For the Kembles, Mrs. Planché, Caroline Boaden, Mary

Ebsworth, and Jane Scott, the familial organization of the theater could be seen as enabling because, although their work was often overshadowed by that of their husbands or fathers, their professionalism, stage experience, and perhaps most importantly their physical presence and influence in the theater and rehearsal room were accepted.

In the first half of the century, most women working in the minor theaters used family networks to gain entry to the profession. By the mid-Victorian period, women's playwriting for the mainstream theater started to achieve some momentum, aided by increasing numbers of educated women entering the profession in a variety of roles. It was at mid-century that the West End of London was established as a prime tourist and entertainment destination, in part because of the new, smaller, more comfortable theaters that produced light and luxurious entertainments. Female theater managers and producers, such as Eliza Vestris, Mary Ann Keeley, Mrs. Alfred Wigan, and Marie Wilton, were at the center of this development, often in partnership with their husbands.[9] New kinds of writing emerged, and comedy and farce about contemporary life flourished. Domesticity, femininity, and female agency stood at the center of these modern entertainments.

Melodrama

Melodrama, a genre imported from France at the beginning of the century, had by the 1860s become naturalized into the English form of domestic drama, concerned with the representation of contemporary life of the middle and working classes. Melodrama focused on ordinary men and women as feeling individuals with intense emotional lives and desires, rather than on the high-ranking hero of Aristotelian tragedy. The content and style of melodrama was not received without controversy, however, and its focus on female characters who transgressed the boundaries of the "proper feminine" was part of the more general moral panic over sensation fiction and the melodramas adapted from it (see Lyn Pykett's discussion of sensation fiction in ch. 9). Criticisms of melodrama accompanied the genre since its first performances on the English stage in 1802, with Thomas Holcroft's *A Tale of Mystery* (an adaptation of Guilbert de Pixérécourt's *Coelina; ou l'enfant de mystère*, 1800). "Melodramatic" is still an easy term of dismissal. That which is melodramatic is regarded as extravagantly emotional, at the cost of imaginative truth; it deals with degrading subjects and degraded characters, going for the easy emotional hit; and it infantilizes its audiences, lulling them with empty affect and artificial resolutions. Yet, sensation novels, and the plays derived from them, are templates for popular entertainment to this day.

By the 1860s, melodramas based on sensation novels, such as *Aurora Floyd*, *Lady Audley's Secret*, and *East Lynne*, shifted the Victorian theater into a new period of creativity and change. In a pattern of remediation typical of the interplay between genres in the nineteenth century, aspects of theatrical melodrama were absorbed into the sensation novel, which in turn gave rise to the long-running sensation dramas of the mid-1860s. Although the first acknowledged sensation novel was Wilkie Collins's *Woman in White* (1859–60) and the first sensation melodrama was theater entrepreneur and playwright Dion Boucicault's *The Colleen Bawn* in 1860, by 1863 one woman's stories dominated the London stage. Adaptations of Mary Braddon's novels *Lady Audley's Secret* and *Aurora Floyd* played across London in bourgeois West End theaters as well as those catering to local working-class audiences in the East End and on the south bank of the Thames. These adaptations were followed by multiple adaptations of Ellen Wood's sensation novel *East Lynne* (1861). *East Lynne* was an international phenomenon, with stage adaptations touring Great Britain, the United States, and the British Empire. It was one of the first stories to be made into film in the early twentieth century, and the story endured in stage, film, and radio drama versions until at least 1939, when a twenty-six part radio drama was broadcast by the Sydney, Australia, radio station 2CH, accompanied by an abridged version of the novel. That broadcast was sponsored by Sydney department store McDowells, underlining the growing cultural and economic connections among consumption, femininity, melodrama, and sensation.

Although the sensation stories of the 1860s constantly replicated patterns of masochistic female suffering and victimization, they also offered many opportunities for women playwrights to explore topics that were otherwise difficult or not fit for "the work of a lady."[10] While Boucicault's popular version of sensation drama focused on extreme physical events represented by spectacular stage effects, such as the rescue of the heroine from a rock isolated in water in *The Colleen Bawn*, women's sensation melodrama drew its power from frank investigations of the conditions of contemporary femininity and dramatized the ways in which female characters could exercise agency and desire within its constraints. The representation of Mary Braddon's and Ellen Wood's bigamous heroines on stage was a marker of a shift in Victorian popular culture to modernity through the representation of women's stories on the popular stage. This shift was intimately bound up with challenges to the Victorian conception of the proper lady in her fictional and material versions and was distinguished by an emphasis on the power of women's emotions and their simultaneous commodification. This intense interest in femininity – particularly its perils – coincided with the fashion in

France for the "well-made play" (*pièce bien faite*) and continued into the late nineteenth century in the problem plays of playwrights such as Arthur Wing Pinero (1855–1934) and George Bernard Shaw (1856–1950), and in translations of Henrik Ibsen's groundbreaking plays, particularly *A Doll's House* (first performed in Copenhagen, 1879; first performance in English, 1889). The interests of the New Women were focused on the exercise of women's agency, especially female suffrage, and explored new futures for women through the theatrical imaginary. The men around them were fascinated by the powers and dangers of late-Victorian femininity and its impact on social structures and order.

Comedy and farce

While sensation melodrama grabbed public attention as part of its basic *modus operandi*, women's playwriting was establishing itself in the genres of comedy and farce in more ordinary circumstances. Farce and comedy offered women writers the chance to satirize the very conditions and ideologies of domesticity and femininity that structured their own lives. Farce particularly played on the precariousness of respectability in the face of threatened chaos through the breakdown of class and gender boundaries. While it is not possible to generalize about the nature of women's playwriting throughout the nineteenth century, as it was various, it ranged from the commercial staple of farce to the experimentation of Baillie and the poetic drama of Augusta Webster and George Eliot. But when women wrote comedy and farce, it threw into high relief the conditions of women's everyday lives. Rather than, as Byron fantasized about Baillie, needing to borrow a man's body to write tragedy, women in the mid-century wrote about the world around them. Of course, their stage version of that world was heightened, exaggerated, and made ridiculous, but mid-century women playwrights had the knack of turning the very quotidian nature of middle-class respectable life into comedy with a particularly feminine point of view.

Writing in the middle of the century, Mrs. Hallett (I can find no other name for her, fl. 1837–45) specialized in comedy for the newly legitimized, but still minor theaters. These were theaters generally near or in the West End of London, but far smaller houses than the Theatres Royal Drury Lane, Covent Garden, or the Haymarket. They catered to an upwardly mobile middle class and were places in which women were central in creating a new kind of entertainment.[11] As Bratton records, women managers created sparkling witty entertainments produced to a high standard in new smaller theaters, where elegancies of domestic comfort prevailed. Mrs. Hallett's play *Nobodies' at Home; Somebodies' Abroad* was first performed in 1847 at the Olympic Theatre, one of these new theaters managed for a long time by the partnership of Eliza Vestris and Charles Mathews.[12] Unlike Catherine Gore's prize comedy, *Quid Pro Quo*, at the Haymarket, Mrs. Hallett's play received approving reviews, perhaps because the play was unpretentiously a farce, not a production at a Theatre Royal trying to save the National Drama. The published edition of the play reprints a series of favorable reviews, praising it as "a ... light and sparkling emanation of humour and fun," "cleverly adapted and an excellent cut at demi-fashionable society, and told well," and "produced with the most decided success" (iii).

Hallett's plot is typical for farce of the period, involving an errant husband and mistaken identity mixed with class consciousness and a comic Irish servant. The farce centers on the Loosecash family arriving in France, having been thrilled at putting their names in the book at the hotel in Dover with "all the great people." Mrs. Loosecash is mocked as an aspirational lower-middle-class woman, "Miss Barbara Buggins, the cheesemonger's only daughter, of Blackman Street, in the Borough, [who] could have picked and chused her a husband" (7), speaking French execrably and English badly. The Buggins daughters are figures of fun – one bookish, tracing the Loosecash family tree back three and a half centuries, and the other a husband-hunting social climbing minx, chatting with her mother about whom they will invite to a "sore-eye" (*soirée*). Their servant, a stock comic figure, pursues any young female servant he thinks likely to kiss him, with the role requiring the actor to do the "stage Irish" turns of comic monologues and songs. The play culminates in a spectacular ballroom scene in which the Loosecashes are almost completely gulled out of their money and the daughters' respectability. They are saved by Mrs. Loosecash's brother, the non-social-climbing Buggins, who has come to bring them home to the East End of London. He exhorts them:

> Now then sister, nieces, friends, let us away for old England. Farewell France and folly. Never let us forget that society forms so many links of a chain, each depending on the other, from high to low. Then never be ashamed of the land that gave you birth, or the honest employment that procures you an honourable independence. (26)

This pat moral lesson is as standard for farce as are the other elements of the play. The farce is in no way out of the ordinary or particularly different from the hundreds of similar such plays produced for the content-hungry mainstream theater of the period. The dicing with respectability and ruin, the comic servant, the quite sharp ridicule of the social climbers – all these elements are normal for comedy and farce in the mid-nineteenth century.

A comparison of Hallett's experiences with those of Catherine Gore or Netta Syrett, picked out as exceptional women playwrights, suggests that there were virtues in being ordinary and in writing commercial plays for the Victorian mainstream theater. There is a tendency for recuperative feminist literary history and criticism to want to see a triumphalist narrative in which the women we recover and celebrate write extraordinary pieces. In this model, women playwrights who participated actively in the professional mainstream can be overlooked. And in one very important sense, even the ordinary is extraordinary when from the pen of a lady. Writing for the theater required physical courage and determination to broach the spaces of bohemian masculinity, along with mental stamina to push the work onto often uninterested managers. That women playwrights, together with the women theater managers of this period, used the theater to play with and about the ordinary ridiculousness of domestic life, and make money from it, was actually quite extraordinary.

The New Woman and the new drama

By the end of the century, representations of femininity were established as essential material for the drama, and women were more visible than ever in a wide range of paid theatrical work. Indeed, George Bernard Shaw wrote (facetiously) in 1894:

> We cannot but see that the time is ripe for the advent of the actress-manageress, and that we are on the verge of something like a struggle between the sexes for the dominion of the London theatres, a struggle which ... must in the long run end disastrously for the side which is furthest behind the times. And that side is at present the men's side.[13]

Shaw's vision of a battle of the sexes had, in fact, been running throughout the century. His pronouncement of women as the eventual winners in the struggle was overly optimistic, and once again focused on exceptional women – in this case, actor Elizabeth Robins (1862–1952) and manager Marion Lea – who – together with Eleanor Marx (1855–98) – were among the leading figures in the introduction of Ibsen's plays to the London stage.

While victory for women in the theater generally, and women playwrights in particular, was not really in sight (and probably still is not given the record of plays by women on the London stage in the twentieth century), in the last decades of the nineteenth century more women than ever before participated in the theater as visible and respected professionals. The theater increasingly provided a platform for the exploration of a variety of challenging and oppositional ideas about contemporary society. Taking their lead from the introduction of new European dramatists, women playwrights started to write explicitly feminist plays that challenged the position of women in late Victorian society. Theatrical events played a prominent part in female suffrage campaigns. The suffrage campaign generated main-stage plays, such as Elizabeth Robins's *Votes for Women* (1907) and Cecily Hamilton and Christopher St. John's *How the Vote was Won* (1909), and suffragette propaganda plays produced in meeting halls around the country, developed by Inez Bensusan in the Play Department of the Actresses' Franchise League, such as Evelyn Glover's *A Chat with Mrs Chicky* (1912). By the end of the Victorian period, the theater had become a place where women could exercise agency and independence. No longer could the profession of playwriting be considered as a solely masculine domain. However, it is the argument of this chapter that playwriting never was a masculine domain, but that successive histories have framed it as such. Paying attention to the work of women playwrights requires that we change the frames of our observation and develop a literary history that accommodates the marginal, the feminine, the popular, and the nonliterary. Writing for the theater offered women money, fame (or notoriety), the excitement of a responsive medium, with immediate contact with the audience. Perhaps most significantly, writing for the theater offered women the opportunity to write themselves into the life of an important national cultural institution, when other forms of citizenship were still denied to them.

NOTES

1. Leslie A. Marchand, ed., *Byron's Letters and Journals, 1816–17* (London: John Murray, 1976), vol. 5, p. 203. Emphasis in original.
2. A. G. L'Estrange, ed., *The Life and Letters of Mary Russell Mitford, Related in a Selection from Her Letters to Her Friends* (London: Richard Bentley, 1870), vol. 2, pp. 161–62.
3. Ibid., vol. 2, p. 213.
4. "Preface," *Quid Pro Quo; or, the Day of the Dupes* (London: National Acting Drama Office, n.d.), p. v.
5. G. H. L. [George Henry Lewes], "The Prize Comedy and the Prize Committee," *Westminster Review* 42:1 (September 1844), 106.
6. Netta Syrett, *The Finding of Nancy*, British Library, Add. Mss. 1902/14J (Lord Chamberlain's Collection of Plays), ff. 7–9.
7. Anonymous [Clement Scott], "The Finding of Nancy: The Playgoers Prize Play at St. James's Theatre," *Daily Telegraph*, May 9, 1902, p. 10.
8. Anonymous, *The Era*, June 21, 1913, p. 17.
9. Jacky Bratton, *The Making of the West End Stage: Marriage, Management and the Mapping of Gender in London, 1830–1870* (Cambridge: Cambridge University Press, 2011), pp. 170–72.
10. "The Drama," *New Monthly Magazine* 35 (August 1832), 348.

11. See Bratton, *The Making of the West End Stage*, *passim*.
12. *Nobodies' at Home: Somebodies' Abroad, A Farce in Two Acts, with Historical Reference to the Poet Churchill* (London: W. S. Johnson, 1847). All further references are to this text.
13. "Preface," William Archer, *The Theatrical 'World' of 1894* (London: Walter Scott, 1894), pp. xxix–xxx.

11

CAROL HANBERY MACKAY

Life-writing

A Victorian woman was in a bind when it came to writing her own life story, for her autobiographical impulse met with charges of pride or egotism for writing an autobiography in the first place. A more acceptable form of life-writing was the family memoir, which ostensibly followed the formula of the multivolumed "life and letters" of a great man but which also allowed the editor to insert herself into a relational narrative. Biography represented yet another alternative, and the selection of biographical subject permitted a Victorian woman to assert interest in other women's lives, perhaps even to discover in them role models who might make full-fledged self-writing more attainable for future female readers. The Victorian women who engaged in life-writing participated in all three approaches, always skirting the edge of propriety by setting in motion the interplay between public and private. Writing her own history, the autobiographer invited into her narrative the life stories of others, usually starting with mini-biographies of family members (sometimes going back several generations) and unfolding through the back stories of a series of influential personages. At the same time, the autobiographical first-person was seldom absent from any biographical endeavor. Letters and journal or diary entries by the biographical subject figured prominently in most memoirs and biographies, occasionally taking over the narrative and often introducing in turn the voices of her correspondents. Complicating this scenario is the question of censorship – self-imposed or executed by well-meaning editors, ultimately reflecting the amorphous Victorian mind-set automatically adopted by the publishing code.

Self-writing by Victorian men tended to follow the dual trajectory inaugurated by St. Augustine and Jean-Jacques Rousseau, creating the narratives of conversion and confession exemplified by John Henry Newman's *Apologia pro vita sua* (A defense of one's life; 1864) and John Stuart Mill's *Autobiography* (1873). Certainly these were generating forces in autobiographies by Victorian women, but gender constraints of the period forced them to introduce additional strategies, both conscious and unconscious, resulting in various hybrid forms. Trying to interpret such texts as narratives of individual subjectivities points up how much they are the product of unreliable narrators for whom self-reflection was a dangerous prospect, often leading writers to conceal what twenty-first-century readers can now penetrate.

Examining autobiographies and other life-writing by Victorian women for insights into cultural history entails recognizing their creative energies as each variously refracts her evolving selves into a self-authorizing voice. Acknowledging their relational roles empowered these women to participate in a larger sense of community, both generally and specifically. As women life-writers read the publications of other women's life stories, they began to establish a nexus of self-reflexive accounting on the published page and in personal correspondence. Public intertextuality merged with personal friendships among such writers as Charlotte Elizabeth Tonna (1790–1846), Anna Jameson (1794–1860), Harriet Martineau (1802–76), and Frances Anne Kemble (1809–93), who paved the way for future life-writers to form their own connective (though sometimes combative) links. By century's end, the interactive publications of Eliza Lynn Linton (1822–98), Edith Simcox (1844–1901), Margaret Oliphant (1828–97), and Mary Augusta Ward (1851–1920) brought into intense scrutiny the genres of both autobiography and biography as they concurrently laid bare the ongoing struggle of the professional woman to tell her own story.

"A life by no means deficient of remarkable incidents"

At the beginning of the nineteenth century, autobiographers of both genders inherited the tradition of the spiritual narrative, particularly represented by the autobiographies of Quakers and Christian missionaries but also driving the religious focus of Charlotte Elizabeth Tonna's *Personal Recollections* (1841), which provides this section's heading.[1] Less hidden than forgotten, Tonna (1790–1846) is recognized today for her industrial novels, most notably *Helen Fleetwood* (1839–40), which exposed the appalling conditions of child labor, and *The Wrongs of Women* (1843–44), which attacked the treatment of women factory workers. But in her own time, she was better known for her anti-Catholicism and the missionary zeal with which she sought to convert London's Irish Catholics to Protestantism. That Tonna should banish from her autobiography any mention of her disastrous first marriage is understandable, but her unwillingness to discuss her fiction points to another concern. Having delighted in the pleasures of an unrestricted reading course in childhood, she undoubtedly realized that writing about being granted "unbounded liberty" (34) from domestic duties required her to counterbalance, probably even surpass, domesticity with the kind of single-minded devotion demanded by her conversion to Evangelicalism. Even recording her activities as editor of the *Christian Lady's Magazine* for twelve years is trumped by her diatribes against evil and extended theological disquisitions.

Tonna's *Personal Recollections* begins assertively, its first chapter performing the usual work of a preface by providing Tonna's rationale for writing her autobiography but then going on to malign the actions of the generic biographer who immediately mines the privacy of journals and confidential letters on the death of his or her subject. She vehemently announces her intention to consign her own private papers to a bonfire before anyone else should draw on them. Yet Tonna also evokes a personal tone by labeling each chapter as a letter, directly addressing her reader from time to time and signing the first missive, "Affectionately yours, C.E." (27). Clearly she had a plan for providing a closing frame to her autobiography when she concluded the final letter with the same biblical invocation with which Charlotte Brontë's Jane Eyre would conclude her eponymous novel, subtitled "An Autobiography," six years later: "Even so, Lord Jesus: come quickly! Amen" (Revelation 22:20). Ironically, that final wording loses its primacy of place when the autobiographer's widower, Lewis H. J. Tonna, appended a thirty-five-page "Memoir" to the 1847 edition of *Personal Recollections*, thereby hijacking his wife's text and interpreting it through his version of a tribute piece. Meanwhile, another repackaging of Tonna's text had already appeared across the Atlantic during her lifetime. Supposedly defending her sister "authoress," Harriet Beecher Stowe supplied a provocative introduction to the M. W. Dodd 1844 publication of Tonna's *Works*, forewarning that the "fastidious may be shocked" to encounter an autobiography published by a living writer.

Like Tonna,[2] Harriet Martineau (1802–76) grew up in Norwich, traveled to North America, became both a novelist and practicing journalist, managed a lifelong hearing disability, and wanted to have the last word as the author of her own life. Two health crises jump-started her autobiographical endeavors. Informed that she had only a short time to live in 1843 and then again in 1855, she treated these diagnoses as the spur to writing her *Autobiography* (1877), and on the second occasion she completed the task to date, printing and binding it in two volumes to await final publication after her death. Thwarting medical science, Martineau lived until 1876, by which time she had assigned to her American friend Maria Weston Chapman the task of editing a third volume of "Memorials," which were to be selected from her journals, letters, and other writings. Like Tonna, Martineau addressed questions of privacy at the outset, asking friends to burn her correspondence. But unlike Tonna, she projected a conclusion beyond her lifetime: she wrote her own obituary for the London *Daily News* (June 29, 1876), which Chapman republished in volume three of the *Autobiography*.[3] Written in the third person, the editorial notice acknowledges that it will provide a "strict and sometimes disparaging view of herself" (660). Nonetheless, Chapman's arrangement and connecting narrative reflect a different sensibility; sharing the wishes of Martineau's circle of friends, she tried to soften the acerbic voice of the autobiographer.

Martineau's exceptional memory served her well in writing her *Autobiography*. Not only does she recall specific incidents of her childhood, she infuses them with their emotional impact. In adulthood, she is astonished to find her same "fears and miseries" (554) described in Brontë's *Jane Eyre*, helping her forge a bond with the pseudonymous "Currer Bell" that she would later break as a result of her harsh review of Brontë's last completed novel *Villette* (1853). Much earlier, Martineau remembers her own emotional turmoil when she contemplated "authorship" and how she overcame it when her brother James praised an article she had published in the *Monthly Repository* (November 1822) under the signatory "V of Norwich": "Now dear, leave it to other women to make shirts and darn stockings; and do you devote yourself to this" (111–12). Given her long and successful career as a woman of letters, Martineau's description of her method of composition is especially intriguing. She tries to write a novel, finding it "excessively dull," but this recollection launches her into denouncing the contemporary practice of revision, not necessary to someone like herself, who boasts an "unconscious preparatory discipline" (113–14). As for trying to create a plot in fiction, she considers it "a task above human faculties," preferring instead to derive it from actual life, for every perfect plot in fiction is taken "bodily from real life" (189).

Intellectual, social economist, philosopher, as well as novelist, journalist, and travel writer – Martineau analyzes herself and others with relentless honesty. Alternately open-minded and fractious, she paints a self-portrait full of contradictions and conundrums. Neither commitment to duty nor allegiance to truth could make her see herself as others saw her. When Oliphant reviewed Martineau's *Autobiography* for *Blackwood's Edinburgh Magazine* (April 1877), she summed it up along with the genre in general by pronouncing it "this terrible instrument of self-murder" (681).

"Leave the letters till we're dead"

Although Virginia Woolf rightly feared the repercussions of publishing her unedited and relentlessly honest correspondence and diaries during her lifetime,[4] Victorian women (and men) silently edited letters and journals for publication in autobiographies and biographies of both the living and the dead. As raw material, these personal documents could be collected and assembled without requiring the organizing principles and rationale that informed a self-consciously undertaken autobiography. Their sense of immediacy supplied ready-made drama, while chronological organization put uncomplicated demands on author/editor and reader alike.

Shakespearian actress "Fanny" Kemble (1809–93) anticipated the public appetite for celebrity gossip by supplying it herself in the form of a series of autobiographical outings based on her personal correspondence and journals. Inspired by a friend returning a trunkful of letters written weekly for more than forty years, Kemble began to compile what she called her "reminiscences."[5] Then, asked by editor William Dean Howells to submit some memoirs to the *Atlantic Monthly* in 1875, she produced twenty monthly installments under the title "An Old Woman's Gossip." This core was expanded into publication of *Records of a Girlhood* (1878), followed by *Records of Later Life* (1882), and concluding with *Further Records, 1848–1883: A Series of Letters* (1890), largely edited by her publisher, Richard Bentley. Admittedly written to entertain, these memoirs invited Victorian readers to vicariously experience the life of a member of an illustrious theatrical family as she crisscrossed the Atlantic, hobnobbing with the rich and famous while still sustaining close personal ties. Becoming a known personality to her readership over time, Kemble transcended the negative judgment usually leveled at the lifestyle of an actress.

Until she starts drawing heavily on her correspondence with Harriet St. Leger, Kemble's *Records of a Girlhood* reads like many other recollections of an active childhood, bringing to the fore such vivid memories as deciding in a pique to run away from home (43) and attending the Parisian theater during holiday visits with her father while she was studying abroad. The letters often seem to be a way for Kemble to practice her story-telling skills, as when she provides a reenactment of her first ride on a locomotive, turning it into an exciting tale of suspense and romance (279–84). Then, without fanfare, she begins to include diary entries when she and her father Charles undertake their theatrical tour of America. Moving in and out of the pattern of regular, daily accounts of her activities gives a false impression of intimacy, however, because such private summaries might just as well be public property. Eventually, the recipients of Kemble's correspondence branch out to include Anna Jameson (1794–1860), who writes that she would like to dedicate her first edition of *Characteristics of Shakespeare's Women* (1832) to Kemble. Admitting Jameson to her circle of confidantes is crucial to Kemble's strategy about how the next record of her life story will open, as Jameson's prominence allows Kemble to strike a discreet balance between telling and not telling anything about her marriage to Pierce Butler, member of a major slave-holding family.

Despite the fact that Kemble obviously knew Butler during their two-year courtship, he appears in *Records of a Girlhood* only once, in its final declarative sentence: "I was married in Philadelphia on the 7th of June, 1834, to Mr. Pierce Butler, of that city" (590). The public history surrounding that heavily censored marriage and subsequent divorce in 1849 appears in an earlier pair of Kemble's journals anchored in the New World. *The Journal of Frances Anne Butler* (1835), covering her American experiences thus far, had a rocky road to public view because her husband first tried unsuccessfully to withdraw it from her Philadelphia publishers but then succeeded in having almost all the names replaced with dashes. She delayed publication of her second American memoir *Journal of a Residence on a Georgian Plantation in 1838–1839* (1863), based on living with her husband and two daughters for five months on the Butler plantation on St. Simons Island off the coast of Georgia. Written in the form of unsent letters addressed to her abolitionist friend Catharine Sedgwick, this journal created quite a stir among Kemble's supporters when it was privately circulated, but the threat of estrangement from her immediate American family led her to hold off publication until she recognized the potential impact of its antislavery message on the outcome of the Civil War.

For novelist, poet, and editor Sara Coleridge (1802–52), letters end up telling her life story as well, even though she laid out a plan of action for writing an autobiographical narrative. But she was too late: she died within eight months of writing to her daughter Edith her opening salvo, which she modestly cast in the guise of a letter: "I have long wished to give you a little sketch of my life."[6] She did not get any further than her ninth year, however, leaving off in mid-sentence, "On reviewing my earlier childhood, I find the predominant reflection ..." (vol. 1, p. 26). Having already performed the dutiful service of editing and publishing much of the canon of her father, Samuel Taylor Coleridge, she undoubtedly felt safe in passing on the legacy of advancing the family record to her daughter. Yet Sara Coleridge's *Memoir and Letters* (1872) contains almost as many letters by friends and relatives as it does those by the author, and limiting the subject's voice proportionately certainly does her a disservice. Furthermore, the editor has already begun to diminish her mother's standing as a writer in her own right, calling Coleridge's letters "unconscious self-portraiture" and circumventing her role in the public sphere: "The letters of Sara Coleridge were not acts of authorship, but of friendship; we feel in reading them, that she is not entertaining or instructing a crowd of listeners, but holding quiet converse with some congenial mind" (vol. 1, p. vii). This is hardly a description of the woman who forthrightly critiques her father's selfish behavior or dissects her own night terrors at the outset of her memoir. Perhaps the passage of time (the *Memoir and Letters* was twenty years reaching fruition) accounts for a daughter's desire to project her mother's image in an unassuming light.

The practice of memorializing a deceased friend or relative by collecting and publishing excerpts from his or her letters and other private papers was widespread in the Victorian period. With little or no editorial input, creating what almost amounts to posthumous autobiographies, these texts grew out of a variety of configurations – for example, a daughter privately circulating a family document in memory of her mother (Laura Stuart's *In Memoriam* [1896] for Caroline Coleman), an intimate friend illuminating the private life of a famous personage (Maria Catherine Bishop's *A Memoir of Mrs. Augustus Craven* [1896] for Pauline de la Feronnays), a daughter following her father's charge (Mrs. Ambrose Myall's *James Hain Friswell: A Memoir* [1898]), and even reversal of the usual generational pattern (Mary Lundie's *Memoir of Mrs. Mary Lundie Duncan: Being Recollections of a Daughter by Her Mother* [1843]). But the case of an established writer – who had already privately published her autobiography and selections from her journals – having her life story repackaged and weighed down by an overabundance of letters written after her death seems less of a tribute than a sacrilege. Novelist Elizabeth Missing Sewell (1815–1906) honed her self-writing skills by writing first-person fiction such as *The Experience of Life* (1852) and educational paradigms for children such as *The Journal of a Home Life* (1867). Toward the end of her life, she published for private circulation among her far-flung family *Extracts from a Private Journal* (1891) and *Autobiography* (1893). Nonetheless, the year after Sewell's death witnessed publication of a bowdlerized version of her *Autobiography*, edited by her niece Eleanor, who transformed it into a hagiographic volume replete with "memories" solicited from a wide range of family, friends, and former students.

Writing the lives of others

Writing the biography of another woman might serve a Victorian woman as preparation for writing her own autobiography or it might constitute a form of surrogate autobiography, either case affording varying degrees of insight into the arc of a woman's life in its particular cultural context. For example, novelist and journalist Charlotte Mary Yonge (1823–1901) had plenty of practice as a biographer, including editing several volumes of *Biographies of Good Women* (1862; 1865) drawn from her journal *The Monthly Packet* and to which she contributed mini-biographies of Sarah Kirby, Sarah

Martin, and Hannah More. She also wrote a full-length biography of the latter (1888), as well as the seven-volume series *Cameos from English History* (1880–90). Although she never completed her own autobiography, she wrote the first three chapters (dated 1877) of what became *Charlotte Mary Yonge: Her Life and Letters* (1907), edited by her colleague Christabel Coleridge (niece of Sara), who was inspired to contribute an appendix listing of "imaginary biographies" that debunk false attacks on Yonge's character. Social reformer Josephine Butler (1828–1906) also treated biography as a precursor to writing autobiography. She wrote two biographies of religious figures and memoirs of her father and husband before tackling *Personal Reminiscences of a Great Crusade* (1896), nonetheless subordinating her private life to her public role in the repeal of the Contagious Diseases Acts.

Novelist Elizabeth Gaskell (1810–65) may not have written an autobiography, but her *Life of Charlotte Brontë* (1857) served as a defense of her own bifurcated existence as private woman and public author. Curiosity about the identity of Currer Bell ran rampant during Brontë's lifetime, hardly satisfied by Charlotte's coy prefatory essay for the 1850 edition of Emily's *Wuthering Heights* and Anne's *Agnes Gray* entitled "Biographical Notice of Ellis and Acton Bell." Memorializing her dead sisters, Charlotte revealed their gendered identity, but it was not until Martineau's obituary notice for Charlotte appeared in the *Daily News* (April 6, 1855; rpt. *Biographical Sketches*, 1868) that the general readership began to learn the details about her sad story and feel a genuine sense of loss. Gaskell's biography was eagerly received, all the more so for the notoriety of its requiring a third edition to excise potentially libelous descriptions of Branwell Brontë's female employer and the Cowan's Bridge Clergy Daughters' School. Using fictional techniques, Gaskell sets each scene dramatically, further grounding the biography in extended quotations from Charlotte's letters, often to the point of their taking over the text as if it were an autobiography. Ultimately, Gaskell splits her subject in two – Charlotte, the dutiful daughter, sister, wife; Currer Bell, the author. Dismissing "the critical, unsympathetic public," Gaskell concludes by appealing to "that larger and more solemn public, who know how to look with tender humility at faults and errors; how to admire generously extraordinary genius, and how to reverence with warm, full hearts all noble virtue."[7]

Brontë's life story aroused the interest of other Victorian women writers, causing them to examine their own relationship to their work and provoking self-commentary that appeared in their autobiographical writings. Most conspicuous of these self-comparisons occurs in Margaret Oliphant's *Autobiography and Letters* (1899).[8] Reading Gaskell's biography of Brontë, she observes, "I don't suppose my powers are equal to hers — my work to myself looks perfectly pale and colourless beside hers — but yet I have had far more experience and, I think, a fuller conception of life" (10). Typically self-deprecating, Oliphant nonetheless proceeds to trade off positive and negative self-judgments, all in response to a sister novelist she believed made a major contribution to the recognition of female autonomy. Oliphant's last publication was the lead chapter she contributed to the Diamond Jubilee volume *Women Novelists of Queen Victoria's Reign: A Book of Appreciation* (1897) entitled "The Sisters Brontë."

Another novelist, critic, and self-writer, Mary Augusta Ward wrote a pivotal two-part review article on "The Literature of Introspection" for *Macmillan's Magazine* (January–February 1884) and eventually published her own autobiography as a family memoir of a professional author, *A Writer's Recollections* (1918). In retrospect, she considered her "Introductions" to the seven-volume Haworth Edition of *Life and Works of the Sisters Brontë* (1899–1900) to be her principal accomplishment. Referring to the Gaskell biography (which constitutes the seventh volume), Ward supplies her own subjective context for the Yorkshire environs, evoking the Brontë sisters as real people and renewing attention to *Wuthering Heights* (1847). Reading their works through their lives, Ward is responsible for generations of future autobiographical interpretations of the Brontë canon.

Charlotte Brontë (1816–55) and George Eliot (Marian Evans, 1819–80) dominated the ranks of successful Victorian women writers, but revelations of Eliot's personal life opened the door to critical attacks that betrayed the envy of her detractors. Eliot had privately found fault with Martineau's *Autobiography*, largely on the basis of the autobiographer's egotism in relating her "triumphs,"[9] but she could not divine how much her own behind-the-scenes success story would rankle her peers. Publication of *George Eliot's Life as Related in Her Letters and Journals* (1885), "arranged and edited by her husband J. W. Cross" and often recast in the third-person, provided the background to a leisured literary life safeguarded by a male confidant who served as a sounding board and handled her business affairs. In particular, the section labeled "How I came to write fiction" introduces an edited journal entry delineating George Henry Lewes's integral role in launching Eliot's career as a novelist (vol. 1, pp. 297–300). For Oliphant, the sole support of several families who needed her to maintain a rigorous publishing schedule, Eliot seemed to have "an almost unfair advantage," as did male authors without wives or family, "who have given themselves up to their art" (Oliphant 15). Building on her comparisons to Brontë, Oliphant here pushes her self-evaluation to ask the hard-hitting question, "Should I have done better if I had been kept, like her, in a mental greenhouse and taken care of?" Circling around a speculative answer in the negative, Oliphant lashes out against Lewes as "caretaker and worshipper unrivalled" (17). Perhaps Cross's disclosure in *Life and Letters* that Eliot had penned the anonymous "Silly Novels by Lady Novelists" for the *Westminster Review* (October 1856) provoked that outburst, for Oliphant had every reason to be offended by Eliot's lack of empathy for the hard-working woman for whom writing was her livelihood and the mainstay for the lives of many others.

Critiquing the genre

Criticism about life-writing as a genre intensified during the course of the nineteenth century, revealing a propensity to be driven by partisan screeds for or against the texts assigned to reviewers (along with an increasingly long list of novels) for a rapidly proliferating periodical press. Had these reviewers the time and inclination for more reflection, they might have put their critiques into disinterested dialogue with Edith Simcox's groundbreaking essay entitled "Autobiographies" for the *North British Review* (January 1870).[10] Ranging from Darius, King of Persia, circa 521–486 BC, to John Henry Newman (the only female autobiographer she mentions is the seventeenth-century letter writer Mme. de Sévigné), Simcox constructs a theory of the genre of autobiography traced through the three historical periods proposed by Auguste Comte: the Elementary, the Positive, and the Analytical. In the scientific spirit of Martineau, Simcox surveys her wide range of samples, utilizing her proficiency in Latin, French, Italian, and German. She conjoins the social scientist with the literary critic when she dispassionately declares, "Autobiographies written for the sake of edification differ amongst each other less in substance and tenor than in the success with which the writer expresses real and genuine feelings as if they were original as well as real" (552), ultimately aligning contemporary introspection with the kind of "mental autobiography" found in fiction (560) and citing examples such as William Makepeace Thackeray's *The History of Pendennis* (1850) and Charlotte Brontë's posthumous *The Professor* (1857).

Oliphant's reviews of Martineau's *Autobiography* for *Blackwood's* (1877) and Eliot's *Life and Letters* for the *Edinburgh Review* (April 1885) joined the ongoing debate in the press over the conflicting issues raised by life-writing. Oliphant often used the occasion of a review to write her own mini-biography of the autobiographer and to pronounce judgment on that life. Just as the Martineau review sometimes degenerates into spiteful attack, the Eliot review embarrasses the reviewer by going beyond knowledge of the text at hand and sinking to character assassination: "It was not long before it became known that this purest preacher of domestic life, of fidelity, and self-sacrifice, had, in her own person, defied the laws and modest traditions that guard domestic life, and had taken a step which in all other cases deprives a woman of the fellowship and sympathy of other women."[11] Yet even in Oliphant's review of Martineau's *Autobiography*, she was already concurring with Eliot's distaste for disclosing private matters. As she noted in the Martineau review, the autobiographer whose work is published after his or her death is the party potentially most culpable: "The right of libeling himself is a right which cannot be taken from any human creature, living or dead; but a posthumous assault on his fellow-creatures is one of the worst and most cowardly, as it is the last sin of which a man is capable" (Martineau 673).

A seasoned reviewer of autobiography, Oliphant also turned her attention to biography and the editing of personal papers that constituted a life and letters publication. James Anthony Froude's edition of *Letters and Memorials of Jane Welsh Carlyle* (1883) particularly fueled Oliphant's rage against what she considered posthumous violation of a woman's privacy: "No woman of this generation, or of any other we are acquainted with, has had such desperate occasion to be saved from her friends: and public feeling and sense of honour must be at a low ebb indeed when no one ventures to stand up and stigmatize as it deserves this betrayal and exposure of the secret of a woman's weakness."[12] Two months later, Oliphant followed her "Mrs. Carlyle" article with a more measured study on "The Ethics of Biography," which distills the same message, even if she could not always adhere to it herself: "In this investigation we are met at once by a rule universally respected and very generally acquiesced in—the first and broadest expression of natural feeling towards our contemporaries who are dead, *De mortuis nil nisi bonum* [Speak no ill of the dead]."[13]

In her article "Literature: Then and Now" for the *Fortnightly Review* (April 1890), Eliza Lynn Linton took contemporary critics of novels and biographies to task for being self-serving and producing partisan assessments. Yet where Eliot was concerned, she had never seemed capable of following her own well-argued precepts. A staunch antifeminist whose lifestyle nonetheless modeled the goals of feminism, Linton had been part of Eliot's and Lewes's inner circle but was later rebuffed by them. Taking out her animosity on both of them in her anonymous review of Eliot's *Life and Letters* for the *Temple Bar* (April 1885), she at once insinuates that Eliot had an unfair advantage in her literary partnership with Lewes and that she was unoriginal in the first place: "The chameleon-like quality of her mind, and her marvellous [sic] power of assimilation, made George Eliot able to profit by outside advantages as those of a more original and independent nature cannot" (Broomfield and Mitchell 366). The same year that this review appeared, Linton published *The Autobiography of Christopher Kirkland* under her own name, its transgendered narrative based on her own life – and confusing not only the general reading public but her intimate friends as well. Her posthumous autobiography, *My Literary Life* (1899), makes an unfortunate return to another extended attack on Eliot. If Linton has only an implied presence in impressions of other writers in this volume, that presence continues to reflect her vindictive attitude toward Eliot and begrudging admiration of her work. Perhaps Linton herself is best served through Beatrice Harraden's forewarning in the preface to *My Literary Life*: "It is to be regretted also that she is not here herself to tone down some of her more pungent remarks and criticisms, hastily thrown off in bitter moments such as come to us all."[14]

Writing her own life

Toward the end of the nineteenth century, some Victorian women still struggled with reservations about the egotism of writing their own life story and the conflict between public disclosure and private reticence. The life-writing of Anne Thackeray Ritchie (1837–1919) illustrates a composite strategy for addressing those concerns. As the daughter of a famous novelist, she became an intimate of many famous writers and artists, both during his lifetime and after his death in 1863. Striking a balance between personal memory and biographical research, she published a series of articles in *Harper's New Monthly Magazine* that she later assembled in a single volume, *Records of Tennyson, Ruskin, and Robert and Elizabeth Browning* (1892). Within another two years, she collected essays that she had published in *Macmillan's Magazine* as *Chapters from Some Memoirs* (1894), featuring (among others) Charlotte Brontë and Fanny Kemble. Along with writing her own fiction, Ritchie had already expressed an interest in several of her "foremothers," first publishing *Madame de Sévigné* (1881) for Oliphant's series of foreign classics and then a string of essays for the *Cornhill Magazine* on Jane Austen, Anna Laetitia Barbauld, Maria Edgeworth, and Amelia Opie, which she collected as *A Book of Sibyls* (1883), dedicated to Oliphant. As a sometime biographer, memoirist, and proto-feminist, Ritchie was primed to find a solution to her father's proscription against writing his biography. So began her major undertaking – writing biographical introductions to Thackeray's canon (1898–99; 1910–11), which constituted a piecemeal biography of her father and her own reflected autobiography, highlighting her apprenticeship as a writer during the years she served as his amanuensis and primary confidante.

Annie Wood Besant (1847–1933) took another incremental approach to writing her life story, although she was more direct than Ritchie in confronting controversial issues and ultimately in reconsidering her life trajectory. Legally separated from her clergyman husband, Besant had joined the ranks of the National Secular Society and was well on her way to becoming a socialist when she launched publication of her monthly journal *Our Corner* in 1883. The following year, she announced to her readership, "I have resolved to pen a few brief autobiographical sketches, which may avail to satisfy friendly questioners, and to serve, in some measure, as defense against unfair attack."[15] A year and a half later, Besant had traced her "deconversion" to atheism, her court case for the right to circulate birth control literature, and the trial for custody of her daughter, at which point she collected and published her monthly installments into the single-volume *Autobiographical Sketches* (1885). Four years later, she converted to theosophy, becoming leader of its European and Indian branches within two more years. These changes caused Besant to review her life from its current perspective, prompting her in turn to engage in another act of self-writing, entitled *An Autobiography* (1893). This recast text is significant for how it reexamines rather than denies her early attraction to Christianity and the logic of her temporary solution in atheism, thereby recognizing the overall curve of her spiritual search for a dynamic synthesis of all religions that could advance the immediate social good and the idealistic goal of world peace.

The relatively self-assured autobiography of Frances Power Cobbe (1822–1904) marked a highpoint for professional women at the end of the Victorian era. Social reformer, anti-vivisectionist activist, suffragist, and all-around feminist journalist, Cobbe already exuded confidence in the straightforward announcement of her title, *Life of Frances Power Cobbe, by Herself* (1894). Yet as a savvy Victorian woman, Cobbe was still careful to counterbalance discussion of her campaigns for reform, such as arguing for a woman's right to earn a university degree, with deference to a woman's role, such as proffered in her series of lectures entitled *Duties of Women* (1881). Another way for her to qualify or tone down her personal accomplishments was to make them seem representative of those of other women: "I have tried to make [my autobiography] the true and complete history of a woman's existence *as seen from within*; a real LIFE, which he who reads it may take as representing fairly the joys, sorrows, and interests, the powers and limitations, of one of my sex and class in the era which is now drawing to a close."[16] As for her intention to provide an account "as seen from within," however, Cobbe falls short of twenty-first-century expectations of introspection, for she remains reticent about her private life and feelings, particularly by making only passing reference to her life companion, the sculptor Mary Lloyd. As a measure of how Cobbe's career in journalism was recognized for its potential to inspire other women to become journalists, her autobiography was widely reviewed and celebrated in the periodical press directed toward female readership, most notably the *Woman's Journal*, *Woman's Signal*, and the *Englishwoman's Review*.

Women's life-writing is still a relatively young field, but it has come a long way since Estelle Jelinek first drew attention to the subject in *The Tradition of Women's Autobiography: From Antiquity to the Present* (1986). Since that time, many out-of-print titles by Victorian life-writers have been uncovered and republished. Most significantly, Regenia Gagnier has promoted interest in working-class autobiographies, prompting publication of collections such as *Factory Lives: Four Nineteenth-Century Working-Class Autobiographies* (2007), which includes *Autobiography, Poems and Songs* (1867) by Ellen Johnston (1835–73), who published poetry under the moniker "the Factory Girl." Scholars have also unearthed previously unpublished life-writing and edited it for publication; a notable example is Edith Simcox's *Autobiography of a Shirtmaker*, completed in 1900 but not published until 1998. Other autobiographical accounts lie in manuscript in rare book and manuscript repositories; two such examples include the life of Emily Davies (1830–1921), co-founder of Girton College at Cambridge University, who prepared her life story for her nephew, and "Works and Days," the thirty-volume journal co-written by Katherine Harris Bradley (1846–1914) and her niece Edith Emma Cooper (1862–1913), who jointly published poetry and verse drama under the pseudonym "Michael Field."

The recovery process sometimes devolves into a rescue mission. One egregious case for Victorian women's life-writing involves the publication history of *The Autobiography and Letters of Mrs. M. O. W. Oliphant* (1899), "arranged and edited" by her friend Annie Coghill, who actually *re*-arranged the order of the entries, deleted or otherwise edited "sensitive" passages, and then added letters totaling double the length of the autobiography itself. Thanks to Elisabeth Jay, who discovered the manuscript of the autobiography among Oliphant's papers at the National Library of Scotland, the original text has been restored almost a century later and republished under the title *The Autobiography of Margaret Oliphant: The Complete Text* (1990). More archival detective work is called for, however, to dismantle what the editors of other life-writing have obscured. Toward the end of Mary Somerville's (1780–1872) life and after her death, the interventions of her friend Frances Power Cobbe, publisher John Murray, and daughter Martha Somerville did a disservice to this scientific author. Comparing the two extant manuscripts of her autobiography with the published version of *Personal Recollections from Early Life to Old Age* (1873) reveals how much they turned her into a proper Victorian lady by diminishing her professional and political accomplishments. Although Kathryn Neeley provides a detailed analysis of many of those changes in her biography of Somerville, the autobiographer deserves a new edition that recovers her original intentions. Twenty-first-century readers of Victorian life-writing unquestionably need to learn more about the publication history of the texts they read to get as close as possible to the lives they seek to encounter.

NOTES

1. Charlotte Elizabeth [Tonna], *Personal Recollections* (1841; New York: John S. Taylor, 1844), p. 11. Further reference to this edition will be given in the text.
2. For a comparative study of Tonna and Martineau, see Linda H. Peterson's chapter, "The Polemics of Piety: Charlotte Elizabeth Tonna's *Personal Recollections*, Harriet Martineau's *Autobiography*, and the Ideological Uses of Spiritual Autobiography," in *Traditions of Victorian Women's Autobiography: The Poetics and Politics of Life Writing* (Charlottesville: University Press of Virginia, 1999), pp. 43–79.
3. For all citations, see Harriet Martineau, *Autobiography*, ed. Linda H. Peterson (1877; Peterborough, ONT: Broadview Press, 2007). This edition includes Martineau's self-authored obituary (660–71) as well as Margaret Oliphant's review of *Autobiography* (673–705), to which further reference will be given in the text; it does not include the third volume of *Memorials* added by Maria Chapman.
4. The heading of this section is a quotation from Virginia Woolf to Ethel Smyth, September 17, 1938, *Letters of Virginia Woolf*, 6 vols., ed. Nigel Nicholson and Joanne Trautmann (London: Hogarth Press, 1980), vol. 6, p. 272. The quotation serves as the subtitle of the sixth volume of *Letters*.
5. Frances Anne Kemble, *Records of a Girlhood* (1878; New York: Cosimo Classics, 2007), p. 1. Further reference to this edition will be given in the text.
6. Sara Coleridge, *Memoir and Letters*, ed. Her Daughter [Edith Coleridge], 2 vols. (London: Henry S. King, 1883), vol. 1, p. 1. Further reference to this edition will be given in the text.
7. Elizabeth Gaskell, *The Life of Charlotte Brontë*, ed. Alan Shelston (1857; Harmondsworth: Penguin Books, 1975), p. 526.
8. For all citations to Oliphant's autobiography, see *The Autobiography of Margaret Oliphant: The Complete Text*, ed. Elisabeth Jay (Oxford: Oxford University Press, 1990), rather than the 1899 edition of *Autobiography and Letters*, ed. Annie Coghill (see the final paragraph of this chapter for further information about its publication history).
9. J. W. Cross, ed., *The Life of George Eliot as Related in Her Letters and Journals*, 3 vols. (London: W. Blackwood, 1885), vol. 3, p. 219. Further reference to this edition will be given in the text.
10. "Autobiographies," rpt. Andrea Broomfield and Sally Mitchell, eds., *Prose by Victorian Women: An Anthology* (New York: Garland Publishing, 1996), pp. 527–63; further reference to this edition will be given in the text.

Broomfield and Mitchell also reprint Linton's review of *The Life of George Eliot*, 366–76; references to this edition will be given later in the text.
11. [Margaret Oliphant], "The Life and Letters of George Eliot," *Edinburgh Review* 161 (April 1885), 515.
12. [Margaret Oliphant], "Mrs. Carlyle," *Contemporary Review* 43 (May 1883), 628.
13. [Margaret Oliphant], "The Ethics of Biography," *Contemporary Review* 44 (July 1883), 78.
14. Eliza Lynn Linton, *My Literary Life* (London: Hodder and Stroughton, 1899), p. 6.
15. Annie Besant, *Autobiographical Sketches*, ed. Carol Hanbery MacKay (1885; Peterborough, ONT: Broadview Press, 2009), p. 57.
16. Frances Power Cobbe, *The Life of Frances Power Cobbe by Herself*, 2 vols. (Boston: Houghton, Mifflin, 1894), vol. 1, p. iv. Emphasis in original.

12

TAMARA S. WAGNER

Travel writing

Victorian women traversed the globe in search of adventure, out of necessity, for health reasons, and to contribute to a growing market for publications on ethnography, geography, botany, or zoology. Many of them went out as the wives, sisters, or daughters of government officials, missionaries, military officers, and scientists; others prided themselves on traveling on their own. The figure of the eccentric female explorer became a Victorian icon of adventurous travel in and beyond an expanding empire. Some of the most intrepid female travelers, however, eschewed this association and instead carefully cultivated an image of preserved femininity in the uncharted spaces into which they ventured. Travel accounts by Victorian women not only reflected the limitations they indisputably faced as women but also their unique opportunities, as they encountered different aspects of the cultures in which they traveled. Their travel writing is therefore often informed by a greater awareness of and attention to the details of everyday living arrangements and domestic concerns. Partly because of their restricted access to scientific and political discourses, female travelers might place more value on personal observation of and contact with the daily lives of other peoples, especially women and children. In *Discourses of Difference*, Sara Mills has influentially speculated that Victorian woman travelers might therefore have had a greater degree of "interaction with members of other nations."[1] One possible result was a degree of identification that might even hint at an awareness of cultural relativity. Yet, women travelers also vehemently criticized what they saw, especially when they focused on the description of domestic manners rather than on political affairs, as signaled in the title of Frances Trollope's influential *Domestic Manners of the Americans* (1832). If many women capitalized on the very confines of their experience, other female travelers also highlighted the insights that were not available to men. Victorian women were able to enter female spaces such as the harem, zenana, or seraglio, and their descriptions of everyday life effectively rebutted the Orientalizing essentialism present in many of the accounts by their male contemporaries. They could go where no man had gone before.

Current critical scholarship on women's travel writing, however, warns against the dangers of an essentialist approach that does a disservice to the wide range of women's experience, attitudes, and writing styles. The 1970s feminist revival prompted vital rediscovery work in the area of women's writing, including their hitherto seldom-studied travel accounts, but the underlying focus on recovering proto-feminist, potentially transgressive material obscured the diversity of women's works. Much early feminist scholarship additionally "suffered from a tendency to see 'woman' as a unitary category" at the expense of broader cultural differences or historical contingencies.[2] In particular, the much-rehearsed truism "that the woman traveller was somehow in flight from something, seeking to escape" domestic confines has been exposed as a fallacy that might reinforce the danger of essentialism.[3] Another important caveat is that so-called feminine approaches or ways of writing can be found in travel accounts written by men. The anecdotal, personal, emotional, and subjective had been defining elements of British travelogues from the eighteenth century onward. As travel writing attained a more professional dimension because of its importance for scientific discovery, however, some female travelers might have continued to assume a particular pose to assert narrative authority. These travel writers felt the need to abide by expected formulae, even to be wary of demonstrating their training and knowledge. Conversely, women writers of adventurous travel deliberately presented themselves as lone explorers flaunting conventions and encountering the extraordinary. Susan Bassnett has gone so far as to suggest that their works should be considered as "self-conscious fictions," as "the persona who emerges from the pages is as much a character as a woman in the novel."[4] There were contradictory images of the Victorian lady-traveler, and these images continue to be redefined and differently deployed in the shifting discourses on women and travel.

The solitary lady-traveler: traveling women's changing self-representation

Perceptions of women, travel, and women's writing about travel changed radically in the course of the nineteenth century, and so did readers' expectations. In her 1908 biography of Isabella Bird Bishop (1831–1904), Anna Stoddard stressed a crucial difference between women who might have traveled into little-known territories while accompanying their husbands and Bird, who undertook most of her adventures without any companion at all. While a traveling wife was "protected by the presence of her husband against the most powerful of terrorizing influences, namely the solitude which magnifies perils and weakens resistance," Bird "nearly always conquered her territories alone ... she faced the wilderness almost singlehanded ... she observed and recorded without companionship."[5] Bird presented herself as an adventurous traveler who despised the beaten track, avoiding European communities in colonial or port cities. In *The Yangtze Valley and Beyond* (1899), she stressed how these enclaves were particularly unappealing to her:

> Those of my readers who have followed me through all or any of my eleven volumes of travels must be aware that my chief wish on arriving at a foreign settlement or treaty port in the East is to get out of it as soon as possible, and that I have not the remotest hankering after Anglo-Asiatic attractions.[6]

Although Bird was aware of how much her works' general popularity rested on her depiction of the extraordinary, including her self-representation as a lone lady-traveler caught up in wild adventures, she was also afraid of being charged with impropriety. She simultaneously worried about possible social censure following the publication of her descriptions of her encounters with the one-eyed outlaw Rocky Mountain Jim Nugent in *A Lady's Life in the Rocky Mountains* (1879) and about the potential lack of interest in her subsequent travel book *Unbeaten Tracks in Japan* (1880), a meticulously researched ethnographic tome. Fortunately, Bird remarked, the "critics have not scented out impropriety in the letters [that comprised her early travel books]. Travellers are privileged to do the most improper things with perfect propriety ... People will find my *Japan* flat and dull after *The Rocky Mountains*."[7] Signaling the underlying ambiguities in the self-representation of Victorian women travelers, what bordered on the improper might guarantee good sales figures. But Bird was wrong. Her book on Japan, in which she entered ethnographical discourses on the Indigenous Ainu, was widely acclaimed. It ensured her the help from the British government that she needed to enter Tibet and sensitive areas in China on her next expedition. Still, as Lorraine Sterry has convincingly argued, the less sensational nature of Bird's later works might account for their relative neglect in feminist studies, in pointed contrast to Bird's titillating Rocky Mountains adventures or her ride astride (rather than sidesaddle) on a horse in Hawaii.[8]

If Bird was self-conscious about her image, despite the fact that this image sold so well, equally adventurous female travelers defined themselves against this image of the eccentric explorer. Traversing the same terrain as Bird in Southeast Asia, for example, Anna Forbes instead emphasized her feminine and domestic nature. She detailed nature as exotically beautiful despite what she termed "the admixture of scientific matter" that arose from her familiarity with her husband's profession as a naturalist: "You must remember that I am only a small and very feminine woman, and no masculine female with top-boots and a fowling-piece."[9] In *Unbeaten Tracks in Islands of the Far East: Experiences of a Naturalist's Wife in the 1880s* (1887), an account of Forbes's visit to "a New Guinean village [as] their first white female visitor," she seamlessly continues the description of domestic interiors and women's clothing that dominates her depiction of colonial Batavia.[10] In focusing on the domestic and insisting that she was traveling as a naturalist's wife (as signaled in her book's subtitle), Forbes epitomizes a compromise that was sought after by the majority of Victorian women travelers.

The role of domesticity in the conceptualization of the Victorian woman traveler as a cultural icon was indeed nothing if not ambiguous, even paradoxical. In her 1845 article on "Lady Travellers," published in the *Quarterly Review*, Elizabeth Rigby (later Lady Eastlake) fascinatingly asserted that it was precisely a lady's domestic knowledge and practices that made her excel as an independent traveler: the "peculiar domestic nature of an Englishwoman's life which made her excel all others in the art of travelling [since] the four cardinal virtues of travelling—activity, punctuality, courage and independence—had already been developed at home, enabling her to achieve so much abroad." Yet, Rigby also proceeded to define one of the traveling woman's "greatest charms, as a describer of foreign scenes and manners [as] that very purposelessness resulting from the more desultory nature of her education ... a woman goes picking up materials much more indiscriminately, and where, as in travelling, little things are of great significance, frequently much more to the purpose."[11] An 1896 article on "Lady Travellers" in *Blackwood's Edinburgh Magazine* similarly lauded Englishwomen's endurance and courage as travelers and emphasised that this "travelling enthusiasm" did not clash with any "domestic duty." Thus, women travelers

> defied hurricanes, ship-wreck, Arctic cold and darkness and all the other dangers and discomforts of sea; and by land, fatigue, hunger and sickness, robbers and extortioners, wild beasts, scorpions and mosquitoes, heat and cold, filth and fever, besides the nameless terrors of savage races, on whose whims they could not count, and whose greed and ferocity shrank from no crime.[12]

Such praise of physical courage needed to be qualified by an assurance of these ladies' "gentleness," and of the adventures' compatibility with domesticity: "In no case had their travelling enthusiasm involved the sacrifice of obvious domestic duty; nor had it brought out any qualities inconsistent with the modesty, the grace, and the gentleness that must always be regarded as the fitting ornaments of the sex."[13] This insistence on the domestic presents perhaps the most persistent continuity in the reception of Victorian women travelers. There were, however, important shifts in the course of the century. These shifts in attitudes involved both the extent of women travelers' participation in scientific discourses and, most controversially perhaps, their role in imperial expansion.

To the empire and beyond: traveling women and colonialism

Victorian women traveled as never before, with new modes of transport making formerly remote places accessible. They covered a vast range of terrain, often as the first white women to enter "untrodden" spaces. Although their journeys were partly facilitated by and, in turn, contributed to empire building, they often reflected critically on colonial policies once they were faced with the realities of colonial life. A double bind was at work. In the British Empire, women were at once complicit in imperialist expansion, while their experience and writing frequently expressed an ambiguous relation to empire. Victorian women were, as Indira Ghose suggests in her study of colonial India, "colonized by gender, but colonizers by race."[14] Women's reactions to this double bind were notably diverse and also changed in the course of the century. When Lady Hester Stanhope (1776–1839) set out for Turkey and the Middle East in 1810, her adventures – which included sporting Turkish male attire – quickly became notorious. Traveling meant freedom of movement to her, but this freedom was largely facilitated by the fact that she was considered an eccentric foreigner and therefore not subject to local customs and conventions in the lands in which she traveled. At the other end of the spectrum, many women who went overseas as the wives of civil servants, military officers, or missionaries openly endorsed the imperial structures that made their travels possible and embraced the colonial enterprise of exporting "civilization."

There was a flourishing subgenre of books about India, chiefly written by those who lived and traveled in the role of wives, daughters, or sisters. Fanny Parkes (1794–1875), Emily Eden (1797–1869), and Mary Carpenter (1807–77) were astute observers of cultural mores, reflecting the contradictions of white women's position in the British colonies. Parkes, for example, lived in the Collector's House in Allahabad, India, as the wife of an East India Company official, yet she traveled independently in northern India and the Himalayas in search of native peoples, their customs, and religious practices. Although she incorporated Arabic and Persian words and mottos in her account, *Wanderings of a Pilgrim in Search of the Picturesque* (1850), and signed herself "a pilgrim" on its title page, Parkes was also inclined to assume the role of memsahib when it suited her needs – as in her address to the native sailors who manned her sailboat on a trip up the Jumna River to see the Taj Mahal. She includes this address as "The Mem Sahiba's Speech," terming it in a tongue-in-cheek fashion "this specimen of eloquence, literally translated from the Hindostanee in which it was spoken."[15] Subtitled *During Four-and-Twenty Years in the East, with Revelations of Life in the Zenana*, the book, moreover, promises a well-informed, detailed account of the everyday, as experienced over a lengthy period of time, and in particular insight into the zenana as an exotic space still shrouded in mystery. While reading Godfrey Charles Mundy's *Pen and Pencil Sketches, being the journal of a tour in India* (1832), Parkes remarks that his book seemed "a much more amusing journal than I can write. I have no tigers to kill, no hurdwar to visit; nor have I even seen the taj."[16] Yet not only did she embark on a detailed journey to the Taj Mahal, but she also knew she could offer very different insights beyond expected tales of tigers and war.

Female missionaries had arguably even better access to rarely presented aspects of the described countries, and yet their own positioning within empire building was also more ambiguous and paradoxical. While the wives of military officers or civil servants often engaged in philanthropic work that was chiefly orchestrated by missionary societies, missionaries at times relocated with their families or were accompanied by a female relative. Their sisters, daughters, or wives were actively involved in the missionary enterprise. This necessarily further complicated their own role as imperial agents and as potential critics of imperialist policies. Missionaries' role in empire building has in itself remained a particularly contested issue. Colonial projects could conveniently be couched in discourses on religious conversion, and yet "key troublemakers" among these missionaries worked against imperial institutions, often deliberately obstructing them.[17] Women, whether writing as observant short-term travelers or as part of an official missionary venture, were placed within a complicated dynamic and might have had to police their reports on missionary efforts in order not to compromise either the missionary societies or themselves.

Discourses on settler colonialism presented similar constraints for travel writers. The latter half of the century saw a rising interest in Britain's geographical antipodes, the new settler colonies in Australia and Aotearoa/ New Zealand. These emergent settler societies might be included as part of a world tour, as in Alice M. Frere's *The Antipodes and Round the World* (1866), but generally women's accounts of their visits to settlements contained detailed minutiae of daily domestic life, blurring the distinction between travel writing and emigration literature. Thus, Lady Mary Anne Barker turned her failed attempt to settle on a farm in New Zealand into a publishing success back in Britain. *Station Life in New Zealand* (1870) and its sequel *Station Amusements in New Zealand* (1873) traded on a growing demand for domestic descriptions of faraway places within the empire. Increasingly, there was also travel writing about London as the imperial metropole, tapping into a rapidly expanding market of colonial readers. This comprised journalistic pieces and manuals containing travel advice targeted specifically at white Australian and New Zealand women traveling "back home" to an England they primarily knew from books.[18] The travel account as advice literature or guidebook, however, formed only a minor strand in a diversifying genre.

While Victorian women traveled for a wide variety of reasons and turned their experience into markedly different forms of writing, several patterns emerge. Frances Trollope, Isabella Bird Bishop, and Mary Kingsley were all well-known figures who covered very different terrain, not only geographically but also socially, and in their writing styles and readerships. Trollope popularized a focus on the everyday, on domestic manners; Kingsley ventured into unbeaten tracks, geographically and scientifically; Bird influentially marketed the image of the adventurous women traveler as she actively sought out the most inaccessible spots. Their works provide insightful case studies that illustrate the genre's diversity and the changing cultural conception of the woman traveler at the time. The remainder of this discussion uses these illustrative cases as specific examples of the most important trends in nineteenth-century women's travel writing.

"Essentially a woman's book": Frances Trollope's *Domestic Manners*

The diary that subsequently formed the basis of Frances Trollope's *Domestic Manners of the Americans* (1832) had never been intended for publication. In 1827, Frances Trollope (1779–1863) took up Frances Wright's invitation to join a utopian community in Nashoba, Tennessee, where Trollope hoped one of her younger sons might find employment. Faced with a swampy, ramshackle settlement, but financially unable to return to England, she instead attempted to establish a bazaar for imported European goods in Cincinnati. This was a failure, too, but *Domestic Manners*, with its acerbic account of everyday life in the United States of America, financially made up for the unprofitable venture. Marketing her work as a travel book ensured that Trollope's experience was read in the tradition of nineteenth-century British travel writing on the renegade colony, and yet it falls into two distinct parts: the first half details personal, domestic experience; the second follows the more conventional tourist routes of the time, including a visit to Niagara

Falls. Trollope was thus an accidental traveler, but her book was to shape perceptions of women travelers and their writing.

As a British travel book criticizing America, *Domestic Manners* formed part of a general trend of books critical of the renegade colony that had become the United States of America. Basil Hall's *Travels in North America* (1829) has been seen as the "immediate catalyst in [Trollope's] literary inclination,"[19] although it chiefly provided the format in which she could couch her personal notes. Following the new trend of satirically presenting and analyzing American institutions and practices, Trollope's book consequently found a ready market, yet it also had a crucial impact on transatlantic relations as well as on women's travel writing. When her son Anthony later published his own travel accounts in *North America* (1862), he found it necessary to distinguish his work from his mother's and not merely because *Domestic Manners* had "created laughter on one side of the Atlantic, and soreness on the other."[20] More significantly, he saw his mother's work as "essentially a woman's book" in its interest in social arrangements.[21] In her first, ultimately discarded preface, Frances Trollope admitted that it might be considered "gossiping": "I greatly doubt if my book contains much valuable instruction," she admits. Yet the domestic details filled a gap in current knowledge about America:

> There is, in fact, so much in America that English ladies and gentlemen know nothing about; the people are so strangely like, and so strangely unlike us; the connection with us is so close, yet the disunion so entire; speaking the same language, yet having hardly a feeling in common, that I am clearly of opinion there is still much untold that is worth telling.[22]

Trollope was keenly aware that she was doing something new in focusing on the everyday instead of chiefly analyzing political agendas and institutions.

Domestic Manners was a popular sensation in 1830s Britain, although it was somewhat acerbically received in the United States. Hostile American reviewers harped on a pettiness that was considered intrinsic to her "mousing out" of domestic detail. The *American Monthly Review* concluded that it could not recommend their "countrymen [to] waste their money in purchasing the trash of a person, who has, according to her own showing, gone mousing about all the resorts of vulgarity for the materials of her abusive picture."[23] By contrast, British reviews stressed how "[i]n depicting the domestic life of the Philadelphian ladies, Mrs Trollope is on her best ground."[24] The *Quarterly Review* welcomed Trollope's approach, asserting, that "this is exactly the title-page we have long wished to see," precisely because there had been "enough of late years of the politics of the United States."[25] Trollope's attention to the everyday influenced Charles Dickens's

American Notes (1842) as well as Harriet Martineau's *Society in America* (1837) and *Retrospect of Western Travel* (1838). Although Martineau strove to refute many of Trollope's observations, their works share the same attention to the everyday. Thus, Martineau asserted how "the nursery, the boudoir, [and] the kitchen, are all excellent schools in which to learn the morals and manners of a people."[26] This emphasis on the domestic did not prevent their books from being taken seriously within political debates of the time. As Pamela Neville-Sington has shown, since the United States was regarded as a democratic experiment, every travel book "was received as if it were a 'party pamphlet.'"[27] The publication of *Domestic Manners* coincided with debates on reform in Victorian Britain and was read as a statement on possible change at home.

The memoir composed by Trollope's daughter-in-law reports that the critic Theodore Hook remarked that "the book is too clever to have been written by a woman," on which Mrs. Trollope commented: "Saucy, that!"[28] There was an underlying perception that women's travel accounts were, or ought to be, different from men's. Trollope's anecdotal diary traded on this expectation in its focus on the domestic and the everyday, yet her virulent exposure of how political and social attitudes determine personal, domestic behavior was at once astute, pointedly satirical at the expense of the Americans, and hence intensely popular in England. Trollope continued to publish travel writing, now purposefully touring various European countries. She likewise kept returning to her American material in her novels. Their reception is a good reminder of the overlapping political, social, and literary discourses of the time. Her Gothic tale *The Refugee in America* (1832) was reviewed together with William Gore Ouseley's nonfiction *Remarks on the Statistics and Political Institutions of the United States* (1832) since both books were "mainly occupied ... with the controversy respecting the comparative cost of government in America and England."[29] Regardless of their focus or style, writing on America fed into these debates, while Trollope's *Domestic Manners* influentially shaped expectations of women's travel writing. The most successful late-Victorian women travelers, in turn, strove to refute precisely these expectations.

Science and adventure: Isabella Bird and Mary Kingsley

Victorian Britain saw growing interest in unbeaten tracks about which little had then been written. Isabella Bird and Mary Kingsley (1862–1900) were to epitomize the solitary woman traveler who sought to leave civilization behind and write about these unknown places. With a self-deflation that was to become characteristic of her writing, Kingsley announced in her first book, *Travels in West Africa* (1897), that she had set out to "go puddling about obscure districts in West Africa after raw fetish and freshwater fish."[30] Kingsley was to sustain this self-ironic presentation of herself, a self-image that could verge on caricature. Bird, by contrast, deliberately moved away from her image as an eccentric lady-traveler in search of adventure to build on her growing reputation as a serious scientific writer. Both women actively participated in current ethnographical debates. Both cultivated double images of themselves as independent, daring explorers overseas and as conventional, domestic women when at home. Both capitalized on shifts in scientific discourses and in attitudes to traveling women. Both used an established link between scientific discovery and travel writing, and as science became increasingly professionalized toward the end of the century, their travel accounts – in association with the personal and subjective – provided an acceptable medium in which they (and other women writers) could present their scientific discoveries and speculations. As Victorian women juxtaposed personal observations and anecdotal material with new scientific data in their publications, they successfully negotiated the shifting demands of the book market as well as those of scientific communities.

Kingsley and Bird were both instrumental in creating what was to become the iconic image of the Victorian female traveler. Kingsley indeed played with this emerging image in a tongue-in-cheek manner. At one point in *Travels in West Africa* (1897), a book prompted by scientific interest, primarily in the classification of hitherto unknown fish species, she describes being stuck in a swamp surrounded by crocodiles, wondering why she had been "such a colossal ass as to come fooling about in mangrove swamps."[31] In another illustrative passage, describing her experience at the Ivory Coast, she showcases at once her sustained ironic style and the many contradictions that underlie her representations of Indigenous people, colonial power, and white traders. She stresses that she "speak[s] from experience," claiming practical knowledge as she identifies with colonial powers. Once, she tells, she had to supervise the transportation of ebony logs "to a bothering wretch of a river steamer that must needs come yelling along for cargo just then" because she just happened to be the only British subject available to handle the situation: "the superior sex being on its back with fever and sending its temperature up with worrying." This description is comically dismissive and deliberately so, while it further asserts an equality of white men and women as part of the same colonial power – an equality that is confirmed when the cargo ship's captain invites her for a drink as an "apologetic invitation" to make up for his damning comments earlier. Yet if Kingsley starts out by demonstrating how "the power of managing Kruboys is a great accomplishment," she depicts her bungling management with humor:

I saw as soon as I had embarked on the affair, from the Kruboys' manner, I was down the wrong path ... The situation was a trying one and the way the captain of the vessel kept dancing about his deck saying things in a foreign tongue, but quite comprehensible, was distracting; but I did not devote myself to giving him the information he asked for, as to what *particular* kind of idiot I was, because he was neither a mad doctor nor an ethnologist and had no right to the information.[32]

What emerges most prominently from this passage is the tone of self-mockery. Kingsley pokes fun at the entire situation and almost caricatures her own ignorance and incapability, and yet this passage reveals a sly assertion of authority. The reference to ethnography, meanwhile, is doubly satirical as it reverses the positions of the observer and observed so as to render the traveler herself the subject of ethnographic study, while the simultaneous hint at the "mad doctor" deflects possible accusations of eccentricity.

This deliberate self-deflation should not detract, however, from Kingsley's achievements as a knowledgeable naturalist and a serious collector, or from her involvement in colonial practices, including the management of native peoples in the ivory trade. Her identification with colonial powers gave her unprecedented opportunities as a female explorer, yet it also explains some of the contradictions in her criticism of cultural colonialism. Kingsley controversially accused missionaries of destroying Indigenous cultures. She showed a genuine interest in these cultures, even as her writing remained embedded in discourse on the management of the colonized.

Travels in West Africa was followed by the equally successful *West African Studies* (1899). Kingsley had three fish species named after her and inspired the formation of the Royal Africa Society. Her tongue-in-cheek complaints about being termed "Sir" or of embarrassments caused when a male explorer was expected as a result of linguistic misunderstandings, however, really express the freedoms that came with traveling into areas where other white women had not yet ventured.[33] Gender constraints were lifted because there simply were no expectations about how a white woman would behave or that she should be treated any differently from her male counterparts.

Bird harnessed the same freedom that came with being the only white woman on her travels. She had started traveling for her health when she was in her early twenties, after an operation on her spine. Her first travel account was the anonymously published *The Englishwoman in America* (1856). Subsequently, she always felt better while traveling, a disjunction that was instrumental in creating a persistent duality at least in her public image. On Bird's death in 1904, the *Edinburgh Medical Journal* summed up this duality:

> When she took the stage as a pioneer and traveller she laughed at fatigue, she was indifferent to the terrors of danger, she was careless of what a day might bring forth in the matter of food; but, stepping from the boards into the wings of life, she immediately became the invalid, the timorous, the delicate, gentle-voiced woman that we associate with the Mrs Bishop of Edinburgh.[34]

Bird became one of the century's most widely traveled women. After making a name as an adventurous lady-traveler, she increasingly undertook specific ethnographic research and consciously sought to contribute to scientific discourses. In 1892, she became a fellow of the Royal Geographical Society. When she published *Among the Tibetans* (1894), the title page announced that the author was "Isabella Bird Bishop, F.R.G.S.; Hon. Fellow of the Royal Scottish Geographical Society, etc.," with the initials lending prestige "in the same way they would to a man's work," as Lila Marz Harper has pointedly put it.[35] Bird's self-representation here signals a significant shift from the insistence that she was a lady even when climbing the Rocky Mountains. By increasingly venturing into areas on which few British travelers had reported, moreover, she at once participated in scientific discourses and made herself useful to the British government, providing potentially important political information on different parts of Asia. After the publication of *Korea and Her Neighbours* (1897), Bird was viewed as an "authority on the political situation in the Far East."[36]

Travel writing by Victorian women continued to be informed by a balancing act between changing conventions and expectations: between an expected attention to domestic detail and a thirst for adventure, between acknowledged participation in scientific discourses and a struggle for professional recognition, between eccentricity as a popular author and the need to preserve a conventional facade. Women's accounts of their travels involved a broad range of perspectives that could accommodate vastly different attitudes to this balancing act as well as to empire, race, and colonization at large. Women's initial motivation, their reasons for traveling, and their preconceptions necessarily shaped the mode of their descriptions. As a result, female travel writers responded differently to limitations and harnessed the different opportunities available to them. They might capitalize on changing popular images or expectations in the market place, even as they helped form them or strove to reshape them.

NOTES

1. Sara Mills, *Discourses of Difference: An Analysis of Women's Travel Writing and Colonialism* (London: Routledge, 1991), p. 99.
2. Susan Bassnett, "Travel Writing and Gender," *The Cambridge Companion to Travel Writing*, ed. Peter Hulme and Tim Youngs (Cambridge: Cambridge University Press, 2002), pp. 225–41, p. 227.
3. Ibid., pp. 226–27. Thus, travel for health has commonly been termed a common excuse that might promise a release from the stifling conventions at home. Compare Lorraine Sterry, *Victorian Women Travellers in Meiji Japan: Discovering A "New" Land* (Folkestone: Global Oriental Ltd, 2009), p. 2.
4. Bassnett, "Travel Writing," p. 234.
5. Anna Stoddard, *The Life of Isabella Bird (Mrs Bishop)* (London: John Murray, 1908), p. v.
6. Isabella Bird (Mrs. Bishop), *The Yangtze Valley and Beyond* (London: John Murray, 1899; rpt., Boston: Beacon Press, 1987), p. 15.
7. Stoddard, *Life of Isabella Bird*, p. 101.
8. Sterry, *Victorian Women Travellers*, p. 239.
9. Anna Forbes, *Unbeaten Tracks in Islands of the Far East: Experiences of a Naturalist's Wife in the 1880s* (Oxford: Oxford University Press, 1987), p. 281.
10. Ibid., p. 123.
11. Elizabeth Rigby, "Lady Travellers," *Quarterly Review* (1845), pp. 99–100; http://digital.library.upenn.edu/women/eastlake/quarterly/travelers.html.
12. [W. G. Blaikie], "Lady Travellers," *Blackwood's Edinburgh Magazine* 160 (July 1896), 49.
13. Ibid., p. 66.
14. Indira Ghose, *Women Travellers in Colonial India: The Power of the Female Gaze* (Oxford: Oxford University Press, 1998), p. 5.
15. Fanny Parkes, *Wanderings of a Pilgrim in Search of the Picturesque* (London: Pelham Richardson, 1850), p. 334.
16. Ibid., p. 268.
17. Anna Johnston, "A Blister on the Imperial Antipodes: Lancelot Edward Threlkeld in Polynesia and Australia," in *Colonial Lives Across the British Empire: Imperial Careering in the Long Nineteenth Century*, ed. David Lambert and Alan Lester (Cambridge: Cambridge University Press, 2006), pp. 58–87, p. 58.
18. Angela Woollacott, *To Try Her Fortune in London: Australian Women, Colonialism, and Modernity* (Oxford: Oxford University Press, 2001), p. 49.
19. Helen Heineman, *Mrs. Trollope: The Triumphant Feminine in the Nineteenth Century* (Athens: Ohio University Press, 1979), p. 71.
20. Anthony Trollope, *North America* (London: Trollope Society, 2001), p. 2.
21. Ibid.
22. Qtd. in Heineman, *Mrs. Trollope*, pp. 79–80.
23. Rev. of Domestic Manners of the Americans, American Monthly Review by Mrs Trollope, rpt. in *American Criticism on Mrs Trollope's 'Domestic Manners of the Americans'* (London: O. Rich, 1833), p. 68 (pp. 65–68).
24. Rev. of Domestic Manners of the Americans by Mrs Trollope, *Quarterly Review* 93 (1832), p. 74 (pp. 39–80).

25. Ibid., pp. 39–40.
26. Harriet Martineau, *Society in America* (London: Saunders and Otley, 1837), vol.1, p. xiv.
27. Pamela Neville-Sington, "The Life and Adventures of a Clever Woman," in *Frances Trollope and the Novel of Social Change*, ed. Brenda Ayres (Westport: Greenwood, 2002), p. 15.
28. Frances Eleanor Trollope, *A Memoir of Frances Trollope* (London: Richard Bentley and Son, 1895), p. 155.
29. Rev. of "Remarks on the Statistics and Political Institutions of the United States, with some Observations on the Ecclesiastical System of America, her Sources of Revenue, &c. by William Gore Ouseley, ... and The Refugee in America: A Novel by Mrs Trollope," *Quarterly Review* 96 (1832), 508.
30. Mary Kingsley, *Travels in West Africa: Congo Francais, Corisco and Cameroons* (London: Macmillan, 1898), p. 8.
31. Ibid., p. 89.
32. Ibid., pp. 477–79. Emphasis in original.
33. Ibid., p. 502, discussed in Lila Marz Harper, *Solitary Travelers: Nineteenth-Century Women's Travel Narratives and the Scientific Vocation* (Madison, NJ: Fairleigh Dickinson University Press, 2001), p. 192.
34. Qtd. in Olive Checkland, *Isabella Bird and "A Woman's Right to Do what she can do Well"* (Aberdeen: Scottish Cultural Press, 1996), p. 177.
35. Harper, *Solitary Travelers*, p. 144.
36. Pat Barr, *A Curious Life for a Lady: The Story of Isabella Bird* (London: Macmillan, 1970), p. 334.

13

MARY ELLIS GIBSON
AND
JASON R. RUDY

Colonial and imperial writing

From verses written on shipboard to poetry published by prestigious London presses, from settler tales written to encourage emigration to autobiographical fiction depicting the often daunting realities of colonial life, British women's writing fully engaged with the nineteenth-century empire. In addressing a topic so global in scope, with parameters still very much under construction, our strategy is to provide an outline of genres written by women in the British Empire and then to focus on poetry published by women in Canada, India, Australia, and New Zealand, drawing parallels and outlining divergences among poetic practices in four quite different colonial settings.

We focus on gender and colonial poetic practices for three reasons. First, in the literature of empire, poetry remains understudied, though many writers considered it the most prestigious of genres at the time. Writing poetry allowed women to establish local and global relationships of literary sociality through newspaper and subscription publication, even in an environment in which they were patronized as poetesses. Moreover, little comparative work has treated Anglophone poetry in global contexts; our comparative approach suggests further work on colonial poetics as global cultural negotiation. Finally, we argue that formal constraints of writing verse in the nineteenth century created aesthetic pressures that magnified the contradictions and ideological impasses of empire. The poems of Emma Roberts and Mary Leslie in India, of Isabella Valancy Crawford in Canada, and of Eliza Hamilton Dunlop in Australia present cogent examples of this phenomenon.

We discuss writings of British women as they traveled or lived abroad and address differences as they emerged in the colonial scene between first- and second-generation writers and between what are commonly distinguished as extraction and settler colonies: that is, colonies the British governed for trade and profit versus colonies British people settled to extend and reproduce their ways of life. We argue that individual cases suggest the limitations of this common antithesis between two kinds of colonial settings. Emigration and settlement, while they appear to result from a straightforward decision, were not always so clearly demarcated from temporary residence or even travel. Many British subjects living in India did not anticipate returning to Britain, a condition common to second-generation residents; conversely, many emigrants to Canada or the antipodes imagined they might one day return "home." The identity of home itself is vexed by the dislocations attendant on travel, temporary residence, and emigration. We situate poetry – in which these dislocations are particularly salient – first in the context of other forms (travel writing, natural history, fiction) and then in the contexts of different literacies and access to print culture, returning to the dominant poetic modes employed by women in the empire.

Narrative and natural history in the colonies

Women's travel writings and narratives of settlement constitute some of the most notable texts of nineteenth-century Anglophone empire. In Canada, most important were the Strickland sisters – Catherine Parr Traill (1802–99) and Susanna Moodie (1803–85) – whose volumes *The Backwoods of Canada* (1836) and *Roughing It in the Bush* (1852), among others, formed many British readers' understandings of Canadian life. Properly speaking, these were narratives of settlement, but they bear significant similarities to Emma Roberts's travel writings in India in that they acquainted British audiences with the domestic manners of British colonialists. Moodie subjoined poems to her prose texts, cannily recirculating verse that had a previous life in periodicals. Joining them was Anna Jameson (1794–1860) who, after her husband Robert Jameson was made chief justice of Upper Canada, followed him to North America seeking a legal end to their unhappy union. Jameson traveled extensively and subsequently published *Winter Studies and Summer Rambles in Canada* (1838) in three thick volumes. Like the Strickland sisters, Emma Roberts (1794–1840) first published much of her writing in periodicals. *Scenes and Characteristics of Hindustan* (3 vols., 1835) was well received in India and Britain and led to further publishing opportunities. Roberts catered to human interest and to what we might call the sociology of emigration. Her *East India Voyager* (1839) collected facts and figures, from salaries in the Indian medical service to itemized packing lists. In *Up the Country* (1867), Emily Eden (1797–1869) reflected her position as sister of the governor-general. Unlike other writers mentioned here, Eden did not rely on writing to support herself, and she made no attempt to learn any Indian language, nor did she seem to have much sympathy with Indians.

Scholars have tended to read nineteenth-century Australian travel writing – by both women and men – as propaganda meant to encourage further emigration. Isabella Bird (1831–1904), for example, emphasizes in an 1877 series for the *Leisure Hour* that the "diffused comfort and prosperity" of Brighton, a suburb of Melbourne, "is very remarkable, and so is the success with which the homelife has been transplanted."[1] Several Australian and New Zealand women's novels of the period straddle the genres of fiction and travel writing. Catherine Helen Spence (1825–1910) opens *Clara Morison: A Tale of South Australia During the Gold Fever* (1854) with young Clara sent out from England to Adelaide because her family cannot afford to keep her. After a second chapter on the voyage out, the novel mixes travelogue and social realism in tracing Clara's adaptation to the harsh colonial environment. Charlotte Evans (1841–82) similarly opens *Over the Hills and Far Away* (1874) with eight chapters detailing the protagonist's departure from England and her voyage to and arrival in New Zealand, after which follows a novel largely in keeping with sensation fiction in its reliance on hidden pasts, a love triangle, and overall Gothic sensibility (Evans's London publisher, Samson Low, also published Wilkie Collins's sensation novels). Ada Cambridge (1844–1926), discussed later for her poetry, was among the more popular Australian women novelists in the later nineteenth century, with works such as *In Two Years' Time* (1879), which was first serialized in the *Australasian*, and *A Woman's Friendship* (1889). Her novels drew attention to experiences of colonial women, in particular the role marriage played in their lives. More politically compelling, in *The Broad Arrow* (1859) Caroline Leakey (1827–81) narrates the experiences of a female convict sent to Van Diemen's Land (Tasmania), eliciting sympathy for those unfairly transported to Australia and for the Indigenous Australians who suffered as a result of colonization (this novel predates Marcus Clarke's *For the Term of His Natural Life* [1874], the best-known Australian convict narrative). Most respected among the early women Australian novelists, Miles Franklin (1879–1954) published *My Brilliant Career* (1901), the narrative of a young woman growing up in rural Australia who eschews marriage to become a professional writer; Australia's top annual literary award is named in Franklin's honor.

Natural history and fiction were also significant forms throughout the colonies. The former ranged from Catherine Traill's *Canadian Wildflowers* (1865) to Maria Graham's *Journal of a Residence in India* (1812) to Mrs. James Cookson's *Flowers Drawn and Painted after Nature in India* (1835). Women were serious botanical investigators, though denied direct admission to scholarly circles or gainful employment. In Australia, Louisa Atkinson (1834–72) pioneered both natural history and fiction, including a long-running series of essays on native flora and fauna in the *Sydney Morning Herald* and the *Sydney Mail*; with the publication of *Gertrude, the Emigrant*

(1857), Atkinson became the first Australian-born woman to publish a novel there. In Canada, Sara Jeannette Duncan (1861–1922) combined journalism and travel writing, turning the tables on Eurocentric models at century's end by persuading her editors to finance a trip around the world. She married in India and wrote Anglo-Indian fiction; years later, she returned to Canada and produced her most famous novel *The Imperialist* (1904), set in small-town Ontario. Duncan created novels that reflected global imperial concerns, while the fiction of Rosanna Lephoron (1829–79) negotiated the divides between French and Anglo Canada.

Fiction published in India became dominant only after 1857, at about the same time it emerged in Australia and New Zealand, but women writers in English turned to fiction early, publishing in Indian periodicals or in London. The earliest novel written by a woman in India (or possibly after her departure), Phoebe Gibbes's *Hartly House, Calcutta* (London, 1789), contains sharp-eyed social analysis in addition to a conventional plot. Gibbes's volume was followed by Elizabeth Hamilton's *Translations of the Letters of a Hindoo Rajah* (1796) and Sydney Owenson's (Lady Morgan's) *The Missionary: An Indian Tale* (1811). Fiction took an evangelical turn in the work of Mary Martha Butt Sherwood, including her neglected adult novel *George Desmond* (1821). Attaching poetry to fiction, Honoria Lawrence (1808–54) likely coauthored with her husband Henry or contributed heavily to *Adventures of an Officer in the Service of Ranjeet Singh* (1842). Even as Flora Annie Steel wrote numerous novels about India after two decades of living there (notably *On the Face of the Waters* [1896], about the uprising of 1857), Indian women writing in English also began to engage with fiction, notably Krupabai Satthianadhan (1862–94) in her autobiographical fiction *Saguna* (1896) and Toru Dutt, discussed later, who wrote both in English and in French.

Contexts for poetry: colonial literacies and romantic legacies

Writers of fiction and travel accounts often embedded poetry in their prose works as epigraphs or affective interludes, but poetry had social, cultural, and aesthetic salience of its own, with a cultural prestige that outweighed that of fiction through much of the century. For poetry, as for other genres, a colonial chronology enables comparison but minimizes differences, including differences in access to print culture. A colonial poetics drawing transnational comparisons necessarily must address what Patrick Williams, following Elleke Boehmer and Ernst Bloch, calls "simultaneous uncontemporaneities."[2] That is, we take the British Empire to have been a heterogeneous space – heterogeneous as to languages, temporalities, technologies of publishing, and notions of history. Metropolitan ideas of Romantic and Victorian literatures do not apply similarly in Britain and the colonies; although we organize our colonial comparisons by rough chronology, we do not wish to minimize the ways that imperial cultural practices were temporally heterogeneous. For example, a lively English-language periodical print culture developed earlier in India than in Australia with the consequence that English-language poets in India, though they sought validation in the metropole, had ample opportunity by the 1820s to publish and even to engage in internecine quarrels, allusions, and ripostes (not until the 1850s would Australia have anything comparable, and in New Zealand not until a decade later). Even Canada came somewhat later to an analogous print culture, when belletristic writing found an ongoing periodical home (and a paying one) in the *Literary Garland* (1838–51).

Access to and varieties of literacy also varied considerably across the empire. English-language poets writing in India emerged in the context of eighteenth-century Orientalism, which recognized and grappled with highly literate elite cultures; women poets were fully conscious that such traditions were both masculine and elite and that male poets operated in conjunction with both elite and popular oral cultures. Women poets in India, particularly second-generation poets such as Mary Carshore, took advantage of their access to oral culture to translate songs and airs. Toru Dutt's narrative poems similarly owe as much to oral Bengali culture as to her study of Sanskrit.[3] While Orientalist poetics in India were early on practiced by men trained in classical languages (Latin, Greek, Persian, Sanskrit), Anglo and Indian women had little access to European classical languages and still less to Asian classical languages, the exceptions being Toru Dutt and Sarojini Naidu. For women such as Mary Leslie (1834–circa 1903) and Emma Roberts, the high rate of illiteracy among Indian woman was a key issue, one they tended to treat directly in their prose rather than in poetry.

English-language poetry provided social and intellectual networks for women, particularly via newspapers and literary annuals. The 1830s saw the publication of annuals in Calcutta deliberately designed to compete with those published in London and Edinburgh, though one Indian proprietor looking toward a British audience felt obliged to defend the "Indianness" of the verse and prose he chose to publish.[4] The contributors to *The Bengal Annual*, in this respect, shared the dilemma of colonial poets generally, that success in Britain often proved illusory even as fear of metropolitan failure shaped the contents and forms of poetry. Canadian poets were under a similar obligation to appear Canadian and to adopt the tropes and themes associated with the "bush" or rural Canadian life, at first satisfying the demands of London editors and later asserting Canadian nationalism.

Australian and New Zealand periodicals reprinted British poetry (Felicia Hemans circulated widely), but the reverse cannot be said. The *Athenaeum*, for example, summarily dismissed Caroline Leakey's *Lyra Australis* along with other Australian poetry: "The Australian muse has not yet learnt to sing."[5] Nonetheless, an increasingly vibrant poetic scene was emerging in both Australia and New Zealand, supported by literacy rates in Melbourne, for example, higher than those of London itself.[6]

Even before arriving in the colonies, British emigrants published poetry (along with short works of fiction) in newspapers aboard ships, often parodically rewriting canonical British and American poems.[7] Maria Jane Jewsbury (1800–33) composed a series of poetic "Oceanides" en route to India in 1832–33; all twelve sections were published in the *Athenaeum*. The journey out and the marked distance from Britain were foundational to colonial writing. Thus, in India, New Zealand, and Australia, poets addressed what Daniel Coleman has described as characteristic of Canadian poets – distance from and belatedness with respect to the metropole.[8] Distance and belatedness, however, were on the whole experienced differently by men and women, for women poets even in Britain were considered belated (i.e., derivative) and distant (i.e., concerned with matters peripheral to the central concerns of culture).

In all the colonial spaces addressed here, we find what Jane Stafford locates in 1840s New Zealand poetry: "settlers did not read or write solely of encounters with the new place." As in Britain, settlers in Canada, Australia, New Zealand, and India inhabited spaces "of introspection, individual reflection and emotion," the purview of Romantic lyricism.[9] Exported to the colonies through British (and pirated U.S.) books and periodicals, Romantic lyricism participated simultaneously in the discourse of interiority common to Romantic lyrics and in the discourse of Anglo gentility. For women poets, as for their male counterparts such as H. L. V. Derozio (1809–31), debts to Hemans and Letitia Landon were particularly important. Sarah Herbert (1824–46), whose poems were published in Halifax, Nova Scotia, in 1857, for example, demonstrated her admiration for Hemans and expressed emotion through tropes of distance, whether from emigration, death at sea, or infant mortality. Still Herbert, of Irish descent, most explicitly praised Tom Moore and lamented the neglect of Ireland by its Anglo-Irish masters. This political subtext merely tinges Herbert's larger domestic and religious agenda – dominated by missionary zeal and temperance. Mary Seyers Carshore (1829–57), her contemporary in India, created a resolutely domestic poetry along similar lines of interiority and gentility, though it was subtly varied by appeals to female friendship. Like Herbert, Carshore invoked her Irish ancestry, but indirectly. In "Lines to a Withered

Shamrock," Carshore ascribed longing for the old country to her father – his nostalgia for an unseen place the poet herself cannot share. Carshore was also the most explicit of all Indian English-language poets in her praise of Landon, whom she memorialized as a fellow colonial in "The Ivied Harp."

A different rhetorical space, endorsing and critiquing Romantic lyricism, was occupied earlier by Ann Cuthbert Knight (1788–1860), whose unjustly neglected *A Year in Canada and Other Poems* (1816) begins with a Wordsworthian evocation of those Canadian "scenes that once could charm—now haply viewed no more!"[10] Knight writes in sophisticated Spenserian stanzas that offer a female intellectual antithesis to Byron's *Childe Harold*. In the title poem, Wordsworth and Childe Harold go to Canada in the spirit of the Scottish Enlightenment, as Knight defends Reason, Freedom, and Justice. Describing the season and the particular beauties of Canada, she turns to sugaring:

> Slow o'er th' inserted wedge the sap distils,
> Beneath the cauldron crackling faggots glow,
> And thickn'ing o'er the fire the sugar boils,
>   Guiltless its sweets, for here no Libyan toils.
>
>   (*A Year in Canada*, 17)

Sympathetic alike to slaves and First Nations women, Knight, though tinged with the notion of the noble savage, extends genuine recognition to Indian women who "spurn / Your pity, should it blend th' ungenerous glance of scorn" (17). European farmers, however, provoke Knight's scorn, for they neglect "improvement," depleting the land's fertility. Knight remakes Wordsworthian tropes and Byronic verse forms in a new critical idiom.

The Australian poet Fidelia Hill (1794–1854) channels both Wordsworth's landscape and Hemans's domestic affections in lyrics composed after arriving in the fledgling town of Adelaide in 1836 and published in *Poems and Recollections of the Past* (1840). Hill was both the first European woman to set foot in the South Australian colony and the first woman to publish a volume of poetry on the Australian continent. In "Adelaide," Hill imagines a vibrant future city, projecting architecture, commerce, and pleasure on the town of mud and tents she encounters. A second poem composed three years later, "Recollections," suggests that Hill's optimism faded:

> Yes, South Australia! three years have elapsed
> Of dreary banishment, since I became
> In thee a sojourner; nor can I choose
> But sometimes think on thee; and tho' thou art
> A fertile source of unavailing woe,
> Thou does awaken deepest interest still.[11]

Like Wordsworth's "Tintern Abbey," which clearly inspired the opening of "Recollections," Hill's poem looks back on a period of years and considers how the poet has matured. No more the naïve optimist anticipating a new version of London in the antipodes, Hill still wants to imagine Adelaide as a potential home; her final stanza privileges the domestic comforts of a loving home: "Here may I dwell, and by experience prove, / That tents with love, yield more substantial bliss / Than Palaces without it, can bestow."[12]

Like Knight in Canada, the Australian Eliza Hamilton Dunlop (1796–1880) marshaled Romantic tropes to elicit sympathy for Indigenous women and children, specifically those killed during the 1838 Myall Creek massacre. The Irish-born Dunlop arrived in Australia only four months before the tragic event, a mass killing of unarmed Indigenous men, women, and children. Her poem "The Aboriginal Mother" was published in the *Australian* later that year, borrowing stylistically from Hemans's "Indian Woman's Death Song" and Lydia Sigourney's "The Cherokee Mother" to generate sympathy: "Oh! hush then—hush my baby," the mother implores, trying to quiet her child and evade the violent colonialists.[13] Dunlop's poem was controversial in its sympathy for Indigenous Australians and its critique of British settlers. Similar modes of sympathy for Indigenous peoples appear in women's poetry across the century. Looking ahead to the turn of the twentieth century, New Zealand poet Dora Wilcox embraces the Romantic trope of the dying Indian to eulogize the Maori who once inhabited the Onawe peninsula outside Christchurch: "Gone is the Atua, and the hillsides lonely, / The warriors dead; / No sight, no sound! the weird wailing only / Of gull instead."[14]

In English India, the more politically compromised Emma Roberts likewise drew on the models of the British Romantic lyric. Roberts was at once indebted to the model of Letitia Landon and, in turn, contributed to Landon's critical success, both as her posthumous memoirist and as the probable source for notes attached to Landon's poems in *Fisher's Drawing-Room Scrapbook*. As the first woman journalist in India, Roberts piloted many of her paratextual techniques in the *Oriental Observer and Literary Gazette* (circa January-June 1831), but her book of poems *Oriental Scenes, Sketches and Tales* (1832; first edn. 1830), first published in India, represents an equally complex negotiation of Romantic interiority. Roberts creates paratexts via lengthy footnotes, in the manner of Orientalist poetics, with special indebtedness to H. L. V. Derozio, to whom she dedicated her poems. Her long poem, "The Rajah's Obsequies," takes up the radical strain of Romantic poetics, combining expression of feeling with political analysis of the place of women in India. Her notes and prefaces anticipate the explanatory footnotes attached to Landon's subsequent poems on Indian subjects.

Like Landon, Roberts furthers the trope of the poetess who expresses feeling, but she too construes this expression through an often ironic agenda.

Thus, Romantic lyricism was transmuted in the colonies in significant ways, and sometimes such transmission returned on its origins with an ironic vengeance. Unlike Sarah Herbert's poems, most of which dwell happily within tropes of domestic gentility in the wake of Hemans, the verses of Roberts and Knight, along with those of Dunlop and Wilcox in the antipodes, retain a topical and critical edge. Roberts indeed struggles with the form of the first person (implicitly male) Romantic speaker in a poem such as "Stanzas Written in a Pavilion of the Rambaugh." As the speaker concludes, the conflicting topoi of nostalgic recollection and present exoticism are a "wreck":

> But all is foreign—'mid the dazzling glare,
>   The pensive gazer would rejoice to see
> The gorgeous pageant melt away in air,
>   While on its wrecks arose the old oak tree.
> The soft green sward with daisies spangled o'er
> . . . . . .
>   The humblest village of his native land.[15]

The instabilities in Roberts's poems, like those of her fellow poets, are as much political as poetical. As they engage with landscape, each of these poets confronts details of the colonial tableau – the sugar bush in spring for Knight or "night on the Ganges" or Muslim tombs for Roberts. Colonial poets were expected to purvey foreign scenes to metropolitan audiences in a way analogous to the expectation some years later that "native" women poets would be themselves the exotic or foreign.

Nature, domesticity, and nation building

In addition to the poetics of Romantic interiority, women poets captured day-to-day challenges of colonial life and contributed to discourses of nationalism, the one often implying the other as they construed nature, domesticity, and nation as ideologically parallel. Susanna Moodie's writings foreground with stark realism challenges of life in an undeveloped frontier. "Oh! Can You Leave Your Native Land?" – subtitled "A Canadian Song" – was first published in 1833, in the *Canadian Literary Magazine*, and later reprinted in *Roughing It in the Bush*. Moodie acknowledges that

> Amid the shades of forests dark,
> Our loved isle [England] will appear
> An Eden, whose delicious bloom
> Will make the wild more drear.[16]

Canada will remain a difficult space; immigration is expulsion from an Edenic England. Moodie aims to discourage Canadian emigration by British "of the higher class [who are] perfectly unsuited ... for contending with the stern realities of emigrant life" (11). Colonial life challenges even the strong of heart, and Moodie especially disdains the "Canada mania" that sent scores of zealots to Canadian shores wholly unequipped to deal with the life they encountered. Like Fidelia Hill, then, Moodie foregrounds the realities of colonial life, balancing optimism with accounts of difficulty.

Caroline Leakey, who in 1847 traveled to Tasmania, represents a second wave of women emigrants: those who arrived in colonies already established. Leakey stayed in Tasmania until 1853 and was ill for much of the time; returning to England, she published *Lyra Australis: or Attempts to Sing in a Strange Land* (1854). In "Pale Oleander of the South," Leakey frames her experience by way of the oleander flower, a poisonous plant common to Europe and Australia. Like the oleander, women, too, are "scattered o'er" the world.[17] The Tasmanian oleander reminds Leakey of an oleander from her youth in England and of a young girl whom she watched die: "So bright a thing was not for earth .... she dropp'd, / In all her beauty, to the earth" (88). Tasmania's "Sweet Oleander!" thus inspires a series of associations, "Threading the mazy past" from the weak flower to the place of women the world over to memories of a dead friend. This experience resembles the process Paul Carter describes whereby Australian colonists worked to classify unknown flora according to established botanical systems, thus making the strange into the familiar.[18] The oleander "of the South" is at once local and universal; it stands as a lynchpin for Leakey's digressive thoughts: her wandering meditation between European and colonial experiences.

As the challenges of the frontier subsided, we find in colonial women poets a rise in nationalist sentiment: enthusiasm for building Canada and Australia as nations (New Zealand was less focused on nationalist concerns, as suggested by its comparative belatedness in self-governance). Isabella Valancy Crawford (1850–87) emigrated from Ireland to Canada as a young girl. Her poems in Toronto newspapers and journals, mostly in the 1880s, as well as her 1884 long poem *Malcolm's Katie* – a foundational work of Canadian literature – anticipate a future Canada earned from the labors of working men rather than from the wealth of the mother country; the poem valorizes the "iron tracks across the prairie lands" and "mills to crush the quartz of wealthy hills" that will build the Canadian nation.[19] Crawford's enthusiastic connection between the North American forests and the emerging Canadian nation was anticipated by Susanna Moodie, whom Crawford knew as a young woman. Moodie's *Roughing It* concludes with "The Maple-Tree. A Canadian Song": "Hurrah! for the sturdy maple-tree! / Long may its green branch wave; / In native strength sublime and free, / Meet emblem for the brave" (332). Like Crawford, Moodie sees Canada as a space for "the poor, industrious working man [for whom] it presents many advantages" (Moodie 330), whereas those of higher class, and less accustomed to work, ought never to have come. The sturdy maple offers a fit metaphor for the strong emigrant who will succeed on Canadian shores: as Crawford's hero Max puts it, "I do truly think that Eden bloom'd / Deep in the heart of tall, green maple groves" (Crawford 86). Nonetheless, Crawford lends such sensuous immediacy to nature that the destruction of the forest, though Edenic for Max, is ambiguous for the poem as a whole. As in the poems of Rosanna Leprohon (1829–79), the conquest of nature in *Malcolm's Katie* evokes its antithetical subtext. Unlike Crawford, Leprohon often represents environmental ambivalence through the dying Indian; moreover, as the wife of a French Canadian physician and a pious Catholic, in representing Canada as nation she shared with the East Indian poet Sarojini Naidu a mission to bridge cultural and political divides.

Whereas Canadian confederation was established in 1867, Australia did not become an independent federation until 1901, and New Zealand in 1907. Women writers in Australia took an active role in building national sentiment. New Zealand granted women voting rights in 1893, Australia in 1902; full voting rights for women throughout Canada were not achieved until 1940. The 1890s were considered a golden age of Australian literature, when the "spirit of democracy" inspired writers to embrace Australia as both geographic space and political ideal. The democratic ideals that resulted in federation were connected to women's suffrage, and we see the intersection of these movements in the work of Louisa Lawson (1848–1920) and Dame Mary Gilmore (1865–1962). Born in New South Wales, Lawson in 1888 founded *The Dawn: A Journal for Australian Women*, a feminist monthly that ran through 1905. She writes in the introduction to a 1903 issue that she always "had in my mind's eye a big, capable, strong, virtuous woman as a representative of Australia." Later in the same issue, her poem "It is Enough" proclaims, "How did she fight? she fought well."[20]

Nationalism and exoticism in *fin-de-siècle* aestheticism

To this point, we have focused on British-born poets in the colonies or on poets of British parentage – though it is a mistake in studying colonial poetry to assume a unitary Britishness, for Scottish or Irish heritage made significant differences in poetic practice. A considerably more complex situation, however, obtained for poets of First Nations or East Indian descent. (Indigenous Australian and Maori writers were not similarly absorbed into the Anglo publishing world during the nineteenth century.)

Several of the most powerful poets we consider brought a quite different sense of nation and identity to their art. E. Pauline Johnson (1861–1913), Toru Dutt (1856–77), and Sarojini Naidu (1879–1949) were published in the aesthetic milieu of *fin-de-siècle* London. All three poets appeared in textual forms that emphasized their femininity, their youth, and their exoticism. All were expected to embody ethnic authenticity, both in their persons (or the recollection of their person in the case of Dutt) and in their poems. When the mixed-race Native American and Anglo poet E. Pauline Johnson published *The White Wampum* (1895) with John Lane, the English publisher of limited Bodley Head editions, Lane selected poems that emphasized First Nations topics. This early in her career Johnson had only written a dozen such poems, seven of which Lane placed at the beginning of the volume. Lane's title page unites Johnson's English and First Nation names with "an elegant art nouveau frame illustration whose authenticity is as specious" as the costume Johnson assumed for her public performances (Figure 3).[21] *The White Wampum* figured in metropolitan culture much the same way as did Dutt's *Ancient Ballads and Legends of Hindustan* (1882) and Naidu's three early volumes of poetry, two of which were brought out by Lane (William Heinemann published her earliest volume in 1905). All five volumes establish the essential Indianness (whether East Indian or First Nations) of their authors through frontispieces, title page art, or prefaces (Figure 4). In short, these poets from the colonies were marketed as exotic and authentic others, whose appeal was judged on the basis of assimilable difference.

All three poets nonetheless exceeded this exotic framing; in fact, Johnson and Naidu are comparable in that both were willing to resist conventions that denied to women poets explicit expression of physical passion. Naidu's early poem "Indian Dancers," first published in Arthur Symons's magazine *The Savoy*, codes passion by claiming a figure celebrated and condemned in earlier English-language poetry in India. Naidu's dancers "bewitch the voluptuous watches of night."[22] Johnson's "Shadow River," "Nocturne," and "The Idlers" present the poet taking physical charge – piloting her lover in her canoe – or claiming a connection to landscape at once erotic and languorous. In "The Idlers," the speaker and her lover have "lost the homeward blowing wind" and found instead

> With easy unreserve,
> Across the gunwale's curve,
> Your arm superb is lying, brown and bare;
> . . . . .
> (I kiss the very wind that glows about your tumbled hair).
> (Johnson, *Collected Poems*, 61)

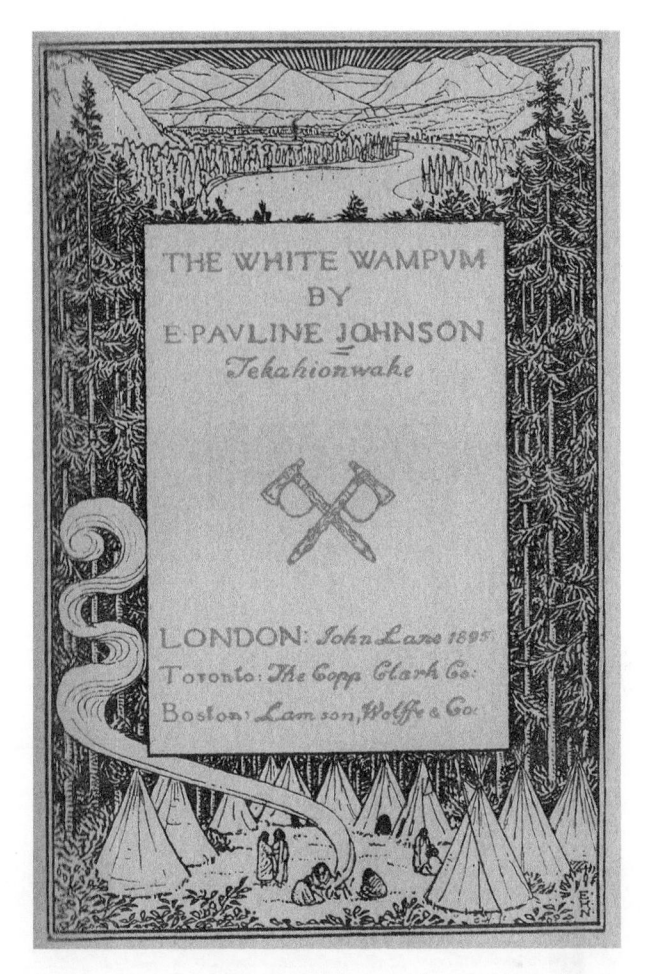

Figure 3. Title page, *The White Wampum*, by E. Pauline Johnson (London: John Lane, 1895).

Yet in "Bass Lake (Muskoka)," nature itself pulses with the power of poetry, and the poet comments indirectly on the culture of exoticism and the "littleness" of social life and art in the Anglo world. The poet/camper among the cedars

> spurns the so-called culture that refines
> Field blossoms to exotics—sweeter is
> The fragrance of those mighty forest pines,
> The littleness of language seems the flower,
> The firs are silence, grandeur, soul and power.
> (Johnson, *Collected Poems*, 47)

Figure 4. Frontispiece, Sarojini Naidu, *The Bird of Time: Songs of Life, Death & the Spring* (London: William Heinemann; New York: John Lane, 1912).

Northern waters, the heron, the loon – these are the land of poetry in "Bass Lake." In India, Naidu could claim nature in a similar way but evoked various traditional tropes of Persian and Urdu poetry, bulbuls and roses, in a paradoxical *fin-de-siècle* aesthetic owing much to her residence in London as a very young woman. Like Johnson, she argued for a poetry that exceeded social "littleness," but within the contexts of Indian nationalism. She came to enact a poetics that owed less to the natural world than Johnson's and much more to an idealized – and deliberate – conflation of various traditional tropes and voices. Having grown up in cosmopolitan circles associated with the court of the Muslim nizam of Hyderabad, Naidu transmuted her late nineteenth-century aesthetic into a political poetry whose subtext was national unity beyond communal differences.

Like Naidu and Johnson, Dutt developed a poetics of late Romanticism. Though posthumously exoticized by British publishers in the same way that Johnson and Naidu were, Dutt engaged in a cosmopolitan negotiation of cultures in a somewhat different way. Unlike Johnson, who literally assembled a costume of native dress and performed her work on stage, Dutt created a texture of literary allusion in her original poetry and triangulated the dominance of British tradition through her translations of contemporary French poetry. In the poetry of Toru Dutt, Wordsworth and Tennyson and even Barrett Browning were matched, if not eclipsed, by Victor Hugo and Lamartine. Nevertheless, the lotus for Dutt held the same central place as the maple tree for Moodie and the field blossoms celebrated by Johnson. Her sonnet "The Lotus" replays the old contest of the flowers, but rather than choose between the lily and the rose (which her source William Cowper associates with the "British fair"), Dutt puts forward the lotus as combining the virtues of both white and red.[23] The British fair, for her, is nothing compared to the virtues of the lotus, including its traditional Indian meaning, purity arising from mud. Just as Johnson defends her own bicultural version of Canadian poetry representing "majesty that lies so far beyond / The pale of culture," so Dutt defends both the lotus and her more famous casuarina tree as sources of comfort, inspiration, poetry (Johnson, *Collected Poems*, 46; Dutt, *Ancient Ballads*, 136). Perhaps she and Johnson are subtly deconstructing the exoticized racism they both encountered. But for Dutt, not wilderness but cultivation marks the superiority of a cosmopolitan poetics. The lotus growing in the tanks in Indian gardens and the casuarina tree evidence a cosmopolitan civilization, one that takes in multiple influences to develop its own intrinsic value.

Toward a transnational comparative poetics: further directions

We have argued that poetry figured in multiple forms of colonial writing, embedded in travel and settler narratives and providing epigraphs to novels. As genres and tropes moved from Britain to the colonies, women poets worked in contexts that presupposed their insignificance and afforded them less access than men to various forms of literacy. Nonetheless, education in modern or classical languages and access to print represented relative privilege and provided women such as Susanna Moodie and Emma Roberts a measure of economic independence.

To compare Toru Dutt and Pauline Johnson, Isabella Valancy Crawford and Emma Roberts, Susanna Moodie and Caroline Leakey is to suggest ways that a comparative poetics of empire allows us to move beyond nationalist constructions of literary canons in English. Such comparisons participate in the vibrant conversations developing in transatlantic and transnational studies and in scholarship organized around cosmopolitanism. They suggest instances as well of networks connecting literary practices along multiple routes of colonial exchange, from newspaper verse to *fin-de-siècle* aestheticism, and offer the prospect of comparative eco-criticism, along with other emerging methodological approaches.

NOTES

1. Isabella L. Bird, "Australia Felix: Impressions of Victoria," *Leisure Hour* (February 10, 1877), 88.
2. Patrick Williams, "'Simultaneous Uncontemporaneities': Theorising Modernism and Empire," in *Modernism and Empire*, ed. Howard J. Booth and Nigel Rigby (Manchester: Manchester University Press, 2000), pp. 13–38.
3. Meenakshi Mukherjee, *The Perishable Empire: Essays on Indian Writing in English* (New Delhi: Oxford University Press, 2000), p. 97.
4. David Lester Richardson, ed., *Bengal Annual* (Calcutta, 1833, 1834).
5. Rev. of *Morbida; or, Passion Past, and other Poems*, *Athenaeum* No. 1377 (March 18, 1854), p. 334.
6. Geoffrey Serle, *The Golden Age: A History of the Colony of Victoria 1851–1861* (Carlton: Melbourne UP, 1977), p. 371.
7. See Jason R. Rudy, "Floating Worlds: Émigré Poetry and British Culture," *ELH: English Literary History* 81 (Spring 2014), 325–50.
8. Daniel Coleman, *White Civility: The Literary Project of English Canada* (Toronto: University of Toronto Press, 2008), p. 16.
9. Jane Stafford, "'No cloud to hide their dear resplendencies': The Uses of Poetry in 1840s New Zealand," *Journal of New Zealand Literature* 28 (2010), 27.
10. Ann Cuthbert Knight, *A Year in Canada, and Other Poems* (Edinburgh: Doig and Stirling, 1816), p. 3. Online, *Early Canadiana*, http://eco.canadiana.ca/view/oocihm.38215/5?r=0&s=1, accessed July 31, 2014.
11. Fidelia Hill, *Poems and Recollections of the Past* (Sydney: T. Trood 1840), p. 64.
12. Ibid., p. 66.
13. Eliza Hamilton Dunlop, "The Aboriginal Mother," *Australian* 5 (December 13, 1838), 4.
14. Dora Wilcox, "Onawe," *Verses from Maoriland* (London: George Allen, 1905), p. 2.
15. Emma Roberts, *Oriental Scenes, Sketches and Tales* (London: Edward Bull, 1832), p. 111.
16. Susanna Moodie, *Roughing It in the Bush* (New York: Norton, 2007), p. 23.

17. Caroline W. Leakey, *Lyra Australis; or, Attempts to Sing in a Strange Land* (London: Bickers and Bush, 1854), p. 85.
18. See Paul Carter, *The Road to Botany Bay* (New York: Knopf, 1988).
19. Isabella Valancy Crawford, *Old Spookses' Pass, Malcolm's Katie, and Other Poems* (Toronto: J. Bain, 1884), p. 52.
20. Louisa Lawson, "To My Countrywomen" and "It is Enough: The House is Come," *The Dawn* 15 (February 1, 1903), 5, 16. Online, *Trove*, http://trove.nla.gov.au/ndp/del/page/7618029.
21. Carole Gerson and Veronica Strong-Boag, eds., *E Pauline Johson Tekahionwake: Collected Poems and Selected Prose* (Toronto: University of Toronto Press, 2002), p. xxi.
22. Sarojini Naidu, *The Golden Threshold* (London: William Heinemann, 1905), p. 71.
23. Toru Dutt, *Ancient Ballads and Legends of Hindustan* (London: Kegan, Paul, Trench, 1882), p. 136.

14

DEBORAH A. LOGAN

History writing

The phrase "Victorian women historians" seems a contradiction in terms. For the Victorians, history was defined by strict notions of gender and genre, a primary tenet being that the recording of history was reserved for those formally educated and trained in archival research and scholarly methodology. Thus, English historians were typically white, socioeconomically privileged males, educated in prestigious public schools and venerable universities, their professional training rounded off by an extended European Grand Tour and an official appointment. The histories they wrote emphasized the actions of men: military exploits, imperial conquests, political machinations, scientific achievements, and technological innovations. Although what they recorded was presented as irrefutable fact treated with the strictest objectivity, modern scholarship has exposed the bias inherent in such a rarified equation; those histories have come to be regarded as representations and replications of a narrowly defined world view with one correct perspective, and that is their own.

Such a tradition precludes the very idea of women historians. Through the late nineteenth century, females were categorically excluded from higher education; depending on familial attitudes toward girls' education and associated economic considerations, relatively few attended primary schools and most were, if educated at all, informally homeschooled. The influence and impact of sociocultural attitudes toward female education should not be underestimated: of the examples offered here, one notable thread linking women historians is a connection with philosophical radicalism. Utilitarian ideology, associated with middle-class prosperity, religious dissent, and sociopolitical reform, fostered a liberalism that promoted and facilitated female education, however informally or haphazardly that was pursued. It is no random coincidence that the city of Norwich, with its strong Unitarian presence and core of philosophical radicals, produced the prominent writers Lucy Aikin, Elizabeth Rigby, Anna Jameson, and Harriet Martineau, all within a span of two decades. Later in the century, just as girls were beginning to benefit from the national education system and make tentative advances into higher education, traditional academics' urge to establish and defend their disciplinary turf intensified; the resulting marginalization of women from scholarly writing served to both discount the palpable evidence of their work and prevent their participation as intellectual equals. Seeming to welcome women historians into the fraternal fold, one reviewer wrote: "We should like to have a discreet lady's opinion... [about] points on which a male historian, who sees everything by the light of Acts of Parliament, cannot be so good a judge as a British matron"; however, her opinions of famous men are emphatically not welcome: "The biography of a prominent man in any age of English history is part of the history of England, and the history of England is a subject a great deal too important and a great deal too difficult to be left to the mercy of half-learned ladies."[1]

Whereas previously it has been fashionable to dismiss Victorian women's intellectual contributions as trivial gossip, unoriginal popularization, or "auxiliary usefulness" to men's endeavors,[2] challenges to disciplinary parameters have enabled scholars to recuperate the work and redeem the reputations of these writers, and to restore the prolific evidence of their accomplishments to its rightful place in intellectual history. The issue concerns both gender and genre; the notion that history can only mean national history (wars, conquests, reigns, politics) leads to the inevitable conclusion that women cannot write history because it involves a realm beyond the domestic sphere, one that does not concern them and that they are not equipped to address. While it is true that few women wrote national history in the conventional sense – Catharine Macaulay (eighteenth century) and Harriet Martineau (nineteenth century) being two exceptions – it is also true that the alternative histories women wrote account for a much broader sociocultural realm than is addressed by national histories. Alternative or complementary histories expand the discipline's parameters by including travel memoirs, biographies, and studies of arts and crafts. Even when these authors ostensibly uphold (or fail to contest) oppressive Victorian gender ideology, their history writing is based on the premise that the separate spheres' division of labor constructs a false dichotomy, and that the public realm concerns women just as surely as the domestic realm shapes the lives of men. A nation's history comprises far more than the interests of privileged and powerful white men, and its narrative is enriched by the fuller picture, enabling the historical record more comprehensively to reflect notions of truth and accuracy.

Social expectations – enforced by religious and political institutions – most certainly confined women to domestic realms, physically and intellectually, and many women historians endeavored to meet both domestic and professional requirements. The prefix "Mrs." functioned as a sort of pseudonym, a precise gender marker denoting social respectability even while asserting professionalism, as with Margaret Oliphant and Elizabeth Gaskell. Countering the claim that hers was a masculine intellect, Harriet Martineau repeatedly emphasized her "thoroughly womanish love of needle-work."[3] Elizabeth Strickland rejected the social aspects of literary fame and published anonymously – effectually sealing her legacy as the silent partner of the more vivacious Agnes – indicating a reluctance to put herself forward professionally, which only an unwomanly woman would do. While the examples here do not adopt masculine or gender-neutral pseudonyms, they do reflect concerns about avoiding the charges of unwomanliness often presented in lieu of critical analysis of their work.

Negotiating the separate spheres ideology is further evidenced by women's literary apprenticeships for nonfiction historical writing, which almost uniformly involved creative writing (poetry and fiction) and children's literature, both viewed as proper genres for females. Some women's training in research methodology involved secretarial service to a male scholar, producing a fair manuscript copy for a male relative or spouse, or translating and editing; in the event of a scholar's death, the amanuensis sometimes completed the work (as with Alice Green) or wrote his biography (Lucy Aikin, Elizabeth Rigby), an achievement that permitted them entry into the literary marketplace. Periodicals writing offered a rigorous (and more lucrative) apprenticeship, often leading to opportunities for literary development through a wide range of topics. Such assignments as obituaries and book reviews required primary research, critical insight, and intellectual vigor; with no little irony, Martineau termed herself the maid-of-all-work for *Daily News*, while Oliphant served as the "general utility woman" for *Blackwood's Magazine*; as self-supporting authors, neither was opposed to such exploitation (*ODNB*).[4]

Travel writing was another staple of women's apprenticeships, travel being regarded as central to one's cultural development. Using travel as an opportunity for extended study, some women produced more enduring sociocultural commentary than the anecdotal memoirs expected of females. Traveling to the great art museums and private collections throughout Europe was itself the "archival" preparation underpinning women's art criticism and histories, although few single women had the economic means for such traveling and the social connections it required. Primary sources, such as manuscripts in the British Museum and other public libraries, were marginally accessible, while state papers in Public Record Offices were typically denied to women, even those supplied with endorsements from influential people. To the extent that women authors had to confront restrictive gender expectations, they were creative in devising ways to transcend the limitations thwarting their professional development.

Late-Victorian intellectual values emphasized pure, unadulterated facts, objectively reported from an unbiased, nonpartisan perspective that constitutes historical *truth*. The masculine professionalization of history as a rarefied scholarly discipline cast Victorian women historians as unprofessional, amateur, and intellectually shallow; often, their writing had a purpose beyond facts – the conveying of moral lessons and useful instruction, the core pillars of Victorian utilitarianism. Harriet Martineau viewed the study of past history as essential for understanding present circumstances so as to intelligently and purposefully shape the future. Children's writer Elizabeth Penrose presented historical figures as instructive vehicles for conveying moral lessons. Biographers Hannah Lawrance and Margaret Oliphant contextualized their subjects' accomplishments in terms of sociocultural significance – not simply reporting the fact of a private action but articulating its public consequence. Ironically, the very concept of history-with-a-purpose challenges the objectivity embraced by modern historiography, for all historians, male or female, write with an agenda.

Just as any authentic national history of nineteenth-century Britain must address royalty and aristocracy, politics and wars, as well as social reforms and the moral regeneration of industrial society, it must also account for progress in the arts and crafts, academics and sciences, and for the achievements of influential people, women and men, living and dead. With instincts sharpened by their own socio-intellectual marginalization, Victorian women historians perceived the historical relevance of topics considered subsidiary to authentic history; with informal educations, limited resources, and self-styled apprenticeships, they established the foundation for modern feminist historiography, through their scholarly industry quietly helping to resolve the "woman question" that so perplexed Victorian men.

National history

Harriet Martineau (1802–76) represents the only example of a Victorian woman historian whose history can be called *national*, in that it is a comprehensive study of contemporary British history and thus of immediate interest. She wrote both in the traditional mode (royal, military, political history) and in the innovative modern mode (socioeconomic reform, industrialization, urbanization), thus effectually bridging old and new and national and subsidiary categories of history. Tutored by her siblings and with only two years of formal schooling, Martineau had an education that was informal but topical. Resources included books and, perhaps more important, periodicals, which were eagerly anticipated, read and discussed, and circulated among friends and family for further discussion. Intellectual endeavors were familial and communal, and reading aloud was central to the social fabric; but her increasing deafness also facilitated private studies, including literature and languages. A disciplined scholar, Martineau accomplished hours of study before breakfast every day, preparing herself to assume the role of governess to the nation, her utilitarian aim in all literary undertakings being to share her insights to benefit the greater good.

Martineau's literary apprenticeship included poetry, hymns, periodicals essays (notably, in the influential, intellectually rigorous *Monthly Repository*), religious analyses, and fiction. Her first critical success, *Illustrations of Political Economy* (1832–34), established her career; subsequent writing includes novels, travelogues, domestic management handbooks, and works in sociology, biography, political economy, journalism, and history. Martineau distinguished herself in virtually every literary undertaking, particularly nonfiction, and this can be attributed to her innate sense of historical practice. In all her writing, she employed a historical model that sought to reveal continuity between past events, present circumstances, and future eventualities. While not all her history writing qualifies as national, everything she wrote was filtered through the distinctly historical lenses of her "author spectacles."[5]

For example, she wrote several series of didactic fiction tales on topics such as industrialization, political economy, taxation, poor laws, and game laws, each carefully researched according to historical methodology – true also of her prodigious periodicals writing, which displayed a broad range of expertise. Her best-known cultural commentary resulted from personal travel (America, 1834–36; Europe, 1839; Middle East, 1847–48; Ireland, 1852; Lake District, 1845–55). *The Martyr Age of the United States* (1839) traces the development of American abolitionism, while *A History of the American Compromises* (1856) aims to interpret for Europeans a bewildering array of congressional legislation concerning slavery. *Eastern Life, Present and Past* (1848) presents a comparative study of world religions in the context of the "practical, moral and intellectual life of antiquity."[6] Two books resulted from her investigative reporting as correspondent for *Daily News*: *Letters from Ireland* (1852), on post-famine socioeconomic reconstruction, and *Endowed Schools of Ireland* (1858), on the impact of religious factions and imperial policies on education reform. Less dramatically and closer to home, both *A Guide to Windermere* (1854) and *A Complete Guide to the English Lakes* (1855) record Lakeland history (past and current) and topography.

Martineau's only conventional biography, *The Hour and the Man* (1841), presents the life of the Haitian liberator Toussaint L'Ouverture embellished as a "historical romance." The many memoirs, character studies, and obituaries she produced for *Daily News* (1852–66) were gathered into *Biographical Sketches* (1869), organized according to literary, scientific, professional, social, political, and royal categories. In the preface, she asserts the material is unedited, so as to remain "true to my own [original] impressions" of the "distinguished dead" of the time;[7] this is consistent with her resistance to revising, which she claimed compromised the content's original accuracy at the expense of style. Insofar as her fiction reads like history and her history reads like fiction, Martineau's signature hybridity explores the natural links between biography and autobiography, journalism and history, literature and social sciences – links less obvious to modern intellects trained in strict disciplinary distinctions.

Martineau's exemplary national history is *A History of the Thirty Years' Peace 1816–46* (1849–50). She added an introduction covering the Peninsular War (1800–15) and a sequel (Irish famine through Crimean War, 1847–54); the complete work was published in America under the title *A History of England from the Commencement of the XIXth century to the Crimean War* (1864). As the record of a crucial half century marked by British imperialism and industrialization, the work emphasizes applied political economy and practical philanthropy, factors particularly relevant to the study of industrialized society. Martineau's career was launched during the First Reform Bill and sustained by its long-lived sociopolitical consequences; her investigation of the impact, benefits, and repercussions of industrialization, particularly the "great ... labour question," reflects an era shaped by "solicitude for the well-being of the people," one wherein "the war of opinion" supplants "feats of arms."[8]

Other contemporary commentary notes the emphasis on human endeavor, best seen through her biographical sketches of influential people of the time; she has particular "merit as a portrait-painter," and her biographies are "picturesque in nature, admirable in character, and impressive in the course of events."[9] Memorials of royalty and aristocrats and the exploits of military men are complemented by the accomplishments of scholars and inventors, performers and creative artists, reformers and craftspeople. The *History* is further distinguished by the contemporaneity of its sources, including the *Annual Register*, *British Almanac*, quarterly reviews and other periodicals, memoirs, Hansard's *Parliamentary Papers*, and Tooke's *History of Prices*.

Critical responses to the *History* highlight its emphasis on sociopolitical and economic reforms. As a woman who, though a taxpayer, had no political voice and had rejected a government pension, Martineau avoided the sort of political partisanship she believed compromised literary integrity; in her view, receiving a pension would have precluded the writing of her history, with its bold critiques of national foibles. In 1833, when she called for a revolution in literature to address "the graver themes [of] the present condition of society," she praised "the birth of political principle, a magnificent subject" whose scenery is "moral" and whose characters are "noble heroes" facilitating "the downfall of bad institutions."[10] These values find fullest expression in her *History*, in which quality of life – advances in liberal and practical arts, equitable economics and education, politics guided by morals and manners – constitutes the palpable measure of modern social principles.

Other national histories include *A History of British Rule in India* (1857) and *Suggestions for the Future Rule of India* (1858), both examining the circumstances resulting in the 1857 Sepoy uprising with a view toward instituting corrective policies. Particularly relevant to a half century of "peace" riddled with military conflicts and territorial aggrandizement is *England and her Soldiers* (1859), which dramatizes the sobering history of preventable, non-combat-related deaths in the military and outlines the basic sanitary reforms needed to avoid such tragedies. For Martineau, the purpose of history is utilitarian: to clarify the present by learning from the past and to anticipate, intelligently and purposefully, the relevance of both to the future.

Complementing the Victorian focus on usefulness, Martineau's *History* records contemporary events and acknowledges the network of influential people on whose expertise she drew, thus lending further insight and authenticity to its account. She also understood that no history is definitive and that all historical narratives require periodic clarification and emendation by those writing retrospectively: "Much is not new: but in writing history one cannot help that. One can only tell it freshly."[11] Martineau initiates a uniquely Victorian contribution to historiography, articulating a modern philosophy of history based on interpreting human experience in the context of social affairs. Praised during her life as "the most complete English historian," by the end of the century Martineau was ignored by the discipline to which she had contributed so much, her only major national history having been published not in England, of which she was critical, but in America, for which she was hopeful.[12]

Alternative histories

While no other Victorian woman historian wrote a sustained, broadly conceived national narrative comparable to Martineau's, many produced biographies of individual figures and dynastic reigns, in both English and European contexts, which furthered the work of interpreting human social experience. Before the literary vogue associated with the popular Strickland sisters, earlier writers established the groundwork, set the tone, and sparked the fashion for royal biographies. Historian Lucy Aikin (1781–1864) is best known for her series of court memoirs: *Elizabeth I* (1818) and *James I* (1822), both of enduring influence, and *Charles I* (1833). She also wrote biographies of John Aikin (1824), Anna Barbauld (1825), and Joseph Addison (1843). Elizabeth Penrose ("Mrs. Markham") (1780–1837), whose popular children's text *A History of England* (1823) was reprinted throughout the century, also wrote *A History of France* (1828) and *Historical Conversations for Young Persons* (1836). Penrose's histories-with-a-purpose feature historical characters who model desirable and undesirable morals and manners. A third early example is Katharine Thomson (1797–1862), historical novelist and sociocultural historian who wrote short biographies for the Society for the Diffusion of Useful Knowledge during the 1820s; her subsequent biographies include Thomas Wolsey (1824), Walter Raleigh (1830), Sarah, Duchess of Marlborough (1839), Viscountess Sundon (1847), the Jacobites (1845–46), George Villiers (1860), and a historical novel about Anne Boleyn (1842).

Writing about female royalty, a topic that figured only marginally in national histories, proved a popular endeavor for women authors. The multi-talented Louisa Costello (1799–1870), a miniaturist, poet, and novelist, wrote *Eminent Englishwomen* (1844) and a biography of Anne, Duchess of Brittany (1855). Historian and journalist Hannah Lawrance (1795–1875) emphasized the generally disparaged domestic realm by highlighting women's less visible contributions to sociocultural developments (if not as creators and inventors, then as art patrons and philanthropists, for example). Lawrance is best known for *Historical Memoirs of the Queens of England* (1838–40), the timing of which preempted the Strickland sisters' first series (discussed later) and compelled them to rename their similar project. The subtitle of her 1843 *History of Woman in England – and Her Influence on Society and Literature* – indicates Lawrance's conviction that domestic interests generally and the contributions of women specifically are essential to national histories, and not to be marginalized or excluded. This crucial understanding and the impetus to do something about it accounts for the impulse to write history-with-a-purpose, seen in the abundance of women writers engaged in recuperating the reputations and intellectual legacies of women. Critics praised Lawrance's "literary excellence of no vulgar kind," noting that her painstaking archival work evidenced womanly "patience and industry" (*ODNB*). Far from being masculinized by intellectual pursuits, she is credited with producing work superior to that of established antiquaries. Elizabeth Barrett claimed Lawrance was intellectually superior to Agnes Strickland and deserved greater recognition in Victorian historiography.

But the superior public reputation belonged to Agnes Strickland (1796–1874), popularizer of historical biographies who welcomed "literary lionizing" and the social whirl it generated. Critics then and now suggest that perhaps the sheer volume of the Strickland sisters' collective works – quantity over quality – accounts for their enduring fame, a publishing phenomenon spanning four decades. As a solo author, Agnes wrote *Historical Tales* (1833), *Tales and Stories from History* (1836), *Victoria from Birth to Bridal* (1837), *English Princesses* (1850–59), *Letters of Mary, Queen of Scots* (1864), and *Stuart Princesses* (1872). But she is better known for the serial biographical histories written in collaboration with her sister Elizabeth (1794–1875) who, as editor of the *Court Journal*, originally conceived the idea. Together they produced *Lives of the Queens of England* (1840–48), *Lives of the Queens of Scotland* (1847–53), *Bachelor Kings of England* (1861), *Seven Bishops* (1866), and *Tudor Princesses* (1868). Jane Margaret, another Strickland sister, (1800–88), wrote *Rome, Republican and Regal* (1854) and a biography of her sister Agnes (1887); two others, Susanna Moodie (1803–85) and Catherine Parr Traill (1802–99), emigrated to Canada, where they wrote of their pioneering experiences and the early history of Canada.

While Agnes Strickland was a regular fixture of the London social season, Elizabeth preferred retirement; it is still unclear to what extent sociable Agnes represented the public face of their work and Elizabeth the marginally credited researcher and writer. Although as a result of their "amateur" status, access to primary material initially met with stiff resistance, they eventually succeeded in acquiring admittance to unpublished official records, letters, private documents, and state papers at libraries and other public and private archives throughout England and Europe. The preface to *Lives of the Queens of England* underscores the authors' historiographical standards: "Facts, not opinions should be the motto of every candid historian; and it is a sacred duty to assert nothing lightly or without good evidence of those who can no longer answer for themselves."[13]

Such scholarly care earns more ridicule than respect. Reviewer Margaret Oliphant offers up a vision of "Clio, the Muse of History: here she is—behold her," working away in the British Library, in poke-bonnet and India rubber boots, armed with an umbrella and fortified by sandwiches – "Agnes Strickland, who introduces to our households the reduced pretension of the historic muse."[14] Significantly, even while dismissed by some as amateurs and denigrated by others as popularizers without substance, attempts to plagiarize their work (by both men and women) necessitated constant vigilance. To her contemporaries, Agnes's prolific work on Mary, Queen of Scots, evidenced Tory sympathies; she was accused of lacking the "masculine gravity and impartiality" expected of a genuine historian (*ODNB*). Immensely popular, then summarily dismissed, the Stricklands suffered from modern commentary condemning the lack of "judicial temper and critical mind necessary for dealing in the right spirit with original authorities"; the writing was deemed "weak" and, despite its primary sources, constituted "trivial gossip and domestic details" (*ODNB*). Modern feminist scholars critique the sisters' conservatism, seen in their failure to question, examine, or challenge the gender ideology they report as a matter of history, which would surely require suspending the historian's objectivity: "Opinions have their date, and change with circumstances, but facts are immutable."[15] Popular and prolific, condemned for impartiality then and critiqued for impartiality now, the case of Agnes and Elizabeth Strickland continues to raise more questions than it resolves.

No such doubts complicate the professional legacy of Mary Ann Green (1818–95), historian and editor of state papers. Green's work includes *Letters of Royal and Illustrious Ladies* (1846); *Lives of the Princesses of England* (1849–55), particularly praised for the thoroughness of her archival research and historical method; and *Life and Letters of Henrietta Maria* (1857). Employed at the Public Record Office as a historian, Green helped the Stricklands gain access to archival materials; as a researcher, she was highly regarded by antiquaries, archivists, and librarians as well as by contemporary history writers. She was the first editor appointed to compile calendars of state papers (1854), a position she held for forty years.

Prolific Scottish author Margaret Oliphant (1828–97) wrote historical fiction (among her hundred novels and novellas), biography, and hundreds of periodical articles and tales. She produced two series of *Historical Sketches* organized around the reigns of George II (1869) and Queen Anne (1894), studies emphasizing certain representative character types to illustrate the values of the time: the poet, reformist, philosopher, painter, journalist, and humorist. In addition to *Child's History of Scotland* (1895), Oliphant wrote three histories of nineteenth-century literature: Romantic (1882), Victorian (1892), and women novelists (1895), as well as many in-depth, single-author studies for various periodicals. A singular contribution to Victorian historiography is her urban histories, based on her travels: *Makers of Florence* (1876), *Makers of Venice* (1887), *Royal Edinburgh* (1890), *Jerusalem* (1891), and *Makers of Modern Rome* (1895). Also unusual is her *Annals of a Publishing House* (1897), a biography of *Blackwood's* publishers drawn from primary sources and still regarded a valuable record of the firm, its journal, and the people who wrote for it. Oliphant herself published more than a hundred articles in *Blackwood's Magazine*.

Oliphant's biographical subjects include Edward Irving (1862), Francis of Assisi (1870), Count de Montalembert (1872), Queen Victoria (1880), John Tulloch (1888), Laurence Oliphant (1891), Thomas Chalmers (1893), and Jeanne d'Arc (1896). Her biographical writing characteristically fuses domestic details with public events, based on her conviction that "the narrowest domestic record widens our experience of human nature, which ... changes least from one generation to another" (*ODNB*). True of many authors who wrote both fiction and nonfiction, Oliphant's narrative style is picturesque, descriptive, and literary; her subjects are presented as characters with whom readers are encouraged to identify. This technique prompts scholar John Clarke to assert that she "cannot be taken seriously as a historian" since even she admits she is not "trained in the ways of knowing."[16] Indeed, none of the historians under consideration here were formally trained, yet they produced work of impressive depth, quality, and innovation. Given her prolific literary output, Oliphant's historical approach seems instinctual, like Martineau's: despite a literariness that is anathema to modern historians, she tempers dramatic events with domestic minutiae, privileging the defining characteristics of her subject's life over dry facts, sterile objectivity, and overdetermined analyses. In this way, she perpetuates Victorian women historians' general aim to incorporate the domestic realm and the women associated with it as a fundamental component of national history.

French royalty evoked lively interest among Victorian women historians. Julia Pardoe (1806–62) produced biographies of Louis XIV (1847), Francis I (1849), and Maria de Medici (1852). Martha Freer (1822–88) wrote French court histories and biographies of Marguerite of Angouleme (1854), Jeanne of Navarre (1855), Elizabeth de Valois (1857), Henry IV (1860–61), and Anne of Austria (1866). In her *Women in France* (1850), Julia Kavanagh (1824–77) asserts: "Though the historians of the period have never fully or willingly acknowledged its existence, their silence cannot efface that which has been" (*ODNB*), a theme further developed in *Women of Christianity* (1852) and *English Women of Letters* (1863). Ranging further afield was Elizabeth Cooper (fl. 1865–74), author of *Popular History of America* (1865), as well as biographies of Arabella Stuart (1866) and Thomas Wentworth (1874). Excepting her *History of England* (1840), Julia Corner (1798–1875) also wrote beyond national concerns, including histories of Europe (1837), France (1840), China (1853), and India (1854).

Despite male intellectuals' objections to women dabbling in theology, religious history and biography were other popular avenues. Along with biographies of St. Philip Neri (1859) and Thomas à Becket (1868), Anne Hope (1809–87) wrote *Acts of the Early Martyrs* (1855), *Conversion of the*

Teutonic Races (1872), *Franciscan Martyrs* (1878), and *First Divorce of Henry VIII* (1894). Grace Aguilar (1816–47) was a short-lived Anglo-Jewish author best known for *Women of Israel* (1845) and "History of the Jews in England" (1847). Catholic historian Mary Helen Allies (1852–1927) wrote *Life of Pius VII* (1875), *Three Catholic Reformers* (1878), *Letters of St. Augustine* (1890), and *History of the Church in England* (1892–97). Representing the Quakers, Irish social reformer Maria Webb (1804–73) wrote biographies of Merle D'Aubigne (1857), *Fells of Swarthmoor Hall* (1865), and *Penns and the Peningtons* (1867).

As British imperialism intensified throughout the nineteenth century, historians of colonial resistance posed a unique challenge to England's national narrative. Welsh historian Jane Williams (1806–85) wrote biographies of the Celtic scholar Thomas Price (1854–55) and Balaclava nurse Betsy Cadwaladyr (1857). Alternately referred to as Ysgafell (after her birthplace), Williams also wrote *The Literary Women of England* (1861) and *History of Wales* (1869). Irish historian and nationalist activist Alice Stopford Green (1847–1929) completed *The Conquest of England* (1884) begun by her husband before writing her own *Henry II* (1888) and *Town Life in the Fifteenth Century* (1894). Green posed a triple threat to an ostensibly seamless national narrative: an Irish Protestant, she moved to Ireland to support the Gaelic cultural renaissance and independence movements; an established historian, she wrote several volumes of Irish history from a nationalist perspective, purposefully designed to confront the existing pro-imperialist version; her extensive social circle included influential Irish intelligentsia as well as radical political activists.

Among this proliferation of intellectual women, three examples stand out in terms of critical recognition. Although her output was small, the short-lived Caroline Halsted (1803–48) exercised considerable impact on the discipline of history. She wrote biographies of Margaret Beaufort (1839) and Richard III (1844), the latter praised for its innovative use of primary materials to contest enduring claims regarding the legitimacy of Richard's political ascendancy. Elise Otte (1818–1903) was perhaps the most internationalized historian; an Anglo-Dane, she visited America and attended classes at Harvard University. Her *History of Scandinavia* (1874) and *Denmark and Iceland* (1881) were praised for their "considerable intellectual achievement," and she was termed "one of the most learned women of her time" (*ODNB*). The self-taught Kate Norgate (1853–1935) earned critical acclaim for her scholarship and narrative skill in *England under the Angevin Kings* (1887); she "represents a transition point in the professionalization of women historians," while the *Times* obituary terms her "the most learned woman historian of the pre-academic period" (*ODNB*).

Arts and crafts featured another field ripe for exploration by women historians. Termed the first woman art historian and critic, Anna Jameson (1794–1860) wrote *Early Italian Painters* (1845), *Sacred and Legendary Art* (1848), *Legends of the Monastic Orders* (1850), and *Legends of the Madonna* (1852); *History of our Lord*, her study of Christian iconography, was unfinished at her death and completed by Elizabeth Rigby (1864). Jameson also wrote biographical studies: *Celebrated Female Sovereigns* (1831), *Characteristics of Women* (1832), and *Women Celebrated by the Poets* (1837). As Harriet Martineau wrote in her obituary of Jameson, she was "a great benefit to her time from her zeal for her sex and for Art."[17] A half century later, John Cousin asserted: "Her works show knowledge and discrimination and ... still retain interest and value."[18]

Three art historians benefited from privileged socioeconomic circumstances (and the titles they held) that enabled them to travel widely and have access to public and private collections. Elizabeth Rigby, Lady Eastlake (1809–93), visited art galleries and museums throughout the world. Journalist and critic for the *Quarterly* and *Edinburgh* reviews, she also translated the *Handbook of the History of Painting* (1851) and *Treasures of Art in Great Britain* (1854) from the German. Maria, Lady Callcott (1785–1842), was best known for her children's text *Little Arthur's History of England* (1835; seventy editions). The same year, she published *Giotto's Chapel in Padua*, the first English analysis of a central figure in pre-Renaissance art, followed by *History of Painting* (1836). Emilia Frances, Lady Dilke (1840–1904), editor of *The Academy*, wrote biographies of Frederic Leighton (1882) and Claude Lorrain (1884). Other studies include *Renaissance of Art in France* (1879), *Art in the Modern State* (1888), and a series on eighteenth-century French art (1899–1902).

Although lacking an honorific title, Julia Cartwright Ady (1851–1924) was born into aristocratic connections, enabling her to travel and gain access to European art collections. Ady wrote for the *Portfolio*, *Magazine of Art*, and *Art Journal*; her biographies include studies of the Italian painters Mantegna and Francia (1881), and of Edward Burne-Jones (1894), G. F. Watts (1896), Sandro Botticelli (1903), Dorothy Sidney (1893), Henriette, Duchess of Orleans (1894), Isabella D'Este (1903), and Giovanni Castiglione (1908). Her work emphasized the cultural aspects of art and is credited with contributing to the establishment of modern Renaissance studies.

Shifting from high art to traditional crafts, many of which were threatened with extinction by industrial manufacturing, women's histories of activities typically associated exclusively with females signal a striking shift in the endeavor to value women's cultural contributions. Elizabeth Stone (1803–81) rejects the art and craft hierarchy in the very title of her *Art of*

Needlework (1840); she further posits the significance of clothing styles as something more than female vanity in *Chronicles of Fashion* (1845). Stone directly challenged the gendered dichotomy of intellectual and cultural pursuits, and the ambivalence and anxiety it engendered, as negotiated by Victorian women historians. Subversively, she presents needlework as a topic worthy of serious study, not merely an activity designed to mask intellectual women's masculine ambitions; indeed, she "praised the needle as an instrument of civilization, superior to the destructive sword" (*ODNB*). Fanny Bury Palliser (1805–78), who published criticism in *Art Journal* and *The Academy*, found more palpable expressions for her interest in needlework, extending her expertise into curatorial work. Her *History of Lace* (1865) was long regarded as the definitive, classic study of the craft; other monographs include *Historic Devices* (1870), *Mottoes for Monuments* (1872), *China Collector's Pocket Companion* (1874), and a translation of *History of Ceramic Art* (1878; from the French). Palliser's most enduring accomplishment is her work establishing the world-class lace collection at the Victoria and Albert Museum, for which she wrote *Descriptive Catalogue of the Lace and Embroidery in the South Kensington Museum* (1871). Demonstrating the persistence of gendered attitudes toward women's intellectual pursuits, Palliser's obituary notes that although her art criticism is "discriminating," she was still a "true woman" (*ODNB*). Nonetheless, the fact remains that distinct from those early women historians who were denied access to archives, Palliser – by official invitation – created one of her own.

To some, women historians' intellectual embrace of so feminine an endeavor as needlework epitomizes their subsidiary role as writers and makers of cultural history. To others, however, it indicates the persistence of their challenges to narrow and outmoded concepts of national historiography. If the pen is mightier than the sword, how much mightier is the needle? Standards of assessment have long been based on measuring the status of women to determine a culture's development as a civilized society. However excluded from a life of the mind, women of the era were not deceived by the spiritualized rhetoric designed to keep their intellects as shuttered as their domestic space; intelligence will out, as evidenced by the creative means they devised to shape apprenticeships that were as informal as their educations. Part of that creativity is expressed through gender – producing woman-centered work – as well as genre – incorporating biography, memoirs, and cultural studies as legitimate historical evidence. Woman, pronounced F. D. Maurice in 1850, "will never get a hearing till her knowledge of the past becomes more organized and methodical."[19] This they did, and evidence abounds that Victorian woman historian is not, after all, a contradiction in terms.

NOTES

1. "Mrs. Thomson's Life of George Villiers," *Saturday Review* 243.9 (June 23, 1860), 815–16.
2. Harriet Martineau, "An Autobiographical Memoir," *Daily News* (June 29, 1876); rpt. in Maria Weston Chapman, *Memorials of Harriet Martineau* (London: Smith, Elder, 1877), p. 468.
3. Harriet Martineau, *Autobiography*, 2 vols. (London: Smith, Elder, 1877), vol. 2, p. 414.
4. Quotations from the Dictionary in the *Oxford Dictionary of National Biography*, online at www.oxforddnb.com, will be cited in the text simply as ODNB.
5. Martineau, *Autobiography*, vol. 2, p. 3.
6. Chapman, *Memorials*, p. 254.
7. Harriet Martineau, "Preface," *Biographical Sketches* (London: Macmillan, 1869), p. vi.
8. "History of England," *British Quarterly Review* 11 (May 1850), 360.
9. "The History of England by Harriet Martineau," *New York Tribune* (March 16, 1877), p. 6.
10. Harriet Martineau, "The Achievements of the Genius of Scott," *Tait's Edinburgh Magazine* 2 (January 1833), 445–60.
11. *Collected Letters of Harriet Martineau*, 5 vols., ed. Deborah Logan (London: Pickering & Chatto, 2005), vol. 4, p. 104.
12. "Miss Martineau's *History of England*," *Christian Examiner* 81:2 (1866), 87.
13. Agnes Strickland, "Preface," *Lives of the Queens of England*, 12 vols. (London: Henry Colburn, 1841–1848), vol. 1, p. vii.
14. "Modern Light Literature – History," *Blackwood's Magazine* 78 (October 1855), 437.
15. Strickland, "Preface," *Queens*, vol. 12, p. xii.
16. John Stock Clarke, *Margaret Oliphant: Nonfictional Writings, A Bibliography* (Queensland, Australia: University of Queensland, 1997), p. 6.
17. Harriet Martineau, "Mrs. Jameson," *Daily News* (March 29, 1860), p. 2, cols. 2–3.
18. John Cousin, *A Short Biographical Dictionary of English Literature* (New York: Dutton, 1910), p. 210.
19. F. D. Maurice, *Letter to the Lord Bishop of London* (London: Parker, 1850), p. 43.

15

MARGARET BEETHAM

Periodical writing

The periodical press was the sea in which all Victorian writers, men and women, big fish and literary minnows, lived and worked. This condition of literary life was obvious to their contemporaries. Looking back from the 1890s, George Saintsbury, himself an energetic writer for periodicals who became a professor of English at Edinburgh University, rated "the development of periodical literature" as perhaps even more significant for the literary history of the nineteenth century than "the enormous popularization and multiplication of the novel."[1] However, this view is not obvious to twenty-first-century readers. We pick up a copy of Elizabeth Barrett Browning's poems or study the works of George Eliot, and it may surprise us to find that the poem we are reading first appeared in a magazine or that George Eliot honed her skills writing for and editing a periodical. Recent scholarship on the press and the digitizing of vast swathes of periodical literature previously available only in specialist libraries are together revolutionizing our understanding of Victorian women's writing. This involves not only reevaluating writers such as Marian Evans (George Eliot) but also bringing back into focus notable women who have been neglected because they worked across different genres and with different pseudonyms such as Rosamund Marriot, recently rediscovered by Linda K. Hughes, or Frances Power Cobbe, who, as Sally Mitchell argues in her biography, was neither novelist nor poet but excelled in other journalistic genres, especially "intellectual prose."[2]

The relationship of the terms "journalism" and "periodical" is contested, a difference rooted in that extraordinary expansion of the press that characterized the Victorian period. The encoding of journalism (associated with newspapers and weeklies) as ephemeral and trashy as against writing of lasting worth to be found in books and periodicals (publications that came out at least monthly) is part of our inheritance from Victorian thinkers. When in 1887 the critic Matthew Arnold (1822–88) famously complained that the "New Journalism" had many good qualities but was "feather-brained," he was expressing a recurring middle-class male anxiety about the press and its lack of seriousness.[3] Ironically, he was himself writing a piece of journalism but assumed that the serious monthly in which he wrote was quite distinct from penny weeklies such as *Titbits* (1881–1984) or the novelettes aimed at working-class women. Without denying that some writing is of more value than others, I argue that we should resist making this the divide. Thinking of serial publication as a category, whatever the intervals of time between one number and the next, enables a fuller understanding and a more sophisticated set of criteria for evaluating Victorian literary production. In using the term "periodical" in this chapter, I seek to keep in mind the range of publication types in which journalism appeared and still appears, all those forms of print that came out at regular intervals: dailies, weeklies, fortnightlies, monthlies, quarterlies, and even annuals. The exuberance and inventiveness of Victorian publishing in all these forms is gradually being recognized and charted, so at its most basic we are constantly revising our estimates of how many Victorian periodicals there were. The second edition of *The Waterloo Directory of English Newspapers and Periodicals: 1800–1900* covers the whole century, but its estimate of 50,000 titles published in England over that period is an indication of its scale.[4]

Victorian writers – women and men – depended on the periodical press to secure notices, advertisements, and reviews of their work and above all to earn money. Periodicals made it possible for men and some women to earn enough by writing to be able to live respectable middle-class lives. As readers, we need to remember that much Victorian literature first appeared in periodicals and in some cases was called into existence and shaped by the demands of periodical publishing. A literary criticism that carries some trace of the Romantic idea of the writer as solitary genius is, therefore, inadequate to an understanding of Victorian literary culture. Periodical writing is always the subject of negotiation between writer and editor and, sometimes, readers. Resisting the idea that a writer has to wait for "inspiration," the journalist L. T. Meade (1844–1914), editor of the girls' magazine *Atalanta* (1887–98) and author of novels, articles, and short stories, argued that "to write against time puts your work into a frame and improves it. To have to write a certain length for a certain publisher who requires a certain kind of work is splendid practice: it makes your brain very supple."[5]

Periodical writing, therefore, differs from other genres discussed in this section of the *Companion* in two respects. First, periodicals included almost every kind of writing practiced by Victorian authors. Dickens's weekly *Household Words* (1850–59) and monthlies such as the *Cornhill* (1860–1975) and *The Argosy* (1865–1901) serialized novels; in fact, such publications were the way in which many – perhaps most – Victorian novels first appeared. Magazines and newspapers, even local papers, frequently published poems, sometimes by the famous, a Tennyson or Elizabeth Barrett Browning, sometimes by unknowns. The practice of literary criticism developed first in the quarterly reviews including *The Edinburgh Review* and *The Westminster* (1824–1914) but spread to monthly magazines such as *The Athenaeum* (1828–1922). Even cheap inexpensive women's magazines such as the penny weekly *Woman* (1890–1912) carried book and theater reviews alongside articles on fashion, gossip, travel writing, jokes, interviews, and short stories. Periodicals were where scientific discoveries and theories were published, social and political commentaries developed, philosophical and literary movements charted and shaped.

Alongside and in dynamic relationship with these verbal texts, visual material in a range of genres and forms (engravings, lithographs, photographs) was important in different kinds of serial publications. Although it is outside the scope of this chapter, the increasingly important relationship between visual and verbal elements was central to Victorian print culture. Visual material was rarely simply secondary. In the beautifully produced annuals and beauty books of the early Victorian period, which were associated with women both as editors and readers, writers were commissioned to write to the illustration. As the century went on, photography had profound effects on ideas of realism, while for all writers, but perhaps particularly for women, the growth of a celebrity culture in which authors' portraits and illustrated interviews with them at home became press staples, the relationship of appearance to persona assumed a new importance in the literary marketplace.[6] Fiction, poetry, essays, reviews, leading articles – these were all journalistic or periodical genres, and women worked in all of them, though in some (fiction) more than in others (political commentary). The kinds of writing by women discussed in other chapters of this *Companion*, therefore, often appeared in or were in their original forms periodical writing.

For – and this is the other significant aspect of Victorian periodicals – they enabled the constant recycling of texts. Despite being characterized by a very particular relationship to time, periodical writing has a surprising capacity for metamorphosis, reappearing in different print formats at different moments. This metamorphosis took several forms from the straightforward recycling of material, both legitimate and illegal, what Victorians called "scissors and paste" journalism, to the regular reissuing of periodical texts in book form. Some genres were designed for this move as were the serialized novels that formed the staple of many magazines, particularly those targeted at women readers in the family. Poems, too, were often subsequently collected into volume form. Some writers republished periodical essays in books of criticism, as did Matthew Arnold in

Culture and Anarchy (published in the *Cornhill*, 1867–68; in book form, 1869). This was all besides the practice of collecting six months' or a year's worth of a magazine's numbers and issuing them in volume format, as many publishers did.

Periodical or journalistic writing, then, is a slippery concept in the Victorian period. Such writing had a habit of turning into something else – a full-length novel, a book of poems, even a bound volume of the magazine or journal. Such transformations, however, were never exact copies. It was not only that writers revised their periodical work for volume publication. It was rather that the meaning of a piece of writing became different when it was no longer embedded in a periodical alongside other kinds of writing by different authors. Reading a poem in a magazine is not like reading a poem as part of a collection of work by one author; a serialized novel sets up its own ways of being read, which have to do with anticipation, memory, and time.[7] Even bound volumes of the magazine that seemed to offer the original context of reading were never exactly like the original. Advertisements, for example, were usually stripped out of the bound volumes, and the whole experience of reading a bound volume differs from leafing through a single issue of a journal, just as reading a print copy of a magazine is quite unlike reading it in an online database.

Some periodical genres regularly migrated into volume form; others did not. Political and social comment, fashion advice, gossip, letters pages, interviews, regular columns or causeries – such genres, though important in periodicals, rarely made it into book form. Yet there were exceptions even here. Eliza Lynn Linton (1822–98) collected her articles from the *Saturday Review* (1855–1938) into a two-volume work with the title of the article that had made her famous, *The Girl of the Period and other Social Essays* (1883); Helen C. Black (1838–1906), a late Victorian journalist, recycled a series of interviews from *The Lady's Pictorial* (1880–1921) in a 1906 volume *Notable Woman Authors of the Day*, though typically she claimed she had "revised, enlarged and brought them up to date."[8] Even when not reissued in book form, political essays and social commentary on issues of the day were often read by and influenced a wide circle of readers – as did the leading articles of Harriet Martineau (1802–76) in the *Daily News* and the powerful "intellectual prose" of Frances Power Cobbe (1822–1904), which I discuss later. These purely journalistic forms were sometimes the place for innovative kinds of writing, as in the case of Alice Meynell's (1847–1922) contributions to the "Wares of Autolycus" column in the *Pall Mall Gazette* (1865–1923).

Arnold's fear of the "feather-brained" press related mainly to publications associated with the new working-class readership that contemporaries believed (rightly or wrongly) was the result of universal schooling brought in by the 1870 Education Act. However, the term "feather-brained" was often associated with women, and Arnold was voicing more obliquely a powerful current of anxiety about the feminization of the press.[9] This association became more acute with the arrival of new kinds of publications aimed at women readers. These ranged from the shilling monthlies the *Cornhill* and *Macmillan's* (1859–1907), which specialized in serial fiction, to the development of a whole section of the press devoted specifically to women defined by their gender. Magazines that addressed their readers as "ladies" dated back to the eighteenth century, but it was in the Victorian period, particularly in the 1880s and 1890s, that the "woman's magazine" became an important part of the press. Though women's reading, particularly that of working-class women, was policed by authority figures, whether librarians or the mistresses of households, Victorian publishers and authors recognized that women constituted an important part of their potential audiences.

Did this female audience mean it was easier for women to enter into journalism and support themselves as writers? Certainly, the growth of the press opened up possibilities for women writers, as Linda Peterson has shown.[10] However, this could mean anything from getting a poem published in a local paper to writing regularly for major publications or even having a paid post on the staff or being an editor. Women could and did enter into print at all these levels. The 1891 census figure of 660 women who listed themselves as "author, editor or journalist" may seem small to the twenty-first-century reader, but that figure almost certainly concealed a number of women who wrote regularly for the press but did not identify primarily as literary professionals. Besides, 660 is a huge growth over the 15 who so registered themselves in 1841.[11] Certainly, women journalists seemed to have arrived by 1894 when the Society of Women Journalists was established.

This generalization conceals, however, a complicated picture, for Victorian women never had access to the press on equal terms with their brothers. The assumptions of women's intellectual inferiority and the continuing importance of the view that women's work was domestic and familial were obstacles that all women writers had to negotiate. The growth of a women's press both in dedicated magazines and in the women's pages of periodicals aimed at a more general readership meant that women continued to find they were more likely to get work in the traditionally feminine areas of fashion, gossip, and domestic advice rather than in reporting or writing editorials. There were exceptions. Flora Shaw (1852–1929), for example, became the hugely influential foreign correspondent and then "colonial editor" on *The Times*, the first woman staff member of the paper.

However, she was just that – exceptional – and did not see it as her role to open up the field to other women.

However, the idea that writing for publication was something the middle-class woman could do from home without transgressing her proper place was increasingly accepted as the century went on, and as middle-class women saw writing as a campaigning tool, an outlet for creativity, or – in most cases – a means of financial support, more attractive and potentially better paid than governessing or needlework. In the 1890s, "Annie S. Swan" (Mrs. Burnett Smith, 1859–1943), the journalist and romantic novelist, regularly complained in her advice column in the monthly magazine *Woman at Home* (1893–1920; subtitled *Annie S. Swan's Magazine*) that she was inundated with letters from women wanting to know how they could earn money by writing. In common with other professional women writers, she tended to discourage her correspondents, arguing that earning your living by writing was not an easy option for women.

"Annie S. Swan" occupied a complex set of personae, writing simultaneously as the romantic novelist associated with that name, as "David Lyall," and very occasionally in her own person as Mrs. Burnett Smith, whose domestic life was allowed now and then to appear in the chatty columns she wrote for "her" magazine. This deployment of multiple and cross-gender pseudonyms was characteristic of the strategies many Victorian women writers adopted. It enabled both a strategic exploitation of different genres and writing opportunities and a defense against the damaging effects of gender politics. This practice was not confined to women, of course. A crucial aspect of the Victorian press was that for much of the period, anonymous or pseudonymous writing was the norm. The struggle over signature, that is, over whether work in periodicals should be signed, was fought out throughout Victoria's reign. By the 1890s, unsigned work was almost confined to newspapers, whereas in the 1830s, it had been the norm in most kinds of periodicals. However, anonymity, like pseudonymity, was used by women in particular ways. It meant that some, like the enormously productive Margaret Oliphant (1828–97), could write far more extensively for one publication (in her case, *Blackwood's Edinburgh Magazine* [1817–1980]) than the average reader would have realized. It enabled some women, such as Christiane Johnstone (1781–1857) of *Tait's Edinburgh Magazine* (1832–61) and Marian Evans in the *Westminster*, to take on masculine editorial roles and experiment with ungendered or masculine writing voices. According to Alexis Easley, Harriet Martineau "actively sought anonymity and objectivity in her work as a means of distancing her gender and identity from her writing."[12] Anonymity enabled complex developments of the first-person voice. However, anonymity was a double-edged weapon. Eliza Lynn Linton, whose anonymous articles attacking those who departed from womanly behavior had been a sensation in the 1860s, twenty years later claimed that she was glad to publish them in book form under her own name because she was tired of other people, including a certain clergyman, claiming to be their author.[13] For women who had become well known as novelists or poets, cashing in on the value of their names in journalistic and editorial work made sense, as it did, for example, for Eliza Cook (1812–89), known as the "popular poetess,"[14] in *Eliza Cook's Journal* (1849–54).

Like anonymity, the use of multiple pseudonyms was also a double-edged weapon, enabling the exploitation of different market niches but distorting or, in some cases, preventing the development of a recognizable authorial voice. According to Linda K. Hughes, the writer Rosamund Marriott Watson (1860–1911) was one for whom the use of pseudonyms proved disastrous rather than enabling. Watson abandoned her earlier, recognizable pseudonym (Graham R. Tomson) when she left her second husband and thus lost what Hughes calls her "meaningful signature" and more or less disappeared from view.[15] The use of pseudonyms also meant that men could adopt a feminine persona where readers might have expected it. In the 1890s, the novelist Arnold Bennett (1867–1931) disguised the fact that he was the editor of the magazine *Woman* (1890–1912) by adopting a series of female pseudonyms, including "Sal Volatile" and "Lady Betty." Periodical culture thus allowed all kinds of literary cross-dressing, a practice that brings into focus the complexities of the relationships between author and text, which are always mediated.

Bearing all this in mind, the rest of this chapter briefly discusses some of the genres of periodical writing that are not dealt with elsewhere in this volume.

Leaders and articles on social and political issues

Though participating in public debate on political and social issues was widely considered inappropriate for women, who, after all, were deemed unfit for the vote until well into the twentieth century, a number of extraordinary women writers nevertheless entered vigorously into periodical debates on such topics. Among the most remarkable was Harriet Martineau (1802–76), whose writing career extended through five decades and who wrote authoritatively on political economy and society in periodicals ranging from the religious *Monthly Repository* (1806–37), (to which she had sent her first, unpaid contribution), to the weighty quarterly *Westminster Review* (1824–1914), through Dickens's *Household Words*, and on to *Once a Week* (1859–80) and the *Daily News* (1846–1912). Martineau became a writer out of financial necessity but also driven by her own intellectual energy and commitment to social causes. Her early work explored the nature of religious faith and doubt, but by the 1830s she was writing on political economy and, following a visit to America, arguing for the abolition of slavery. In the 1850s and 1860s, she also wrote astringent articles on the role of women, arguing that the idea that women did not have to work was a myth proposed by "the jealousy of men" and that women needed education and access to work as well as democratic rights.[16] Despite suffering from deafness and intermittent ill health, she combined authoritative writing with huge productivity, writing books, treatises, novels, an autobiography, and thousands of articles, including hundreds of leaders (editorials) for the *Daily News* between 1852 and 1866 when she was living in the Lake District but at the center of current debates. She experimented with writing on economic and social issues in expository and narrative modes, hoping to make her extensive reading available to ordinary readers.[17]

Equally remarkable was Frances Power Cobbe (1822–1904), another radical writer with a long career (forty-five years) as a working journalist and a keen and incisive style. A generation younger than Martineau, she was like the older writer in that she began publishing before a change in her family circumstances forced – or perhaps enabled – her to become a full-time writer, earning a living by her pen. Like many of her contemporaries, Cobbe explored issues of faith and doubt. She rejected what she saw as narrow religious doctrine but stressed the importance of a generous theism. Cobbe became a powerful campaigner for women's suffrage and was increasingly involved in campaigning against vivisection, seeing a continuity between men's, particularly medical men's, treatment of women and their disregard of animal suffering. Her article on "Wife Torture in England," which arose out of this concern, pioneered later feminist concern about what we now call domestic violence.[18] According to her biographer Sally Mitchell, Cobbe published well over one hundred articles in leading periodicals; produced some two hundred tracts for the antivivisection movement; wrote more than a thousand unsigned (and ungendered) second leaders on politics, public issues, and social causes for the London halfpenny paper the *Echo* (1868–1905), where she was on the staff between 1868 and 1875. She also wrote for the evening daily *Standard* (1827–1916) and served as a daily news correspondent in London and Florence.[19] She lived openly with another woman, whom she acknowledged as her life partner.

Eliza Lynn Linton, mentioned earlier, though she also had a long career, was a very different kind of journalist from either of these two – not least because she was a conservative, attacking "women's rightists" in virulent tones. The first woman to have a regular paid post on the staff of a journal, her articles on "The Girl of the Period" in the *Saturday Review* (1855–1938) caused a public storm. Her capacity to coin a telling phase was evident, too, in later coinages such as "The Shrieking Sisterhood" and "The Wild Women." Her public persona as a harsh critic, particularly of other women seeking to follow her pioneering example, was apparently belied by her private kindness to younger women writers.[20]

These women found a public voice in the general press. Others were notable for the role they played in periodicals that were set up specifically to put forward a case or champion a cause. These included feminist periodicals, temperance journals, and religious magazines, publications for which financial support from religious or political organizations or from committed individuals ensured the continuance of loss-making projects or for which writers were prepared to work for little – or even no – money to further the cause.

Though the term "feminist" is a later coinage, we can talk of a feminist press that developed in the second half of the century, beginning with the *Englishwoman's Review* (1857–59) and the monthly *English Woman's Journal* (1858–64), edited by Bessie Parkes (1828–1925) and Barbara Bodichon (1827–91).[21] This *Journal* was printed by Emily Faithfull (1835–95) at the Victoria Press, which she had set up to train and employ women as typesetters. Typesetting was part of what Barbara Onslow has called "the back-room" work of the periodical press, that collaborative effort among writers, editors, proofreaders, and printers needed to bring each number of a journal out on its due day.[22] Faithfull wanted women to be enabled to enter properly paid employment at every level of the press. She went on to help set up the ambitious literary *Victoria Magazine* (1863–80), which, though not exclusively female, was notable for publishing the work of women poets, fiction writers, and essayists including Christina Rossetti, Adelaide Proctor, Frances Power Cobbe, and Margaret Oliphant, alongside well-known male authors. As well as her work on *Victoria* and in the press, Faithfull continued to write for other journals including *The Lady's Pictorial* (1880–1921), for which she wrote its women's column until the 1890s. Other able women writers set up, edited, and wrote for journals that existed to further women's rights. These ranged from Lydia Becker's (1827–90) *Women's Suffrage Journal* (1870–90), based in Manchester, which carried reports from regional societies and published campaigning articles and letters, through Henrietta Muller's (1845/6–1906) *Women's Penny Paper* (1888–90), which aimed at a broader readership but was short lived, to more specialist publications such as the *Women's Industrial News* (1895–1919). This organ of the Women's Industrial Council, a forerunner of the Women's Trades Union Association, was edited by the energetic Clementina Black (1853–1922). Black, like Emily Faithfull and other women involved in campaigning and radical journals, also wrote extensively in general periodicals and in the women's press, a growing sector of the market in print that targeted women with articles, stories, advice, and pictures on what were deemed to be traditional feminine interests.

Religious journalism

A very different genre of periodical, but one also more concerned with spreading a message than competing in the market, was the religious magazine, vast numbers of which appeared during this period. The domestication of Protestant Christianity and the definition of womanliness as having particular spiritual and moral qualities meant that it was acceptable for women to write for religious periodicals as long as they upheld doctrinal and gender norms. Early nineteenth-century pioneers such as Sarah Trimmer (1741–1810) and Hannah More (1745–1833), founder of the Religious Tract Society, had opened up this field, but it was women such as Charlotte Elizabeth Tonna (1790–1846), dubbed the "muslin divine," and Mrs. Bakewell (?fl. 1845–64) of the *British Mother's Magazine* (1845–64) who carried their commitment into regular periodical publications.[23] Tonna was identified with the *Christian Lady's Magazine* (1834–49), which she edited and for which she probably wrote a good deal of copy, but she also edited and wrote anonymously for *The Protestant Magazine* (dates unknown). She walked a fine line between arguing that women were subordinate to men and encouraging them to be actively engaged in campaigns for the abolition of slavery and reform of conditions in factories where so many women worked. Emma Worboise, who edited and wrote for the *Christian World Magazine* (1857–1961) for twenty years, carried this kind of journalism into the next generation, as did her fellow worker in the publishing house of James Clarke, the gifted Mary Anne Hearn, one of the few "Victorian women of humble birth" to become a full-time professional journalist.[24] However, it was Charlotte Yonge (1823–1901) who was the most successful of the Victorian women who engaged in explicitly religious journalism. In Yonge's case, her success at *The Monthly Packet* (1851–99), which she edited for more than forty years, owed much to the serialization of her novels and also to the engaging tone of her editorial persona and encouragement of other young women writers. Yonge's magazine, subtitled "for Younger Members of the Church of England," shared with several other such journals a desire to address girls and young women with a religious message that would be at once instructive and enjoyable. *The Magazine for the Young*, edited by Anne Mozley (1809–91), was another High Church periodical, although the Religious Tract Society's *Girls' Own Paper* (1880–1956), the most popular and long-running magazine in this genre, was edited throughout the Victorian period by Charles Peters. Other specifically Christian journals aimed at a target group included Mrs. Bakewell's *British Mother's Magazine* (1845–64), which offered advice on bringing up children. Just as the religious girls' magazines gradually gave way to publications with a more secular agenda, for example, L. T. Meade's *Atalanta* (1887–98), so toward the end of the century writing addressed to mothers became more thoroughly secular with titles such as *Baby* (1887–1915), edited by Ada Ballin (1862–1906) who specialized in writing on health and rational dress. This journal was both more child centered and more driven by advertising, a process discernible in the next genre of writing to which I turn.

The "causerie" and the advice column

Among the most completely journalistic genres were the special columns or causeries, which might include gossip, snippets of news, and moral stories or jokes – depending on the nature of the publication. Such columns existed in a range of periodicals. Sometimes the title of the column provided an umbrella covering a number of different writers, as in "The Wares of Autolycus" column in the *Pall Mall Gazette* to which Alice Meynell and Rosamund Marriott contributed. However, with the development of signature and the growth of celebrity authorship in the latter part of the period, columns focused round a particular writerly persona were more common. Andrew Lang's "At the Sign of the Ship" in *Longman's Magazine* (1882–1905) was perhaps the most famous. In the women's magazine press, these columns often took the forms of advice on domestic matters or on fashion and dress. As early as the 1850s, in the first magazine aimed specifically at the middle-class woman, Beeton's *Englishwoman's Domestic Magazine* (1852–79), Isabella Beeton (1836–65) wrote a regular monthly column on the latest Paris fashions, giving her readers detailed advice, accompanied by paper patterns so that they could ensure they were always *a la mode*. Isabella became her husband Samuel Beeton's coeditor and fellow worker in the Beeton publishing house, where they pioneered not only new kinds of women's journals but also developed the format of the advice column.

However, it was another writer who had learned her trade in Beeton publications, Matilda Browne (?–1936), in her column "Spinnings" in the *Englishwoman's Domestic Magazine*, who developed the women's column in two significant ways. First, she created a chatty persona to engage with readers as though she were a personal friend; second, she gave advice not only on fashion but on where to shop. Her column pioneered what contemporaries described as the "shopping column," where editorial copy in the form of advice overlapped with advertising, what we today might call "advertorials." Isabella Beeton's premature death in 1865 precipitated Browne into taking on more and more work in the Beeton titles. When she and Samuel Beeton parted company from Ward and Lock, to whom he had sold his titles, Browne set up her own journal, taking the names "Myra" or "The Silkworm" and the conceit of her column as a "Spinning" into the new monthly. There she developed both of these devices with such success that, according to Christopher Breward, *Myra's Journal of Dress and Fashion* (1875–1912) signaled a significant shift both in the periodical industry and in discussions of women's position in relation to work and to the department store, developed though the discourse of dress.[25] In her column, fashion and shopping were combined, and a tone of gossipy intimacy was developed round a particular female persona, characteristics incorporated in various forms in the penny magazines of the New Journalism such as *Woman's Life* (1895–1934), where "Lady Veritas" offered readers a whole column on the "serious business" of shopping.[26]

The regular column, whether or not identified with a named journalist, sometimes overlapped with that other most journalistic of spaces – the letters page or correspondence column where readers' contributions were invited or problems answered. The nature of serial forms, that they come out over time, means they engage readers in ways a book cannot. Early Victorian convention had been to print only answers to correspondences rather than the original letters. However, by the end of the century, as journalism became more professionalized and the difference between writer and reader more demarcated, printing readers' letters (suitably edited) and commenting on them became a staple of a range of magazines and newspapers; in some cases, the running commentary was developed through a persona with whom readers were invited to engage. Anne S. Swan's columns "Over the Tea Cups" and "Love, Courtship and Marriage" in *Woman at Home* were prime examples of this trend. However, correspondence columns took many forms from the serious debates of *The Englishwoman's Review* through to the chatty exchanges of the cheap weeklies for women that proliferated in the 1890s and continued into the twentieth century.

Interviews

The other journalistic genre that became an important element of the New Journalism was the interview. Though potted biographies of notable people had been a staple of many kinds of periodicals throughout the century, it was only in the 1880s and 1890s that the interview appeared as a significant genre, part of that growing personalization that was associated particularly with W. T. Stead's (1849–1912) campaigning New Journalism and that gradually extended its reach alongside the use of signature and more personalized style. In this kind of writing, Hulda Friederichs was preeminent. Friederichs, the first woman to be employed and paid on the same terms as her male colleagues, eschewed exclusively feminine subjects. She was appointed by George Newnes (1851–1910) to be chief interviewer on the *Pall Mall Gazette*, subsequently working for him on the *Westminster Gazette* (1893–1928) and editing the *Westminster Budget* (1893–1904).[27] As an interviewer, she did not confine her attentions to the famous but sought out subjects of interest among circus performers, music hall artists, a tattooer, and other marginal groups of workers. Venturing into places where respectable women did not go, Friederichs explored the tensions of class and gender without sensationalizing them.

Other women notable for their work as interviewers were Sarah Tooley (1857–1946) and Helen Black. Both worked across a range of journals including those addressed to women and, unlike Friederichs, concentrated on celebrity interviews, especially those with other journalists and writers. This practice was becoming an important part of the press by the 1890s. The penny weekly *Woman* ran a series of interviews with editors in 1898, and Black wrote her "notable women authors" interviews for the more upmarket *Lady's Pictorial*. These made the women writer doubly visible as both interviewer and interviewee. Ironically, the interviews routinely stressed the domestic virtues and womanliness of those interviewed, qualities made more pointed because they were usually conducted in their homes. Even a notoriously advanced woman such as Sarah Grand (1854–1943), whose novels dealt with venereal disease and gender bending, was described in terms that stressed her womanly spirituality and delicate appearance.[28] Eliza Lynn Linton's table might be covered "with a mass of journals, magazines and periodicals," but it is the beautiful cushions and fire screen she has embroidered with her own needle that the interviewer notices.[29]

In this paradox, the position of the Victorian woman in the periodical press is made clear. The very moment that seems to confirm that she has arrived as a professional, indeed as a celebrated, writer is also when she must conform to the ideals of domestic femininity and womanly appearance.

NOTES

1. George Saintsbury, *A History of Nineteenth Century Literature, 1780–1895* (London: Macmillan, 1896), p. 166.
2. Finnuala Dillane, *Before George Eliot: Marian Evans and the Periodical Press* (Cambridge: Cambridge University Press, 2013); Linda K. Hughes, *Graham R: Rosamund Marriott Watson; Woman of Letters* (Athens: Ohio University Press,

2005); Sally Mitchell, *Frances Power Cobbe: Victorian Feminist, Journalist, Reformer* (Charlottesville: University of Virginia Press, 2004), p. 3.
3. Matthew Arnold, "Up to Easter," *Nineteenth Century* 21 (1887), 638–39.
4. John S. North, ed., *Waterloo Directory of Newspapers and Periodicals, 1800–1900*, Series 2 (Waterloo: North Waterloo Academic Press, 2003).
5. Anon., "How I write my Books: An interview with L.T. Meade," *The Young Woman* 6 (1892), 123.
6. Alexis Easley, *Literary Celebrity, Gender, and Victorian Authorship, 1850–1914* (Newark: University of Delaware Press, 2011).
7. Natalie Houston, "Newspaper Poems: Material Texts in the Public Sphere," *Victorian Studies* 51 (2008), 233–42; Linda K. Hughes and Michael Lund, *The Victorian Serial* (Charlottesville: University of Virginia Press, 1991).
8. Helen C. Black, *Notable Women Authors of the Day* (London: Maclaren and Company, 1906), n.p.
9. Margaret Beetham, *A Magazine of her Own? Domesticity and Desire in the Woman's Magazine 1800–1914* (London: Routledge, 1996), pp. 119 ff.
10. Linda H. Peterson, *Becoming a Woman of Letters: Myths of Authorship and Facts of the Victorian Market* (Princeton: Princeton University Press, 2009), pp. 2–3 and *passim*.
11. Qtd. in F. Elizabeth Gray, "Introduction," *Women in Journalism at the Fin de Siècle*, ed. F. Elizabeth Gray (Basingstoke: Palgrave Macmillan, 2012), p. 4.
12. Easley, *Literary Celebrity*, p. 80.
13. E. Lynn Linton, *The Girl of the Period and Other Social Essays* (London: Richard Bentley, 1883), pp. 1, 3.
14. Qtd. in Laurel Brake and Marysa Demoor, eds., *Dictionary of Nineteenth-Century Journalism in Great Britain and Ireland* (Ghent and London: Academia Press and The British Library, 2009), s.v. "Cook, Eliza," p. 140.
15. Linda K. Hughes, "Journalism's Iconoclast: Rosamund Marriott Watson," in Gray, ed., *Women in Journalism*, p. 214 and Hughes, *Graham R., passim* .
16. Harriet Martineau, "Female Industry," *Edinburgh Review* 1859, p. 109, qtd. in Barbara Caine, "Feminism, Journalism and Public Debate," in *Women and Literature in Britain, 1800–1900*, ed. Joanne Shattock (Cambridge: Cambridge University Press, 2001), p. 110.
17. Barbara Onslow, *Women of the Press in Nineteenth-Century Britain* (Basingstoke: Macmillan, 2000), pp. 230–31; Peterson, *Becoming a Woman of Letters*, pp. 61–95.
18. Frances Power Cobbe, "Wife Torture in England," *Contemporary Review* 37 (April 1878), 55–87.
19. Mitchell, *Frances Power Cobbe*, p. 2 and *passim*.
20. See, e.g., Black, *Notable Women Authors*, pp. 1–10.
21. Caine, "Feminism, Journalism and Public Debate," pp. 99–118.
22. Onslow, *Women of the Press*, pp. 149–56.
23. Ibid., p. 238; Beetham, *Magazine of her Own?* pp. 48–56.
24. Brake and Demoor, eds., *Dictionary of Nineteenth-Century Journalism in Great Britain and Ireland*, p. 278.
25. Christopher Breward, "Femininity and Consumption: The Problem of the Late Nineteenth-century Fashion Journal," *Journal of Design History* 7:2 (1994), 71–89.

26. Anon., *Woman's Life*, 1 (1895), 3.
27. Dillane, "A Fair Feld and no Favour: Hulda Frederichs, the Interview, and the New Woman" in Gray, ed., *Women in Journalism*, pp. 148–64; Brake and Demoor, eds., *Dictionary of Nineteenth-Century Journalism*.
28. See Beetham, *Magazine of her Own?* pp. 128–30.
29. Black, *Notable Women Authors*, pp. 5–8.

16

JOANNE WILKES

Reviewing

One of the most famous pieces of literary criticism of the Victorian period appeared in the prestigious periodical the *Quarterly Review* in December 1848. It covered the literary sensation *Jane Eyre*, published the preceding year under the mysterious pseudonym "Currer Bell." The review became notorious for its hostility to the novel: it calls the work "pre-eminently an anti-Christian composition," infused with "the tone of mind and thought which has overthrown authority and violated every code human and divine abroad, and fostered Chartism and rebellion at home." The reviewer joins in the speculation about the true identity of the novelist, including theories that the name "Currer Bell" concealed a female. But the reviewer discounts this notion, on account of the ignorance that the novelist supposedly shows about things every woman should know, declaring that "no woman trusses game and garnishes dessert-dishes with the same hands, or talks of so doing in the same breath," and "no woman attires another in such fancy dresses as Jane's ladies assume."[1]

The reviewer sources this specifically female knowledge to "a lady friend, whom we are always happy to consult," creating the impression that the critic is male. This impression was confirmed when in her 1857 biography of Charlotte Brontë, Elizabeth Gaskell attacked the reviewer as if male. But the culprit was actually Elizabeth Rigby (later Eastlake, 1809–93). Although Charlotte Brontë and Elizabeth Gaskell actually knew this fact, the true attribution was only publicly confirmed more than forty years later by Brontë scholar W. Robertson Nicoll, who had picked up a reference in the published letters of Elizabeth Rigby's friend Sara Coleridge.

The reason for the obscurity of the review's authorship, and also for Rigby's adopting a male persona, is that the *Quarterly Review* in 1848 practiced what was at that time a near-universal custom of publishing its articles and reviews anonymously. This periodical continued to do so for many years longer, but from the late 1850s, it became increasingly common for the contents of periodicals to be signed: the new monthly *Macmillan's*

Magazine pioneered the practice from 1859. The convention of anonymity did, however, have important implications for women reviewers.

The convention has made identifications of authorship for many Victorian reviews difficult, so researchers owe much to the successive editors of the *Wellesley Index to Victorian Periodicals*, whose investigations have led to numerous authorial attributions. They have covered in particular the more prestigious Victorian periodicals: the quarterlies and monthlies. Meanwhile, scholars of the weekly *Athenaeum*, which published a comprehensive range of reviews in many fields from 1828 onward, have benefited from the results of an indexing project based on the files still extant, some of which findings were published in Marysa Demoor's *Their Fair Share* (2000). For the *Christian Remembrancer*, an intellectual High Church Anglican periodical for which records do not survive, innovative computer analyses by the Centre for Literary and Linguistic Computing at the University of Newcastle (Australia) have assisted in authorial attribution – notably as regards the critic Anne Mozley. The outlets for reviews increased astronomically over the century, doubling over the decade 1854–64 (from 624 to 1,250); with advances in both literacy and printing technology, numbers continued to rise. But the concentration of much modern research on high-end to middlebrow periodical titles, dominated by male contributors, and the lack of research on women's or niche magazines have meant that much of women's output as reviewers remains obscure. In particular, knowledge of women's activity in reviewing for newspapers is piecemeal because of the sheer volume of this material, most of which awaits research. Hence, my coverage in this chapter will necessarily be slanted toward reviewing in periodicals.

As the practice of anonymity came to be contested mid-century, there was considerable debate about its implications. Anthony Trollope, whose *Fortnightly Review* (1865–) championed signature, claimed in his *Autobiography* that anonymity could give a factitious prestige to the views of a nonentity, when expressed in a respected organ of criticism: "an ordinary reader would not care to have his books recommended to him by Jones; but the recommendation of the great unknown comes to him with all the weight of *The Times*, the *Spectator*, or the *Saturday* [*Review*]." But the counterargument, advanced by critic E. S. Dallas, was that writing in a respected periodical helped divest the nonentity critic (here called "Smith") of his egotism, such that he is "forced to regard only that part of his consciousness which identifies him with every other member of the community – Smith, no longer the individual unity, but the representative man."[2] Such a contributor, opined regular periodical writer W. R. Greg, would also have a sense of responsibility to the wider "we" of the publication: rather than serving primarily to conceal his own insignificance, his contributions would show him adjusting his writing to his sense of the journal's collective voice.[3]

A major argument against anonymity, nonetheless, was that it offered scope for personal attacks for which the writer did not have to take personal responsibility. In her review of *Jane Eyre*, Elizabeth Rigby also claimed that were Currer Bell really a woman, then she must be "one who has, for some sufficient reason, long forfeited the society of her own sex."[4] That is, she was unchaste, and it was this comment that especially offended both Charlotte Brontë and Elizabeth Gaskell. There was a tradition of hard-hitting and sometimes personally directed writing in the *Quarterly*, as well as in the other long-established quarterly, the *Edinburgh Review*. The founding of these periodicals, in 1809 and 1802 respectively, had a major impact on the literary scene and raised the standard of reviewing, but also gave rein to attacks on individuals. It is also important to note that, in the first half of the century in particular, works that were not straightforwardly political could be judged on political grounds. The *Quarterly* was a strongly Tory publication, actually founded to counter the influence of the more liberal *Edinburgh*: hence, writers could be attacked for their known political affiliations or, in the case of Currer Bell, because of a perceived political tendency in their work.

The overall assumption about periodical and newspaper writing was that it was done by men. This is the implication behind Trollope's "Jones" and Dallas's "Smith." Men did indeed predominate, yet in 1865, proto-feminist activist Bessie Rayner Parkes ruefully observed that "if editors were ever known to disclose the dread secrets of their dens, they would only give the public an idea of the authoresses whose unsigned names are legion; of their rolls of manuscripts, which are as the sands of the sea."[5] Given that a male voice generally carried more authority than a female one, women did on occasion write reviews using an overtly male persona. This was sometimes the case, for example, for Margaret Oliphant (1828–97), who was by far the most prolific woman contributor to periodicals identified in research to date. She published in a variety of outlets, but her mainstay was the monthly *Blackwood's Edinburgh Magazine*, for which she wrote many reviews and articles from the early 1850s till her death more than forty years later. From its inception in 1817, this magazine had a masculine image, promoted in particular by the early "Noctes Ambrosianae" – fictional conversations among a group of men who were fictionalized versions of actual male contributors – and continuing via the tendency of its articles to assume a masculine coterie in its readership. Oliphant's overtly male persona is more evident in her earlier rather than her later contributions, but near the end of her career she ran a column of general reviews called "The Old Saloon"

(1887–92), which deliberately evoked the masculine-coterie domain of Blackwood's publishing offices in Edinburgh. Later in the century, too, the reviews of poetry that appeared in the early 1890s as by "Graham R. Tomson," in the intellectual weekly *The Academy* and the newspaper the *Illustrated London News*, made forthright judgments of prominent male poets – but when their author Rosamund Tomson lost access to the pseudonym because of divorce and remarriage, becoming Rosamund Marriott Watson, she lost prestige and thus access to prestigious reviewing work.[6]

Using a male persona could be a strategic way of commenting on women's condition from a supposedly sympathetic masculine perspective. Anne Mozley, for instance, reviewing Dinah Mulock Craik's *A Woman's Thoughts About Women* for the *Christian Remembrancer* in June 1858, takes a generally conservative stance, emphasizing women's biblically ordained social subordination. But she also observes that it can be male self-interest, rather than women's incapacity, which makes men unwilling to sacrifice their wives' or daughters' attentions by allowing them paid work away from home. Meanwhile, in October 1856 Marian Evans, on the eve of her career as the published writer of fiction "George Eliot," produced for the quarterly *Westminster Review* (October 1856) a caustic article called "Silly Novels by Lady Novelists." From an implied male perspective, this review ridicules and castigates contemporary "ladies" who write fiction for their intellectual pretentiousness, weak and convoluted writing, and implausible representations of life. But the more serious point here is that these ladies have relished praise without understanding how much it is saturated with condescension. It is badly written and pseudo-intellectual fiction by women that encourages negative judgments of women's literary potential, and Evans adopts a male persona to make this point.

Women's use of male personae in periodical reviewing should not, nonetheless, be overstated. Much anonymous reviewing was written in a gender-neutral voice. And what might be seen as a countertrend to male ventriloquism is evident in the establishment, from mid-century, of periodicals conducted by women that advocated proto-feminist ideas and policies to do with education, employment opportunities, and property rights for women. Published by the activist Langham Place Group in London, both the *English Woman's Journal* (1858–64) and *Englishwoman's Review* (1866–1910) had significant review sections highlighting women's achievements in literature. The female reviewers of the *English Woman's Journal* began to establish "a pantheon of notable women writers," while those in the *Englishwoman's Review* evaluated works according to whether or not they supported feminist values. The latter's column "Women's Books of the Month" covered works by women authors in all fields, while "Women's

Books – A Possible Library," Helen Blackburn's substantial article of May 1889, lists women's contributions to a variety of genres, including travel, biography, translation, history, political economy, and science, as well as creative writing.[7]

Other aspects of the convention of anonymity are of particular import to Victorian women reviewers. One is the potential for women to review in genres that demanded expertise they were not generally thought to possess. Although Elizabeth Rigby is now mainly known for her savaging of *Jane Eyre*, she had a long career as a periodical writer (from the early 1840s till her death half a century later), and her subjects ranged through books for children, travel writing, biography, Russian literature and culture, and, above all, European art. Margaret Oliphant, although she reviewed much fiction, also covered poetry, history, biography and autobiography, art, and religion. Theological matters were considered especially beyond women's competence, so Anne Mozley, in proposing in 1866 to review publications by recent Catholic converts for *Blackwood's* so as to illustrate these writers' divergences of opinion, emphasizes to editor John Blackwood that the identity "*& sex*" of the writer would have to be concealed, since "people don't generally suspect ladies of writing on such subjects."[8] She would have encountered the patronizing treatment noted in Marian Evans's "Silly Novels" review, risked by women writers who ventured beyond what was considered their competence. In the case of the translation of Homer's *Iliad* by Lord Derby, Blackwood had not needed to be advised to conceal the reviewer's sex. This was the formidably erudite Elizabeth Julia Hasell (1830–87). He asked her in 1865 to do the *Iliad* review – an important one to him, since *Blackwood's* had always strongly supported the Tories, and Lord Derby was the current leader. Hasell supplied the review and Blackwood published it, but in writing to Derby himself, he represented the reviewer as male.

A particularly interesting case is the prominent and prolific Harriet Martineau (1802–76), who had come to the public's attention in the early 1830s as the author of a popular series of stories called *Illustrations of Political Economy* (1832–34). She had encountered some misogynist criticism – including from the *Quarterly Review* – for daring to write on this supposedly masculine subject. Martineau went on to publish under her own name in a range of genres, but also to contribute widely to periodicals, sometimes anonymously. She is one of the newspaper reviewers whose work has been identified, and her most sustained journalistic output was in fact as a leader (editorial) writer and reviewer for the London *Daily News* from 1852 to 1866. Most of these contributions were leaders, but there were forty-seven reviews published between 1853 and 1865, and they covered a great variety of topics. These included British and American politics, foreign policy, novels, education, science, agriculture, and history. According to Dallas Liddle, the prospect of exerting influence as an anonymous writer had become attractive to Martineau by the early 1850s: it offered "all the benefits of work, and of complete success, without any of the responsibility."[9] And the gendered implications of this choice would be spelled out by Martineau's admiring biographer Florence Fenwick Miller in 1884: "I wonder how many of the men who have presumed to say that women are 'incapable of understanding politics' or of 'sympathising in great causes,' received a large part of their political education, ... from those journalistic writings by Harriet Martineau?"[10]

Another corollary of anonymous reviewing was that as each periodical or newspaper had a characteristic outlook, tone, and style, women reviewers could adapt their own voices and attitudes to those of the periodical they were targeting. Anne Mozley reviewed for the *Christian Remembrancer*; she also wrote four reviews during 1859 and 1860 for each issue of the short-lived *Bentley's Quarterly Review*, produced articles on various subjects for *Blackwood's* through the 1860s and 1870s (including a few reviews such as the one on Catholic converts), and wrote shorter articles for the weekly *Saturday Review*, covering social mores and general literary issues. The articles for the first three outlets are long, reflective, and analytical – although a retrospective of the career of the famous novelist Edward Bulwer Lytton in *Bentley's* skewers his pretensions to profundity much as Marian Evans does those of "lady novelists." For the *Saturday Review*, however, in which short epigrammatic articles and reviews were valued, Mozley needed to make her points more concisely.

The ability to adapt material to different outlets was especially useful when reviewers needed to maximize income. So Mary Margaret Busk (1779–1863), always struggling to publish work, might review the same book for different periodicals, mimicking the style expected for each: lively and impertinent for *Bentley's Miscellany*, scholarly for the *Foreign Quarterly Review*, subdued and straightforward for the weekly *Athenaeum*. Similarly, when Marian Evans was supporting herself in the 1850s largely through reviewing, she covered in 1855 a book on John Milton for both the weekly *Leader* and the quarterly *Westminster Review*. Although the two publications shared a politically radical outlook, the article for the weekly had to be briefer, more conversational, subjective, and generalized, whereas the review for the quarterly took a more scholarly approach, investigating Milton's theories on education and the overall impact of his works. Indeed, what regular readers expected of an organ such as the *Westminster* might become so familiar that a personal friend of Evans's could read the "Belles Lettres" section of the periodical's reviews for April 1854 and assume that it had been written by Evans – as that section often was – whereas the actual writer was another regular contributor, Jane Sinnett. This periodical, according to Judith Johnston, encouraged "a certain forthright tone, erudite reference, and a caustic humour."[11]

Marian Evans was well aware that she was writing in a particular style considered appropriate to a quarterly, so she went in for "slashing" reviews. But as Liddle has argued, this antagonistic rhetoric came to seem to her inconsistent with the kind of engagement with readers that she believed appropriate to morally effective writing. Indeed, although intellectually more cogent, it was too much like the kind of hectoring that she had criticized in the "silly novels" themselves. Genuine teaching, Evans believed, worked through arousing a sympathetic response in readers and thus extending their world view outside their immediate experience, and this effect is what she aspired to in the fiction she published as George Eliot.[12]

In this context, it is interesting to compare the discussion of some of the novels treated in "Silly Novels" with their handling by the notable *Athenaeum* reviewer, Geraldine Jewsbury (1812–80). Jewsbury was a prolific, and anonymous, reviewer for this weekly through the 1850s and 1860s, and she covered mainly new fiction. In 1856, she happened to review three of the novels dealt with in Evans's article: *Laura Gay*, *Compensation*, and *The Old Grey Church*. Evans characterizes *Laura Gay* and *Compensation* as part of the "*mind-and-millinery* species"[13] of fiction, with a veneer of pretentious intellectualism over the conventional concerns of high-society courtship. The heroine of *Compensation* cannot speak intelligible English, while her fatuous counterpart in *Laura Gay* parades her classical learning. For Evans, the writers of these novels simply exemplify "poverty of brains," showing no familiarity at all with real life, while their heroines' "genius and morality" are worth little unless "backed by eligible offers." The Evangelical *The Old Grey Church*, meanwhile, is also fixated on high life, eschewing the "real drama of Evangelicalism" among the middle and lower classes. The novel is, Evans declares, "utterly tame and feeble," with both its dialogue and its narrative "drivelling."[14] As for Geraldine Jewsbury, she is as unimpressed as Evans by both *Laura Gay* and *Compensation*: in the former, she finds the story uninteresting, the heroine too oracular, and the style "feeble," while *Compensation* is both implausible and "foolish." She does not, however, cast aspersions on the actual authors (*Athenaeum*, January 26, 1856, p. 104; July 19, 1856, p. 896); in discussing *The Old Grey Church*, she does not attack it but just observes that it is an "unexceptionable novel for family reading" (*Athenaeum*, May 24, 1856, p. 648).

One reason for the difference here is that a priority for Jewsbury, reviewing for a weekly that covered a broad range of publications, was to specify what kind of novel each one under review was and what sort of readership would appreciate it. So while she makes no claims for the aesthetic quality of *The Old Grey Church*, she realizes that there is a market for fiction of this type. On the other hand, she can commend to another kind of reader Margaret Oliphant's *A Son of the Soil* as a serious text, different from "the ordinary run of novel" (*Athenaeum*, June 9, 1866, pp. 765–66), while George Eliot's first full-length fiction *Adam Bede* is "of the highest class" and so "to be accepted, not criticised" (*Athenaeum*, February 26, 1859, p. 284).

Very judicious in her habitual tone was a remarkable critic of a generation before Jewsbury's – Christian Isobel Johnstone (1781–1857). The politically more liberal counterpart to *Blackwood's* was *Tait's Edinburgh Magazine*, and Johnstone was its editor from 1832 to 1846. She was also responsible for the book review section, and her own numerous contributions covered a broad variety of genres: travel and geography, politics, finance, religion, history, science, anatomy, mathematics, biography and autobiography, criticism, poetry, drama, and fiction. She was evidently no friend to either royalty or Tories, but she avoided the partisan stridency common during the period, offering balanced judgments of a range of writers, including Maria Edgeworth, Mary Howitt, William Cobbett, Lady Mary Wortley Montagu, Charles Lamb, Benjamin Disraeli, Mary Shelley, Elizabeth Barrett, Fanny Kemble, Jeremy Bentham, Charles Dickens, Harriet Martineau, M. G. Lewis, and James Fenimore Cooper. Johnstone was interested in women writers: for example, when reviewing poetry collections from Elizabeth Barrett and Fanny Kemble in 1844, in conjunction with the work of Coventry Patmore, she announces at the outset that she is putting the women poets first because of "their merits." Moreover, in treating Hannah Lawrance's *Historical Memoirs of the Queens of England from the Commencement of the Twelfth Century* (1838), she claims that Lawrance had "dug deeper in the tumulus of antiquity, than many accredited excavators of the other sex."[15]

Although Hannah Lawrance (1795–1875) published *Historical Memoirs*, as well as *The History of Woman in England* (1844), her main literary activity in her long career was as a reviewer. From the 1830s to the early 1850s, she reviewed regularly for the *Athenaeum*, wherein her specialty was the history of the British Isles from the earliest days to the sixteenth century. She was clearly a woman of considerable scholarship, including knowledge of unpublished records and an ability to read Middle English, Anglo-Saxon, Anglo-Norman, Old French, and Latin. Among several periodical outlets, her principal one was the *British Quarterly Review*, to which she made more than sixty contributions from 1847 to 1870. This was a Nonconformist quarterly founded in the 1840s, which, like the *Athenaeum* and *Tait's*, offered more scope for contributions by women than the two long-established quarterlies. Here, Lawrance's subjects were diverse: as well as many articles about medieval, premedieval, and Early Modern literature, there were also pieces on art, African explorations, and the education and employment of women. She ventured into contemporary literature too, reviewing Tennyson's *Idylls of the King* and Gaskell's *Life of Charlotte Brontë*, and offering a posthumous retrospect of Elizabeth Barrett Browning's work in 1865.

Women such as Hannah Lawrance, Christian Johnstone, Harriet Martineau, Marian Evans, Margaret Oliphant, and Elizabeth Rigby Eastlake were remarkable for the broad range of areas in which they reviewed. In the later part of the century, two new trends affected women's activity as reviewers: the increasing prevalence of signature and the development of specialization. The generalist reviewer continued to exist, but the range of subjects studied at universities increased, with the growing prominence of history in particular and the introduction of English literature as an academic field of study. The burgeoning of periodicals, too, included the growth of specialist journals, adding to the demand for specialist knowledge in reviewers. Although women gained access to universities only in the last thirty years of the century, and in small numbers, some women reviewers, like their predecessors, embarked on the kind of self-education that enabled them to adapt to a new environment.

Edith Simcox (1844–1901) continued in the tradition of the polymath reviewer, contributing essays and reviews to a variety of periodicals. But after publishing initially as "H. Lawrenny," she started signing her own name and thus disclosed the impressive knowledge of which a female reviewer was capable. As Barbara Onslow notes, "she moved as easily from economics to ethics, or history to science, as between the literatures of Britain and Germany."[16] She could both operate within the "spacious arenas" of the monthly *Fortnightly Review* and *St Paul's Magazine* and write incisively for *The Academy*, whose male critics were often Oxford dons: these contributions were largely under her own name. She wrote for the latter weekly for twenty-five years, from its inception in 1869, covering topics such as French and German literature; Anglophone writers such as Emerson, Mill, Godwin, and Charles and Mary Lamb; and contemporary fiction by Bulwer Lytton, not to mention popular women novelists such as Ouida, Rhoda Broughton, and M. E. Braddon. She was especially interested in the lives and works of women, paying tribute in *The Academy* to the achievements of an earlier generation including astronomer Mary Somerville and writers

Dorothy Wordsworth and Anna Letitia Barbauld. In the larger space afforded by the *Fortnightly*, she commented on the "Ideals of Feminine Usefulness" represented by the founder of Ragged Schools, Mary Carpenter, and the devout Dora Pattison, who gave her life to hospital work in the slums (*Fortnightly Review*, May 27, 1880, pp. 656–71). Two other notable articles, both written in her twenties, were a wide-ranging analysis of different kinds of autobiographies (*North British Review*, January 1870, pp. 383–414) and an erudite commentary on the philosopher Schopenhauer (*Contemporary Review*, December 1872, pp. 440–63).

Emilia Dilke (1840–1904), of the same generation as Simcox, did reviewing that was more specialist in orientation. Mindful of the recommendation of her first husband, Oxford don Mark Pattison, to become "*the* authority on some subject,"[17] she decided to make that subject art history, especially French art of the Renaissance and subsequent centuries. She had studied art at the South Kensington School of Art under John Ruskin but went on to research her specialist area independently. Having contributed (anonymously) to the weekly *Saturday Review* in the 1860s, she went on to write for the *Westminster*, and then to become the art editor of *The Academy*, where her contributions were signed; she also published in the *Magazine of Art*. In her art criticism, she distanced herself from both her mentor Ruskin and the champion of "art for art's sake," Walter Pater, to reach an aesthetic that combined a valuing of technical execution and an awareness of social and historical contexts. These priorities carried over to her work for the nonspecialist *Athenaeum*. Here, while she demonstrated her knowledge of art terminology and the development of art criticism, she recalls Geraldine Jewsbury in being attuned to the implied reader of the periodical. For her, explains Marysa Demoor, this reader is someone "interested in the narrative of paintings as well as in the artists' technical excellencies." Hence, in her regular reviews of a German yearbook on art (1880–1904), she argues that "art criticism and art history had to tread a middle way between the academic exposé and the popularising story."[18]

One field in which women regularly reviewed throughout the Victorian period was European literature. This trend is worth highlighting – partly because European literature in the original and in translation loomed larger in the literary world than it does now – but also because it was an area in which women could gain competence. Education in European languages, especially French and Italian, was open to middle- and upper-class women in a way that learning in classical languages usually was not. Of the reviewers already mentioned, Busk, Evans, Hasell, Lawrance, Sinnett, Oliphant, and Simcox were all notable for reviewing texts in European languages: Evans, Sinnett, and Busk were especially expert about writing in German, while

Hasell educated herself in Spanish literature, and Oliphant made substantial contributions to the reviewing of French and Italian literature. Of later writers, significant figures include Helen Zimmern (1846–1934), a professional translator of German and Italian, who reviewed for a variety of periodicals, especially in the translation field, where she emphasized the quality of the translation as well as the content, and Mary Robinson (later Darmesteter, 1857–1944), with similar priorities, who reviewed translations for the *Athenaeum* in the 1880s and 1890s.

The *Athenaeum* was especially salient for its employment of women reviewers in the last thirty years of the nineteenth century, under the editorship of Norman McColl and the proprietorship of Sir Charles Dilke (Emilia's husband). In general, the convention of anonymity continued, its having been an article of faith with Sir Charles's grandfather Charles Wentworth Dilke, who believed that the practice relieved reviewers from possible pressure from authors and publishers. Important contributors in fields normally considered male preserves included Millicent Garrett Fawcett (1847–1929), who reviewed twenty-eight books on political economy, and Jane Ellen Harrison (1850–1928), a classical scholar and anthropologist who, unlike most women reviewers, did have academic training (at the British Museum) and also held a research fellowship at Newnham College in Cambridge (1898–1903). Harrison reviewed regularly on archaeology and ancient religion from 1893 to 1901.

Women also continued to review fiction in the *Athenaeum*, a prolific contributor being Katherine de Mattos (1851–1939), who wrote 1,300 reviews over twenty-two years from 1886. She could be hard hitting, as in her criticism of veteran popular novelist Rhoda Broughton for weak plots and slapdash writing. Nor did she spare the established and respected Henry James, although for the opposite reason – his writing was oversubtle. So in *The Awkward Age*, despite its "adroitness, and suppleness of diction," the reader, she says, can become wearied by "a sense of ineffectual striving with shadows" created by "rarified psychology" and "general bloodlessness" (*Athenaeum*, May 27, 1899).[19] De Mattos was usually more enthusiastic about James's short stories where, she claims in reviewing *The Lesson of the Master, and Other Stories* in 1892, "space does not allow of circumlocution or prolonged fencing with direct issues" (*Athenaeum*, March 19, p. 369). Like other *Athenaeum* reviewers, she is aware of the difference between general readers and those with more recondite tastes.

In the later years of the nineteenth century, the *Athenaeum* also featured several women who regularly reviewed poetry, including Mathilde Blind (1841–96) and Edith Nesbit (1858–1924). Especially cogent was the work of Augusta Webster (1837–94), who contributed from 1884 to her death 228 book reviews, mostly of poetry, and who was sometimes given the opportunity to write quite extensively and/or to open an issue. Many of the volumes she covered have sunk without trace, and Webster found most of them dross. But in 1893, she did offer a positive review of Yeats's *The Countess Kathleen and Various Legends and Lyrics* (January 7, 1893, p. 16) and welcomed *Underneath the Boughs* by "Michael Field" (Katherine Bradley and Edith Cooper) (September 9, 1893, pp. 345–46). Both her praise and her blame reveal that she values spontaneity combined with evidence of thought, often revealed by imagery that comes across as "natural" rather than as strained or artificial. Again, the effect of the text on the reader is a salient consideration – poetry should offer the reader new insights by setting his or her imagination to work.

In surveying women journalists of the nineteenth century, Barbara Onslow contrasts the work of Elizabeth Rigby Eastlake with that of later critic Alice Meynell (1847–1922), observing that the essays of the two were "scarcely recognizable as belonging to the same genre." Although Onslow acknowledges that the demands of periodicals as much as the writer herself determined formats, she notes that briefer, snappier essays and reviews were more in demand later in the century. Meynell wrote essays and reviews for many outlets – including several newspapers – and cultivated brevity and elegance. Thus "arresting phrases and swift turns of argument illuminate what is praised and just save the sharpness of criticism from sinking into malice."[20] She became famous in particular for her contributions to the "Wares of Autolycus" column in the daily *Pall Mall Gazette* in the 1890s, which often covered literature, though it was not concerned primarily with reviewing books. She also wrote on literature for the *Scots Observer* (1889–92) and on art for the *Art Journal*, *Magazine of Art*, and *Pall Mall Gazette*.

For all that Meynell's style differed from that of many earlier female reviewers, one thing she shared with most of them was that reviewing was part of a larger literary repertoire: Meynell's main other literary endeavor was publishing poetry. Much of her journalism was not in the form of reviews, and this was also the case with other writers discussed here, such as Anne Mozley, Christian Johnstone, Harriet Martineau, and Edith Simcox. Indeed, Eliza Lynn Linton (1822–98), one of the most prolific writers for periodicals and newspapers, and the first woman on the staff of a daily newspaper (*The Morning Chronicle*, 1849–51), has not been covered here, since she was not prominent primarily as a reviewer; prodigiously industrious in journalism, Linton was also a novelist. It is important to register just how versatile many women reviewers were. Other poets included Augusta Webster, a remarkable practitioner of the dramatic monologue; Rosamund Tomson/Marriott Watson; and Edith Nesbit (still known for her children's fiction). Harriet Martineau translated philosophy and, as well as *Illustrations of Political Economy*, produced novels, history, and travel books on America. Both Emilia Dilke and Edith Simcox were activists in the women's trade union movement and wrote in that area accordingly, while Millicent Fawcett was a prominent suffragist. Geraldine Jewsbury was also a novelist and had a long career as a publisher's reader. Under her own name, Margaret Oliphant was known primarily for her fiction, publishing more than eighty novels, but she also brought out biographies, histories, and literary histories.

It is not always possible to determine how largely financial considerations loomed in the careers of women reviewers. In the cases of Rigby Eastlake, Hasell, and Mozley, it seems that they wrote so as to express themselves about subjects that interested them and that they enjoyed researching; for Hasell and Mozley, too, writing diversified the life of a lady of leisure given otherwise to local good works. But unlike many male reviewers, women who needed to earn a living had few options: men might practice a profession or gain a university post, whereas women sufficiently educated to write for publication had few other choices besides teaching or governessing. Women also had less access than men to literary and publishing networks, not to mention male-only clubs and university connections, although they were never without networks of their own. They might also lack male financial backing, as became the case when Martineau's family business failed in the 1820s; or when they were widowed with children to support, as happened to Oliphant and Sinnett; or when their male partners were also reliant on writing, as with Marian Evans's partner George Henry Lewes and Alice Meynell's husband Wilfrid; or when their husbands were feckless, like those of Katherine de Mattos and Edith Nesbit.

Margaret Oliphant did enjoy writing for its own sake: she received the proofs of her first novel on her wedding day in 1849. But as her financial commitments increased, she found she had to publish anything she could place, and she resented never achieving the regular income that a man with an editorship would have had. By contrast, Harriet Martineau found her family's financial misfortune gave her a rationale for publishing; in the autobiography that she wrote in the 1850s, she constructed a heroic image of herself, struggling and succeeding in the marketplace.

Finally, Alice Meynell's and Edith Simcox's cases give interesting indications of what might be achieved by the turn of the century. Writing reviews and essays for the income that her poetry could not garner, Meynell not only cultivated her prose style but also produced collections of her journalism in book form, with high production values. Together with her poetry, Meynell's journalism contributed to creating for her a high-culture reputation as a woman of letters.[21] Union activist Simcox's priorities were different, but in February 1880, when she had returned home from central London on foot for lack of money, she aspired to earn £50 a year from writing. When she died in 1901, her death certificate described her as a "Gentlewoman of independent means," and she scored an obituary in *The Times*.

NOTES

1. [Elizabeth Rigby], "Vanity Fair – and Jane Eyre," *Quarterly Review* 84 (December 1848), 153–85, 173–75.
2. Anthony Trollope, *Autobiography* (Oxford: Oxford University Press, 1980), chap. 10, p. 153; [E. S. Dallas], "Popular Literature: The Periodical Press," *Blackwood's Magazine* 85 (February 1859), 180–95, 187.
3. Greg's views are discussed by Dallas Liddle, "Salesmen, Sportsmen, Mentors: Anonymity in Mid-Victorian Theories of Journalism," *Victorian Studies* 41 (1997), 31–58; see also Sarah Nash, "What's in a Name? Signature, Criticism, and Authority in the *Fortnightly Review*," *Victorian Periodicals Review* 43 (2010), 57–82.
4. [Rigby], p. 176.
5. Bessie Raynor Parkes, *Essays on Woman's Work* (1865), qtd. in Alexis Easley, *First-Person Anonymous: Women Writers and Victorian Print Media, 1830–1870* (Aldershot and Burlington, VT: Ashgate, 2004), p. 2.
6. Linda K. Hughes, "Journalism's Iconoclast: Rosamund Marriott Watson ('Graham R. Tomson')," in *Women in Journalism at the Fin de Siècle: Making a Name for Herself*, ed. F. Elizabeth Gray (Houndsmill, Basingstoke: Palgrave Macmillan, 2012), pp. 202–17.
7. See Solveig C. Robinson, "'Amazed at our Success': The Langham Place Editors and the Emergence of a Feminist Critical Tradition," *Victorian Periodicals Review* 29 (1996), 159–72.
8. Qtd. in Joanne Wilkes, *Women Reviewing Women in Nineteenth-Century Britain: The Critical Reception of Jane Austen, Charlotte Brontë and George Eliot* (Farnham, Surrey, and Burlington, VT: Ashgate, 2010), pp. 91–92.
9. Dallas Liddle, *The Dynamics of Genre: Journalism and the Practice of Literature in Mid-Victorian Britain* (Charlottesville: University of Virginia Press, 2009), p. 58.
10. Florence Fenwick Miller, *Harriet Martineau*, Eminent Women Series, ed. J. H. Ingram (London: W. H. Allen, 1884), p. 194.
11. Judith Johnston, *Victorian Women and the Economies of Travel, Translation and Culture, 1830–1870* (Farnham, Surrey, and Burlington, VT: Ashgate, 2013), p. 137.
12. Liddle, *Dynamics of Genre*, pp. 99ff.
13. This phrase and several that follow come from "Silly Novels by Lady Novelists," *Westminster Review* 66 (October 1856), 442–61; rpt. Thomas Pinney, ed., *Essays of George Eliot* (London: Routledge and Kegan Paul, 1963), pp. 300–24, at p. 301. Emphasis in original.
14. Ibid., pp. 304, 307, 318, 320.

15. *Tait's Edinburgh Magazine*, N.S. 2 (1838), 257, qtd. in Rosemary Mitchell, *Picturing the Past: English History in Text and Image, 1830–1870* (Oxford: Clarendon Press, 2000), p. 150.
16. Barbara Onslow, *Women of the Press in Nineteenth-Century Britain* (Houndmills, Basingstoke: Macmillan; New York: St. Martin's, 2000), p. 76.
17. Onslow, *Women of the Press*, pp. 78–79; see also Elizabeth Mansfield, "Articulating Authority: Emilia Dilke's Early Essays and Reviews," *Victorian Periodicals Review* 31 (1998), 75–86. Emphasis in original.
18. Marysa Demoor, *Their Fair Share: Women, Power and Criticism in the Athenaeum from Millicent Garrett Fawcett to Katherine Mansfield, 1870–1920* (Aldershot: Ashgate, 2000), pp. 72–73.
19. Quoted in Demoor, *Their Fair Share*, p. 97.
20. Onslow, *Women of the Press*, p. 84.
21. Linda H. Peterson, *Becoming a Woman of Letters: Myths of Authorship and Facts of the Victorian Market* (Princeton: Princeton University Press, 2009), pp. 173ff.

17

CLAUDIA NELSON

Children's writing

The business of writing for children

In his adult novel *New Grub Street* (1891), set in the London literary world, George Gissing sketches the career of two young middle-class women left in straitened circumstances by their mother's death. Their brother submits to a publisher under their names a proposal for a book to be titled *A Child's History of the English Parliament*, which the young women then complete and publish. Subsequently, the sisters embark on freelance work for a magazine that Gissing calls *The English Girl* (the title suggests that it resembles such real-life publications as *The Young Ladies' Journal* and *The Girl's Own Paper*), because their brother knows the editor and has prevailed on her to provide employment for them even though they have little previous experience. Their earnings are steady; unlike many other women authors of the period, neither has to combine writing with other forms of paid employment; and at least one sister finds the work pleasant enough that she continues it even after marriage has made her financially secure. All in all, the portrait of their literary career is considerably less gloomy than the corresponding account of the struggle of many of the male writers with whom *New Grub Street* is primarily concerned.

While sketchy, Gissing's discussion of the sisters' enterprise is founded on an accurate understanding that if writing for pay was a career relatively open to middle-class women in the nineteenth century, children's literature was arguably the most welcoming segment of the field. To be sure, almost any kind of writing could have been produced at home to a schedule that made it possible for an author to attend also to the domestic duties that Victorian ideology identified as paramount for a woman, but because teaching and guiding children was often considered to be the most important of those duties, writing juvenile literature could be seen

251

as an extension of her natural womanly capacities. That women were presumed to have a special affinity for the young meant that earning money as a children's author was likely to be viewed as socially positive rather than as an unfeminine attempt to thrust oneself into the public sphere.

Moreover, Victorian women were already well ensconced in this profession, having inherited a thriving tradition of women's writing for children from their Georgian predecessors. Sarah Fielding (1710–68), whose *The Governess* (1749) was at once the first novel written explicitly for girls and the first full-length children's novel in English, and Maria Edgeworth (1768–1849), whose *Harry and Lucy* (1827) was a childhood favorite of the future Queen Victoria and who was also well known as a writer for adults, were among the many literary foremothers who achieved success as storytellers. But before the Victorian period, women were also prolific producers of children's poetry, primers, geographies, histories, biographies, science writing, travel writing, and religious tracts, among other genres. All these modes within children's literature continued to flourish as the nineteenth century progressed. Children's nonfiction was already a mature form by the Victorian period, and like children's fiction it was produced as often by women as by men. While the fact that a single writer might use multiple pen names, including cross-gendered ones, makes it difficult to estimate the relative proportion of male and female Victorian children's writers, women make up not quite half of the figures (thirty-one out of sixty-eight) listed in two volumes of the *Dictionary of Literary Biography* devoted to nineteenth-century British authors prominent within the field of children's literature.

To be sure, becoming a published children's author did not guarantee a continued living after one's literary productivity ended; applicants to the Royal Literary Fund charity included a number of prolific, if minor, children's writers on the order of Eliza Meteyard. Yet literary historian Susan Mumm notes that proportionate to their numbers in the general population of writers, women authors of children's books are underrepresented in the lists of people requesting such aid, and that even some of the petitioners had formerly earned a better living by their pen than was the case for their peers working in other forms. She instances Emma Marshall (1830–99), whose 200-odd domestic novels and historical romances for children and adults had once brought her £500 a year and enabled her to educate five sons for assorted professions.[1] Children's literature was at once potentially profitable and generically rich, diverse, and hospitable to women; during Victoria's reign, it furnished a significant arena both for female self-expression and for female community. In addition to mapping some landmarks within women-authored texts for children, this chapter discusses ways in which juvenile literature served these functions for Victorian women.

Children's literature as pulpit: didacticism and the woman's voice

Although not all works for children were didactically inclined even at the beginning of the Victorian era (and certainly not by the end), adult arbiters generally assumed that children's literature would communicate something worthwhile – morals or information or both – to its young consumers. This expectation could function as an inducement rather than a constriction for women, in that children's literature thus afforded them a platform from which to advocate a cause, critique behaviors or attitudes that they found unacceptable, or otherwise seek to shape the next generation. Writing for children, in short, held out the promise of social power. Consider the influence exerted by Anna Sewell's *Black Beauty* (1877), which, like its predecessors Sarah Trimmer's *The History of the Robins* (1786) and Mary Wollstonecraft's *Original Stories from Real Life* (1788), belongs to a largely feminine tradition of didactic works presenting kindness to animals as foundational to a rational and admirable adulthood. Narrated from the point of view of the title character as he moves through a succession of good and bad owners and descends from riding horse to carriage horse to cab horse, Sewell's *roman à thèse* exposes and condemns the ill effects on horses of human ignorance and thoughtlessness; various humane societies and allied groups used it to explain to young members how to behave toward animals. Sewell (1820–78), the daughter of children's author Mary Sewell (1797–1884), was not a writer by trade – *Black Beauty* was her only novel, completed at the end of her life when her health was at its worst – and her literary efforts were prompted much more by a desire to teach than by a desire to earn money.

Black Beauty was informed by Sewell's Quaker upbringing, which early instilled in her a sense of her duty toward less fortunate fellow creatures and encouraged her (and other women) to take an active role in efforts to improve the world. While other religions such as Judaism had at best a small presence in British children's literature at this time, it is difficult to overestimate the influence that various Christian denominations exerted on the field, particularly in the early and mid-Victorian years. In 1865, the Copyright Sub-Committee of the Religious Tract Society (RTS) identified children's books as "among the most saleable issues of the society";[2] the RTS's focus on marketability here was not only about profit but also about getting out the message. For that matter, profit could even be a source of anxiety if it seemed likely to undermine didacticism. When in 1879 and 1880 the RTS established *The Boy's Own Paper* and *The Girl's Own Paper* and these magazines proved enormously popular, some members of the organization's leadership were distressed by the degree of success achieved, taking the impressive sales figures as a sign that the magazines were striking too secular a note. Whether or not this was the case, the magazines continued on their best-selling way, and *The Girl's Own Paper* both inspired a number of profit-directed alternatives such as *Atalanta* (founded 1887) and *The Girl's Realm* (founded 1898) and provided a continuing forum for writers of moral fare for young women.

Of the religious writers for children working in these years, Evangelical women were among the most successful at making their voices heard, potentially to positive social effect beyond the making of livelihoods for themselves. The tract, an effort at persuasion that often took narrative form, was commonly associated with Christianity and with other forms of social engineering such as the temperance movement. While pamphlet-length tracts had a built-in circulation advantage because they were bought in bulk for distribution by the charitably inclined, longer tracts sometimes proved competitive in the general literary marketplace. The waif tales of Hesba Stretton (née Sarah Smith, 1832–1911), for example, were among the best-selling works in any genre over the course of the Victorian period; at the time of Stretton's death, some two million copies of her most successful children's book, *Jessica's First Prayer* (1867), had been sold. Through its pathetic portrait of a London street child who has been neglected by parents, church, educational system, and nation and yet remains a child of God, *Jessica's First Prayer* castigates middle-class snobbery and seeks to bring readers to a sense of their duty to their neighbor. Simultaneously, it explores the power of the outcast to change hearts, indicating that Jessica's ability to convert the (bourgeois) heathen may exceed that of even an earnest and well-disposed clergyman. Lord Shaftesbury, a contemporary reader, rhapsodized over the novel's "depth of Christian feeling" and remarked that "no man on earth could have completed a page of it."[3] Shaftesbury's comment both harmonizes with Stretton's own feminist leanings and suggests the extent to which Christian-themed children's writing afforded a socially acceptable – even socially welcome – pulpit to women whose own denominations generally denied them entry to the ministry.

While Sewell and Stretton set their novels in England and used an English cast of characters, both authors' works circulated internationally. *Jessica's First Prayer* was translated into fifteen languages and, for a time, was a required text in the Russian school system, while by 1897 George Angell, founder of the Massachusetts Society for the Prevention of Cruelty to Animals, had distributed more than two million copies of *Black Beauty* worldwide and had helped get the novel translated into six languages. Sewell's American fans seem to have found the work particularly potent; Aidan Chambers reports that as late as 1924, a Texas judge sent a cowhand who was convicted of mistreating his horse to spend a month in jail, noting as part of the sentence that the prisoner was to read *Black Beauty* three times.[4]

Other Christian women writers took as their stage not England but the British Empire, mingling their religious message with an imperial one. Fiction such as *Edith and Her Ayah, And Other Stories* (1872), by A.L.O.E. (Charlotte Maria Tucker, 1821–93, writing as "A Lady of England"), which drew on the firsthand knowledge of India that its author had gained as a missionary in Amritsar, and nonfiction such as Anne Maria Sargeant's *Mamma's Lessons on the History and Geography of Palestine* (1850) sought to acculturate young readers both as Christians and as citizens of a world power. The title story in *Edith and Her Ayah*, for instance, explains that while words alone may accomplish little in bringing Indigenous peoples to Christ, setting a virtuous example may do more. Above all, it contends that a child's sincere love and prayers for the souls of the natives may effect genuine conversions. The young reader is thus to understand both that the child colonist may bring about real change for the better and that the British presence in India and other non-Christian lands constitutes a kind of sacred trust. If empire is good to the extent that it furthers the Christian mission, the British child must think of colonized lands not as assets to be exploited but as patients to be brought to health. While such texts establish a hierarchy that takes British cultural superiority for granted, they also urge the development of a sense of responsibility toward non-British citizens of the Empire, an attitude not always on display in secular adventure fiction.

Genre and setting: fairylands, schoolrooms, and homes

Black Beauty, *Jessica's First Prayer*, A.L.O.E.'s many writings, and other widely reprinted didactic works suggest the appeal of children's literature as a platform for reform during the Victorian period. Yet while the open espousal of any number of causes may certainly be found in Victorian women's fiction for children, some genres tend to subordinate teaching moments to other elements, resulting in texts that offer instruction either perfunctorily or covertly. Such texts foreground the detailed description of the social environment that their characters occupy and may be found across a spectrum ranging from the fantastic to the familiar.

To be sure, during the first half of the Victorian period, works of fantasy by women were in many cases openly didactic. A case in point is A.L.O.E.'s *The Crown of Success* (1863), an allegory about four children competing under the guidance of the magical figure Mr. Learning to furnish cottages shaped like heads. The successful child, a girl whose physical disability and modest disposition might have seemed to put her at a disadvantage in the race, wins because she has affiliated herself with the good nymph Duty rather than with Folly or Pride; little Nelly works steadily and consistently, always with pleasing her mother as her objective, and consequently outpaces her brilliant but less virtuous older brother. The moral here is highly visible. But after Lewis Carroll (Charles Lutwidge Dodgson) published *Alice's Adventures in Wonderland* in 1865, the success of this fantasy that openly mocks the adult passion for instructing children set a fashion for imaginative literature that did not seem obviously calculated to teach the young.

Indeed, by the end of the century women (and men as well) were often employing the fairy tale to comment on the shortcomings not of children but of the adult world. Gender was a particular focus of these efforts, and accordingly the 1890s, a decade in which women made notable advances in career and educational options, witnessed a boom in the feminist fairy tale. Typical examples include E. Nesbit's "The Island of the Nine Whirlpools" (1899), in which the witch (who will initially strike readers as conventionally wicked, since she lives in a cave decorated with live snakes, but who turns out to be motivated by sisterly solidarity) makes common cause with the princess and her mother against the unpleasant and sexist king, and suffragist Evelyn Sharp's "The Boy Who Looked Like a Girl" (1896), which asserts the superiority of girls over loud and quarrelsome boys.

More proximate to the *Alice* books, Christina Rossetti's *Speaking Likenesses* (1874) responded to them, as critic U. C. Knoepflmacher has argued, by attacking Carroll's hostility toward adult women, including promulgators of didacticism. Rossetti's work followed other female-authored fantasies, such as Jean Ingelow's *Mopsa the Fairy* (1869) and Juliana Horatia Ewing's "Amelia and the Dwarfs" (1870), that examine and critique Victorian attitudes toward femininity and explore their damaging repercussions through unhappy or ambiguous endings. While such work certainly has its socially didactic implications, instruction here is much less evident than it is in texts such as *The Crown of Success*. The message, too, is very different from A.L.O.E.'s "Do your duty and work hard"; it seems closer to "Question the status quo," a moral not characteristic of early Victorian juvenile literature with its eighteenth-century roots.

Consider also the girls' school story, a genre that profited from the expanded educational opportunities available to Victorian girls in the latter part of the century. Woman-authored school stories did not originally take the form that later became conventional for them. To name some early examples, Sarah Fielding's eighteenth-century *The Governess*, cited earlier as the first full-length children's novel in English, deals with the education of a small group of girls by a female preceptor, and in 1841 Harriet Martineau (1802–76) published *The Crofton Boys*, a boys' school story that follows young Hugh's experiences (including the amputation of one of his feet after schoolyard roughhousing leads to an injury) at his preparatory school. In contrast, tales set in girls' boarding schools and secondary schools did not come into vogue until the 1880s and 1890s, when such institutions began to outpace home instruction as part of the training of middle-class girls.

Some late-century children's writers, for instance Sharp in *The Making of a Schoolgirl* (1897), wrote school stories only infrequently, while others were particularly associated with the form. Elizabeth Meade Smith (1844–1914), better known as L. T. Meade, is an example of the latter type of author. Her most popular school story was *A World of Girls* (1886), which, like many twentieth-century examples (and like the Lowood School portion of Charlotte Brontë's *Jane Eyre* before them), focuses on the schoolgirl within her peer group and traces her development – in this case from prickly and traumatized victim of recent bereavement to popular and well-adjusted member of the school. Works such as Jessie Mansergh's *Tom and Some Other Girls: A Public School Story* (1901) indicate that girls may expect their school life to look much like that vouchsafed to privileged boys and should look forward to it accordingly, while critic Sally Mitchell observes that stories set in high schools often suggest that an important function of the school is to compensate for the deficiencies and constrictions of the home environment.[5] Girls' school stories, in other words, typically celebrate female community, even when such celebration comes at the expense of a critique of domesticity.

Meanwhile, the dominant genre within woman-authored fiction for children, the domestic novel, often engaged in its own critiques of domesticity, making use of ambiguity and humor to dilute its more earnest moments, and anatomizing and making recommendations for the improvement of family life. This subversiveness may be found even early in the period. Catherine Sinclair's novel *Holiday House* (1839) is a striking example of the complexities possible within domestic didacticism. The tale chronicles the exploits of naughty Harry and Laura and their virtuous older brother, a configuration that might in more conventional hands have resulted in a cautionary tale in which Harry and Laura's misbehavior brings them to disaster while Frank's goodness is rewarded. Instead, Sinclair lampoons adult harshness in the person of the children's censorious caretaker, Mrs. Crabtree, and provides a parodic cautionary tale as a high point of the novel. The ending of this interpolated fairy tale mocks adults' fixation on child improvement, in that the protagonist grows up to become a thrasher of chance-met boys who, he believes, share the idle propensities that he himself evinced in childhood – a display of adult brutality that recalls the misconduct of the villainous giant who menaced him at that time. Meanwhile, in the frame tale Harry and Laura's native high spirits are tamed not by adult influence, which this novel represents as largely ineffective, but by their experience of tragedy when Frank contracts a fatal illness. In short, while *Holiday House* sometimes strikes a melancholy and spiritually uplifting note characteristic of much Christian fiction of the mid-nineteenth century, it also celebrates playfulness, critiques adult disciplinary enterprises, and questions gender stereotypes.

As *Holiday House*'s interest in both boys and girls illustrates, women's domestic fiction for children often has as much to say about masculinity as it does about femininity – and its message is not always complimentary. The title and subtitle of Annie Keary's *The Rival Kings, or, Overbearing* (1857) identify the novel's theme, namely the problems that may arise when boys assert their desire for dominance within the domestic setting. The story follows Maurice Lloyd, "king" within a sibling group of which he is the oldest, and the consequences of his jealous anger when a neighbor boy, Roger Fletcher, attracts the fealty of three children staying in the Lloyd household. Maurice's mother is aware of his feelings and attempts to teach him better ways by telling him didactic stories and urging him to put his faith in Christ, but neither her narratives nor her exhortations have a significant effect on Maurice's implacability. Keary provides a happy ending when a near-tragedy brings Maurice to a sense of his sin in time, but the novel hints that in the absence of some such dramatic turn of events, the male tendency to be "overbearing" and to insist on hegemony will often trump female virtue and, indeed, the power of female domestic narratives. The implications for domestic life are decidedly edgy.

Arguably, ambiguity characterizes iconic children's domestic fiction throughout the Victorian period. Consider, for instance, the two ways of reading Charlotte M. Yonge's best-selling novel *The Daisy Chain* (1856) that are described in Nesbit's *The Wouldbegoods* (1901), itself a sympathetic yet humorous treatment of children's efforts at virtue by an author who was in her day an admirer of *Jessica's First Prayer*. Daisy, whose own goodness the child narrator considers excessive, says that Yonge's story is

> about a family of poor motherless children who tried so hard to be good, and they were confirmed, and had a bazaar, and went to church at the Minster, and one of them got married and wore black watered silk and silver ornaments. So her baby died, and then she was sorry she had not been a good mother to it.

At this point, one of the other children gets up and tries to leave the gathering in protest at the tale's apparent dullness and earnestness, at which Daisy's brother explains that "*The Daisy Chain* is not a bit like that really. It's a ripping book. One of the boys dresses up like a lady and comes to call, and another tries to hit his little sister with a hoe. It's jolly fine, I tell you."[6] Like many other Victorian domestic tales, *The Daisy Chain* is a complex narrative that invites radically different readings.

While Daisy's way of reading Yonge's novel is the more conventional, her brother's emphasis on the text's antic qualities is legitimate as well, judging by the uses to which some later writers put it. Yonge (1823–1901) did not consider herself a feminist, but her novel nonetheless exerted a strong influence on more outspoken writers; Ethel, *The Daisy Chain*'s protagonist, is a gawky and brilliant teenage girl who contributed to Louisa May Alcott's portrayal of Jo March. Ethel's hunger for classical learning and her grief when other responsibilities require her to abandon study enable the narrator to focus on female frustration over the limitations of domestic life, and this theme is one to which Yonge would return many times over the course of her long and productive career. Yonge herself, while concurring with her father's view that women who were not in need of money should not earn it, nonetheless reaped substantial profits from her writing, which she turned over to various religious causes. She thus became not only a successful professional author but also a philanthropist who sought to change her world for the better.

Community, mentorship, and magazines

Yonge had a shrewd understanding of Victorian audiences and their needs. She wrote variously for audiences that we would now describe as middle grade, adolescent, and adult; for working-class and more privileged readers; and in a variety of genres including biography, historical fiction and nonfiction, and domestic fiction. While her view of her own writing was in part instrumental inasmuch as she would earmark the earnings from a particular publication for a particular philanthropic project, she was also conscious of her role as guide to multiple generations of younger women writers. Writing, she understood, is constitutive of community, and she nurtured community both through her editorship of a magazine, *The Monthly Packet*, and by serving as mentor and "Mother Goose" to a group of young women who came to know themselves as "The Goslings." The Goslings produced their own hand-lettered and handsomely illustrated magazine, *The Barnacle* (the title comes from the barnacle goose but also connotes a colony of small individuals clustering around a larger center), passing it in person and by post to members in different parts of Britain so that all who wanted to could contribute their own poetry, travel writing, instructive essays, or serialized fiction written in close imitation of Yonge. At least one Gosling, Christabel Coleridge (1843–1921), became in due course a professional writer herself, taking over the editorship of *The Monthly Packet*, publishing the first biography of Yonge, and producing more than a dozen novels.

This model of community and mentorship among women writers for children was by no means unique to Yonge. Much of Juliana Ewing's work, for instance, including her popular novellas *Jackanapes* (1879) and *The Story of a Short Life* (1883), debuted in *Aunt Judy's Magazine*, a periodical founded by her mother, Margaret Gatty (1809–73); named after the young Juliana; and edited at various times by Gatty, Ewing's sister Horatia Eden, and Ewing herself. After Gatty's death, the magazine continued to publish works by members of the Gatty family as well as by outsiders such as Carroll, early installments of whose novel *Sylvie and Bruno* appeared in *Aunt Judy's* in 1867. Nevertheless, Ewing's own initial publication was not in *Aunt Judy's* but in *The Monthly Packet*, a detail illustrating the overlap possible within different feminine writing communities. Indeed, Yonge's magazine was a productive venue for Ewing, whose first book, *Melchior's Dream and Other Tales* (1862), was a collection of her stories from that periodical. Similarly, Meade founded *Atalanta* in part as a way of furthering feminist ideals; the magazine sought to mentor its readers, providing them with career advice and opportunities to make their voices heard by winning critical essay competitions.

Of course, established women could serve as literary benefactors in the field of book publishing as well. For instance, the noted Scottish fantasist George MacDonald (1824–1905) owed the publication of his first successful novel, *David Elginbrod* (1863), to Dinah Mulock Craik (1826–87), who recommended it to her publishers. Nevertheless, magazine publishing was an enterprise particularly open to new women writers, inasmuch as children's periodicals developed explosively over the course of the Victorian period; critic Diana Dixon puts at 160 the number of titles published during 1900. Editors of girls' magazines, many of whom were female, were perennially hungry for material and ready to work with unknown authors. In this regard, too, Gissing's portrait of the business in *New Grub Street* is an accurate one.

One by-product of the thriving magazine market was that writers might feel encouraged to work in multiple genres. Even a periodical clearly aimed at a particular segment of the reading public typically contained a wide range of forms. Thus, a glance at the January and February 1847 numbers (to take a sample at random) of the *Juvenile Missionary Magazine* reveals entries classifiable as biography, history, anthropological commentary, wild beast adventures, sheet music, arts and crafts, and comparative culture in the shape of a juxtaposition of Chinese proverbs with their English counterparts, in addition to free-standing illustrations; narrative forms here range from dialogues and letters to third-person storytelling and sermons. With the possible exception of the sermons, any of these contributions might come from a female pen. Such variety was typical of the Victorian children's magazine and made it easy for a writer who had sold one kind of work to an editor to branch out into another kind of work – moving from short poems to more remunerative stories or serials, for instance, as happened with Nesbit.

Crossing over: writing for multiple audiences

That Nesbit (1858–1924) built much of her career on selling work to adult middlebrow or "family" magazines also reminds us of the large body of crossover literature, works that might be read with pleasure by both children and adults. Her first major success after a career of hack work not dissimilar to the model described in *New Grub Street* came with *The Story of the Treasure Seekers*, published in volume form in 1899 after having appeared piecemeal not only in *Nister's Holiday Annual* (aimed at children) but also in the family periodicals *The Illustrated London News*, *Pall Mall*, and *Windsor Magazine*. Subsequent works appeared serially in *The Strand*, a middlebrow magazine predominantly aimed at adults but offering a fine line in quality children's literature as well.

Women writers who had made a success in the book market by writing for adults sometimes crossed over into writing for children because such writing offered particular benefits. Martineau made her name with her work on political economy in the 1830s but had also written tracts for the Calvinist publishing firm F. Houlston and Son early in her career, some of them addressed to children. She returned to children's literature in the 1840s with the Playfellow series, four short volumes published quarterly in 1841, noting in her autobiography that her health had become so poor at this point in her life that the "light and easy work ... of a series of children's tales" was all she could manage.[7] Craik, who as Dinah Mulock had produced one of the major best sellers of the era in the 1856 adult novel *John Halifax, Gentleman*, was prompted to write works of children's fantasy, including *The Adventures of a Brownie* (1872) and *The Little Lame Prince* (1874), when she married and, in 1869, adopted a daughter. And Rossetti, who had in 1862 turned down an invitation to contribute to a collection of poetry about children on the ground that "*children* are not amongst my suggestive subjects,"[8] gravitated toward children's poetry and fiction in the early 1870s with *Sing-Song* (1872) as well as with *Speaking Likenesses*, in both cases with the expressed hope of succeeding in the lucrative children's Christmas book market. Among them, these three authors' motivations for taking up children's writing, namely its perceived ease, compatibility with family life, and potential for profit, resemble those of many other women writers for children during this period.

One reason that the discussion of crossover writing becomes relevant here is that the Victorian era was characterized by a marked segmentation of the reading public. Whereas mid-Victorian literature saw considerable success on the part of "family novelists" on the order of Charles Dickens, whose works could be read aloud to the entire family circle and enjoyed by old and young alike, later and more Modernist writers such as Henry James addressed their works to a more select group, what they saw as the mature, discerning reader. This trend followed on what was largely an eighteenth-century innovation, the creation of a separate literature for children, and also on the nineteenth-century innovation of producing separate texts for girls and for boys. Increased literacy and decreased production costs gradually opened the door to specialized periodicals for readers of every political or religious stripe and for many different socioeconomic levels. Magazines aimed at working-class youths, for instance, included both strongly didactic titles and sensational story papers available for a halfpenny to the economically enfranchised shopgirl or office boy. Book publishing, too, ranged from the luxury item of the lavishly illustrated gift book to the penny tract and from the gendered novel for older girl or boy readers to the genderless story for young children, of which the most famous late-Victorian example may be Beatrix Potter's *The Tale of Peter Rabbit* (1901).

The market for children's literature thus developed a large number of niches over the course of the Victorian period, a feature that in some cases worked to women's advantage. Writing for girls or young children was considered women's work; when male bylines appear in *The Girl's Own*

Paper, for instance, they often belong to clerics. Yet women did not remain within a literary purdah. While male writers dominated books and periodicals aimed at boys, successful authors of boys' school stories included such writers as Elizabeth Eiloart and Annie Forsyth Grant, and women also contributed to boys' magazines, sometimes under male pseudonyms. Moreover, some forms, such as fantasy and many kinds of nonfiction, were not strongly gendered, and men and women competed there on a more or less equal basis. While Charles Kingsley, for example, first made his mark in children's literature by producing a work of popular science, *Glaucus, or the Wonders of the Shore* (1855), Gatty, author of *Parables from Nature* (1855–71, 5 vols.) and an authority on seaweeds, was one of a number of woman writers who also succeeded in this form.

Conclusion

Just as children's literature took a wide variety of forms from fiction to poetry to nonfiction and from magazine to single volume, it represented different things to different women writers. To some, certainly, it was drudgery or disappointment; Nesbit was one of many who might have preferred to win fame as a poet or as a novelist for adults. To others, among them many religious writers, it was a high calling, a chance to disseminate to a receptive audience social or moral messages about which they were passionate. Some considered it primarily play, some a congenial livelihood, some a forum in which they could engage with other woman writers as pupil or teacher. Inevitably, the degree of artistry achieved also varied considerably.

Yet at its best, Victorian children's literature by women reaches a high standard of excellence. Often innovative, it still more frequently affords a valuable glimpse at the social priorities and attitudes of individual writers, hinting at aspects of daily life that they found particularly frustrating or rewarding and giving today's reader a sense of how these women understood their place in the world. As historical documents and sometimes also as works of art, these works of juvenile literature richly repay adult scrutiny.

NOTES

1. Susan D. Mumm, "Writing for Their Lives: Women Applicants to the Royal Literary Fund, 1840–1880," *Publishing History* 27 (1990), 32–33.
2. Qtd. in Elaine Lomax, *The Writings of Hesba Stretton: Reclaiming the Outcast* (Burlington, VT: Ashgate, 2009), p. 54.
3. Qtd. in Lomax, *The Writings of Hesba Stretton*, p. 57.

4. Aidan Chambers, "Letters from England: A Hope for Benefit," *The Horn Book* 53 (1977), 356–59.
5. Sally Mitchell, *The New Girl: Girls' Culture in England, 1880–1915* (New York: Columbia University Press, 1995), p. 80.
6. E. Nesbit, *The Wouldbegoods, in The Story of the Treasure Seekers and The Wouldbegoods*, ed. Claudia Nelson (Houndmills: Palgrave Macmillan, 2013), pp. 263–64.
7. Qtd. in Ainslie Robinson, "Playfellows and Propaganda: Harriet Martineau's Children's Writing," *Women's Writing* 9:3 (2002), 395.
8. Qtd. in Lorraine Janzen Kooistra, *Christina Rossetti and Illustration: A Publishing History* (Athens: Ohio University Press, 2002), p. 91. Emphasis in original.

GUIDE TO FURTHER READING

Introduction: Victorian women's writing and modern feminist criticism

Adams, Kimberly van Esveld. "Women and Literary Criticism." In *The Cambridge History of Literary Criticism: The Nineteenth Century*, vol. 6, ed. M. A. R. Habib. Cambridge: Cambridge University Press, 2013. Pp. 72–94.

Donovan, Josephine. *Feminist Theory: The Intellectual Traditions*. New York: Continuum, 2012.

Eagleton, Mary (ed.). *Feminist Literary Theory: A Reader*. 2nd edn. Malden, MA: Wiley-Blackwell, 2011.

Federico, Annette R. (ed.). *Gilbert & Gubar's* The Madwoman in the Attic *After Thirty Years*. Columbia: University of Missouri Press, 2009.

Friedman, Susan Stanford. "Post/Poststructuralist Feminist Criticism: The Politics of Recuperation and Negotiation," *New Literary History*, 22:2 (Spring 1991), 465–90.

Gilbert, Sandra M. *Rereading Women: Thirty Years of Exploring Our Literary Traditions*. New York: Norton, 2011.

Gilbert, Sandra M. and Susan Gubar. *The Madwoman in the Attic: The Woman Writer and the Nineteenth-Century Literary Imagination*. New Haven: Yale University Press, 1979.

Moers, Ellen. *Literary Women: The Great Writers*. New York: Oxford University Press, 1976.

Shattock, Joanne (ed.). *The Oxford Guide to British Women Writers*. Oxford: Oxford University Press, 1993.

(ed.). *Women and Literature in Britain, 1800–1900*. Cambridge: Cambridge University Press, 2001.

Showalter, Elaine. *A Literature of Their Own: British Women Novelists from Brontë to Lessing*. Princeton: Princeton University Press, 1977.

"'A Literature of Their Own' Revisited." *NOVEL: A Forum on Fiction* 31:3 (Summer 1998), 399–413.

Warhol-Down, Robyn and Diane Price Herndl (eds.). *Feminisms Redux: An Anthology of Literary Theory and Criticism*. New Brunswick, NJ: Rutgers University Press, 2009.

Part I: Victorian women writers' careers

1 Making a debut

Bernstein, Susan David. *Roomscape: Women Writers in the British Museum from George Eliot to Virginia Woolf.* Edinburgh: Edinburgh University Press, 2013.

Easley, Alexis. *First-Person Anonymous: Women Writers and Victorian Print Media, 1830–70.* Aldershot: Ashgate, 2004.

  Literary Celebrity, Gender, and Victorian Authorship, 1850–1914. Newark: Delaware University Press, 2011.

Fraser, Hilary, Stephanie Green, and Judith Johnston. *Gender and the Victorian Periodical.* Cambridge: Cambridge University Press, 2003.

Onslow, Barbara. *Women of the Press in Nineteenth-Century Britain.* Basingstoke: Macmillan, 2000.

Peterson, Linda H. *Becoming a Woman of Letters: Myths of Authorship and Facts of the Victorian Market.* Princeton: Princeton University Press, 2009.

Phegley, Jennifer. *Educating the Proper Woman Reader: Victorian Family Literary Magazines and the Cultural Health of the Nation.* Columbus: Ohio State University Press, 2004.

Shattock, Joanne. "Professional Networks: Masculine and Feminine." *Victorian Periodicals Review* 44.2 (Summer 2011), 128–40.

Tuchman, Gaye and Nina Fortin. *Edging Women Out: Victorian Novelists, Publishers and Social Change.* New Haven: Yale University Press, 1989.

2 Becoming a professional writer

Colón, Susan E. *The Professional Ideal in the Victorian Novel: The Works of Disraeli, Trollope, Gaskell, and Eliot.* New York: Palgrave Macmillan, 2007.

Cross, Nigel. *The Common Writer. Life in Nineteenth-Century Grub Street.* Cambridge: Cambridge University Press, 1985.

Gleadle, Kathryn. *The Early Feminists. Radical Unitarians and the Emergence of the Women's Rights Movement, 1831–1850.* Basingstoke: Macmillan, 1995.

Oliphant, Margaret. *The Autobiography of Margaret Oliphant,* ed. Elisabeth Jay. Oxford: Oxford University Press, 1990.

Peterson, Linda H. *Becoming a Woman of Letters: Myths of Authorship and Facts of the Victorian Market.* Princeton: Princeton University Press, 2009.

Shattock, Joanne. "Professional Networks: Masculine and Feminine." *Victorian Periodicals Review* 44:2 (Summer 2011), 128–40.

3 Working with publishers

Ashton, Rosemary. *George Eliot: A Life.* London: Penguin, 1997.

Finkelstein, David. *The House of Blackwood: Author-Publisher Relations in the Victorian Era.* University Park: Pennsylvania State University Press, 2002.

Glynn, Jenifer. "Charlotte Brontë" and "Mrs Gaskell." In *Prince of Publishers: A Biography of George Smith.* London: Allison & Busby, 1986. Pp. 49–75, 87–99.

Jay, Elisabeth. *Mrs Oliphant, A Fiction to Herself: A Literary Life*. Oxford: Clarendon Press, 1995.
Newbolt, Peter. *William Tinsley (1831–1902): "Speculative Publisher."* Aldershot: Ashgate, 2001.
Shattock, Joanne. "Professional Networking, Masculine and Feminine." *Victorian Periodicals Review* 44:2 (Summer 2011), 131–32.
Tuchman, Gaye and Nina E. Fortin, *Edging Women Out: Victorian Novelists, Publishers, and Social Change*. New Haven, CT: Yale University Press, 1989.

4 Assuming the role of editor

Beetham, Margaret. *A Magazine of her Own? Domesticity and Desire in the Woman's Magazine, 1800–1914*. London: Routledge, 1996.
Beetham, Margaret and Kay Boardman (eds.). *Victorian Women's Magazines: An Anthology*. Manchester: Manchester University Press, 2001.
Brake, Laurel. *Subjugated Knowledges: Journalism, Gender and Literature in the Nineteenth Century*. Basingstoke: Macmillan, 1994.
Easley, Alexis. *First-Person Anonymous: Women Writers and Victorian Print Media, 1830–1870*. Aldershot: Ashgate, 2004.
Feldman, Paula (ed.). "Introduction." In *The Keepsake for 1829*. Peterborough, Ontario: Broadview Press, 2006.
Fraser, Hilary, Stephanie Green, and Judith Johnston. *Gender and the Victorian Periodical*. Cambridge: Cambridge University Press, 2003.
Harris, Susan (ed.). *Blue Pencils and Hidden Hands: Women Editing Periodicals, 1830–1910*. Boston: Northeastern University Press, 2004.
Ledbetter, Kathryn. *British Victorian Women's Periodicals: Beauty, Civilization, and Poetry*. Basingstoke: Palgrave Macmillan, 2009.
Onslow, Barbara. *Women of the Press in Nineteenth-Century Britain*. Basingstoke: Palgrave Macmillan, 2000.
Patten, Robert and David Finkelstein. "Editing *Blackwood's*; or, What Do Editors Do?" In *Print Culture and the Blackwood Tradition*, ed. David Finkelstein. Toronto: University of Toronto Press, 2006. Pp. 146–83.
Wiener, Joel H. (ed.). *Innovators and Preachers: The Role of the Editor in Victorian England*. Westport, CT: Greenwood Press, 1985.

5 Achieving fame and canonicity

Brown, Susan. "The Victorian Poetess." In *The Cambridge Companion to Victorian Poetry*, ed. Joseph Bristow. Cambridge: Cambridge University Press, 2000.
The Brownings' Correspondence: An Online Edition, www.browningscorrespondence.com
Chapman, Alison (ed.). *The Database of Victorian Periodical Poetry*, http://web.uvic.ca/~vicpoet/database-of-victorian-periodical-poetry/.
Easley, Alexis. *Literary Celebrity, Gender, and Victorian Authorship, 1850–1914*. Newark: University of Delaware Press, 2011.

Guy, Josephine. "Authors and Authorship." In *The Cambridge Companion to English Literature 1830–1914*, ed. Joanne Shattock. Cambridge: Cambridge University Press, 2010.
Henry, Nancy. *The Cambridge Introduction to George Eliot*. Cambridge: Cambridge University Press, 2008.
Kooistra, Lorraine Janzen. *Christina Rossetti and Illustration: A Publishing History*. Athens: Ohio University Press, 2002.
Lootens, Tricia. *Lost Saints: Silence, Gender, and Victorian Literary Canonization*. Charlottesville: University of Virginia Press, 1996.
Marsh, Jan. *Christina Rossetti: A Literary Biography*. London: Pimlico, 1994.
Peterson, Linda. Elizabeth Gaskell's *The Life of Charlotte Brontë*. In *The Cambridge Companion to Elizabeth Gaskell*, ed. Jill L. Matus. Cambridge: Cambridge University Press, 2007). Pp. 69–74.

Part II: Victorian women writers' achievements

6 Poetry

Armstrong, Isobel and Virginia Blain (eds.). *Women's Poetry, Late Romantic to Late Victorian: Gender and Genre, 1830–1900*. New York: St. Martin's Press, 1999.
Boos, Florence (ed.). *Working-Class Women Poets in Victorian Britain: An Anthology*. Peterborough: Broadview Press, 2008.
Chapman, Alison (ed.). *Victorian Women Poets*. Cambridge: D. S. Brewer, 2003.
Dieleman, Karen. *Religious Imaginaries: The Liturgical and Poetic Practices of Elizabeth Barrett Browning, Christina Rossetti, and Adelaide Procter*. Athens: Ohio University Press, 2012.
Harrington, Emily. *Second Person Singular: Late Victorian Women Poets and the Bonds of Verse*. Charlottesville: University of Virginia Press, 2014.
Ledbetter, Kathryn. *British Women's Victorian Periodicals: Beauty, Civilization and Poetry*. Houndmills: Palgrave Macmillan, 2009.
Leighton, Angela. *Victorian Women Poets: Writing Against the Heart*. Charlottesville: University Press of Virginia, 1992.
Leighton, Angela and Margaret Reynolds (eds.). *Victorian Women Poets*. Oxford: Blackwell Publishers, 1995.
Prins, Yopie. *Victorian Sappho*. Princeton: Princeton University Press, 1999.
Scheinberg, Cynthia. *Women's Poetry and Religion in Victorian England: Jewish Identity and Christian Culture*. Cambridge: Cambridge University Press, 2002.

7 Silver-fork, industrial, and Gothic fiction

Bodenheimer, Rosemarie. *The Politics of Story in Victorian Social Fiction*. Ithaca: Cornell University Press, 1988.
Botting, Fred. *Gothic*. London: Routledge, 1996.
Copeland, Edward. *The Silver Fork Novel: Fashionable Fiction in the Age of Reform*. Cambridge: Cambridge University Press, 2012.

Gallagher, Catherine. *The Industrial Reformation of English Fiction: Social Discourse and Narrative Form 1832–1867.* Chicago and London: University of Chicago Press, 1985.
Gilbert, Sandra M., and Susan Gubar. *The Madwoman in the Attic: The Woman Writer and the Nineteenth-Century Literary Imagination.* New Haven: Yale University Press, 1979.
Guy, Josephine. *The Victorian Social-Problem Novel: The Market, the Individual and Communal Life.* Basingstoke: Macmillan, 1996.
Harman, Barbara Leah. *The Feminine Political Novel in Victorian England.* Charlottesville: University of Virginia Press, 1998.
Hughes, Winifred. "Silver Fork Writers and Readers: Social Contexts of a Best Seller." *NOVEL: A Forum on Fiction* 25 (1992), 328–47.
Jacobus, Mary. "The Buried Letter: Feminism and Romanticism in Charlotte Brontë's Villette." In *Women Writing and Writing About Women*, ed. Mary Jacobus. London: Croom Helm, 1979. Pp. 42–60.
Krueger, Christine L. *The Reader's Repentance: Women Preachers, Women Writers, and Nineteenth-Century Social Discourse.* Chicago: Chicago University Press, 1992.
O'Cinneide, Muireann. *Aristocratic Women and the Literary Nation, 1832–1867.* Basingstoke: Palgrave Macmillan, 2008.
Wagner, Tamara (ed.). "Special Issue: Silver Fork Fiction." *Women's Writing*, 16:2 (2009).
Zlotnick, Susan. *Women, Writing, and the Industrial Revolution.* Baltimore and London: John Hopkins University Press, 1998.

8 The realist novel

Greiner, Rae. *Sympathetic Realism in Nineteenth-Century British Fiction.* Baltimore: Johns Hopkins University Press, 2012.
Langbauer, Laurie. *Novels of Everyday Life: The Series in English Fiction, 1850–1930.* Ithaca: Cornell University Press, 1999.
Levine, Caroline. "Victorian Realism." *The Cambridge Companion to the Victorian Novel*, 2nd edn., ed. Deirdre David. Cambridge: Cambridge University Press, 2013.
Levine, George. *The Realistic Imagination: English Fiction from Frankenstein to Lady Chatterley.* Chicago: University of Chicago Press, 1981.
Morris, Pam. *Realism.* New York: Routledge, 2003.
Shaw, Harry E. *Narrating Reality: Austen, Scott, Eliot.* Ithaca: Cornell University Press, 1999.
Showalter, Elaine. "Queen George." In *Sexual Anarchy: Gender and Culture at the Fin de Siecle.* New York: Penguin Books, 1990.
Yeazell, Ruth Bernard. *Art of the Everyday: Dutch Painting and the Realist Novel.* Princeton: Princeton University Press, 2008.

9 Sensation and New Woman fiction

Ardis, Ann. *New Women, New Novels: Feminism and Early Modernism.* New Brunswick, NJ: Rutgers University Press, 1990.

Flint, Kate. *The Woman Reader 1837–1914*. Oxford: Clarendon Press, 1993.
Gavin, Adrienne E. and Carolyn Oulton (eds.). *Writing Women of the Fin de Siècle: Authors of Change*. London: Palgrave Macmillan, 2012.
Gilbert, Pamela (ed.). *A Companion to Sensation Fiction*. Oxford: Wiley-Blackwell, 2012.
Hager, Lisa. "Embodying Agency: Ouida's Sensational Shaping of the British New Woman." *Woman's Writing* 20 (2013), 235–46.
Harrison, Kimberly and Richard Fantina (eds.). *Victorian Sensations: Essays on a Scandalous Genre*. Columbus: Ohio State University Press, 2006.
Heilmann, Ann. *New Woman Fiction: Women Writing First-Wave Feminism*. Basingstoke: Macmillan, 2000.
  New Woman Strategies: Sarah Grand, Olive Schreiner, Mona Caird. Manchester: Manchester University Press, 2004.
Ledger, Sally. *The New Woman: Fiction and Feminism at the Fin de Siècle*. Manchester: Manchester University Press, 1997.
Mangham, Andrew (ed.). *The Cambridge Companion to Sensation Fiction*. Cambridge: Cambridge University Press, 2013.
O'Toole, Tina. *The Irish New Woman*. Basingstoke: Palgrave Macmillan, 2013.
Pykett, Lyn. *The Improper Feminine: The Women's Sensation Novel and the New Woman Fiction*. London: Routledge, 1992.
  The Nineteenth-Century Sensation Novel. Tavistock: Northcote House, 2011.
Showalter, Elaine. *A Literature of Their Own: British Women Novelists from Brontë to Lessing*. Princeton: Princeton University Press, 1977, revised and expanded 1997.

10 Drama and theater

Bratton, Jacky. *The Making of the West End Stage: Marriage, Management and the Mapping of Gender in London, 1830–1870*. Cambridge: Cambridge University Press, 2011.
Burroughs, Catherine. *Closet Stages: Joanna Baillie and the Theater Theory of British Romantic Women Writers*. Philadelphia: University of Pennsylvania Press, 1997.
Davis, Tracy C. and Ellen Donkin (eds.). *Women and Playwriting in Nineteenth-Century Britain*. Cambridge: Cambridge University Press, 1999.
Donohue, Joseph (ed.). *The Cambridge History of British Theatre*, vol. 2: *1660 to 1895*. Cambridge: Cambridge University Press, 2004.
Holledge, Julie. *Innocent Flowers: Women in the Edwardian Theatre*. London: Virago Press, 1981.
Marshall, Gail. *Actresses on the Victorian Stage: Feminine Performance and the Galatea Myth*. Cambridge: Cambridge University Press, 1998.
Newey, Katherine. *Women's Theatre Writing in Victorian Britain*. Basingstoke: Palgrave Macmillan, 2005.
Powell, Kerry. *Women and Victorian Theatre*. Cambridge: Cambridge University Press, 1997.
Stephens, John Russell. *The Profession of the Playwright*. Cambridge: Cambridge University Press, 1992.

11 Life-writing

Atkinson, Juliette. *Victorian Biography Reconsidered: A Study of Nineteenth-Century "Hidden" Lives*. Oxford: Oxford University Press, 2010.
Bell, Susan Groag and Marilyn Yalom (eds.). *Revealing Lives: Autobiography, Biography, and Gender*. Albany: State University of New York Press, 1990.
Benstock, Shari (ed.). *The Private Self: Theory and Practice of Women's Autobiographical Writings*. Chapel Hill: University of North Carolina Press, 1988.
Bloom, Abigail Burnham (ed.). *Personal Moments in the Lives of Victorian Women: Selections from Their Autobiographies*. 2 vols. Lewiston, NY: Edwin Mellon Press, 2008.
Brodski, Bella and Celeste Schenck (eds.). *Life/Lines: Theorizing Women's Autobiography*. Ithaca: Cornell University Press, 1988.
Corbett, Mary Jean. *Representing Femininity: Middle-Class Subjectivity and Victorian and Edwardian Women's Autobiography*. Oxford: Oxford University Press, 1992.
Gagnier, Regenia. *Subjectivities: A History of Self-Representation in Britain, 1832–1920*. New York: Oxford University Press, 1991.
Heilbrun, Carolyn G. *Writing a Woman's Life*. New York: W. W. Norton, 1988.
Lionnet, Françoise. *Autobiographical Voices: Race, Gender, Self-Portraiture*. Ithaca: Cornell University Press, 1989.
Mackay, Carol Hanbery. *Creative Negativity: Four Victorian Exemplars of the Female Quest*. Stanford: Stanford University Press, 2001.
Newey, Vincent and Philip Shaw (eds.). *Mortal Pages, Literary Lives: Studies in Nineteenth-Century Autobiography*. Aldershot: Scolar Press, 1996.
Peterson, Linda H. *Victorian Women's Autobiography: The Poetics and Politics of Life Writing*. Charlottesville: University of Virginia Press, 1999.
Sanders, Valerie. *The Private Lives of Victorian Women: Autobiography in Nineteenth-Century England*. London: Harvester Wheatsheaf, 1989.
Smith, Sidonie and Julia Watson (eds.). *Women, Autobiography, Theory: A Reader*. Madison: University of Wisconsin Press, 1998.

12 Travel writing

Bassnett, Susan. "Travel Writing and Gender." *The Cambridge Companion to Travel Writing*, ed. Peter Hulme and Tim Youngs. Cambridge: Cambridge University Press, 2002. Pp. 225–41.
Blunt, Alison. *Travel, Gender, and Imperialism: Mary Kingsley and West Africa*. New York and London: Guildford Press, 1994.
Brisson, Ulrike. "Fish and Fetish: Mary Kingsley's Studies of Fetish in West Africa." *Journal of Narrative Theory* 35:3 (2005), 326–40.
Harper, Lila Marz. *Solitary Travellers: Nineteenth-Century Women's Travel Narratives and the Scientific Vocation*. Madison, NJ: Fairleigh Dickinson University Press, 2001.
Korte, Barbara. *English Travel Writing: From Pilgrimages to Postcolonial Explorations*. Basingstoke: Palgrave, 2002.

Mills, Sara. *Discourses of Difference: An Analysis of Women's Travel Writing and Colonialism*. London: Routledge, 1991.
Morgan, Susan. *Place Matters: Gendered Geography in Victorian Women's Travel Books about Southeast Asia*. New Brunswick, NJ: Rutgers University Press, 1996.
Pratt, Mary Louise. *Imperial Eyes: Travel Writing and Transculturation*. New York: Routledge, 1992.
Robinson, Jane. *Unsuitable for Ladies: An Anthology of Women Travellers*. Oxford: Oxford University Press, 2001.
Sterry, Lorraine. *Victorian Women Travellers in Meiji Japan: Discovering a "New" Land*. Folkestone: Global Oriental, 2009.
Thompson, Carl. *Travel Writing*. London: Routledge, 2011.
Thurin, Susan Schoenbauer. *Victorian Travelers and the Opening of China, 1842–1907*. Athens: Ohio University Press, 1999.

13 Colonial and imperial writing

Adelaide, Debra (ed.). *A Bright and Fiery Troop: Australian Women Writers of the Nineteenth Century*. Ringwood, VIC: Penguin, 1988.
Chilton, Lisa. *Agents of Empire: British Female Migration to Canada and Australia, 1860s–1930*. Toronto: University of Toronto Press, 2007.
Das, Sisir Kumar. *A History of Indian Literature, 1800–1910*. New Delhi: Sahitya Akademi, 1991.
David, Deirdre. *Rule Britannia: Women, Empire, and Victorian Writing*. Ithaca: Cornell University Press, 1995.
Howells, Coral Ann and Eva-Marie Kröller (eds.). *The Cambridge History of Canadian Literature*. Cambridge: Cambridge University Press, 2009.
Gibson, Mary Ellis. *Anglophone Poetry in Colonial India, 1780–1913: A Critical Anthology*. Athens: Ohio University Press, 2011.
  Indian Angles: English Verse in Colonial India from Jones to Tagore. Athens: Ohio University Press. 2011.
Hanson, Carter. *Emigration, Nation, Vocation: The Literature of English Emigration to Canada, 1825–1900*. East Lansing: Michigan State University Press, 2009.
Joshi, Priya. *In Another Country: Colonialism, Culture, and the English Novel in India*. New York: Columbia University Press, 2002.
Leask, Nigel. *British Romantic Travel Writers and the East: Anxieties of Empire*. Cambridge: Cambridge University Press, 1993.
Mehrotra, Arvind Krishna. *History of Indian Literature in English*. New York: Columbia University Press, 2003.
Stafford, Jane, and Mark Williams. *Maoriland: New Zealand Literature, 1872–1914*. Wellington: Victoria University Press, 2006.
Tasker, Meg and E. Warwick Slinn (eds.). "Nineteenth-Century Australian Poetry." Special issue of *Victorian Poetry* 40:1 (Spring 2002).
White, Daniel E. *From Little London to Little Bengal: Religion, Print, and Modernity in Early British India, 1793–1935*. Baltimore: Johns Hopkins University Press, 2013.

14 History writing

Felber, Lynette (ed.). *Clio's Daughters. British Women Making History, 1790–1899.* Newark: University of Delaware Press, 2007.
Fraser, Hilary. *Women Writing Art History in the Nineteenth Century.* Cambridge: Cambridge University Press, 2014.
Jay, Elisabeth. *Mrs. Oliphant: 'A fiction to herself.' A Literary Life.* Oxford: Clarendon, 1995.
Johnston, Judith. *Anna Jameson.* Aldershot: Scolar, 1997.
Lawrence, Anne. "Women Historians and Documentary Research." In *Women, Scholarship and Criticism. Gender and Knowledge c. 1790–1900,* ed. Joan Bellamy et al. Manchester: Manchester University Press, 2000. Pp. 125–41.
Levine, Philippa. *The Amateur and the Professional: Antiquarians, Historians and Archaeologists in Victorian England, 1838–1886.* Cambridge: Cambridge University Press, 1986.
Logan, Deborah. *Harriet Martineau's Writing on British History and Military Reform.* 6 vols. London: Pickering & Chatto, 2005.
Maitzen, Rohan. *Gender, Genre, and Victorian Historical Writing.* New York: Garland, 1998.
Mitchell, Rosemary. "A Stitch in Time: Women, Needlework, and the Making of History." *Journal of Victorian Culture* 1:2 (Autumn 1996), 185–202.
  "The Busy Daughters of Clio: Women Writers of History from 1820 to 1880." *Women's History Review* 7:1 (Spring 1998), 107–34.
Pope-Hennessy, Una. *Agnes Strickland: Biographer of the Queens of England.* London: Chatto & Windus, 1940.

15 Periodical writing

Beetham, Margaret. *A Magazine of her Own? Domesticity and Desire in the Woman's Magazine 1800–1914.* London: Routledge, 1996.
Brake, Laurel and Marysa Demoor (eds.). *Dictionary of Nineteenth-Century Journalism in Great Britain and Ireland.* Ghent and London: Academia Press and The British Library, 2009.
Dillane, Finnuala. *Before George Eliot: Marian Evans and the Periodical Press.* Cambridge: Cambridge University Press, 2013.
Easley, Alexis. *Literary Celebrity, Gender, and Victorian Authorship, 1850–1914.* Newark: University of Delaware Press, 2011.
Fraser, Hilary, Stephanie Green, and Judith Johnston. *Gender and the Victorian Periodical.* Cambridge: Cambridge University Press, 2003.
Gray, F. Elizabeth (ed.). *Women in Journalism at the Fin de Siecle.* Basingstoke: Palgrave Macmillan, 2012.
Hughes, Linda K. *Graham R: Rosamund Marriott Watson, Woman of Letters.* Athens: Ohio University Press, 2005.
Hughes, Linda K. and Michael Lund. *The Victorian Serial.* Charlottesville: University of Virginia Press, 1991.
Mitchell, Sally. *Frances Power Cobbe: Victorian Feminist, Journalist, Reformer.* Charlottesville: University of Virginia Press, 2004.

North, John S. (ed.). *Waterloo Directory of Newspapers and Periodicals, 1800–1900*, Series 2. Waterloo: North Waterloo Academic Press, 2003.
Onslow, Barbara. *Women of the Press in Nineteenth-Century Britain*. Basingstoke: Macmillan, 2000.
Peterson, Linda. *Becoming a Woman of Letters: Myths of Authorship and Facts of the Victorian Market*. Princeton: Princeton University Press, 2009.

16 Reviewing

Adams, Kimberly van Esveld. "Women and Literary Criticism." In *The Cambridge History of Literary Criticism, Vol. 6: The Nineteenth Century*, ed. M. A. R. Habib. Cambridge: Cambridge University Press, 2013. Pp. 72–94.
Demoor, Marysa. *Their Fair Share: Women, Power and Criticism in the Athenaeum from Millicent Garrett Fawcett to Katherine Mansfield, 1870–1920*. Aldershot: Ashgate, 2000.
Dillane, Fionnuala. *Before George Eliot: Marian Evans and the Periodical Press*. Cambridge: Cambridge University Press, 2013.
Fryckstedt, Monica C. *Geraldine Jewsbury's Athenaeum Reviews: A Mirror of Mid-Victorian Attitudes to Fiction*. Acta Universitatis Upsaliensis: Studia Anglistica Upsaliensia 61, 1986.
Gray, F. Elizabeth (ed.). *Women in Journalism at the Fin de Siècle: Making a Name for Herself*. Houndmills, Basingstoke: Palgrave Macmillan, 2012.
Houghton, Walter et al. *The Wellesley Index to Victorian Periodicals*. Toronto: University of Toronto Press, 1966–, and online at http://wellesley.chadwyck.com/home.do.
Johnston, Judith. *Victorian Women and the Economies of Travel, Translation and Culture, 1830–1870*. Farnham, Surrey: Ashgate, 2013.
Liddle, Dallas. *The Dynamics of Genre: Journalism and the Practice of Literature in Mid-Victorian Britain*. Charlottesville: University of Virginia Press, 2009.
Mansfield, Elizabeth. "Articulating Authority: Emilia Dilke's Early Essays and Reviews." *Victorian Periodicals Review* 31 (1998), 75–86.
Onslow, Barbara. *Women of the Press in Nineteenth-Century Britain*. New York: St. Martin's, 2000.
Robinson, Solveig C. (ed.). *A Serious Occupation: Literary Criticism by Victorian Women Writers*, Peterborough, ONT: Broadview, 2003.
Wilkes, Joanne. *Women Reviewing Women in Nineteenth-Century Britain: The Critical Reception of Jane Austen, Charlotte Brontë and George Eliot*. Farnham, Surrey: Ashgate, 2010.

17 Children's writing

Chapman, Alison. "Phantasies of Matriarchy in Victorian Children's Literature." In *Victorian Women Writers and the Woman Question*, ed. Nicola Diane Thompson. Cambridge: Cambridge University Press, 1999. Pp. 60–79.
Dixon, Diane. "From Instruction to Amusement: Attitudes of Authority in Children's Periodicals before 1914." *Victorian Periodicals Review* 19 (1986), 63–67.

Gubar, Marah. *Artful Dodgers: Reconceiving the Golden Age of Children's Literature*. New York: Oxford University Press, 2009.

Knoepflmacher, U. C. *Ventures into Childland: Victorians, Fairy Tales, and Femininity*. Chicago: University of Chicago Press, 1998.

Kooistra, Lorraine Janzen. *Christina Rossetti and Illustration: A Publishing History*. Athens: Ohio University Press, 2002.

Lomax, Elaine. *The Writings of Hesba Stretton: Reclaiming the Outcast*. Burlington, VT: Ashgate, 2009.

Mitchell, Sally. *The New Girl: Girls' Culture in England, 1880–1915*. New York: Columbia University Press, 1995.

Mumm, Susan. "Writing for Their Lives: Women Applicants to the Royal Literary Fund, 1840–1880." *Publishing History* 27 (1990), 27–49.

Nelson, Claudia. *Boys Will Be Girls: The Feminine Ethic and British Children's Fiction, 1857–1917*. New Brunswick, NJ: Rutgers University Press, 1991.

Norcia, Megan A. *X Marks the Spot: Women Writers Map the Empire for British Children, 1790–1895*. Athens: Ohio University Press, 2010.

Reynolds, Kimberley. *Girls Only? Gender and Popular Children's Fiction in Britain, 1880–1910*. New York: Harvester Wheatsheaf, 1990.

Robinson, Ainslie. "Playfellows and Propaganda: Harriet Martineau's Children's Writing." *Women's Writing* 9:3 (2002), 395–412.

Talairach-Vielmas, Laurence. *Moulding the Female Body in Victorian Fairy Tales and Sensation Novels*. Aldershot: Ashgate, 2007.

Thiel, Elizabeth. *The Fantasy of Family: Nineteenth-Century Children's Literature and the Myth of the Domestic Ideal*. New York: Routledge, 2008.

INDEX

A.L.O.E. (Charlotte Maria Tucker)
   Edith and Her Ayah, And Other Stories 9, 255
   The Crown of Success 256
abolitionism 94, 164, 210, 228, 230
Academy, The 218, 219, 239, 244, 245
Actresses' Franchise League 157
Addison, Joseph 213
author's guides 25–6, 59
advertising 23, 48, 50, 231–2
Ady, Julia Cartwright 218
aesthetic essay 9
aestheticism 96, 199–203
Aguilar, Grace
   Women of Israel 217
   "History of the Jews in England" 217
Aikin, John 213
Aikin, Lucy 206, 208
   Charles I 213
   Elizabeth I 213
   James I 213
Ainsworth's Magazine 17
Ainu (indigenous population) 177
Alexandra Magazine 135
All the Year Round 15, 35, 61
Allen, Grant
   The Woman Who Did 133
Allen, W. H. 81
Allies, Mary Helen
   History of the Church in England 217
   Letters of St. Augustine 217
   Life of Pius VII 217
   Three Catholic Reformers 217
American civil war 37, 164
American Monthly Review 182,
Angell, George 254
Anglican Church 110, 230, 237
Anne of Austria 216
Anne, Duchess of Brittany 213

Annual Register 211
annuals 8, 47, 53, 62–3, 68, 70, 83, 95, 193, 222, 223
anonymous publication 7, 16, 21, 36, 38, 46, 49, 83, 124, 126–7, 168, 169, 185, 208, 227, 230, 236, 240–1, 242, 245
   anonymity and personae 17–8, 108, 226, 238–9
   debate over practice 236–7
   novel 114
   playwriting competition 148
   poetry 77, 89
Anonymous, "A Woman's Struggles: the True Account of an American Shorthand Writer" 66
anthologies 73, 74, 77, 83, 84, 101
Anthony, Susan B. 93
Argosy 60, 76, 222
Armstrong, Isobel 97
Armstrong, Nancy 121
Arnold, Edward 51
Arnold, Matthew 97, 221, 224–5
   Culture and Anarchy 223–4
Art Journal 48, 218, 219, 247
Ashley-Cooper, Anthony (Lord Shaftesbury) 254
Atalanta 40, 75, 222, 231, 254, 260
Athenaeum 36, 37, 38, 83, 90, 91, 112, 194, 223, 237, 241–3, 245, 246–7
Atkinson, Louisa 191–2
   Gertrude, the Emigrant 191–2
Atlantic Monthly 163
Augustine, Saint 159, 217
Aunt Judy's Magazine 67, 260
Austen, Jane 2, 6, 41, 84, 107, 128, 170
Austin, Alfred 74
Australasian 191
autobiography 4–5, 19, 134, 159–162, 163, 165, 168–73, 211, 240, 243

276

INDEX

Baby 231
Baillie, Joanna 84, 144, 154
  Plays on the Passions 144
Bakewell, Mrs. 230–1
Ballin, Ada 231
Bancroft, Marie 151
Barbauld, Anna Letitia 170, 213, 245
Barker, Juliet 44
Barker, Lady Mary Anne 180–1
  Station Amusements in New Zealand 181
  Station Life in New Zealand 181
Barnacle, The 62, 260
Barrett Browning, Elizabeth 4, 10, 16, 74, 78, 81–2, 92–6, 97, 100, 102, 203, 213, 221, 223, 243, 244
  Aurora Leigh 4, 76, 78, 84, 89, 92–4
  Battle of Marathon 15
  Casa Guidi Windows 78, 94–5
  "The Cry of the Children" 94
  A Drama of Exile 91
  "L.E.L.'s Last Question" 100
  Letters 78
  Poems Before Congress 78
  "A Reed" 95–6
  "The Romaunt of the Page" 95
  "Runaway Slave at Pilgrim's Point" 94
  The Seraphim 91
  Sonnets from the Portuguese 78, 95
Barthes, Roland 119
Bartholomew, Anne 22
Bassnett, Susan 176
Beaufort, Margaret 217
Becker, Lydia 64, 229
Becket, Thomas à 216
Beer, Rachel 59
Beeton, Isabella 231–2
Beeton, Samuel 231
Belgravia 61, 70, 74
Bell, Henry Mackenzie
  Christina Rossetti: A Biographical and Critical Study 80
  "To Christina G. Rossetti (Greater as a Woman than even as a Poet)" 80
Bengal Annual, The 193
Bennett, Arnold 227
  Journalism for Women: A Practical Guide 59
Bensusan, Inez 157
Bentham, Jeremy 243
Bentley, George 24, 45, 51
Bentley, Richard (father of George) 17, 74–5
Bentley, Richard (son of George) 51, 163
Bentley's Miscellany 241

Bentley's Quarterly Review 241
Beringer, Aimée 151
Bernstein, Susan David 25
Besant, Annie Wood 6, 66–7, 71
  An Autobiography 171
  Autobiographical Sketches 171
  Our Corner 67
Bildungsroman 107, 134
Biographies of Good Women 165
biography 3, 6, 8, 10, 34, 37, 38, 39, 47, 73, 74, 77, 159, 160, 165–8, 169, 207, 210, 211, 232, 240, 243, 248, 252, 259, 261
  and canonicity 79–80, 82
  historical biography 212–8
  and personal correspondence 163
Bird, Isabella 9, 176–7, 181, 183–6, 191
  Among the Tibetans 186
  The Englishwoman in America 185
  Korea and Her Neighbours 186
  A Lady's Life in the Rocky Mountains 177
  Unbeaten Tracks in Japan 177
  The Yangtze Valley and Beyond 177
Bishop, Maria Catherine
  A Memoir of Mrs. Augustus Craven 165
Bishop, Mary 3
Black and White Magazine 141
Black, Clementina 64, 229
Black, Helen C.
  Notable Woman Authors of the Day 10, 224
Blackburn, Helen
  "Women's Books – A Possible Library" 239–40
Blackett, Ellen 47, 55
Blackett, Henry 38, 47, 55, 56
Blackwood (publishing house) *See* William Blackwood and Sons
Blackwood, Isabella 47
Blackwood, John 32, 38, 46, 49–50, 240
Blackwood, "Major" William (nephew of John) 46, 50
Blackwood, William 46, 74
Blackwood's Edinburgh Magazine 6, 16, 17, 18, 32, 38, 39, 40, 46, 49, 68, 162, 168, 178, 208, 215, 226, 238, 240, 241, 243
Blaikie, W. G. 178
Blair, Kirstie 20
Blessington, Countess of *See* Marguerite Gardiner
Blind, Mathilde 79, 81–2, 84, 246
Bloch, Ernst 192
Boaden, Caroline 151
Bodenheimer, Rosemarie 111

Bodichon, Barbara 229
Bodley Head Press 9, 48, 200
Boehmer, Elleke 192
Boleyn, Anne 213
Bookman, The 80
Book of Beauty, The 62–3
book reviewing See also periodicals, review articles 5, 30, 36–7, 38–9, 46, 83–4, 208, 236–49
   anonymity 236–41
   European literature 245–6
   male personae 238–9
   poetry 246–7
   specialization 244–5
Boos, Florence 20
Botticelli, Sandro 218
Boucherett, Jessie 65
Boucicault, Dion
   The Colleen Bawn 153
Bouquet from Marlybone Gardens, The 47
Bourdieu, Pierre 121
Boy's Own Paper, The 254
Braddon, Mary Elizabeth 29, 61, 70, 74, 77, 133, 138, 151, 244
   Aurora Floyd 153
   Lady Audley's Secret 7, 136, 153
Bradlaugh, Charles 6, 66–7
Bradley, Katherine (see Michael Field)
Bray, Charles 18
British Almanac 211
British Library Reading Room 25
British Magazine 68
British Mother's Magazine 231–2
British Quarterly Review 243
Brontë, Anne 18, 44, 79, 107, 115
   Agnes Gray 166
   The Tenant of Wildfell Hall 116
Brontë, Charlotte 5, 6, 35, 37, 41, 43–5, 55, 74–5, 78–9, 81, 82, 105, 107 115–6, 125, 126, 166, 167, 170, 236, 238, 244
   "Biographical Notice of Ellis and Acton Bell" 79, 166
   Jane Eyre 1, 5, 6, 18, 44, 105, 115–7, 161, 162, 236, 238, 240, 257
   The Professor 43–4, 168
   Villette 105, 115–7, 162
Brontë, Emily 18, 81, 107, 115
   Wuthering Heights 18, 43, 45, 79, 116, 166, 167
Brooks, Peter 114, 117
Broughton, Rhoda 51, 133, 138, 244, 246
   Cometh up as a Flower 139

Browne, Matilda
   "Spinnings" 231–2
Browne, Phillis, *What Girls Can Do* 25
Browning, Robert 82, 97, 170
Bulwer-Lytton, Edward 46, 107, 241, 244
   England and the English 105–6
   Pelham 106
Bulwer-Lytton, Rosina 106, 116
   Cheveley; or, the Man of Honour 106, 108
Burne-Jones, Edward 218
Burns Centenary Prize 75–6
Burns, Robert 75–6
Busk, Mary Margaret 241, 245
Butler, Josephine 64, 166
   Personal Reminiscences of a Great Crusade 166
Byatt, A.S. 130
Byron, George Gordon 3, 62, 144, 149, 154
   Childe Harold's Pilgrimage 195

Cadwaladyr, Betsy 217
Caird, Mona 82, 130, 133, 135, 139
   The Daughters of Danaus 137
   The Morality of Marriage and Other Essays on the Status and Destiny of Woman 135
Callcott, Lady Maria
   Giotto's Chapel in Padua 218
   History of Painting 218
   Little Arthur's History of England 218
Calvert, Adelaide 151
Cambridge, Ada
   In Two Years' Time 191
   A Woman's Friendship 191
Canadian Literary Magazine 197
canon 73–4, 204
   formation and women writers 80–5
   relationship to market 74–80
Carey and Hart (publisher) 54
Carlile, Richard 64
Carlyle, Jane Welsh
   Letters and Memorials of Jane Welsh Carlyle 169
Carlyle, Thomas
   Sartor Resartus 55
Carpenter, Mary 179, 245
Carroll, Lewis
   Alice's Adventures in Wonderland 256
   Sylvie and Bruno 260
Carshore, Mary Seyers 193
   "The Ivied Harp" 195
   "Lines to a Withered Shamrock" 194–5
Carter, Paul 198
Cassell, John 19–20

INDEX

Literature of Working Men 20
Castiglione, Giovanni 218
Chalmers, Thomas 216
Chambers, Robert 34, 74
Chambers, William 34, 74
Chambers's Edinburgh Journal 32, 35
Chapman and Hall (publishers) 5, 16, 31
Chapman, John 49, 65
Charles Fox (publisher) 55
Chartism 5, 113, 236
children's writing 9, 34, 77, 89, 208, 209, 213, 218, 247–8, 251–63
  adult audience 261–3
  community 259–61
  didacticism 253–5
  empire 255
  fantasy 256–7
  magazines 259–61
  setting 255–9
cholera 54
Cholmondeley, Mary 49, 51–2, 130, 133
  The Danvers Jewels 51
  A Devotée 51
  Diana Tempest 51
  Red Pottage 51, 139, 140
  Sir Charles Danvers 51
Christ 98, 102, 255, 258
Christianity *See also* Religion 5, 96, 171, 230, 254
Christian Lady's Magazine 111, 161, 230
Christian Remembrancer 237, 239, 241
Christian Socialist 35
Christian World Magazine 230
Churchill, Sarah (Duchess of Marlborough) 213
circulating library 77, 141
Civil List pension 34, 211–2
Clarke, Marcus
  For the Term of His Natural Life 191
Claybaugh, Amanda 124, 126
Clayton, Charlotte (Viscountess Sundon) 213
Clive, Mrs. 83
Cobbe, Frances Power 59, 171–2, 221, 224, 228, 229
  Duties of Women 171
  Life of Frances Power Cobbe, by Herself 171
  "Wife Torture in England" 228
Cobbett, William 243
Coghill, Annie 172
Colburn and Bentley (publisher) 54
Colburn, Henry 43, 46
Colby, Vineta 124
Coleman, Daniel 194

Coleridge, Christabel 62, 166, 260
Coleridge, Samuel Taylor 55, 84, 90, 164
Coleridge, Sara 166, 236
  Memoir and Letters 164–5
Collins, Wilkie 133, 191
  Woman in White 153
Comte, Auguste 126, 168
Conquest, Elizabeth 151
Contagious Diseases Act 64, 137, 166
Contemporary Review 245
Cook, Eliza 5–6, 22, 31
  Eliza Cook's Journal 6, 19, 32, 34, 63, 92, 227
  Lays of a Wild Harp, 21
  Melaia and Other Poems 21
  Poems, Second Series 21
  "The Old Armchair" 21
Cookson, Mrs. James
  Flowers Drawn and Painted after Nature in India 191
Cooper, Edith Emma *See* Michael Field
Cooper, Elizabeth, *Popular History of America* 216
Cooper, James Fenimore 243
co-operative movement 32
Corelli, Marie
  "One of the World's Wonders" 24
  A Romance of Two Worlds 24
Corner, Julia, *History of England* 216
Cornhill Magazine 23, 36, 37, 39, 55, 61, 129, 170, 222, 224, 225
Costello, Louisa, *Eminent Englishwomen* 213
Court Journal 214
Cousin, Victor 36
Cousins, John 218
Covent Garden Theatre 146, 151, 154
Coventry Herald and Observer 18
Cowden-Clarke, Charles 68
Cowden-Clarke, Mary 68
Cowper, William 203
Craig, Isa 75–6, 76–7
  Poems: An Offering to Lancashire 76
  Poems by Isa 76
Craik, Dinah Maria Mulock 29, 55–6, 83, 260
  The Adventures of a Brownie 262
  John Halifax, Gentleman 56, 262
  The Little Lame Prince 262
  A Woman's Thoughts About Women 239
Craik, George 47
Crawford, Isabella Valancy
  Malcolm's Katie 198–9
Crimean War 211

Cross, John
  George Eliot's Life as Related in her Letters and Journals 79, 167–8
Crowe, Catherine 83, 151
Crystal Palace, the 75
Cummins, Maria S.
  Mabel Vaughan 36

D'Aubigne, Merle 217
D'Este, Isabella 218
Daily News 162, 166, 208, 211, 224, 227, 228, 240
Daily News: Letters from Ireland 210
Daily Telegraph 135, 149
Dallas, E.S. 237, 238
Dante 100
Darcy, Ella 133
Darwin, Erasmus 3
Darwinism 82
Davies, Emily 65, 66, 172
Dawn 64
Dawn: A Journal for Australian Women, The 199
de Courcy, Beatrice 67
de Courcy, Margaret 67
de Lamartine, Alphonse 203
de Mattos, Katherine 246, 248
de Medici, Maria 216
de Montalembert, Charles Forbes René (Count) 216
de Pixérécourt, Guilbert
  Coelina; ou l'enfant de mystère 153
de Sablé, Madame (Madelene de Souvré) 36
de Sévigné, Madame (Marie de Rabutin-Chantal) 37, 168, 170
de Staël, Germaine
  Corinne, Or Italy 76, 92
de Valois, Elizabeth 216
de Vere, Aubrey 48
decadence 48
Denvil, Mrs. 151
Derozio, H. L. V. 4, 194, 196
devotional writing *See also* poetry, devotional 3, 46, 100–1
Dickens, Charles 31, 60, 123, 243, 262
  American Notes 182-3
  Hard Times 35, 109
  Household Words 32, 34, 35, 36, 61, 222, 227
  Nicholas Nickleby 150
Dictionary of Literary Biography 252
Dictionary of National Biography 34, 37
digitization of texts 84–5, 221

Dilke, Charles 246
Dilke, Emilia 245, 248
  Art in the Modern State 218
  Renaissance of Art in France 218
Dillane, Fionnuala 18
Disraeli, Benjamin 106, 107, 243
  Sybil 109
Disraeli, Isaac
  Calamities of Authors 4, 15
divorce 7, 38, 135–6, 164, 239
  Divorce Act of 1857 135
Dixon, Ella Hepworth 133
Dodd, M.W. 161
domestic fiction *See also* novel, domestic 6, 21, 83, 92, 105, 107, 110, 111, 115–7, 124, 128, 134, 252, 257–9
domesticity 17, 31, 63, 69, 79, 90, 91, 97, 139, 160–1, 257
  and advice columns 231
  and colonies 196, 197–9
  domestic ideology 15, 75, 113, 121, 136, 207–8, 219, 225, 251–2
  domestic violence 108, 228
  in drama and theater 152, 154, 156
  and editorial work 59–60
  and George Eliot 168–9
  and national history 213, 216
  and periodical interviews 233
  in travel writing 9, 175, 177–9, 180–1, 181–3
Douglas Jerrold's Shilling Magazine 31, 32, 33
Douglas Jerrold's Weekly Newspaper 22, 31, 32, 33
Dowie, Menie Muriel 133
Drabble, Margaret 130
Dramatic Authors Society 146
Drury Lane 146, 151, 154
Duffy, Carol Ann 74
Duncan, Sara Jeannette
  The Imperialist 192
Dunlop, Eliza Hamilton 4, 189, 197
  "The Aboriginal Mother" 196
Dutt, Toru 192, 193, 204
  Ancient Ballads and Legends of Hindustan 200
  "The Lotus" 203

Easley, Alexis 4, 5, 56, 84, 226
Easson, Angus 35
East India Company 179
Ebsworth, Joseph 151

Ebsworth, Mary 151–2
Eccles, Charlotte O'Conore
  "The Experiences of a Woman Journalist" 68
Echo 228
Eden, Emily 179
  Up the Country 190
Eden, Horatia 260
Edgeworth, Maria 2, 170, 243
  Harry and Lucy 252
Edinburgh Medical Journal 186
Edinburgh Review 168, 218, 223, 238
editorship 59–71
  celebrity editorship 61–3
  collaborative editorship 67–70
  political editorship 64–7
Education Act 225
Egerton, George 130, 133, 140–1
  Discords 140
  Keynotes 138, 140
  The Wheel of God 140
Eiloart, Elizabeth 263
Elford, William 145
Eliot, George (Marian Evans) 3, 6–7, 17–8, 41, 49–51, 55, 65, 74, 81, 82, 83, 84, 91, 127, 128, 129–30, 154, 167–8, 169–70, 221, 226, 239, 241–2, 244, 245, 248
  Adam Bede 6, 50, 51, 119, 122–3, 126, 127, 129, 243
  Daniel Deronda 7, 51, 129
  Felix Holt 50
  George Eliot's Life as Related in Her Letters and Journals 79–80
  "Janet's Repentance" 126, 127
  Middlemarch 107, 119–21, 124, 128–9, 130
  "The Natural History of German Life" 123–4
  Romola 50
  "The Sad Fortunes of the Reverend Amos Barton" 49, 127
  Scenes of Clerical Life 35, 49, 123, 129
  "Silly Novels by Lady Novelists" 7, 18, 23, 123, 124–5, 168, 239, 240, 242
Eliza Cook's Journal See Eliza Cook
Ellis, Sarah Stickney 63
Elwood, Anne Katharine 2, 10
  Memoirs of the Literary Ladies of England 1
Emerson, Ralph Waldo 244
  Representative Men 44
Eminent Women 79, 81, 82
English Woman's Journal 7, 65, 66, 135, 229, 239

Englishwoman's Domestic Magazine 67, 231
Englishwoman's Review 7, 65, 135, 172, 229, 232, 239
Ermath, Elizabeth Deeds 120
ethnography 175, 185
Evans, Charlotte
  Over the Hills and Far Away 191
Ewing, Juliana Horatia
  "Amelia and the Dwarfs" 256
  Jackanapes 260
  Melchior's Dream and Other Tales 260
  The Story of a Short Life 260

Fabian Society 67
Fairbrother, Robert 151
fairy tale 9, 256
Faithfull, Emily 65, 66, 229
fallen women 97, 99, 126
fame 17, 23, 47, 48, 61, 62, 69, 73–85, 148, 157, 208
  celebrity 73, 233
fantasy (genre) 9, 256, 262, 263
Fauriel, Jean Claude
  Chants Populaires de la Grèce Moderne 36
Fawcett, Millicent Garrett 246, 248
"Feast of the Poets" (special edition of *Tait's Edinburgh Magazine*) 20
Federico, Annette 24
Female Middle Class Emigration Society 65
Feminism 29–30, 82, 94, 110, 117, 135, 137, 138, 157, 171, 199, 228, 229–30, 238, 239, 259, 260
Feminist Literary Criticism 2, 9–10, 84, 113, 134, 156, 176, 209, 215
  Second-wave Feminism 93
Femininity 5, 63, 75, 84, 96, 116, 117, 137, 139, 146, 152, 153–4, 156, 175, 200, 233, 256, 258
Ferrier, Susan 2, 6, 124
Field, Michael (Katherine Bradley and Edith Emma Cooper)
  Underneath the Boughs 247
  "Works and Days" 172
Fielding, Sarah
  The Governess 252, 257
Finden's Tableaux 68
Finkelstein, David
  The House of Blackwood 39, 50
Fisher's Drawing-Room Scrapbook 196
Flint, Kate
  The Woman Reader 134

Forbes, Anna 177–8
  Unbeaten Tracks in Islands of the Far East: Experiences of a Naturalist's Wife in the 1880s 178
Foreign Quarterly Review 241
Forman, Henry Buxton 78
Forster, John 16
Forster, Margaret 16
Fortin, Nina 23, 52
Fortnightly Review 169, 237, 244, 245
Fox, William J. 5, 31
Francis I 216
Francis of Assisi 216
Franklin, Miles
  My Brilliant Career 191
Fraser, James 54
Fraser's Magazine 37, 52–5
  "The Fraserians" (illustration) 52–5
Freer, Martha 216
French Revolution 2, 144
Frere, Alice M.
  The Antipodes and Round the World 180
Friederichs, Hulda 233
Friedman, Susan Stanford 9
Froude, James Anthony 169

Gaelic (cultural renaissance, independence movement) 217
Gagnier, Regenia 172
Gardiner, Marguerite (Countess of Blessington) 62–3, 83, 106, 107
  Conversations with Lord Byron 62
  The Victims of Society 107
Garrick Club 146
Gaskell, Elizabeth 7, 29, 30–2, 34–7, 40–1, 83, 105, 121, 125, 126–7, 208, 236, 237
  "Bessy's Troubles at Home" 35
  "Christmas Storms and Sunshine" 35
  "Clopton Hall" 16
  "Company Manners" 36
  "Cousin Phillis" 129
  Cranford 35, 107, 126
  "Half a Life-time Ago" 34
  "Hand and Heart, " 35
  "The Last Generation in England" 34
  The Life of Charlotte Brontë 35, 37, 78–9, 126, 166–7, 244
  "Life in Manchester: Libby Marsh's Three Eras" 16, 21
  "Lizzie Leigh" 35
  "Martha Preston" 34
  Mary Barton 1, 5, 16, 31, 34, 36, 109, 113–4, 126, 127–8
  "Modern Greek Songs" 36
  North and South 35, 36–7, 109, 113, 114–5, 126, 127, 128
  Ruth 36, 115, 126
  Sylvia's Lovers 129
  Wives and Daughters 36, 90, 129
Gatty, Margaret 67, 260
  Parables from Nature 263
Gender 1, 33, 124, 125, 135, 154, 159, 160, 170, 206, 207, 208, 209, 215, 219, 225, 230, 233, 241, 256, 258, 262
  and anonymity 226, 228, 239
  and author-publisher relations 52–6
  and canonicity 73–85
  gender equality 6, 63, 115
  gender roles in poetry 93–4, 95, 96
  gender roles in fiction 107–9, 111, 114, 115, 115–7, 121, 128, 139, 233
  and literary influence 4
  male personae in periodical reviewing 226
  and playwriting 144, 147, 148
  and pseudonyms 18, 84, 126, 166, 226, 252, 263
  and travel writing 179, 185
  See also domesticity; feminism; femininity
General Federation for the Abolition of the State Regulation of Vice 64
George II 39, 215
Germ 16, 47
Ghose, Indira 179
Gibbes, Phoebe
  Hartly House, Calcutta 192
Gilbert, Sandra M. and Susan Gubar
  The Madwoman in the Attic 2, 117
Gillies, Mary 22
Gilmore, Dame Mary 199
Girl's Realm, The 254
Girls' Own Paper, The 251, 254
Gissing, George
  New Grub Street 24–5, 251, 261
  The Odd Women 133
Gladstone, William Ewart 34, 79
Glover, Evelyn
  A Chat with Mrs Chicky 157
Golden Gates (*See Winter's Weekly*)
Good Words 39, 77
Gore, Catherine 106, 124, 148, 150, 156
  Cecil 105, 107, 108–9, 115
  The Hamiltons 107
  Quid Pro Quo 155
Graham, Maria
  Journal of a Residence in India 191

Grand, Sarah 25, 133, 233
  The Beth Book 137, 140
  The Heavenly Twins 137, 139
Grant, Annie Forsyth 263
Graphic 39
Green, Alice Stopford
  The Conquest of England 217
  Henry II 217
  Town Life in the Fifteenth Century 217
Green, Mary Ann
  Letters of Royal and Illustrious Ladies 215
  Life and Letters of Henrietta Maria 215
  Lives of the Princesses of England 215
Greenwell, Dora 101
Greenwood, Frederick 129
Greg, W.R. 237–8
Grimaldi, Josheph 151
Grimstone, Mary Leman 5
Grogan, Mercy
  How Women May Earn a Living 25
Gubar, Susan (see Sandra M. Gilbert and Susan Gubar)

Haight, George 50
Haldane, Elizabeth 35
Hall, Anna Maria 61, 63, 68–70
  Can Wrong be Right? 69
  "Something of What Florence Nightingale Has Done and Is Doing" 69
Hall, Basil
  Travels in North America 182
Hall, Samuel Carter 68–9
Hallett, Mrs. 154–6
  Nobodies' at Home; Somebodies' Abroad 154–5
Halsted, Caroline 217
Hamilton, Cecily and Christopher St. John
  How the Vote was Won 157
Hamilton, Elizabeth
  Translations of the Letters of a Hindoo Rajah 192
Hamilton, Janet 19–20
  "Counteracting Influences" 19
  Poems and Essays of a Miscellaneous Character 20
Hansard
  Parliamentary Papers 211
Hardy, Thomas 7, 137
  Jude the Obscure 133
Harper, Lila Marz 186
Harper's New Monthly Magazine 36, 133, 170
Harraden, Beatrice 170

Harris, Janice 23
Harrison, Jane Ellen 246
Hasell, Elizabeth Julia 240, 245, 246, 248
Hauptmann, Gerhardt 147
Haymarket Theatre 148, 149, 154, 155
Hazlitt, William 106
  Essays 44
Hearn, Mary Anne 60, 230
Heath, Charles 63
Heinemann, William 200
Hemans, Felicia 4, 82, 89–92, 97, 102, 194, 195, 197
  "Arabella Stuart" 90
  "Casabianca" 90
  The Forest Sanctuary 91
  "Imelda" 90
  "Indian Woman's Death Song" 196
  "Joan of Arc Rheims" 90
  "The Peasant Girl of the Rhone" 90
  "Properzia Rossi" 90
  Records of Woman 90, 93
  "A Spirit's Return" 91–2
Henriette, Duchess of Orleans 218
Herbert, Sarah 4, 194, 197
Hill, Fidelia 4, 198
  "Adelaide" 195
  Poems and Recollections of the Past 195
  "Recollections" 195–6
Hodgson, Mrs. 22
Hogg, James 89, 90
Holcroft, Thomas
  A Tale of Mystery 152
Homer
  Iliad 240
Hook, Theodore 106, 183
Hope, Anne
  Acts of the Early Martyrs 216
  Conversion of the Teutonic Races 216–7
  First Divorce of Henry VIII 217
  Franciscan Martyrs 217
Hope, Eva
  Queens of Literature of the Victorian Era 82
Hopkins, Gerard Manley
  "Carrion Comfort" 101–2
Houlston and Son (publisher) 54, 261
Household Words See Charles Dickens
Howells, William Dean 163
Howitt, Anna Mary 70
Howitt, Mary 5, 6, 22, 31, 33, 34, 70, 243
  Visits to Remarkable Places 16
Howitt, William 5, 6, 16, 31
  Visits to Remarkable Places 16

Howitt's Journal 5–6, 19, 20, 21, 31, 32, 70
  publication of Gaskell's fiction 5, 16
Hughes, Linda K. 4, 25, 221, 227
Hugo, Victor 203
Humphreys, Eliza 26
Hungry Forties, the 109
Hurst and Blackett (publisher) 33, 38, 39, 43, 46, 54
Hurst and Robinson (publisher) 54

Ibsen, Henrik 147, 156
  A Doll's House 154
Illustrated London News, The 48, 148, 239, 261
illustration 52–5, 67, 70, 112, 200, 201, 202, 223, 261
indigenous peoples 4, 184, 196, 255
industrialization 46, 64, 109–15, 209, 210, 211, 218, 229
Ingelow, Jean
  Mopsa the Fairy 256
Ingram, John H. 81–2
Institute of Journalists 25
Iota (Kathleen Caffyn) 133
Irish Famine 211
Irving, Edward 39, 53, 216
Isis 64
ivory trade 185

J. Warren (publisher) 54
Jacobites 213
James, Henry 39, 130, 262
  The Awkward Age 246
  The Lesson of the Master, and Other Stories 246
Jameson, Anna 160, 163–4, 206
  Celebrated Female Sovereigns 218
  Characteristics of Shakespeare's Women 163
  Characteristics of Women 218
  Early Italian Painters 218
  History of our Lord 218
  Legends of the Madonna 218
  Legends of the Monastic Orders 218
  Sacred and Legendary Art 218
  Winter Studies and Summer Rambles in Canada 190
  Women Celebrated by the Poets 218
Jameson, Robert 190
Jay, Elisabeth 46, 47, 172
Jeanne d'Arc 218
Jeanne of Navarre 216

Jelinek, Estelle
  The Tradition of Women's Autobiography: From Antiquity to the Present 172
Jerrold, Douglas 22, 31, 32, 33
Jerrold's Weekly Newspaper see *Douglas Jerrold's Weekly Newspaper*
Jewsbury, Geraldine 38, 74, 83, 242–3, 248
Johnson, E. Pauline 200–3, 204
  "Bass Lake (Muskoka)" 201, 202
  Collected Poems 201, 203
  "The Idlers" 200
  "Nocturne" 200
  "Shadow River" 200
  The White Wampum 200, 201
Johnston, Ellen
  Autobiography, Poems and Songs 172
Johnstone, Christian Isobel 6, 20, 31, 64, 226, 243, 244, 247
Journalism 8–9, 26, 35, 39, 59, 93, 172, 221–33
  interviews 232–3
  leaders 227–30
  New Journalism 8, 221, 232–3
  religious journalism 230–1
  remuneration 26, 63, 222
Juvenile Forget Me Not 68
Juvenile Missionary Magazine 261

Kavanagh, Julia 2, 10
  English Women of Letters 1, 216
  Women of Christianity 216
  Women in France 216
Keary, Annie
  The Rival Kings, or, Overbearing 258
Keeley, Mary Anne 152
Keepsake, The 62
Kemble, Charles 145, 151
Kemble, Fanny 151, 160, 163–4, 170, 243
  Further Records, 1848–1883: A Series of Letters 163
  The Journal of Frances Anne Butler 164
  Journal of a Residence on a Georgian Plantation in 1838–1839 164
  Records of a Girlhood 163, 164
  Records of Later Life 163
Kemble, John Philip 151
Kemble, Marie-Therese 151
Kenyon, Frederic G. 78
King, Henry S. 48
Kingsley, Charles 83
  Alton Locke 109
  Glaucus, or the Wonders of the Shore 263
Kingsley, Mary 9, 181, 183–6

Travels in West Africa 184–5
West African Studies 185
Knight, Ann Cuthburt 196, 197
A Year in Canada and Other Poems 195
Knoepflmacher, U. C. 256
Kooistra, Lorraine Janzen 80

L'Ouverture, Toussaint 232
Ladies Cabinet of Fashion, Music and Romance 67
Lady's Pictorial xix, 45, 224, 229, 233
Lamb, Charles 243, 244
Lamb, Mary 244
Lamb, William (Lord Melbourne) 106
Lancashire cotton famine of 1862 37
Landon, Letitia Elizabeth (L.E.L.) 54, 62, 63, 83, 92, 100, 194, 195, 196–7
  The Fate of Adelaide 54
  The Golden Violet 54
  The Improvisatrice 54
  "Night at Sea" 100
  The Troubadour 54
Lane, John 9, 48, 200
Lane, Sarah 151
Lang, Andrew 231
Langford, Joseph 50
Langham Place Group 60, 65, 76, 239
Law, Alice 97
Lawrance, Hannah 209, 213, 243–4, 245
  Historical Memoirs of the Queens of England 213, 243
  The History of Woman in England 213, 243
Lawrence, Henry
  Adventures of an Officer in the Service of Ranjeet Singh 192
Lawrence, Honoria 192
Lawson, Louisa 199
Leakey, Caroline 198, 204
  The Broad Arrow 191
  Lyra Australis: or Attempts to Sing in a Strange Land 194, 198
  "Pale Oleander of the South" 198
Ledbetter, Kathryn 17
Leigh-Smith, Barbara 65
Leighton, Frederic 218
Leisure Hour 191
Lephoron, Rosanna 192
Leslie, Mary 189, 193
Lessing, Doris 130
Levy, Amy 25, 83–4
Lewes, George Henry 1–2, 30, 49–50, 65, 79, 126, 148, 167–8, 169, 248

Lewis, M.G. 243
Liddle, Dallas 241, 242
Linton, Eliza Lynn 17, 130, 160, 169–70, 227, 228–9, 233, 247
  Amymone: A Romance in the Days of Pericles 17
  The Autobiography of Christopher Kirkland 170
  Azeth, the Egyptian 17
  "The Girl of the Period" 135
  The Girl of the Period and other Social Essays 224
  "Literature: Then and Now"
  My Literary Life 170
  "The Revolt Against Matrimony" 135
  "The Wild Women: As Politicians" 135
  "The Wild Women: As Social Insurgents" 135
literary annuals 8, 47, 53, 62–3, 68, 70, 83, 95, 193, 222, 223
Literary Garland 193
Literary Ladies (dining club) 25
literary societies, women's 19, 25–6, 31, 55, 62, 63, 225
Literary World 80
Lloyd, Mary 171–2
London Review 92
London Society 61
London Theatres Royals 145, 148, 151, 154, 155
Longfellow, Henry Wadsworth
  The Golden Legend 36
Longman, Brown, Green, and Longmans (publisher) 54
Longman's Magazine 39, 231
Lootens, Tricia 80
Lorrain, Claude 218
Louis XIV, King 216
Lovell, Maria 151
Low, Frances
  Press Work for Women 25–6
Low, Samson 191
Lundie, Mary
  Memoir of Mrs. Mary Lundie Duncan: Being Recollections of a Daughter by Her Mother 165

Macaulay, Catharine 207
MacDonald, George 260
  David Elginbrod 260
Mackay, Mary. *See* Corelli, Marie
Macmillan (publishing house) 23–4, 47–8, 52, 84

Macmillan, Alexander 36, 38, 39, 47–8, 51–2, 74
Macmillan's Magazine 23, 47, 167, 170, 225, 236–7
Macready, William 145
Madge, Travers 35
Magazine for the Young 230
Magazine of Art 48, 218, 245, 247
Maidment, Brian 19
Malthus, Thomas Robert
  Essay on the Principle of Population 109
Malthusianism 33
Mansergh, Jessie
  Tom and Some Other Girls: A Public School Story 257
Marguerite of Angouleme 216
marriage 7, 33, 36, 91, 95, 107–8, 114–5, 116, 139–40, 191
  marriage plot 128
  The Marriage Problem 135–7
Marryat, Florence 61, 133
Marryat, Frederick 61, 63
Marsh, Jan 74
Marshall, Emma 252
Martin, Sarah 165–6
Martineau, Harriet 3, 5, 8, 10, 19, 54, 65, 82, 112, 113, 114, 117, 125, 126, 160, 161–2, 166, 168, 206, 207, 208, 209–12, 216, 218, 224, 226, 227–8, 240–1, 243, 244, 247, 248, 261–2
  Autobiography 19, 161, 168–9
  Biographical Sketches 211
  A Complete Guide to the English Lakes 210
  The Crofton Boys 257
  Deerbrook 107, 126
  Eastern Life, Present and Past 210
  Endowed Schools of Ireland 210
  England and her Soldiers 212
  A Guide to Windermere 210
  A History of the American Compromises 210
  A History of British Rule in India 212
  A History of England from the Commencement of the XIXth century to the Crimean War 211
  A History of the Thirty Years' Peace 1816–46 211–2
  The Hour and the Man 210–1
  Illustrations of Political Economy 54, 105, 109–11, 126, 210, 240, 248
  Letters from Ireland 210
  The Martyr Age of the United States 210

Retrospect of Western Travel 183
Society in America 183
Suggestions for the Future Rule of India 212
Marx, Eleanor 156
Mary, Queen of Scots 214
Masson, David 29, 31, 47
Maurice, F. D. 219
Mayer, Joseph 33
Mayne, Fanny 35
Mazzini, Giuseppe 65
McColl, Norman 246
McGann, Jerome 97
Meade, L. T. (Elizabeth Meade Smith) 25, 222, 231, 260
  A World of Girls 257
melodrama 7, 105, 113–4, 147, 152–4
Meredith, George 23
Merivale, Elizabeth (Mrs. Herman) 151
Merry England 48
Meteyard, Eliza 5, 6, 22, 29, 30–4, 40–1, 64, 252
  Life of Josiah Wedgwood from his private correspondence and family papers 33–4
  Struggles for Fame 32, 33, 34
  Scenes in the Life of an Authoress 22, 32
  "The Whittington Club and the Ladies" 32–3
  "Time versus Malthus" 33
  "The Works of John Ironshaft" 33
Metropolitan 61
Meynell, Alice 8–9, 46, 48, 49, 74, 224, 231, 247, 248–9
  The Children 9
  Later Poems 48
  Poems 48
  Preludes 48
  The Rhythm of Life and Other Essays 48
  The Spirit of Place 9
Meynell, Wilfrid 48, 248
Miles, Alfred H.
  The Poets and the Poetry of the Century, Charles Kingsley to James Thomson 83, 84
Mill, John Stuart 65, 244
  Autobiography 159
  The Subjection of Women 1, 2
Miller, Florence Fenwick 241
Mills, Sarah
  Discourses of Difference 175
Milton, John 91, 241
missionaries 160, 175, 179, 185
  and travel writing 180
Mitford, Mary Russell 6, 54, 64, 83, 145–6

Dramatic Scenes, Sketches, and Other Poems 54
Our Village 54
modernism 97
Moers, Ellen
  Literary Women 2, 4
Montagu, Lady Mary Wortley 243
Monthly Packet 61–2, 71, 165, 230, 260
Monthly Repository 19, 54, 162, 210, 227
Moodie, Susanna 190, 197–9, 203, 204, 214
  The Backwoods of Canada 190
  Roughing It in the Bush 190, 198
  "The Maple-Tree. A Canadian Song" 198–9
  "Oh! Can You Leave Your Native Land?" 197–8
Moore, George 133, 141
  A Drama in Muslin 133
  Esther Waters 133
Moore, Thomas (novelist) 3
  The Bachelor 3
Moore, Thomas (poet) 3, 63, 194
More, Hannah 3, 81, 124, 166, 230
Morley, John
  "English Men of Letters" series 84
Morning Chronicle 247
Morning Post 149
Mozley, Anne 230, 237, 239, 240, 241, 247, 248
Mrs Ellis' Morning Call 63
Mudie's Circulating Library 141
Muller, Henrietta 229
Mulock, Dinah. *See* Craik, Dinah Maria Mulock
Mundy, Godfrey Charles
  Pen and Pencil Sketches 180
Musical Times 68
Myall, Mrs. Ambrose
  James Hain Friswell: A Memoir 165
Myra's Journal of Dress and Fashion 232

Naidu, Sarojini 193, 199, 200–3
  "Indian Dancers" 200
National Association for the Promotion of Social Sciences 65
National Reformer 6, 66–7
National Secular Society 66, 171
natural history 190–2
  George Eliot on 123–4
needlework 16, 219, 226
Nesbit, Edith 246, 247–8, 261, 263
  "The Island of the Nine Whirlpools" 256
  The Story of the Treasure Seekers 261

The Wouldbegoods 258–9
networks, networking 3, 5–6, 15–6, 19, 22, 23, 25, 31–5, 59–60, 65–6, 67–71, 145–6, 150–2, 193, 204, 212, 238–9, 248
New Monthly Magazine 16
New Woman fiction 6, 7, 133–42
Newby, Thomas (publisher) 17, 18, 43–5
Newman, John Henry 168
  Apologia pro vita sua 159
Newnes, George 233
newspapers 21, 134, 204, 221–2, 226, 237, 240, 247
  See also journalism; periodicals
Nicoll, W. Robertson 236
Nister's Holiday Annual 261
Norgate, Kate
  England under the Angevin Kings 217
North British Review 168, 245
Norton, Caroline 62
novel, the 1, 45, 52, 105, 221
  for children 252, 257–9, 262
  domestic 6, 83, 92, 105, 107, 110, 111, 115–7, 124, 128, 134, 252, 257–9
  gothic 6, 105, 111, 115–7, 191
  historical 46, 213
  industrial 6, 105, 107, 109–15
  New Woman 6, 7, 133–42
  and the railway 141
  realist 6–7, 107, 110, 119–30, 141
  sensation 6–7, 29, 51, 77, 83, 116, 133–42, 152–3, 191
  serialized 16, 22, 35, 36, 39, 46, 55, 61, 69, 71, 77, 111, 112, 129, 133, 136, 141, 191, 222–4, 225, 230, 260, 261
  silver-fork 6, 33, 105–9, 110, 148
Novello, J. Alfred 68
Novello, Vincent 68
Nugent, Jim 177
Nussey, Ellen 81

Oliphant, Laurence
Oliphant, Margaret 2, 3, 5, 6, 10, 16, 29, 30–2, 37–41, 46–7, 49, 55–6, 68, 115, 121, 129–30, 137, 138, 160, 162, 167–9, 170, 208, 209, 214, 215–6, 226, 229, 238–9, 240, 244, 245–6, 248
  Annals of a Publishing House 39, 215
  Autobiography 37–8, 46–7, 55, 166–7, 172
  Child's History of Scotland 215
  Christian Melville 16
  Chronicles of Carlingford 39, 47, 129
  "The Ethics of Biography" 169

Oliphant, Margaret (cont.)
  "The Executor" 47
  Historical Sketches of the Reign of George II 39, 215
  Jerusalem 215
  Katie Stewart 16, 46
  Literary History of England 1–2, 3–4, 6
  Makers of Florence 215
  Makers of Modern Rome 215
  Makers of Venice 215
  "Mrs. Carlyle" 169
  Passages in the Life of Margaret Maitland 16
  The Perpetual Curate 39
  The Quiet Heart 38
  Royal Edinburgh 215
  Salem Chapel 133
  "The Sisters Brontë" 6, 167
  Son of the Soil 243
Once a Week 227
Opie, Amelia 170
Oriental Observer and Literary Gazette 196
Otte, Elise 217
  Denmark and Iceland 217
  History of Scandinavia 217
"Ouida" (Marie Louise de la Ramée) 133, 244
Oulton, Carolyn 51
Our Corner 6, 67, 171
Ouseley, William Gore 183
Owenson, Sydney (Lady Morgan) 112
  The Missionary: An Indian Tale 192

Paine, Thomas
  The Age of Reason 64
Pall Mall Gazette 23, 48, 233
  "The Wares of Autolycus" 8–9, 224, 231, 247
Palliser, Fanny Bury 219
  China Collector's Pocket Companion 219
  Descriptive Catalogue of the Lace and Embroidery in the South Kensington Museum 219
  Historic Devices 219
  History of Ceramic Art 219
  History of Lace 219
  Mottoes for Monuments 219
Pardoe, Julia 216
Parkes, Bessie Rayner 29–30, 31, 41, 65, 229, 238
  Essays on Woman's Work 30
Parkes, Fanny 179–80
  "The Mem Sahiba's Speech" 180
  Wanderings of a Pilgrim in Search of the Picturesque 179–80
Pater, Walter 245
paternalism 46, 55–6, 111, 113
Patmore, Coventry 48, 74, 243
Pattison, Dora 245
Pattison, Mark 245
Pearn, Violet 149
  The Minotaur 149
Peninsular War 211
Penrose, Elizabeth 209, 213
  Historical Conversations for Young Persons 213
  A History of England 213
  A History of France 213
People's Journal 19, 20, 32
periodicals 4, 8, 17, 22–6, 30, 74–5, 77, 89, 141, 192, 193–4, 208, 210, 221–33, 259–61, 263
  and advice columns 20, 224, 225, 226, 230, 231–2
  and causeries 224, 231
  for children 260–3
  circulation of 21, 64, 74
  and correspondence columns 20, 61–2, 232
  digitization of 221
  editing of 6, 21, 48, 59–71, 74, 83, 111, 221, 229–31, 233, 260
  and female readers 17, 23, 172, 225, 237, 261
  and interviews 223, 224, 232–3
  and leaders (editorials) 227–30, 240–1
  and new journalism 221–2, 232–3
  poetry in 21, 76–7, 89, 189, 190, 193–4, 198, 222–3
  progressive 19–22, 32, 64–7, 135, 229–30
  religious 17, 161, 229, 230–1, 254
  and review articles 30, 36–7, 73, 83–4, 168–70, 223, 236–49
  working-class 19–20, 262
  and George Eliot 17–8, 49, 50, 123, 221, 226, 241–2
  and Elizabeth Gaskell 31–2, 34–7
  and Harriet Martineau 54, 208, 210, 226, 227–8, 240–1
  and Eliza Meteyard 31, 32, 34
  and Alice Meynell 9, 48, 231, 247, 248–9
  and Margaret Oliphant 16, 32, 38–40, 46–7, 208, 215, 226, 229
  and Christina Rossetti 16, 47, 101, 229
  See also annuals, literary; journalism; newspapers
Peters, Charles 231

Peterson, Linda H. 30, 70, 78–9, 225
Petrarch 100
Phegley, Jennifer 23
philanthropy 17, 33, 115, 180, 211, 213, 259–60
Phillips, Elizabeth 151
Pike, Holden 26
Pinero, Arthur Wing 154
Planché, Eliza 151
Poet Laureateship 74, 76
poetry 3, 4, 8, 15–6, 18, 23, 47–8, 55, 63, 80, 82–4, 89–103, 123–4, 172, 223, 239, 243, 246–7, 248
   children's 252, 260, 262
   colonial 4, 189–90, 192–204
   devotional 80, 89, 91, 96, 97–9, 101–2
   epic 92
   landscape 4, 195
   poetess 77–8, 84, 92, 95, 100, 189, 197, 227
   political 78, 89, 94–5, 203
   prize 75–7
   sentimental 21, 89
   working-class 6, 19–21, 114
Polack, Elizabeth 151
poor laws 32, 210
Portfolio 218
Potter, Beatrix
   The Tale of Peter Rabbit 262
pottery, history of 34
Pre-Raphaelite Brotherhood 16, 47
Price, Thomas 217
Procter, Adelaide Anne 101
professionalism 2–3, 5, 10, 25–6, 29–41, 69, 73, 74, 76–7, 126, 133, 160, 167, 171, 207
   and book reviewing 36–7, 38–9
   and editorship 59–60, 63
   and income 32, 38, 39, 50–1, 55–6, 259
   and professional associations 25, 32–3, 55, 146
   of literature 10
   and overproduction 37–8, 40
   and the periodical press 30–2, 37, 38, 225, 232
   and relationships with publishers 43–56
   standards for assessing 29–30, 37, 38, 74, 233
   and theater 150–2, 156
   tension with domesticity 75, 140, 191, 207–8, 225–6, 233
   of travel writing 176, 184, 186
   of women's history writing 8, 206, 208–9
   and work space 59–60
   See also networks, networking
prostitution 32
Protestant Magazine 230
pseudonymous publication 16–8, 22, 23, 33, 47, 63, 77, 84, 124, 162, 172, 208, 221, 226–7, 236, 239, 263
Public Record Office 208, 215
publicity
   as masculine domain 145–6

Quarterly Review, The 5, 17, 178, 182, 218, 236, 238, 240
Queen Anne 215
Queen Victoria 82, 214, 216, 252
Quiver 20

Radcliffe, Ann 81
   The Mysteries of Udolpho 215–6
Raleigh, Walter 213
Reader, The 36, 37
realism 6–7, 105, 107, 110, 113–4, 119–30, 134, 191, 197, 223
   and painting 122–3
   and social reform 7, 123–4
Reform Act, 1832 54, 106, 112, 124
"Regina's Maids of Honour" 52–4
religion 5, 54, 61–2, 70, 171, 179–80, 194, 206, 210, 216–7, 228, 229, 230–1, 240, 243, 252, 259, 263
   in literature 80, 91–2, 94–6, 97–102, 111–4, 125, 160–1, 166, 253–5
   influence on writers 39, 207
Religious Tract Society 230–1, 253–4
   Copyright Subcommittee 253
repression
   in the sensation novel 138–40
Review of Reviews 23
Revue des Deux Mondes 36
Richard Bentley & Son 51
Richard III, King 217
Riddell, Charlotte 45–6, 60, 70, 133
   George Geith of Fen Court 45
   The Rich Husband 45
   A Struggle for Fame 45
   Too Much Alone 45
   The World and the Church 45
   Zuriel's Child 45
Riehl, Wilhelm Heinrich von 123
Rigby, Elizabeth (Lady Eastlake) 5, 178, 206, 208, 218, 236, 238, 240, 244, 247, 248
   Handbook of the History of Painting 218
   Treasures of Art in Great Britain 218

Risorgimento 78, 95
Ritchie, Anne Thackeray 170–1
  A Book of Sibyls 170
  Chapters from Some Memoirs 170
  Madame de Sévigné 170
  Records of Tennyson, Ruskin, and Robert and ElizabethBrowning 170
Roberts, Emma 189, 190, 193, 196–7, 204
  East India Voyager 190
  Oriental Scenes, Sketches and Tales 196
  Scenes and Characteristics of Hindustan 190
  "The Rajah's Obsequies" 196
  "Stanzas Written in a Pavilion of the Rambaugh" 197
Robins, Elizabeth 156
  Votes for Women 157
Robinson, A. Mary F. 81–2
Robinson, F. W. 39
Robinson, Mary 246
Romanticism 82, 92, 94, 192–7, 203, 215, 222
Roscoe, Margaret. *See* Sandbach, Margaret
Rossetti, Christina 4, 15, 16, 23, 46–8, 49, 74, 78, 80, 81–2, 83–4, 89, 91, 92, 96–103, 229, 262
  "Alas my Lord" 101–2
  Annus Domini: A Prayer for Each Day of the Year
  "A Better Resurrection" 101
  "A Birthday" 47, 99
  Fata Morgana 97
  Goblin Market 47, 97–9
  "Monna Innominata: A Sonnet of Sonnets" 100
  New Poems 47
  Pageant and Other Poems 100
  "Paradise: in a Symbol" 101
  Poetical Works of Christina Georgina Rossetti 47
  The Prince's Progress and Other Poems 47
  "Remember" 99–100
  Sing-Song 262
  "Song" 99, 100
  Speaking Likenesses 256, 262
  "Uphill" 47
  Verses 80, 101
  Verses: Dedicated to Her Mother 15
  "Weary in Well-Doing" 101
Rossetti, Dante Gabriel 16, 83
Rossetti, Lucy Madox Brown 81
Rossetti, William Michael 47, 80, 92
Rotunda, the 64
Rousseau, Jean-Jacques 2, 159

Royal Africa Society 185
Royal Geographical Society 186
Royal Literary Fund 32, 252
Ruskin, John 23, 48, 92, 170
  Modern Painters 44, 123, 245

Saintsbury, George 221
Sand, George 1
Sandbach, Margaret
  Spiritual Alchemy 36
sanitary reform 64, 212
Sappho 48
Sargeant, Anne Maria
  "Edith and Her Ayah" 9
  Mamma's Lessons on the History and Geography of Palestine 255
Sartain, John 34
Sartain's Union Magazine 34
satire 105, 106
Satthianadhan, Krupabai
  Saguna 192
Saturday Review 48, 74, 224, 228, 237, 241, 245
Saunders and Otley 54
Savoy, The 200
Schellenberg, Betty 10
Schreiner, Olive 130, 133
  Dreams 141
  The Story of an African Farm 141
Scots Observer 9, 48, 247
Scott, Clement 149
Scott, Jane 151–2
Scott, Walter 50, 84, 90
Scotsman, The 76
Sedgwick, Catharine 164
self-marketing 23, 24
Sepoy Uprising 212
Seward, Anna 3
Sewell, Anna 253
  Black Beauty 9, 253, 254–5
Sewell, Elizabeth 124
  Autobiography 165
  The Experience of Life 165
  Extracts from a Private Journal 165
  Journal of a Home Life 165
Sewell, Mary 253
sexuality 7, 76, 90, 93–4, 97–9, 107, 110, 116–7, 136, 144
  in the sensation novel 137–40, 142
Shakespeare, William 149, 163
Sharp, Elizabeth
  Women Poets of the Victorian Era 82–3

Sharp, Evelyn
  "The Boy Who Looked Like a Girl" 256
  The Making of a Schoolgirl 257
Sharpe's London Magazine 32, 68, 69
Sharples, Eliza 64
Shaw, Flora 23, 225–6
Shaw, George Bernard 154, 156
Shelley, Mary 81–2, 243
Shelley, Percy Bysshe 84
Sheridan, Louisa Henrietta 62
Sheridan, Richard Brinsley 149, 151
Sherwood, Mary Martha Butt 192
  George Desmond 192
Shield 64
Shillingsburg, Peter L. 55
Shipley, Orby
  Lyra Messianica 101
Shobal, Frederic
  Biographical Dictionary of the Living Authors of GreatBritain and Ireland 3
short story 35, 37, 140–2
Showalter, Elaine 130
  A Literature of Their Own 2, 4, 134
Siddons, Sarah 151
Sidney, Dorothy 218
Sigourney, Lydia
  "The Cherokee Mother" 196
Simcox, Edith 160, 244–5, 247–9
  "Autobiographies" 168
  Autobiography of a Shirtmaker 172
  "Ideals of Feminine Usefulness" 245
Sinclair, Catherine
  Holiday House 257–8
Sinnett, Jane 242, 245, 248
Skeet, Charles 45
Sketch, The 48
Smith, Adam
  Wealth of Nations 109, 126
Smith, Elder 18, 44–5, 55
Smith, Elizabeth Meade. See Meade, L. T.
Smith, George 18, 44–5, 74, 78
Smith, William H. 93
Smith-Stanley, Edward (Lord Derby) 240
social reform 6, 7, 21–2, 32–3, 64–7, 93, 106–14, 124–5, 135, 166, 171, 183, 206, 209–12, 215, 217, 230, 255–6
socialism 6, 66–7, 171
Society for Promoting Christian Knowledge 101
Society for the Diffusion of Useful Knowledge 213
Society for the Promotion of the Employment of Women 65
Society of Authors 25
Society of Women Journalists 25, 63, 225
Somerville, Mary 82, 172–3, 244
  Personal Recollections from Early Life to Old Age, 172–3
Somerville, Martha 172
South Place Chapel 5, 31
Southey, Robert 75
Spasmodism 92
Spectator 40, 48, 237
Spence, Catherine Helen
  Clara Morrison: A Tale of South Australia During the Gold Fever 191
Spirit and Manners of the Age 68
St James's Gazette 40
St James's Magazine 60, 61, 68, 69, 70
St Paul's Magazine 39, 244
St. Philip Neri 216
Stafford, Jane 194
Standard 228
Stanhope, Lady Hester 179
Stannard, Henrietta (John Strange Winter) 60, 63
Stead, W. T. 23, 26, 136–7, 233
Stedman, Edmund Clarence
  Victorian Poets 83
Steel, Flora Anne 192
  On the Face of the Waters 192
Sterry, Lorraine 177
Stoddard, Anna 176–7
Stone, Elizabeth 218–9
  Art of Needlework 218–9
  Chronicles of Fashion 219
Stone, Marjorie 114
Stowe, Harriet Beecher 125, 161
Strand, The 141
Stretton, Hesba 254
  Jessica's First Prayer 254
Strickland, Agnes 208, 212–5
  Bachelor Kings of England
  English Princesses 214
  Historical Tales 214
  Letters of Mary, Queen of Scots 214
  Lives of the Queens of England 214
  Lives of the Queens of Scotland 214
  Seven Bishops 214
  Stuart Princesses 214
  Tales and Stories from History 214
  Tudor Princesses 214
  Victoria from Birth to Bridal 214
Strickland, Elizabeth 208, 212–15
  Lives of the Queens of England 214

Strickland, Elizabeth (cont.)
  Lives of the Queens of Scotland 214
  Bachelor Kings of England 214
  Seven Bishops 214
  Tudor Princesses 214
Strickland, Jane Margaret
  Rome, Republican and Regal 214
Stuart, Arabella 90, 216
Stuart, Laura
  In Memoriam 165
subscription (funding method) 47, 189
suffrage, women's 64, 154, 157, 199, 228, 229
Sunday School Penny Magazine 35
Sunday School Times 60
Sunday Times 59
Sutherland, John 24
Swan, Annie S. (Mrs. Burnett Smith) 63, 226, 232
Sydney Mail 191
Sydney Morning Herald 191
Symons, Arthur 200
Syrett, Netta 148–9, 156
  The Finding of Nancy 148–9
  The Sheltering Tree 149

Tait's Edinburgh Magazine 6, 21, 22, 31, 32, 64, 226, 243, 244
  "Feast of the Poets" 20
Taylor, Mary 18
temperance 19, 32, 229, 254
Temple Bar 24, 169
Ten Hours Bill 109, 111–3
Tennyson, Alfred 4, 48, 74, 90, 91, 92, 97, 170, 203, 223
  "Columbus" 91
  Idylls of the King 244
  In Memoriam 91–2
  "The Lady of Shalott" 99
  "To the Marquis of Dufferin and Ava" 91
Thackeray, William Makepeace 44, 46, 55, 61, 123, 170
  The History of Pendennis 168
  Vanity Fair 105, 108
theater 5, 7, 144–57, 163
  comedy 148–9, 150, 152, 154–6
  decline of the drama 149–50
  farce 147, 150, 152, 154–6
  melodrama 7, 147, 152–4
  playwriting competitions 147–50
  "well-made play" 153–4
Theism 228
Theosophy 171

Thomson, Katharine 213
Tillotson's (fiction agency) 39
Times, The 23, 148, 217, 225, 237, 249
Tinsley Brothers (publishers) 45–6, 52
Titbits 222
Tomson, Graham R. *See* Watson, Rosamund Marriott
Tonna, Charlotte Elizabeth 111, 112–3, 114, 116, 160–2, 230
  Helen Fleetwood 109, 111, 112–3, 160
  Personal Recollections 160
  The Wrongs of Woman 113, 160, 161
Tooke, Thomas
  History of Prices 211
Tooley, Sarah 233
Torrens, W. T. M.
  Lancashire's Lesson; or the Need of a Settled Policy in Times of Exceptional Distress 36
Tractarianism 61, 70
trade unionism 64, 113, 229, 248, 248
Traill, Catherine Parr 214
  The Backwoods of Canada 190
  Canadian Wildflowers 191
  Roughing It in the Bush 190
travel writing 9, 16, 38, 39, 77, 162, 175–86, 189–92, 203, 207, 208, 210, 223, 240, 248, 252, 260
Trimmer, Sarah 230
  The History of the Robins 253
Trollope, Anthony 40, 123, 129
  Autobiography 237, 238
  History of Barset
  North America 182
Trollope, Frances 111–3, 181–3
  Domestic Manners of the Americans 175, 181–3
  The Life and Adventures of Michael Armstrong, the Factory Boy 109, 111–3
  The Refugee in America 183
True Briton 35
Tuchman, Gaye 23, 52
Tucker, Charlotte Maria. *See* A.L.O.E.
Tulloch, John 216
Tynan, Katherine, "Santa Christina"

Unitarianism 5, 30, 31, 54, 114, 206
utopian communities 181

Vestris, Eliza 151, 152, 155
Vicinus, Martha 19
Victoria and Albert Museum 219

Victoria Magazine 65–6, 135, 229
Victoria Press 75, 76, 229
Victoria, Queen 82, 214, 216, 252
Villiers, George 213

W. Pickering (publisher) 55
Walpole, Horace
   The Castle of Otranto 115
Ward, A. W. 37
Ward and Lock 232
Ward, Mary Augusta 160, 167
   "Introductions" to *Life and Works of the Sisters Brontë* 167
   "The Literature of Introspection" 167
   A Writer's Recollections 167
Waterloo Directory of English Newspapers and Periodicals: 1800–1900 222
Watkins, John
   Biographical Dictionary of the Living Authors of Great Britain and Ireland 3
Watson, Rosamund Marriott (Graham R. Tomson) 8, 227, 239, 247
Watts, G. F. 218
Webb, Maria 217
   Fells of Swarthmoor Hall 217
   Penns and the Peningtons 217
Webb, Sidney 67
Webster, Augusta 83, 154, 246–7
   "Poets and Personal Pronouns" 84
Webster, Benjamin 148
Wedgwood, Josiah 33–4
Weekly Dispatch 21
Weekly Register 48
Wellesley Index to Victorian Periodicals 237
Wells, H. G. 241
Wentworth, Thomas 216
Westminster Budget 233
Westminster Gazette 233
Westminster Review, The 1, 6–7, 17, 49, 65, 83, 123, 124–5, 135, 148, 168, 223, 227, 239, 241–2, 245
Whittaker, George 54
Whittington Club 5, 22, 32–3
Wigan, Leonora (Mrs. Alfred) 152
Wilcox, Dora 196, 197
Wilde, Oscar 83–4
William Blackwood and Sons 32, 43, 46
Williams, Jane (Ysgafell) 217
   History of Wales 217
   The Literary Women of England 217
Williams, Patrick 192
Williams, Raymond 113

Keywords 123
Williams, William Smith 44
Wilson, Margaret 151
Wilton, Marie (Marie Bancroft) 151, 152
Windsor Magazine 261
Winter's Weekly 60, 63
Wise, Thomas 78
Wollstonecraft, Mary 3–4, 117
   Original Stories from Real Life 253
   Vindication of the Rights of Women 3
Wolsey, Thomas 213
Woman 233
Woman at Home: Annie S. Swan's Magazine 63, 226, 232
Woman Question 105, 135, 209
Woman's Journal 172
Woman's Life 232
Woman's Signal 172
Woman's World 83
Women of England, The 63
Women Novelists of Queen Victoria's Reign: A Book of Appreciation 6, 10, 83, 130, 167
Women's Industrial Council 64, 229
Women's Industrial News 64, 229
Women's Penny Paper 229
Women's Suffrage Journal 64, 229
Wood, Ellen (Mrs. Henry) 29, 60, 77, 83, 133, 153
   East Lynne 7, 136, 153
Woolf, Virginia 92, 97, 121, 162–3
Worboise, Emma 230
Wordsworth, Dorothy 245
Wordsworth, William 4, 74, 123–4, 195, 203
   "Extempore Effusion upon the Death of James Hogg" 89–90
   "Lines Written a Few Miles above Tintern Abbey" 196
   The Prelude 4, 92
working hours, regulation of 32, 109, 111–3
Working-Man's Friend and Family Instructor 19–20
Wright, Frances 181

Yeats, William Butler
   The Countess Kathleen and Various Legends and Lyrics 247
Yeazell, Ruth Bernard 122
Yellow Book 141
Yellowbacks 141

Yonge, Charlotte 61–2, 71, 81, 124, 165–6, 230, 259–60
  Cameos from English History 166
  Charlotte Mary Yonge: Her Life and Letters 166
  The Daisy Chain 258–9
  The Heir of Redclyffe 61
Young Woman 26
Young, Melinda 151

Zimmern, Helen 246

Cambridge Companions to ...

AUTHORS

Edward Albee edited by Stephen J. Bottoms

Margaret Atwood edited by Coral Ann Howells

W. H. Auden edited by Stan Smith

Jane Austen edited by Edward Copeland and Juliet McMaster (second edition)

Beckett edited by John Pilling

Bede edited by Scott DeGregorio

Aphra Behn edited by Derek Hughes and Janet Todd

Walter Benjamin edited by David S. Ferris

William Blake edited by Morris Eaves

Jorge Luis Borges edited by Edwin Williamson

Brecht edited by Peter Thomson and Glendyr Sacks (second edition)

The Brontës edited by Heather Glen

Bunyan edited by Anne Dunan-Page

Frances Burney edited by Peter Sabor

Byron edited by Drummond Bone

Albert Camus edited by Edward J. Hughes

Willa Cather edited by Marilee Lindemann

Cervantes edited by Anthony J. Cascardi

Chaucer edited by Piero Boitani and Jill Mann (second edition)

Chekhov edited by Vera Gottlieb and Paul Allain

Kate Chopin edited by Janet Beer

Caryl Churchill edited by Elaine Aston and Elin Diamond

Cicero edited by Catherine Steel

Coleridge edited by Lucy Newlyn

Wilkie Collins edited by Jenny Bourne Taylor

Joseph Conrad edited by J. H. Stape

H. D. edited by Nephie J. Christodoulides and Polina Mackay

Dante edited by Rachel Jacoff (second edition)

Daniel Defoe edited by John Richetti

Don DeLillo edited by John N. Duvall

Charles Dickens edited by John O. Jordan

Emily Dickinson edited by Wendy Martin

John Donne edited by Achsah Guibbory

Dostoevskii edited by W. J. Leatherbarrow

Theodore Dreiser edited by Leonard Cassuto and Claire Virginia Eby

John Dryden edited by Steven N. Zwicker

W. E. B. Du Bois edited by Shamoon Zamir

George Eliot edited by George Levine

T. S. Eliot edited by A. David Moody

Ralph Ellison edited by Ross Posnock

Ralph Waldo Emerson edited by Joel Porte and Saundra Morris

William Faulkner edited by Philip M. Weinstein

Henry Fielding edited by Claude Rawson

F. Scott Fitzgerald edited by Ruth Prigozy

Flaubert edited by Timothy Unwin

E. M. Forster edited by David Bradshaw

Benjamin Franklin edited by Carla Mulford

Brian Friel edited by Anthony Roche

Robert Frost edited by Robert Faggen

Gabriel García Márquez edited by Philip Swanson

Elizabeth Gaskell edited by Jill L. Matus

Goethe edited by Lesley Sharpe

Günter Grass edited by Stuart Taberner

Thomas Hardy edited by Dale Kramer

David Hare edited by Richard Boon

Nathaniel Hawthorne edited by Richard Millington

Seamus Heaney edited by Bernard O'Donoghue

Ernest Hemingway edited by Scott Donaldson

Homer edited by Robert Fowler

Horace edited by Stephen Harrison

Ted Hughes edited by Terry Gifford

Ibsen edited by James McFarlane

Henry James edited by Jonathan Freedman

Samuel Johnson edited by Greg Clingham

Ben Jonson edited by Richard Harp and Stanley Stewart

James Joyce edited by Derek Attridge (second edition)

Kafka edited by Julian Preece

Keats edited by Susan J. Wolfson

Rudyard Kipling edited by Howard J. Booth

Lacan edited by Jean-Michel Rabaté

D. H. Lawrence edited by Anne Fernihough

Primo Levi edited by Robert Gordon

Lucretius edited by Stuart Gillespie and Philip Hardie

Machiavelli edited by John M. Najemy

David Mamet edited by Christopher Bigsby
Thomas Mann edited by Ritchie Robertson
Christopher Marlowe edited by Patrick Cheney
Andrew Marvell edited by Derek Hirst and Steven N. Zwicker
Herman Melville edited by Robert S. Levine
Arthur Miller edited by Christopher Bigsby (second edition)
Milton edited by Dennis Danielson (second edition)
Molière edited by David Bradby and Andrew Calder
Toni Morrison edited by Justine Tally
Nabokov edited by Julian W. Connolly
Eugene O'Neill edited by Michael Manheim
George Orwell edited by John Rodden
Ovid edited by Philip Hardie
Harold Pinter edited by Peter Raby (second edition)
Sylvia Plath edited by Jo Gill
Edgar Allan Poe edited by Kevin J. Hayes
Alexander Pope edited by Pat Rogers
Ezra Pound edited by Ira B. Nadel
Proust edited by Richard Bales
Pushkin edited by Andrew Kahn
Rabelais edited by John O'Brien
Rilke edited by Karen Leeder and Robert Vilain
Philip Roth edited by Timothy Parrish
Salman Rushdie edited by Abdulrazak Gurnah
Shakespeare edited by Margareta de Grazia and Stanley Wells (second edition)
Shakespearean Comedy edited by Alexander Leggatt
Shakespeare and Contemporary Dramatists edited by Ton Hoenselaars
Shakespeare and Popular Culture edited by Robert Shaughnessy
Shakespearean Tragedy edited by Claire McEachern (second edition)
Shakespeare on Film edited by Russell Jackson (second edition)
Shakespeare on Stage edited by Stanley Wells and Sarah Stanton
Shakespeare's History Plays edited by Michael Hattaway

Shakespeare's Last Plays edited by Catherine M. S. Alexander
Shakespeare's Poetry edited by Patrick Cheney
George Bernard Shaw edited by Christopher Innes
Shelley edited by Timothy Morton
Mary Shelley edited by Esther Schor
Sam Shepard edited by Matthew C. Roudané
Spenser edited by Andrew Hadfield
Laurence Sterne edited by Thomas Keymer
Wallace Stevens edited by John N. Serio
Tom Stoppard edited by Katherine E. Kelly
Harriet Beecher Stowe edited by Cindy Weinstein
August Strindberg edited by Michael Robinson
Jonathan Swift edited by Christopher Fox
J. M. Synge edited by P. J. Mathews
Tacitus edited by A. J. Woodman
Henry David Thoreau edited by Joel Myerson
Tolstoy edited by Donna Tussing Orwin
Anthony Trollope edited by Carolyn Dever and Lisa Niles
Mark Twain edited by Forrest G. Robinson
John Updike edited by Stacey Olster
Mario Vargas Llosa edited by Efrain Kristal and John King
Virgil edited by Charles Martindale
Voltaire edited by Nicholas Cronk
Edith Wharton edited by Millicent Bell
Walt Whitman edited by Ezra Greenspan
Oscar Wilde edited by Peter Raby
Tennessee Williams edited by Matthew C. Roudané
August Wilson edited by Christopher Bigsby
Mary Wollstonecraft edited by Claudia L. Johnson
Virginia Woolf edited by Susan Sellers (second edition)
Wordsworth edited by Stephen Gill
W. B. Yeats edited by Marjorie Howes and John Kelly
Zola edited by Brian Nelson

TOPICS

The Actress edited by Maggie B. Gale and John Stokes
The African American Novel edited by Maryemma Graham
The African American Slave Narrative edited by Audrey A. Fisch
Theatre History by David Wiles and Christine Dymkowski

African American Theatre by Harvey Young

Allegory edited by Rita Copeland and Peter Struck

American Crime Fiction edited by Catherine Ross Nickerson

American Modernism edited by Walter Kalaidjian

American Poetry Since 1945 edited by Jennifer Ashton

American Realism and Naturalism edited by Donald Pizer

American Travel Writing edited by Alfred Bendixen and Judith Hamera

American Women Playwrights edited by Brenda Murphy

Ancient Rhetoric edited by Erik Gunderson

Arthurian Legend edited by Elizabeth Archibald and Ad Putter

Australian Literature edited by Elizabeth Webby

British Literature of the French Revolution edited by Pamela Clemit

British Romanticism edited by Stuart Curran (second edition)

British Romantic Poetry edited by James Chandler and Maureen N. McLane

British Theatre, 1730–1830, edited by Jane Moody and Daniel O'Quinn

Canadian Literature edited by Eva-Marie Kröller

Children's Literature edited by M. O. Grenby and Andrea Immel

The Classic Russian Novel edited by Malcolm V. Jones and Robin Feuer Miller

Contemporary Irish Poetry edited by Matthew Campbell

Creative Writing edited by David Morley and Philip Neilsen

Crime Fiction edited by Martin Priestman

Early Modern Women's Writing edited by Laura Lunger Knoppers

The Eighteenth-Century Novel edited by John Richetti

Eighteenth-Century Poetry edited by John Sitter

Emma edited by Peter Sabor

English Literature, 1500–1600 edited by Arthur F. Kinney

English Literature, 1650–1740 edited by Steven N. Zwicker

English Literature, 1740–1830 edited by Thomas Keymer and Jon Mee

English Literature, 1830–1914 edited by Joanne Shattock

English Novelists edited by Adrian Poole

English Poetry, Donne to Marvell edited by Thomas N. Corns

English Poets edited by Claude Rawson

English Renaissance Drama, second edition edited by A. R. Braunmuller and Michael Hattaway

English Renaissance Tragedy edited by Emma Smith and Garrett A. Sullivan Jr.

English Restoration Theatre edited by Deborah C. Payne Fisk

The Epic edited by Catherine Bates

European Modernism edited by Pericles Lewis

European Novelists edited by Michael Bell

Fairy Tales edited by Maria Tatar

Fantasy Literature edited by Edward James and Farah Mendlesohn

Feminist Literary Theory edited by Ellen Rooney

Fiction in the Romantic Period edited by Richard Maxwell and Katie Trumpener

The Fin de Siècle edited by Gail Marshall

The French Enlightenment edited by Daniel Brewer

The French Novel: from 1800 to the Present edited by Timothy Unwin

Gay and Lesbian Writing edited by Hugh Stevens

German Romanticism edited by Nicholas Saul

Gothic Fiction edited by Jerrold E. Hogle

The Greek and Roman Novel edited by Tim Whitmarsh

Greek and Roman Theatre edited by Marianne McDonald and J. Michael Walton

Greek Comedy edited by Martin Revermann

Greek Lyric edited by Felix Budelmann

Greek Mythology edited by Roger D. Woodard

Greek Tragedy edited by P. E. Easterling

The Harlem Renaissance edited by George Hutchinson

The History of the Book edited by Leslie Howsam

The Irish Novel edited by John Wilson Foster

The Italian Novel edited by Peter Bondanella and Andrea Ciccarelli

The Italian Renaissance edited by Michael Wyatt

Jewish American Literature edited by Hana Wirth-Nesher and Michael P. Kramer

The Latin American Novel edited by Efraín Kristal

The Literature of the First World War edited by Vincent Sherry

The Literature of London edited by Lawrence Manley

The Literature of Los Angeles edited by Kevin R. McNamara

The Literature of New York edited by Cyrus Patell and Bryan Waterman

The Literature of Paris edited by Anna-Louise Milne

The Literature of World War II edited by Marina MacKay

Literature on Screen edited by Deborah Cartmell and Imelda Whelehan

Medieval English Culture edited by Andrew Galloway

Medieval English Literature edited by Larry Scanlon

Medieval English Mysticism edited by Samuel Fanous and Vincent Gillespie

Medieval English Theatre edited by Richard Beadle and Alan J. Fletcher (second edition)

Medieval French Literature edited by Simon Gaunt and Sarah Kay

Medieval Romance edited by Roberta L. Krueger

Medieval Women's Writing edited by Carolyn Dinshaw and David Wallace

Modern American Culture edited by Christopher Bigsby

Modern British Women Playwrights edited by Elaine Aston and Janelle Reinelt

Modern French Culture edited by Nicholas Hewitt

Modern German Culture edited by Eva Kolinsky and Wilfried van der Will

The Modern German Novel edited by Graham Bartram

The Modern Gothic edited by Jerrold E. Hogle

Modern Irish Culture edited by Joe Cleary and Claire Connolly

Modern Italian Culture edited by Zygmunt G. Baranski and Rebecca J. West

Modern Latin American Culture edited by John King

Modern Russian Culture edited by Nicholas Rzhevsky

Modern Spanish Culture edited by David T. Gies

Modernism edited by Michael Levenson (second edition)

The Modernist Novel edited by Morag Shiach

Modernist Poetry edited by Alex Davis and Lee M. Jenkins

Modernist Women Writers edited by Maren Tova Linett

Narrative edited by David Herman

Native American Literature edited by Joy Porter and Kenneth M. Roemer

Nineteenth-Century American Women's Writing edited by Dale M. Bauer and Philip Gould

Old English Literature edited by Malcolm Godden and Michael Lapidge (second edition)

Performance Studies edited by Tracy C. Davis

Piers Plowman by Andrew Cole and Andrew Galloway

Popular Fiction edited by David Glover and Scott McCracken

Postcolonial Literary Studies edited by Neil Lazarus

Postmodernism edited by Steven Connor

The Pre-Raphaelites edited by Elizabeth Prettejohn

Pride and Prejudice edited by Janet Todd

Renaissance Humanism edited by Jill Kraye

The Roman Historians edited by Andrew Feldherr

Roman Satire edited by Kirk Freudenburg

Science Fiction edited by Edward James and Farah Mendlesohn

Scottish Literature edited by Gerald Carruthers and Liam McIlvanney

Sensation Fiction edited by Andrew Mangham

The Sonnet edited by A. D. Cousins and Peter Howarth

The Spanish Novel: from 1600 to the Present edited by Harriet Turner and Adelaida López de Martínez

Textual Scholarship edited by Neil Fraistat and Julia Flanders

Travel Writing edited by Peter Hulme and Tim Youngs

Twentieth-Century British and Irish Women's Poetry edited by Jane Dowson

The Twentieth-Century English Novel edited by Robert L. Caserio

Twentieth-Century English Poetry edited by Neil Corcoran

Twentieth-Century Irish Drama edited by Shaun Richards

Twentieth-Century Russian Literature edited by Marina Balina and Evgeny Dobrenko

Utopian Literature edited by Gregory Claeys

Victorian and Edwardian Theatre edited by Kerry Powell

The Victorian Novel edited by Deirdre David (second edition)
Victorian Poetry edited by Joseph Bristow
Victorian Women's Writing edited by Linda H. Peterson
War Writing edited by Kate McLoughlin
Women's Writing in Britain, 1660–1789 edited by Catherine Ingrassia
Women's Writing in the Romantic Period edited by Devoney Looser
Writing of the English Revolution edited by N. H. Keeble